Leading Schools Legally: A Practical Anthology of School Law

By: David Emmert
Contributing Editors: Jeffery J. Qualkinbush and Bruce D. Donaldson
Copy Editor: Debbie Dewitt

ISBN 0-9748391-6-7

Power Publishing
7168 Zionsville Road
Indianapolis, IN 46268
(317) 347-1051

This book is manufactured in the United States of America.

Library of Congress Cataloging in Publication Data in Progress.

Published by Power Publishing
7168 Zionsville Road
Indianapolis, IN 46268

Special thanks to Barnes & Thornburg LLP for providing the funding for the Leading Schools Legally project.

DEDICATION

To my mother, Vivian Emmert, for her amazing intuition in
predicting that someday I'd be an attorney and write a book.

CONTENTS

CHAPTER

1

THE SYSTEM: SOURCES OF LEGAL AUTHORITY

"Power corrupts and absolute power corrupts absolutely."

- Lord John Acton

Educational leaders have a responsibility to know the laws, which will guide their decisions and the legal ramifications of the choices and decisions they make regarding the day-to-day functioning of their respective institutions. This book explains those laws and provides examples and case studies, which demonstrate how the laws affect the various entities involved in education.

The government of the United States uses a balance of power system intended to distribute legal authority in such a way as to create checks and balances among governmental decision makers. Governmental leaders at all levels including teachers, administrators, principals, school board members, state governors and even the President of the United States are governed by this system in order to ensure that no one entity becomes too powerful to lead effectively. Some examples of how this checks and balances system works in the public school arena are listed below:

1. **A school board member who exercises personal power inconsistent with legal power is checked by the judicial system.**

    Example: A school board member, who without express delegation from school board, defies policy by repeatedly entering classrooms without first reporting to the office and gaining consent, is ordered by a court to cease the practice.

2. **A school principal is checked by a state administrative agency.**

    Example: An administrator who defies collective bargaining law and offers a wage-related benefit to a teacher without negotiating with the exclusive representative of all the teachers is ordered by the administering agency to rescind the benefit.

3. **A school board or state legislature is checked by the judicial system.**

    Example: A policy established by the school board (or statute from the legislature) such as requiring everyone to begin each day by listening to a prayer interferes with students' and teachers' free exercise of religion and is ruled void.

I. FLOW OF LEGAL POWER TO SCHOOLS

Systems of public education act as governmental representatives and as such, are subject to the legal constraints and authority that apply to governmental entities. The term "legal power" means the action of an individual governmental actor or a governmental body that will be upheld if challenged in court (or in an administrative agency empowered to hear the particular dispute). The following briefly-annotated outline gives a general overview of the major sources of legal authority from federal, to state, to local systems of public education.

   I. *Federal Constitution*
- A. **Silent** (no express provision concerning education)
- B. **Bill of Rights** (personal freedoms impacting public schools)
    1. First Amendment freedoms of speech and religion and prevention of religious establishment;
    2. Fourth Amendment prevention of unreasonable searches and seizures
- C. **Fourteenth Amendment** (states, including their local schools, prohibited from denying:)
    1. Privileges and immunities of U.S. citizens;
    2. Life, liberty, or property without due process of law (procedural and substantive due process required);
    3. Equal protection of the law

    D. **Powers of Congress** (Art. 1, Sec. 8)
1. General Welfare Clause (No Child Left Behind Act, Individuals with Disabilities Education Act, Family Education Rights and Privacy Act, Title VII of Civil Rights Act, etc.)
2. Commerce Clause (Fair Labor Standards Act)
3. Necessary and Proper Clause (power to enact all laws "necessary and proper" in executing its specifically granted powers and "all other powers" granted in the federal constitution)

    E. **Supremacy Clause** (Art. 6, Clause 2)
1. Federal constitution and laws of Congress declared to be "supreme law of the land"
2. Judges in all states bound to grant such federal supremacy over state constitution and laws

    F. **Ex Post Facto Clause** (Art. 1, Sec. 10, Clause 1) (states prohibited from penalizing conduct that was engaged in before the law was passed)

    G. **Impairment of Contracts Clause** (Art. 1, Sec.10, Clause 1) (except in the valid use of its police powers, states prohibited from enacting laws that impair existing obligations under prior contracts:

        Example: *State ex rel. Anderson v. Brand*, 303 U.S. 95 (1938), where the Supreme Court ruled that the Indiana legislature's repeal of a 1927 tenure law, that had previously created a system of continuing, indefinite contracts for permanent teachers, illegally impaired the continuing contract of such a teacher who had been dismissed.

    H. **Judicial Authority** (Art. 3) (establishment of and vesting judicial power in the Supreme Court and those lesser courts that Congress deems necessary to establish)

    I. **Reservation of State Rights** (Tenth Amendment) (powers in the U.S. Constitution that are not granted to the United States, nor prohibited to the states, are reserved to the states; since the power to create a system of education is neither given to Congress nor prohibited to the states, it is deemed a state power)

II. *State Constitution*

    A. **Delegation of legal power to the state legislature to provide an educational system** (such phraseology as "general and uniform," "tuition without charge," "tuition free," and "equally open to all")

    B. Establishment of and vesting judicial power in the state supreme court (and those lower courts deemed needed by the legislature)

III. *State Legislature*

    A. **Creation of and delegation of legal power to state-level education agencies** (state board and department of education, teacher/administrator licensing board, labor relations board)

    B. Creation of and delegation of legal power to local community boards of education

IV. School Boards
A. **Specific Powers** (express authority in only those specific areas stated in legislation, e.g., employ and compensate staff; implied authority from what can reasonably be deduced from a specific power, e.g., as part of compensation, pay, moving expenses)
B. **Homerule Powers** (grant of broad powers in the conduct of the school district, limited only by what is expressly prohibited in constitutions, statutes, and agency regulations)

V. Judicial System
A. Interpretation of meaning of constitutions, statutes, regulations, and school board policies
B. Determining the existence of legal authority in governmental decision-makers and whether such authority was applied consistent with law
C. Deciding conflicts between parties with real interests at stake

II. FEDERAL COURT SYSTEM

The judicial authority, which arbitrates justice regarding constitutional rights within the educational system, is the Federal court system. This system is accessed by and available to all those associated with the educational process. After hearing a case, the court's decision then becomes the standard by which future cases will be judged, and to which school leaders can look for guidance. The procedure by which these precedents and standards are determined is described below, followed by an example of the application of this process to a specific case.

A. Access to Federal District (Trial) Court: "Section 1983"

As applied to public schools, a person or entity has initial access to a federal district (trial) court when the plaintiff has a real (as opposed to hypothetical) stake in a federal question that will involve application of the U.S. Constitution, federal statutes, or federal agency regulations. The specific avenue of access created by Congress in the Civil Rights Act of 1871 is codified at Title 42, section 1983 of the United States Code, which reads in relevant part:

> Every person who, under color of any statute, ordinance, regulation, custom, or usage, of any State or Territory or the District of Columbia, subjects, or causes to be subjected, any citizen of the United States or other person within the jurisdiction thereof to the deprivation of any rights, privileges, or immunities secured by the Constitution and laws, shall be liable to the party injured in an action at law, suit in equity, or other proper proceeding for redress. . . .

Courts have interpreted the term "person" to include a corporation, an unincorporated entity or group, or particular entity of government, including the board of education of a school district.

Students of education law will frequently see reference to the phrase "section 1983 action," which is used when a plaintiff sues in federal district court (or a state court) alleging that an individual school board member, administrator, teacher, and/or the corporate school district, has acted under "color of state law" to deprive the plaintiff of a right established by the federal constitution, statutes, or agency regulations.

B. Appeal to Federal Circuit Court

The party that loses a particular issue (or issues) before the federal trial court may appeal to the federal circuit court that has jurisdiction to hear appeals from district courts in specific states. Normally, the appeal is heard by a three-judge panel, which renders a decision after a **review** of the trial court record, the briefs of the parties, and of the laws at issue. No witness testimony or other evidence is introduced at the appellate level. A non-prevailing party may ask all the circuit judges to review the panel's decision, and if granted, the decision of the entire circuit is called an *en banc* ruling.

The following is a list of the twelve federal circuit courts of appeal that consider education-related cases. The first eleven are the numbered circuits with the abbreviations of those states or territories comprising each circuit.

First:	ME, MA, NH, PR,* RI
Second:	CT, NY, VT
Third:	DE, PA, NJ, VI*
Fourth:	MD, NC, SC, VA, WV
Fifth:	LA, MS, TX
Sixth:	KY, MI, OH, TN
Seventh:	IL, IN, WI
Eighth:	AR, IA, MN, MO, NE, ND, SD
Ninth:	AL, AZ, CA, ID, HI, MT, NV, OR, WA
Tenth:	CO, KS, NM, OK, UT, WY
Eleventh:	AL, FL, GA
Twelfth:	District of Columbia

* PR is Puerto Rico and VI is Virgin Islands.

It is important to note that there may be inconsistencies and discrepancies among the different circuits. Federal circuit courts may examine a particular issue with the same or similar set of facts and arrive at opposite conclusions.

For example, as to the question of whether or not the use of drug-detecting canines to sniff students is a search within the meaning of the Fourth Amendment, the Seventh Circuit has ruled that it is not a search, *Doe v. Renfrow*, 631 F.2d 91 (7th Cir. 1980), *cert. denied*, 451 U.S. 1022 (1981), whereas the Fifth Circuit ruled it a search in *Horton v. Goose Creek Indep. Sch. Dist.*, 690 F.2d 470 (5th Cir. 1982). Because the Supreme Court has not decided this question, the two circuits remain divided. This means that students in Illinois, Indiana, and Wisconsin (Seventh Circuit) may have their persons sniffed by a dog without there being a Fourth Amendment "search," but such actions are a search in the Fifth Circuit states of Louisiana, Mississippi, and Texas. <u>Only if the Supreme Court decides the issue does it become the legal standard in all of the states</u>.

It should be further noted: A decision of a federal district court or circuit court of appeals may or not be "published" at the court's discretion. A published decision may be cited as authority in subsequent cases and will be cited at the district (trial) court level with the abbreviation for "Federal Supplement", i.e., either "F.Supp.", "F.Supp.2d," or "F.Supp.3d," followed in parentheses by the abbreviation of the district's state location and the year of the decision. Hypothetical example: *Doe v. Smith*, 788 F.Supp.2d 102 (N.D.Ind. 1998). This would be volume 788 of the second series of the Federal Supplement, starting at page 102, with the court being the northern district of Indiana and the year, 1998). Some states are divided into east-west districts, with some, due to lower populations, having the entire state as one district. An example of the latter would be the district of New Hampshire, or "D.N.H."

At the circuit court of appeals level, if a decision is published, the citation after the names of the parties will contain an "F," "F2d," or "F3rd" reference to the Federal Reporter using the volume number preceding the "F" and page number following, and concluding with a parenthetical notation naming the particular circuit and the year of the decision.

C. *Appeal to the United States Supreme Court*

A non-prevailing party at the circuit court level may appeal to the Supreme Court via what is termed a "petition for certiorari." The Supreme Court, on average, accepts only about five percent of the petitions for review. (Many of the circuit court citations, like the one in *Doe v. Renfrow*, above, are followed by "cert. denied," which means the losing party's attempted appeal was rejected.)

When the Supreme Court accepts a certiorari petition, it will normally set the matter for oral argument, and then issue a decision by the end of its term, thus establishing national precedent on the litigated point(s) of law. State and federal courts are bound to follow such precedent when deciding cases based on the same facts. However, since fact situations differ from case to case, and since the Supreme Court's language is subject to different interpretations, lower courts will not always follow what some would believe to be the Court's "precedent." This will then initiate another cycle of appeals to the Court.

Basis for appeals to the Supreme Court

-- Setting a legal standard that, when followed and applied by the lower courts to a different set of facts, results in the Court reversing the circuit court because the outcome is not what it could have originally intended.

For example, the Court in *Tinker v. Des Moines Indep. Sch. Dist.*, 393 U.S. 503 (1969) established a substantial disruption/material interference standard when judging a public school's discipline of personal speech of a student. When the federal trial court and the Ninth Circuit Court of Appeals applied the *Tinker* standard to a student's lewd speech at a convocation to nominate student council officers, the lower courts found a lack of evidence of substantial disruption or material interference and ruled for the student. On appeal, however, the Supreme Court in *Bethel Sch. Dist. No. 403 v. Fraser*, 478 U.S. 675 (1986) reversed the circuit court, distinguished the *Fraser* facts from those of *Tinker*, and ruled that speech that is lewd, vulgar, indecent, or plainly offensive is unprotected and can be regulated by school officials.

-- Challenges to prior Supreme Court precedent are also based on changes in social thought and opinion.

For example: Although the Court in its 1896 "separate but equal" ruling, upheld racial segregation by state officials in Louisiana railway cars, *Plessy v. Ferguson*, 163 U.S. 537 (1896), it unanimously ruled in 1954 that segregated schools are "inherently unequal," *Brown v. Board of Education of Topeka*, 347 U.S. 483, 495 (1954).

-- Changes in the makeup of the justices on the Court.

For example: In the second quickest turnaround in school-related Court rulings (twelve years) the Court reversed itself on the issue of public school teachers giving instruction in parochial schools.

In *Agostini v. Felton*, 521 U.S. 203 (1997), the Court ruled that the First Amendment's "Establishment Clause" is not violated by having public school teachers, under a federal program commonly called "Title I," teach in religious schools. The 1997 decision overruled two of its 1985 rulings that found just the opposite.

Note: The quickest turnaround was three years. See *West Virginia State Bd. of Ed. v. Barnette*, 319 U.S. 624 (1943) that upheld a Jehovah Witness student's freedom of speech not to stand and participate in the Pledge of Allegiance, and overruled *Minersville Sch. Dist. v. Gobitis*, 310 U.S. 586 (1940) that upheld the expulsion of two Jehovah Witness students who had refused to participate in the required pledge.

D. Liability under Section 1983

The school district, as a separate legal entity, may only be held liable in a section 1983 action when the district's policy, custom, or practice violates the federal Constitution, statutes, or regulations. *Monell v. Department of Social Services of New York,* 436 U.S. 658 (1978). The district may **not** be held liable for the actions of its employees as long as they are not acting pursuant to the district's policy, custom, or practice. A school employee may be found individually liable under section 1983, but depending on state immunity statutes, the damages caused by the employee's actions may be paid by the school district if such actions were taken in good faith within the scope of employment.

The following case is an example and discussion of the appeals procedure used in a specific case:

CASE
Springdale Education Association v. Springdale Sch. Dist.,
133 F3d 649 (8th Cir. 1998) (emphasis added)

The Springdale Education Association and its president, Wendell Ridenour, and Ridenour and Susan Rowe, individually (hereinafter, collectively, "the union"), brought this action pursuant to 42 U.S.C. § 1983 against the Springdale School District and its superintendent, Jim Rollins, in both his individual and official capacities. The union appeals from the district court's dismissal of each claim with prejudice, and from the denial of its motion to reconsider the dismissals. We affirm in part, reverse in part, and remand.

[Facts:] This appeal arises from an apparent conflict between Rollins and those individuals in the district's employ who have associated themselves with the Springdale Education Association, a local union.

-- In its initial complaint, **the union charged that certain actions and statements by Rollins** (and other unnamed district employees) **evincing an anti-union sentiment were violative of the First Amendment. The union sought to assign liability for its alleged constitutional injuries both to the district and Rollins under section 1983**. . . .

-- The union's amended complaint alleged that on May 29, 1996, Rollins directed the Springdale school board attorney to research the legal question whether the district could legally terminate the employment of teachers for involvement in union activities.

-- In addition, Rollins stated at a public meeting that as long as he was superintendent "classified or non-certified district personnel were not going to be members of the Springdale Education Association" and that "he would 'not stand for it.'"

-- Moreover, "Rollins or those under his direction or control" encouraged or coerced employees of the district not to join the union, subjected district employees to "ridicule and contempt in public and private meetings," and placed Rowe, a non-certified district employee, on probation "in direct retaliation for her lawful activities" on behalf of the union.

-- Further, "[s]upervisors under the direction of and with the knowledge of Rollins" had expressed to members of the union the hope that they could "be saved from this 'satanic organization,' referring to the Springdale Education Association, AEA, and/or NEA." . . .

Legal issue of school board liability due to the act of the superintendent: The legal precedent: To state a claim under section 1983, a plaintiff must set forth facts that allege an action was performed under color of state law that resulted in a constitutional injury. . . . **A local government, however, cannot be held liable under section 1983 for an injury inflicted solely by its employees or agents on a theory of respondeat superior**. *See Andrews v. Fowler* , 98 F.3d 1069, 1074 (8th Cir. 1996) (citing *Monell v. Department of Social Servs. of City of New York, 436 U.S. 658, 694* (1978)). Rather, **a plaintiff seeking to impose such liability is required to identify either an official municipal policy or a widespread custom or practice that caused the plaintiff's injury**. . . .

The identification of an official policy as a basis upon which to impose liability ensures that a municipality is held liable only for constitutional deprivations "resulting from the decisions of its duly constituted legislative body or of those officials whose acts may fairly be said to be those of the municipality." . . . Similarly, **actions performed pursuant to a municipal "custom" not formally approved by an authorized decision maker "may fairly subject a municipality to liability on the theory that the relevant practice is so widespread as to have the force of law."**

As the district court noted, **neither the union's complaint nor amended complaint, read liberally, alleges that any constitutional injury was the result of an official policy or widespread custom of the school district.** Instead, **every alleged action is attributed specifically to Rollins, or to unnamed persons "under his direction or control."** . . . The amended complaint is thus insufficient, on its face, to state a claim against the district. *See, e.g. , Baxter by Baxter v. Vigo County Sch. Corp.,* 26 F.3d 728, 735-36 (7th Cir. 1994) (**dismissal of county school corporation proper when complaint failed to adequately allege policies or customs on part of corporation**).

Nevertheless, **the union attempts in its brief to attribute the actions of Rollins to the district by asserting that Rollins is an authorized district policymaker**. Any action taken by Rollins, it contends, must therefore have constituted official district policy. We have summarized the applicable law regarding this theory as follows:

-- Although municipal liability for violating constitutional rights may arise from a single act of a policy maker, that act must come from one in an authoritative policy making position and represent the official policy of the municipality . . . . Therefore, "[w]hen an official's discretionary decisions are constrained by policies not of that official's making, those policies, rather than the subordinate's departures from them, are the act of the municipality."

-- Whether a person is an authorized policymaker for purposes of assigning municipal liability is a question of state law. *See Jett v. Dallas Indep. Sch. Dist. , 491 U.S. 701, 737* (1989). . . .

-- The **district court determined that Rollins was not an authorized policymaker for the school district under Arkansas law,** precluding any claim against the district for his actions under the "official policy" theory of municipal liability. We agree with this conclusion.

-- With regard to all school district policies, a school superintendent is empowered only to "recommend" changes, which may or may not become "proposals." . . .

The union argues, however, that Rollins was, in fact, the district's final policymaker with respect to Rowe's being placed on probation in retaliation for union activities. Arkansas law does not establish procedures for placing school district employees on some sort of explicit probation. A superintendent does have authority to place a teacher or a non-certified district employee on suspension. . . . However, those suspended are entitled to a hearing within ten days, and only the school board may terminate employment or continue a suspension for any definite period of time. . . . An employee cannot lose compensation without action by the board. . . .

-- Arkansas law is clear, then, that a school board, and not a superintendent, has ultimate responsibility for all district policies, including policies involving unfavorable employment action. . . . Nowhere in the union's amended complaint is it alleged that any "probation" suffered by Rowe was ever ratified or approved by the board, tacitly or otherwise. Accordingly, we agree with the district court that municipal liability for such an action cannot be premised upon a vague allegation directed solely at Rollins or the anonymous subordinates to which the union has repeatedly referred.

The union also briefly argues that the amended complaint is sufficient to state a section 1983 claim against the district under the theory **that actions and statements by Rollins and others indicate that the district has a widespread custom of unconstitutional anti-union practices. Under such a theory, liability may be established through proof that the alleged conduct was so pervasive among nonpolicymaking employees of the municipality as to constitute a custom or usage with the force of law**. . . .

-- We have held that in order to state such a claim, a plaintiff must allege facts, which if true, would tend to prove:

(1) **The existence of a continuing, widespread, persistent pattern of unconstitutional misconduct by the governmental entity's employees;**

(2) **Deliberate indifference to or tacit authorization of such conduct by the governmental entity's policymaking officials after notice to the officials of that misconduct;**

(3) **That plaintiff was injured by acts pursuant to the governmental entity's custom,** i.e., that the custom was the moving force behind the constitutional violation.

-- We agree with the district court that the amended complaint does not allege facts which, if true, would be sufficient to demonstrate the district's deliberate indifference to or tacit authorization of any sort of pervasive custom of unconstitutional conduct by district employees as measured by such a standard. . . .

Issue of individual liability of superintendent under section 1983:

. . . [A] supervisor may be subject to individual liability under section 1983 "**if he directly participates in a constitutional violation.**" . . . This is true regardless of whether the supervisor is an authorized policymaker for purposes of municipal liability. . . . In other words, Rollins need not be a final policymaker for the district in order to be subject to individual liability for actions that he himself performed.

-- **Teachers have the right to associate with the union of their choice.** . . . School officials, in turn, while "free to express their views on unions and to urge teachers to join or not to join a union," may not "terminate or otherwise discriminate against employees who act against their wishes."

-- **Accepting as true her allegation that Rollins was responsible for placing her on probation and that he took such action intending to punish her for involvement in union activities, we conclude that Rowe has stated a claim against Rollins that is sufficient to survive a motion to dismiss.** The dismissal of all claims against the district is affirmed. The dismissal of claims by the union and Ridenour against Rollins is affirmed. The dismissal of Rowe's claim against Rollins in his individual capacity is reversed, and the case is remanded to the district court for further proceedings consistent with this opinion.

CASE

Porter v. Ascension Parish School Board,
393 F.3d 608 (5th Cir. 2004) (emphasis added):

. . . Because Adam raised a material fact question with respect to his First Amendment claim, **we must proceed to ascertain whether Adam's rights were "clearly established" such that "it would be clear to a reasonable [official] that his conduct was unlawful in the situation he confronted." "This is not to say that an official action is protected by qualified immunity unless the very act in question has previously been held unlawful, but it is to say that in the light of pre-existing law the unlawfulness must be apparent." Even if we find that Adam's right to First Amendment protection is clearly established, Principal Braud will still receive qualified immunity if his actions were objectively reasonable in light of the circumstances he faced at the time he acted. Qualified immunity should be recognized if officials "of reasonable competence could disagree on [whether a particular action is lawful]."** The Supreme Court has observed that the protection afforded by qualified immunity is broad, protecting "all but the plainly incompetent or those who knowingly violate the law."

It is indisputable that expressions such as Adam's drawing, provided that they do not constitute a true threat, are entitled to First Amendment protection. It is also clear that such drawings are entitled to **diminished First Amendment protection when composed by a student on-campus, or purposefully brought onto a school campus where they become on-campus speech subject to special limitations.** The line dividing fully protected "off-campus" speech from less protected "on-campus" speech is unclear, however, in cases such as this involving off-campus speech brought on-campus without the knowledge or permission of the speaker.

Many courts have applied the *Tinker* standard in evaluating off-campus student speech later brought on-campus by persons other than the speaker. These cases have dealt with such things as "underground" student newspapers distributed off-campus, student run websites created on off-campus computers, and various writings brought on-campus by students other than their original author.

Although reaching differing conclusions as to the legality of restrictions placed upon the speech in question, these cases consistently approach off-campus speech brought on-campus as subject to regulation under *Tinker*'s "material and substantial" disruption test.

Not all courts have adopted this approach, however, and some have found that off-campus speech is entitled to full First Amendment protection even when it makes its way onto school grounds without the assistance of the speaker. Still others have adopted a combination approach, analyzing off-campus speech under a flurry of standards in an effort to comprehensively address all possible legal approaches. Frustrated by these inconsistencies, commentators have begun calling for courts to more clearly delineate the boundary line between off-campus speech entitled to greater First Amendment protection, and on-campus speech subject to greater regulation.

Because Adam's drawing was composed off-campus, displayed only to members of his own household, stored off-campus, and not purposefully taken by him to EAHS or publicized in a way certain to result in its appearance at EAHS, we have found that the drawing is protected by the First Amendment. Furthermore, we have found that it is neither speech directed at the campus nor a purposefully communicated true threat. However, **a reasonable school official facing this question for the first time would find no "preexisting" body of law from which he could draw clear guidance and certain conclusions. Rather, a reasonable school official would encounter a body of case law sending inconsistent signals as to how far school authority to regulate student speech reaches beyond the confines of the campus**.

Given the unsettled nature of First Amendment law as applied to off-campus student speech inadvertently brought on campus by others, the contours of **Adam's right to First Amendment protection in the present case cannot be deemed "clearly established" such that it would be clear to a reasonable EAHS official that sanctioning Adam based on the content of his drawing was unlawful under the circumstances. Thus, Braud is entitled to qualified immunity**.

Even if Adam's rights were clearly established at the time of his expulsion, **Braud's determination that the drawing was not entitled to First Amendment protection was objectively reasonable. The Supreme Court has observed that, even when a particular legal doctrine is clearly established, "[i]t is sometimes difficult for an [official] to determine how the relevant legal doctrine . . . will apply to the factual situation the [official] confronts."** The record indicates that, at the time he recommended Adam for expulsion, Braud was aware that Adam was responsible for the drawing, that the drawing was two or three years old, and that the drawing had been brought to Galvez Middle School by Adam's younger brother. **These facts raise the subtle but important legal questions of whether the drawing constitutes on-campus speech, or an intentionally communicated threat. Although we have answered both of these queries in the negative, we cannot say that all reasonable school officials facing these circumstances would reach the same conclusion. . . .**

Without condoning violations of student's constitutional rights, qualified immunity recognizes that school officials, such as Principal Braud, must be allowed to make reasonable mistakes when forced to act in the face of uncertainty. Given the benefit of hindsight, the effort to fault Principal Braud for failing to conduct a more thorough investigation into the facts has purpose. For instance, Braud could have spoken with Andrew Breen about how he acquired the drawing, or queried Kendall Goudeau and other members of Adam's friend group about whether Adam had recently discussed the drawing or shown it to them. In fairness, however, it was reasonable for Braud to forego further investigation given LeBlanc's waiver of Adam's right to a hearing. By waiving the hearing, LeBlanc eliminated an important opportunity for Braud and the Ascension Parish School Board to develop the facts more fully.

Given the unique facts of the present case, we find that Braud acted without the benefit of established law that was clear in its application to these facts, and in an objectively reasonable manner. Thus, he is entitled to qualified immunity with respect to Adam's First Amendment claim. . . .

III. STATE COURT SYSTEM

A. *Trial Courts*

The state constitution establishes the judicial system, including trial courts. The constitution may create particular trial courts and specifically state their jurisdictions, or it may name them and leave it to the state legislature to set their jurisdictions. (Interestingly, trial courts in New York are called supreme courts.)

The main function of trial courts is to hear and admit the factual evidence in original cases and decide the dispute. A secondary function is to serve as reviewing courts in appeals of state agency (and some school board) determinations. In some states, the constitution or legislature has trial courts act in a review capacity, which would include reviewing a school board's decision to dismiss a teacher or expel a student. In this review capacity, the trial court will generally determine if the administrative body has followed proper procedure, based its decision on substantial evidence of record, and conducted a fair proceeding.

State trial courts also have the power to decide "Section 1983" disputes where, for example, a school employee or board of education is alleged to have violated the federal constitutional rights of a person while acting under color of state law. Often times, school boards will have Section 1983 actions that are filed in state court removed to a federal district court.

B. Appellate Courts

The state constitution establishes an initial court of appeals to review trial court decisions and a final court of appeals, called the Supreme Court in all states except New York and Maryland, to review the court of appeals' decision. The ruling of the state's highest court is final in all cases except those involving a federal question. When a federal issue is involved, the non-prevailing party may petition the U.S. Supreme Court to hear it, but the Supreme Court has the discretion to deny the appeal.

SCENARIOS
STATE AND APPLY THE RELEVANT LEGAL RULE(S) TO THE FACTS.

1. School Board had no policy governing student searches. Over each of the past 10 years, Board received at least two written or oral complaints at its meetings that a particular sixth grade teacher frequently made all students in the class completely empty their book bags, pockets, purses, and shoes and socks. Superintendent reported to Board that Teacher was outstanding, produced very high test scores, and, in fact, conducted such searches. Board and Superintendent took no action to stop the searchers because they believed the searches were a positive tool in deterring drug and weapon possession even in light of school attorney's written opinion (also given Teacher) that case law was clear that such searches violated the Fourth Amendment.

When Teacher's suspicionless search produced a loaded handgun taped to Student's lower leg that resulted in expulsion, parents on Student's behalf filed Section 1983 action against Teacher and Superintendent in both their individual and official capacities, and School Board in its official capacity. School Attorney filed motion to dismiss the complaint against the two employees and against the School Board claiming there would be no liability against any of them.

2. School Board was given the express power by State Legislature to employ teachers and all other employees deemed necessary and to set their compensation, including fringe benefits. Superintendent asked Board President if it would be "OK" to pay an additional ten sick days to Teacher Aide because she had exhausted those granted by board policy, but had run into complications following surgery and needed additional days. Superintendent stated that she was an outstanding employee who had been offered a job in the private sector and wanted to induce her to stay with some added fringe benefits. President agreed and payroll was instructed to pay the days. Payroll Clerk complied but called State Auditing Agency which informed Superintendent and Board President that they had to get the extra ten day's pay back from Teacher Aide.

When School Board failed to act, State Auditing Agency referred the matter to the State Attorney General who filed a civil suit in state trial court for the money's return.

CHAPTER 2

COMMON LAW OF TORTS

This chapter discusses tort law as it applies to the public and private school context. When an individual claims injury to one's person or property by the wrongful act of another, the courts of each state, via common (or case) law, have established legal standards for determining whether a civil wrong (tort) was committed. If liability is found, the court will decide the appropriate remedy by awarding damages against the one committing the tort.

State legislatures have passed statutes, commonly called "tort claims acts," which usually cover such matters as the length of time to file a tort claim action (statute of limitations), the allocation of damages when partial liability is found against the plaintiff (comparative negligence), governmental immunity, individual liability, and damage limitations when the injury was caused by an agent of a governmental body.

In the public or private school context, the subjects that will be addressed under state common law tort subjects are negligence, defamation, assault and battery, parent liability for tortuous acts of children, and constitutional torts.

I. COMMON LAW NEGLIGENCE

Liability for negligence occurs when injury to a person or property directly results from the failure of a public or private school board of education or any school employee (or agent) to exercise the requisite standard of care while acting on behalf of the school within the scope of the employment (or agency) relationship.

A. *Respondeat Superior*

Under the common law doctrine of "respondeat superior," the entity that is superior is required to respond, via the payment of damages, to the injurious acts committed within the scope of the employment or agency relationship by those employed by, or designated as agents of, the superior. The responsibility of the superior (or "master") to respond with damages for the tortuous acts of its employees or agents (or "servants") is sometimes referred to as "vicarious liability," i.e., the superior (master) is liable in place of the employee or agent (servant).

The common law of agency refers to the superior as the "principal," and those who are designated to act for the principal as "agents." It is somewhat rare in the school context to have a "principal/agent" issue arise, but it did in two Indiana cases. As to whether or not a person is acting as an "agent" of the school, the following judicial statement is helpful:

> Agency is a relationship resulting from the manifestation of consent by one party to another that the latter will act as an agent for the former. In addition, the agent must acquiesce to the arrangement and be subject to the principal's control. An apparent agency is also initiated by a manifestation of the principal. However, the necessary manifestation is one made by the principal to a third party who in turn is instilled with a reasonable belief that another person is an agent of the principal. It is essential that there be some form of communication, direct or indirect, by the principal, which instills a reasonable belief in the mind of the third party. Statements or manifestations made by the agent are not sufficient to create an apparent agency relationship.

Swanson v. Wabash College, 504 N.E.2d 327, 331-32, (Ind.App. 1987) (citations omitted).

Example of application: In the case of *Wickey v. Sparks, Peru Comm. Sch. Corp., and Heartland Career Center*, 642 N.E.2d 262 (Ind.App.2Dist. 1994), the court ruled that a Peru school student, who was permitted by the school to drive from the Career Center (where vocational courses were taken) back to Peru for afternoon classes, was not the agent of either school when she caused an auto accident that injured a third party. The injured person failed to prove that an agency relationship had been created by either of the schools manifesting that the student was their agent.

B. Acting within the Scope of Employment

In a case involving an employee's sexual abuse of a student, where the school was relieved of liability, the Iowa Supreme Court clearly expressed the legal standard for scope of employment as follows:

> [F]or an act to be within the scope of employment the conduct complained of "must be of the same general nature as that authorized or incidental to the conduct authorized." . . . Thus, an act is deemed to be within the scope of one's employment "where such act is necessary to accomplish the purpose of the employment and is intended for such purpose." . . . The question is whether the employee's conduct "is so unlike that authorized that it is 'substantially different.'" . . . Said another way, "a deviation from the employer's business or interest to pursue the employee's own business or interest must be *substantial in nature* to relieve the employer of liability."

Godar v. Edwards, 588 N.W.2d 701 at 705-706 (Iowa 1999) (internal citations omitted; court's emphasis).

Example of application of the standard: In applying the legal standard to the facts, the court concluded "that any alleged sexual abuse by Edwards was not an act committed within the scope of his employment for which the school district may be held liable." *Id.* at 706. Said the court:

> First, we believe that it cannot reasonably be said that sexual abuse by Edwards is "of the same general nature" as that authorized by the school district in connection with his duties as curriculum director . . . Nor can it be said that any inappropriate acts by Edwards were committed in furtherance of his duties as curriculum director. To the contrary, any alleged sexual abuse by Edwards would be a substantial deviation from his duties as curriculum director and "substantially different" in nature from that authorized by the school district. . . .

There simply was no evidence to show that Edwards' alleged conduct was expected, foreseeable, or sanctioned by the school district. We do not believe that sexual abuse by a teacher is a "normal" risk associated with the objectives of educating students such that it should be borne by the school district. *Id.* at 706-07.

C. Legal Standard for Negligence

The legal standard created by common (case) law consists of the following elements, which the plaintiff has the burden of proving: (1) legal duty of care owed the plaintiff; (2) breach of the legal duty of care; (3) injury to plaintiff or plaintiff's property; and (4) injury was a direct or proximate cause of the breach.

C1. Legal Duty of Care

Generally, schools, via their employees (and other agents, e.g., parent volunteers who help chaperone a field trip), owe a duty of care to students once they come under the responsibility and supervision of school personnel. For example, students who walk to school or are waiting at the bus stop are under the supervision, not of the school, but of their parents until the point that school personnel take responsibility for their care. Similarly, at the end of the school day, the school's duty to supervise ends, and the parent's duty begins when the students have safely walked off school property or away from the school bus.

The Minnesota Supreme Court in the case of *Anderson by Anderson v. Shaughnessy*, 526 N.W.2d 625 (Minn. 1995), which involved a student injured from a paint ball shot by another student right after the school bus pulled away at the end of the day, stated that "[t]he duty of care with respect to transporting school children has yet to be expanded beyond the safe deposit of the children at their scheduled destinations in a manner designed to allow their safe crossing of streets after disembarkment. . . ." *Id.* at 626.

An exception to the requirement that students be under the responsibility and supervision of school personnel before the legal duty of care attaches is when an employee, while acting within the scope of employment, gains knowledge that creates a reasonable foreseeability of harm when the student is no longer under the school's supervision. For example, when a teacher during school hours learns that Student A plans to "beat up" Student B after getting off the school bus that day, a legal duty of care arises on the part of the teacher to take reasonable measures, such as contacting the parents and warning the students, to prevent the now foreseeable event.

A school's legal duty of care has been expressed by the Iowa Supreme Court as:

> Duty is a question of whether the relationship between the actor and the injured person gives rise to any legal obligation on the actors (*sic*) part for the benefit if the injured person.

Godar v. Edwards, 588 N.W.2d 701 at 707 (Iowa 1999).

As to the extent of the legal duty that may be owed to an injured person, the court stated at 708:

> The duty of a school district concerning the supervision and safety of students is not unlimited. Rather the scope of the school's duty is limited by what risks are reasonably foreseeable. . . . Wrongful activities will only be foreseeable "if the district knew or in the exercise of reasonable care should have known of the risk that resulted in the occurrence.

Application example of a case wherein the legal duty of care standard was applied:

CASE BRIEF

Mangold v. Dept. of Natural Resources and Switzerland County Sch. Corp.,
756 N.E.2d 970 (Ind. 2001)

[Facts:] Junior high school as part of science curriculum had a state conservation officer instruct students on firearm safety wherein a shotgun shell was dismantled and its parts explained with officer telling students that they should never handle ammunition unless an adult was present. Twelve-year-old went home, partially took apart father's shotgun shell without adult supervision, struck firing pin with hammer and chisel, caused explosion, and blinded himself in one eye.

[Legal issue:] Under the common law of negligence, did school owe a legal duty of care toward student who was injured at home?

[Lower court action:] Court of Appeals affirmed trial court's summary judgment for school because no legal duty of care was created in that the injury occurred at student's home and not on school property. It cited earlier appellate court precedent, which ruled that no duty of care was created when teacher allowed student to take golf club home and he was injured when younger brother accidentally hit him with club.

[Supreme Court ruling:] Summary judgment for school reversed in favor of student. Trial court erred as matter of law in finding school owed no duty of care to student simply because accident occurred off school property.

[Rationale:] Generally, in determining if a legal duty exists, courts must balance (1) the relationship between the parties, (2) the existence of reasonable foreseeabilty of harm, and (3) public policy considerations. However, because in prior school cases the Supreme Court (Ind.) has established "a duty for school authorities to exercise reasonable care for the safety of children under their control," *Miller v. Griesel*, 308 N.E.2d 701, 706 (Ind. 1974), where "we essentially have made a policy decision that a school's relationship to its students, the foreseeability of harm, and public policy concerns entitle students to protection." *Mangold*, 756 N.E.2d at 974, "and the focus shifts to whether a given set of facts represents a breach of that duty."

"As applied to the facts in this case, the question is whether School breached its duty of reasonable care and supervision by providing . . . [student] with inaccurate information and inaccurate warnings when it instructed him on firearm safety. . . we see no relationship between the location of . . . [student's] injuries and School's duty of reasonable care and supervision."

C2. Breach of Legal Duty

Generally speaking, one's duty to others is to act as a reasonable or ordinary person would act. What actions are reasonable varies with the circumstances. For example, a kindergarten teacher's actions in supervising class are very different from a college professor's actions due to differences in maturity. The element of foreseeability of harm is important in assessing whether reasonable care was exercised. The jury will decide if a reasonable person would have foreseen a risk and taken sufficient steps to prevent any foreseeable harm. Thus, one's actions in response to a foreseeable harm is not measured by what the defendant actually knew or did, but it is determined by an objective standard—what a reasonable or ordinary person in the defendant's place should have known or done.

Once the duty of care is established by showing how a reasonable or ordinary person would have acted under the circumstances, the defendant's conduct will be measured against that standard of care. If the defendant's conduct does not conform to the reasonable standard of care, then a breach of one's duty to the plaintiff is shown.

Application example of a case wherein the standard for reasonable care was applied:

CASE BRIEF
Miller v. Griesel, 308 N.E.2d 701 (Ind. 1974)

[Facts:] Ten fifth graders without apparent discipline problems remained in class during recess to work on a salt relief map project. The teacher, pursuant to her principal's verbal directive that permitted teachers to leave the room if another teacher was secured to check in on the students, did so. While absent and after another teacher had already checked on them once and then departed, the student who had brought a small tackle box from home opened it to show student Miller its contents because Miller was thinking of trading some pencils for it. Two batteries and what was thought to be a Christmas tree light with two wires attached were removed by Miller who wanted to see if the light worked. When he touched the wires of what was in reality a dynamite-blasting cap to the batteries, it exploded, causing permanent damage and possible future blindness to one eye.

[Legal issue:] Did the school, via the actions of the two teachers and the principal, breach its duty of reasonable care toward the injured student?

[Lower court action:] The Court of Appeals affirmed the trial court's ruling in favor of the school district's motion on the evidence that was made following the student's presentation of evidence.

[Supreme Court ruling:] Upheld judgment on the evidence ruling in favor of the school district, but for reasons different than stated by the trial court.

[Rationale:] Trial court must answer three questions of law when addressing common law negligence issues before submitting the case to the jury: (1) Does the law recognize any duty on defendant's part to conform his conduct to a requisite standard of care? (2) What standard of care should be imposed on the relationship between the plaintiff and defendant if a legal duty exists? (3) Is the evidence introduced by the plaintiff sufficient as a matter of law to permit the jury to find that the plaintiff has established the required elements of common law negligence?

<u>Legal duty question</u>: "The relationship between the parties here is one of grammar school students and school personnel in the respective positions of teacher, principal, and school board. The specific and initial question of law presented, therefore, is whether the law of this State recognizes a duty for school authorities to exercise reasonable care and supervision for the safety of the children under their control. We believe that schools have such a responsibility and that the relationship of school pupils and school authorities should call into play the well recognized duty in tort law that persons entrusted with children, or others whose characteristics make it likely that they may do somewhat unreasonable things, have a special responsibility recognized by the common law to supervise their charges. . ."

<u>Standard of care question</u>: ". . . The traditional standard to be applied is whether the defendants exercised their duty with the level of care that an ordinary prudent person would under the circumstances. . . . The answers to the first two questions of law posed by this case therefore may be summed up by stating that **the common law of this State recognizes a duty on the part of school personnel to exercise ordinary and reasonable care for the safety of the children under their authority.** [Emphasis added.]

"It should be emphasized here, however, that schools are not intended to be insurers of the safety of their pupils, nor are they strictly liable for any injuries that may occur to them. The duty imposed by this legal relationship is a practical recognition by the law that school officials are required to exercise due care in the supervision of their pupils; that while they are neither an insurer of safety nor are they immune from liability. It is not a harsh burden to require school authorities in some instances to anticipate and guard against conduct of children by which they may harm themselves or others. . ."

<u>Sufficiency of evidence question</u>: "A court should not direct a verdict for a defendant at the close of a plaintiff's evidence unless there is a total absence of evidence or reasonable inference on at least one essential element of plaintiff's case. . . .'

"Applying evidence elicited at trial to the requisite elements of negligence we believe that the plaintiffs failed to meet the basic evidentiary standard outlined above . . . Of course what constitutes due care and adequate supervision depends largely upon the circumstances surrounding the incident such as the number and age of the students left in the classroom, the activity in which they were engaged, the duration of the period in which they were left without supervision, the ease of providing some alternative means of supervision and the extent to which the school board has provided and implemented guidelines and resources to insure adequate supervision. Since the plaintiff failed to show the actual length of time the students were left unattended or that the activity in which they were engaged was particularly hazardous or that any of the students in the room were of a troublesome, mischievous nature we believe the trial court correctly granted the TR. 50 motion."

Second application example:

The *Miller* case was also relied upon in the *Wickey v. Sparks* case, discussed above, where the court had to decide if there was a duty to supervise a student who was allowed to drive between a vocational school and her regular school and caused an accident that injured a member of the general public.

The *Wickey* court examined the factor of the relationship between the parties and found that unlike *Miller*, where the relationship was between students and school authorities, there was no such relationship between the two schools and a stranger who was a member of the general public driving along a highway when she was injured by the student driver.

Secondly, *Wickey* considered the foreseeability of harm factor and determined that the student was a responsible, licensed driver who posed no foreseeable risk of harming other drivers.

Thirdly, *Wickey* discussed the public policy concern factor, cited *Miller's* thinking that "schools are not intended to be insurers of the safety of their pupils, nor are they strictly liable for any injuries that may occur to them," 308 N.E.2d at 706, and concluded that public policy concerns did not impose a common law duty on the two schools to protect the injured member of the general public.

C3. Injury

The plaintiff in a negligence action has the burden of proving that an injury directly resulted from the defendant's action. The injury can be damage to the plaintiff's person or property. Historically, courts have required proof of the existence of a physical impact on the body of the person, so that merely suffering fright from a "close call" is not sufficient to meet this standard and establish liability. However, modern-day courts have softened this rigid standard to some extent in situations where a plaintiff, such as a parent, has been in close proximity to a loved-one, such as a child, and witnessed an injury to the child as a result of the negligent act of another.

C4. Injury as Direct (Proximate) Cause

The plaintiff is required to prove that the injury was a direct or proximate cause of the defendant's negligent act (or failure to act). This need for a causal connection between the breach of duty to use reasonable care and resulting injury is also termed "legal cause."

In some situations, a negligent act of a school employee can be the initial act in a chain of events that leads to a student's injury. However, it may be an intervening factor that was not foreseeable, which actually causes the injury. For example, improper instructions by a chemistry teacher may lead to chemicals becoming unstable and overflowing the test tube, but it could be the intervening events of a student accidentally dropping his book (not caused by the foaming chemicals) that makes a loud noise that startles a girl whose piercing scream causes the teacher, who is about ready to pour a neutralizing agent on the spill, to drop the bottle of agent that shatters and cuts the hand of a nearby student. Here, the original negligent act of the improperly mixed chemicals due to faulty instructions of the teacher would likely not be found to have been the direct, proximate, or legal cause of the injured student's cut hand.

D. Common Law Defenses to Negligence

D1. Contributory Negligence

Although a student may suffer injury due to the negligence of a school employee, the school may escape liability if it can prove that the student's actions were also negligent and contributed to the injury. The age and mental capacity of the student as it relates to the ability to recognize and appreciate the potential consequences of the student's actions leading to injury plays an important role in the determination of contributory negligence. In nearly all cases, the jury makes this decision, but in the following case, the evidence of contributory negligence was so clear and beyond dispute that the court made the determination in a summary judgment ruling.

Although the court in the *Mangold case*, (the exploding shotgun shell case discussed above) did not give the school district the easier and much less expensive route of summary judgment (thus requiring the issue to be set for full trial), it did permit the school to prevail due to the legal defense of contributory negligence. In Indiana, via the Tort Claims Act, a jury at the trial level is not permitted to compare and assess percentages of fault and damages when the defendant is a governmental body, such as a public school. (See I.C. 34-51-2-2.) Therefore, the common law standard applied, which permits a defendant to escape total liability if the plaintiff is found in even the slightest degree to be partially at fault in the cause of his/her injury.

A court majority determined as a matter of law that student Mangold was at least "minimally negligent" and barred him from any recovery of damages.If Mangold had been a nonpublic school student, the private school would have had to face a full trial because it did not have the benefit of the complete common law defense of contributory negligence that prevents recovery of any damages.

Application example of a case wherein the standard for contributory negligence was applied:

CASE BRIEF
Izard v. Hickory City Bd. of Educ., 315 S.E.2d 756 (N.C. Ct.App. 1984).

[Facts:] Plaintiff Izard, a 14-year-old intermediate school student, severed three fingers on his left hand when he attempted to cut a piece of wood on the power saw in industrial arts class. In a previous school he had learned about and used a similar saw. The teacher had spent 20 minutes prior to the injury explaining the proper use and operation of the saw.

[Legal issue:] Did the school establish that the student's conduct amounted to contributory negligence, thus absolving the school of any liability for his injury?

[Lower court action:] The trial court found contributory negligence by the student and ruled in favor of the school on its motion for summary judgment.

[Court of Appeals ruling:] Affirmed the summary judgment ruling in favor of school.

[Rationale:] "A 14-year-old boy is presumed capable of contributory negligence to the same extent as an adult in the absence of evidence that he lacked the capacity, discretion and experience which would ordinarily be possessed by a boy of that age. . . All the evidence indicates that, at the time of the accident, Michael Izard was a normal 14-year-old boy of ordinary capacity, discretion and experience. He was, therefore, capable of contributory negligence."

"In the case at bar, the evidence presented to the trial court appears un-contradicted that, despite being fully instructed and warned about the proper use of the power saw, Michael Izard carelessly moved his hand into the path of the blade, thereby injuring himself. As his own deposition testimony states:

I knew I was supposed to take a board and sweep the other board away so I wouldn't cut my hand but I moved my hand across there and got it up into the blade . . . I was not looking at the blade when I got my hand into it. I was looking at the piece of wood that I was going to push off the floor.

"Even when considered in the light most favorable to the plaintiffs, we find this testimony clearly establishes that Michael Izard's injury was the result of his own contributory negligence."

D2. Assumption of Risk Defense

Assumption of risk, which in some states is termed "incurred risk," is a complete defense to a suit in negligence. It is similar to contributory negligence in that the age and mental competence of the student also plays an important role. The key elements to the legal standard for measuring assumption of risk are: (1) whether the **student knew and understood the danger** of what would happen if a certain action were taken (the same as contributory negligence), and (2) **intentionally** (as opposed to negligently) undertook the action in face of the known danger.

Application example of a case wherein the standard for assumption of risk was applied:

CASE

Beckett v. Clinton Prairie School Corp., 504 N.E.2d 552 (Ind. 1987).

. . . The background facts were well summarized by the Court of Appeals, as follows.

On April 25, 1984, Beckett was injured while participating in baseball practice at Clinton Prairie High School. Beckett, a senior, was in his fourth year as a player on the team. Beckett was an outfielder.

On the day of the injury, the outfielders practiced under assistant coach Dan Hilgedick (Coach Hilgedick) on a long and wide field south of the high school. The regular playing field was too wet for use. Coach Hilgedick conducted an outfielder's drill, in which he was the hitter. Thirty yards directly in front of him was the cut off man (freshman Kent Wein). Thirty to forty yards beyond the cut off man were the outfielders, lined up facing the hitter and approximately perpendicular to the ball's line of flight.

Coach Hilgedick would hit fly balls to the outfielder on the end of the line, who would catch the ball and relay it to the cut off man, who would throw the ball to a shag man standing next to the coach.

The accident occurred after Coach Hilgedick hit a high fly ball to Beckett. The wind was blowing hard and it was difficult for the players to hear. Beckett called for the ball.

Meanwhile, Coach Hilgedick called for the cut off man (Wein) to catch the ball. Beckett said he did not hear Wein call for the ball. Wein said he was only to catch the ball upon receiving instructions from the coach. Neither the coach nor Wein heard Beckett call for the ball. Wein and Beckett collided head-on. Beckett suffered a broken jaw and Wein's nose was broken.

The theory of Beckett's case against Clinton Prairie is that Coach Hilgedick failed to warn Beckett of the danger of the collision, failed to adequately and reasonably supervise the practice, failed to post sufficient personnel to watch for possible collisions, conducted the practice in an unreasonably dangerous manner, and allowed supervisory personnel to participate directly in the practice...

This Court has clearly recognized that there exists a duty on the part of school personnel to exercise ordinary and reasonable care for the safety of the children under their authority. *Miller v. Griesel* (1974), . . .

While expressly noting that schools are not intended to be insurers of the safety of their pupils, nor are they strictly liable for any injuries that may occur to them, this Court in *Miller* held that the appropriate standard is whether a defendant exercised his duty with the level of care of an ordinary prudent person under the same or similar circumstances. Such a factual determination is generally a jury question.

As to this first issue, we therefore agree with the following statement of the Court of Appeals:

Viewing the facts liberally in a light most favorable to Beckett as we must, it is apparent a dispute of material fact exists as to whether Coach Hilgedick's conduct conformed to the requisite standard of care.

On the day of practice, the wind blew at a speed which made coaching commands difficult to hear. Beckett, seventy yards away from the coach, responded to the fly ball in compliance with the written instruction "outfielders have preference over infielders." Coach Hilgedick, knowing his written instructions to outfielders and the wind conditions that day which made hearing difficult, called for the cut off man to catch the ball. It cannot be said his action under the circumstances conformed to the requisite standard of care as a matter of law. 494 N.E.2d at 990. We hold that the trial court erroneously determined as a matter of law that Clinton Prairie did not breach its duty of care to Beckett.

The remaining issue is whether the trial court erred in granting summary judgment on the basis of it's finding that the plaintiff incurred the risk as a matter of law.

Various components of the doctrine of incurred risk were effectively synthesized in a definition of the doctrine of incurred risk as presented by Judge Ratliff in *Power v. Brodie* (1984), Ind.App., . . .:

It involves a mental state of venturousness on the part of the actor, and demands a subjective analysis into the actor's actual knowledge and voluntary acceptance of the risk. By definition ... the very essence of incurred risk is the conscious, deliberate and intentional embarkation upon the course of conduct with knowledge of the circumstances. It requires much more than the general awareness of a potential for mishap. Incurred risk contemplates acceptance of a specific risk of which the plaintiff has *actual* knowledge.

In the present case, however, we need not evaluate whether there is adequate circumstantial evidence of actual knowledge. From our review of the record, we are satisfied that plaintiff's actual knowledge is conclusively shown, and that the trial court correctly determined that Clinton Prairie was entitled to summary judgment on the issue of incurred risk. While the plaintiff at one point in his deposition stated that he never heard of baseball players colliding and that he had no knowledge of any kinds of accidents happening on baseball fields, the other detailed admissions in his deposition provided unequivocal evidence of actual knowledge and appreciation of this specific risk involved. . . .

Therefore, notwithstanding the trial court's error on Issue I, it correctly found on Issue II that the plaintiff incurred the risk of injury as a matter of law, and properly entered summary judgment against plaintiff. Judgment affirmed.

In the *Beckett* case, the court overruled the trial court's finding that there was no negligence on the part of the school. However, even though the actions of the coach that caused the collision and resulting injury to Beckett may have been negligent, the defense of assumption (incurrence) of risk completely absolved the school from any liability for his broken jaw.

E. State-Created Defenses to Negligence: Governmental Immunity

State legislatures, via tort claims acts, have stepped in as a matter of public policy, and modified common law judicial principles. Originally, as a matter of common law, based on the theory that "the king could do no wrong," governmental bodies could not be found liable for the injurious acts of their employees and agents.

Courts began modifying this principle in various situations and now states have enacted legislation declaring that their agencies and local units of government may be sued and required to pay damages for the tortuous acts of their employees. The technical advantage for schools is that a successful defense of governmental immunity means the case never goes to trial, and via a motion to dismiss is dispensed with early at much less cost in time, energy, and litigation fees, which keeps liability insurance rates lower.

Indiana, for example has established twenty-two specific areas of complete immunity for the state and local entities of government (I.C. 34-13-3-3). Four examples of state or governmental immunity appear in section F. below.

F. Immunity of Governmental Entity or Employee

Sec. 3. A governmental entity or an employee acting within the scope of the employee's employment is not liable if a loss results from the following:

> (1) The natural condition of unimproved property. . .
> (3) The temporary condition of a public thoroughfare . . . that results from weather. . .
> (7) The performance of a discretionary function. . .
> (20) Injury to a student or a student's property by an employee of a school corporation if the employee is acting reasonably under a discipline policy adopted under IC 20-33-8-7(b). . . .

As to provision (1), if a school purchases or is given land in its natural condition, and before any improvement is made, a person is injured thereon, the school is immune from any damages (assuming that in the case of a student under the care of the school there was no negligence that allowed the student to escape supervision and wander onto the unimproved property).

In (3), there is immunity if a person is injured due to a slip and fall on an icy school sidewalk or parking lot due to a temporary condition caused by weather. Indiana case law has found that a school sidewalk and university parking lot were "public thoroughfares" and governmental immunity protected the entities because the weather conditions occurred so quickly it did not permit employees to remove the ice in a timely fashion. See *Yerkes v. Heartland Career Center*, 661 N.E.2d 558 (Ind. App. 1995), (sidewalk); *Brunner v. Trustees of Purdue Univ.*, 702 N.E.2d 759 (Ind. App. 1998) (parking lot). A third case, however, did not grant immunity when the snow remained on the school parking lot for six days before a spectator to a wrestling meet fell and was injured. *Hertz v. School City of East Chicago*, 744 N.E.2d 484 (Ind.App. 2001).

In provision (7), a "discretionary function" means a function that as a matter of policy the governmental body may, but is not required to, perform. For example, a school board may decide to purchase a slide for the playground and as a result, a child slips going up the steps and breaks an arm through no fault of the school. If sued, the board's decision to purchase the slide would be granted immunity. (The school, however, could be found liable in negligence for injury caused by its failing in its "ministerial" function to inspect and repair defects in the slide.)

In (20), as long as the court would find that a school employee's action that caused injury to a student or a student's property was reasonable and taken pursuant to a properly adopted discipline policy, immunity would be granted. If the policy prohibits the possession of a cellular device during the school day, and the teacher, after having a student refuse his request to hand it over, starts to remove it from the inside pocket of the student's jacket when it falls to the floor and is broken as a result of getting snagged in the lining, immunity should be found due to the teacher's reasonable actions.

G. Negligent Hiring and Retention

The state common law negligence elements of legal duty, breach of duty by failing to utilize reasonable care, and injury as a direct or proximate cause of such failure have been applied in cases alleging that a school's system of screening candidates for employment and/or its implementation of the system was inadequate and directly resulted in injury to a student. Similarly, state courts have recognized negligence actions when a school is alleged to have used inadequate efforts in investigating and dealing with employees whose actions are known, or could have reasonably have been known, to have caused injury to students.

In the case of *Godar v. Edwards*, 588 N.W.2d 701 (Iowa 1999), the school district was charged with negligent hiring when its curriculum director was alleged to have committed sexual acts upon a student. The court explained the legal standard for negligent hiring, which it expanded to cover the torts of negligent retention and of negligent supervision of employees, as follows:

A party asserting a claim for negligent hiring generally bases the claim upon Restatement (Second) of Agency § 213 (1957). Section 213 provides as follows:

> A person conducting an activity through servants or other agents is subject to liability for harm resulting from his conduct if he is negligent or reckless: . . . . (b) in the employment of improper persons or instrumentalities in work involving risk of harm to others; (c) in the supervision of the activity; or (d) in permitting, or failing to prevent, negligent or other tortuous conduct by persons, whether or not his servants or agents, upon premises or with instrumentalities under his control.

> As one authority from 27 Am. Jur. 2d *Employment Relationship* § 473, at 913 (1996) has explained: The tort of negligent hiring is based on the principle that a person conducting an activity through employees is subject to liability for harm resulting from conduct in the employment of improper persons involving risk of harm to others.

Thus, in order to recover based on a claim of negligent hiring, a plaintiff must prove the following:

(1) that the employer knew, or in the exercise of ordinary care should have known, of its employee's unfitness at the time of hiring;

(2) that through the negligent hiring of the employee, the employee's incompetence, unfitness, or dangerous characteristics proximately caused the resulting injuries;

(3) that there is some employment or agency relationship between the tortfeasor and the defendant employer. . . .

We now join those jurisdictions that have recognized a claim by an injured third party for negligent hiring and conclude that an employer has a duty to exercise reasonable care in hiring individuals, who, because of their employment, may pose a threat of injury to members of the public. We believe that such a claim likewise includes an action for negligent retention and negligent supervision.

588 N.W.2d at 708-09. The *Godar* court upheld the trial court's granting of the school's motion for a directed verdict following the trial, and concluded that the alleged victim failed to produce sufficient evidence that the school superintendent knew at the time the curriculum director was hired of any past history of inappropriate conduct or that the superintendent failed to follow the school's hiring procedures. Likewise, the court found a lack of evidence presented by the plaintiff that the school knew or reasonably should have known that its employee was engaged in the alleged sexual conduct. Hence there was no negligent retention or supervision by the school district.

H. *Intentional Misrepresentation in Hiring Recommendations*

School officials who make recommendations to prospective school employers about present or past employees may be subject to the tort action intentional misrepresentation.

Application example of a case wherein the standard for intentional misrepresentation was applied:

CASE BRIEF

Randi W. v. Muroc Joint Unified Sch. Dist., 929 P.2d 582 (Cal. 1997)
(emphasis added).

[**Facts:**] Plaintiff, who alleged that she was a victim of a sexual assault by her assistant principal (Gadams), when she was 13, sued three previous employers and their administrators for negligent and intentional misrepresentation because of letters of recommendation they had written to Gadams' college placement office after he had left their employ. The letters stressed only positive attributes of Gadams and recommended him without reservation. She alleged that the three writers of the letters knew that Gadams was the subject of alleged sexual misconduct complaints while employed at their respective schools and that the letters formed the basis of his being hired at her school.

[Legal issue:]   Under the common law of negligence and fraud, is a school employer liable for favorable recommendations made about an employee to future school employers without disclosing relevant negative information bearing on the person's fitness to perform the duties of the position?

[Lower court action:] The Court of Appeals reversed the ruling of the trial court that had dismissed the case in favor of the three school districts. The appellate court held that plaintiff's complaint sufficiently alleged a cause of action for negligent misrepresentation and fraud in that the facts alleged that an official in each of the defendant schools negligently or intentionally gave false information to another person that resulted in physical injury to the letter's recipient or a third person.

[Supreme Court ruling:]   Upheld Court of Appeals decision in favor of the student.

[Rationale:]   "[T]he general rule is that all persons have a duty to use ordinary care to prevent others from being injured as the result of their conduct. . . .

[As to forseeability of harm:]   "Based on the facts alleged in the complaint, defendants could foresee that Livingston's [School District] officers would read and rely on defendants' letters in deciding to hire Gadams. Likewise, defendants could foresee that, had they not unqualifiedly recommended Gadams, Livingston would not have hired him. And, finally, defendants could foresee that Gadams, after being hired by Livingston, might molest or injure a Livingston student such as plaintiff.

"[T]he law certainly recognizes a policy of preventing future harm of the kind alleged here. One of society's highest priorities is to protect children from sexual or physical abuse. . . .

". . . **we hold**, consistent with Restatement Second of Torts sections 310 and 311, **that the writer of a letter of recommendation owes to third persons a duty not to misrepresent the facts in describing the qualifications and character of a former employee, if making these misrepresentations would present a substantial, foreseeable risk of physical injury to the third persons**. . . .

". . . we view this case as a "misleading half-truths" situation in which defendants, having undertaken to provide some information regarding Gadams's teaching credentials and character, were obliged to disclose all other facts which "materially qualify" the limited facts disclosed. . . .

As the Court of Appeal observed, defendants' letters offered general and unreserved praise for Gadams's character and personality (e.g., "dependable [and] reliable," "pleasant personality," "high standards," "relates well to the students"). According to the Court of Appeal, having volunteered this information, defendants were obliged to complete the picture by disclosing material facts regarding charges and complaints of Gadams's sexual improprieties. . . .

"We conclude that these letters, essentially recommending Gadams for any position without reservation or qualification, constituted affirmative representations that strongly implied Gadams was fit to interact appropriately and safely with female students. These representations were false and misleading in light of defendants' alleged knowledge of charges of Gadams's repeated sexual improprieties. **We also conclude that plaintiff's complaint adequately alleged misleading half-truths that could invoke an exception to the general rule excluding liability for mere nondisclosure or other failure to act.** . . ."

Second application example of a case wherein the standard for intentional misrepresentation was applied: The Indiana Supreme Court in the non-school case of *Passmore v. Multi-Management Services, Inc.*, 810 N.E.2d 1022 (Ind. 2004) relied on the *Randi W.* case when it adopted, for the first time, the tort of intentional misrepresentation in situations where an employer purposely misrepresents the truth about an employee's work performance to a prospective employer knowing that, if hired, the employee could cause harm to other persons.

The Passmore court, however, refused to adopt the tort of *negligent* misrepresentation for the public policy reason that it would cause many employers not to comment about an employee to prospective employers, other than giving the dates of employment, if it would mean that employers could be held liable for *negligence* in what was unintentionally said about an employee's performance.

II. DEFAMATION

The common law tort of defamation refers to a claimed injury to the plaintiff's reputation caused by the publication, either spoken (slander) or written (libel), to a third party.

Application example of a case wherein the standard for defamation was applied:

CASE

Poyser v. Peerless, 775 N.E.2d 1101 (Ind. App. 2002) (emphasis added)

Karen Poyser filed a defamation lawsuit against St. Richard's School, her former employer, David Peerless and Claudia Hilligoss, her supervisors at the school, the St. Richard's Board of Directors, and Karen Dorfman, president of the Board (collectively referred to as "the School").

The School moved for summary judgment, which motion was granted by the trial court.

Poyser now appeals the summary judgment against her. We affirm.

Poyser raises three issues for our review, which we consolidate and restate as one: whether the trial court properly granted summary judgment to the School on finding that the statements the School made in a letter to the School community about Poyser's departure from the School were true, were made without malice, or were protected by the common interest privilege.

[Facts:] Karen Poyser was employed beginning in 1991 as a second-grade teacher at St. Richard's School, a private Episcopal grade school in Indianapolis. While Poyser was employed at St. Richard's, her ultimate supervisor was the Headmaster, David Peerless. Her immediate supervisor at the relevant time was Claudia Hilligoss, the "Lower School Head."

Poyser and Hilligoss experienced "communication difficulties" in their dealings with one another. Poyser did not sign and return her contract for the 1999-2000 school year, but she did begin teaching that fall. In September of 1999, Poyser composed a letter to Peerless explaining her complaints and concerns about the school administration and Hilligoss in particular. She indicated in her letter that she was "considering turning in [her] resignation.". . . She requested a meeting with Peerless at his convenience, and sent a copy of the letter to Hilligoss and to the St. Richard's Board of Directors.

After Peerless received this letter, he directed Hilligoss to meet with Poyser to try to resolve their difficulties and he sent a letter to Poyser informing her that she should follow the chain-of-command and attempt resolution first with Hilligoss before he became involved. Appellant's Appendix at 257.

Because Hilligoss was reluctant to meet one-on-one with Poyser due to their past difficulties, Peerless ultimately agreed to attend a meeting between the two. Hilligoss e-mailed Poyser on September 22, 1999, and informed her that she had scheduled a meeting for the two of them that afternoon, that Peerless would also attend, and that arrangements had been made to cover her classroom during this time. . . .

Poyser responded by e-mail that the meeting was not at a good time for her and that she would not meet with Hilligoss and Peerless at the same time. . . . Hilligoss responded by e-mail that "the issues you raised in your letter are serious enough to require a meeting" that afternoon, and that she and Peerless expected her to meet with them as scheduled. . . .

Poyser did not attend the meeting. Peerless sent an e-mail that afternoon informing Poyser that her failure to attend the meeting was a serious violation, scheduling another meeting for the morning of September 24, and asking her not to discuss the issue "in any way that negatively affects the school's reputation, ability to function smoothly, or the quality of the working conditions." . . .

That evening was the school open house, and following her presentation to the parents of her students, one of whom was a Board member, Poyser answered questions regarding her employment situation at the school and read to them parts of her letter to Peerless and his response.

At the September 24 meeting, Peerless informed Poyser that her actions, both in failing to attend the September 22 meeting and in talking with parents about her situation, were insubordination and grounds for termination.

Poyser responded that he could not terminate her because she had never turned in her contract and that she was resigning. However, she refused to discuss her resignation further with Hilligoss in the room. Peerless then asked that she turn in her key to the school and he escorted her from the school. . . .

At the next regularly scheduled Board meeting, the Board addressed the apparent discrepancy between Poyser's position that she had resigned from St. Richard's and Peerless' position that he had terminated her employment. To address concerns that Peerless had violated school policies and procedures in his handling of Poyser's departure and to end the discord in the school community over the situation, the Board formally addressed Poyser's departure by sending a letter from the Board to all St. Richard's parents. After speaking with Peerless, Karen Dorfman, the president of the Board, composed and signed the letter, which reads in part:

There has been much speculation as to the circumstances surrounding Mrs. Poyser's departure from St. Richard's. For the privacy of its employees, St. Richard's makes every effort to maintain confidentiality with respect to personnel issues. However, in this case, there seems to be a general misunderstanding as to what occurred. The incidents surrounding Mrs. Poyser's departure were instigated by her and not her supervisor, Mrs. Hilligoss. The Administration attempted to address Mrs. Poyser's concerns within the School's published guidelines and policies. It was only after Mrs. Poyser ignored School policies and the Administration's directives, and refused to meet with the Administration to resolve her concerns, that the School decided to terminate her contract. . .

Poyser thereafter initiated a lawsuit against Peerless, Hilligoss, Dorfman, St. Richard's School, and St. Richard's Board of Directors, alleging that they had defamed, slandered and libeled her through the publication of Peerless' notices regarding her termination and Dorfman's above-quoted letter.

The School moved for summary judgment, alleging that the statements made were true, there was no evidence of malice in the making of the statements, and the School was protected by the "common interest privilege." Poyser opposed the motion. Following a hearing, the trial court granted the School's motion for summary judgment. . .

Mrs. Poyser's claims fail as a matter of law for three reasons: (1) Mrs. Poyser has not demonstrated a prima facie case as the undisputed facts demonstrate that the allegedly defamatory statements were true. . .; (2) Mrs. Poyser has not shown a prima facie case as the undisputed facts demonstrate that there was no malice. . .; and, (3) the comments were protected by the common interest privilege as parents and schools have "corresponding interests" in the free flow of information about teachers, the school environment, and the education of children. . . .

[Legal Standard] **Defamation is "that which tends to injure reputation or to diminish esteem, respect, good will, or confidence in the plaintiff, or to excite derogatory feelings or opinions about the plaintiff."**

To establish defamation, the **plaintiff must prove the following elements: (1) a communication with defamatory imputation; (2) malice; (3) publication; and (4) damages.**

In general, the determination of whether a communication is defamatory is a question of law for the court. The determination becomes a question of fact for the jury if the communication is reasonably susceptible of either defamatory or non-defamatory interpretation. **However, a communication is defamatory per se if it imputes: (1) criminal conduct; (2) a loathsome disease; (3) misconduct in a person's trade, profession, office, or occupation; or (4) sexual misconduct. Damages are presumed** even without proof of actual harm to the plaintiff's reputation **if the communication is defamatory per se.**

The trial court determined that Poyser had not stated an actionable claim for defamation for three reasons: the allegedly defamatory statements were true, they were made without malice, and they were protected by the "common interest" privilege. . .

Malice

A private individual bringing a defamation action must show "actual" malice in matters of public or general concern. . . . The question of whether there is sufficient evidence to support finding actual malice is a question of law for the court. **Actual malice exists when "the defendant publishes a defamatory statement 'with knowledge that it was false or with reckless disregard of whether it was false or not.' "** . . .

Poyser contends that Dorfman, in relying exclusively on the version of events related to her by Peerless, wrote the letter with reckless disregard for the truth. In order to prevail, Poyser must show that the School was aware of the inaccuracy of the statements in Dorfman's letter at the time of publication or had serious doubts as to their accuracy. Poyser has failed in this regard. . . .

Poyser contends that because Dorfman relied upon Peerless as her sole source of information prior to writing the letter, she demonstrated reckless disregard for whether the statements she made concerning the encounter were true. She contends that this is at least sufficient to create a question of fact regarding the malice element, thus precluding summary judgment. We disagree.

In defamation cases arising in the journalism arena, we have held that it is not sufficient to show that the reporting in question was speculative or even sloppy, *Cochran v. Indianapolis Newspapers, Inc.*, . . . , and that the failure to investigate does not in itself establish malice. *Kitco*, . . .

Despite Dorfman's reservations about Peerless as an administrator, she made it quite clear in her deposition that she believed he was truthful in relaying to her and the Board the events surrounding Poyser's departure and that she had no reason to doubt his version of events. . . .

[Conclusion:] As Poyser has failed to raise a genuine issue of material fact as to the element of malice required to sustain her defamation suit, we hold that the trial court properly granted summary judgment to the School. The judgment of the trial court is affirmed.

The *Poyser* case discusses the elements of the legal standard for defamation. The plaintiff has the burden of proving (1) communication of a statement that injured the reputation, diminished the esteem, good will, or confidence in the plaintiff; (2) actual malice, which means a knowingly false statement or a statement made with reckless disregard for the truth; (3) publication to someone other than the plaintiff; and (4) damages (injury), which must be established with proof of actual harm, or in the case of defamation *per se* with proof that the statement imputed "criminal conduct, a loathsome disease, misconduct in one's trade, profession, office, or occupation, or sexual misconduct,"), where damages are presumed without proof of actual harm being required.

A. Defense of Privilege

State common law recognizes the complete defense of privilege, either absolute or qualified, against a charge of defamation. In the school context, a privilege defense can be applied in such situations as parents making critical statements regarding teachers, administrators commenting about why employees were disciplined, administrators making negative comments when asked to give a job reference, and as in the following case, a university instructor who wrote a letter to a school about an education student who had applied for a teaching position.

Application example of a case wherein the standard for defense of privilege was applied:

CASE

Olsson v. Indiana University, 571 N.E.2d 582 (Ind. App. 4th Dist. (1991).

[Facts:] School of education Student filed defamation action against University when its instructor wrote a letter to a school district that did not hire her after requesting an evaluation of Student when she applied for a teaching position. Letter stated that she was a "marginal student teacher," described her as "enthusiastic, willing to work, and comfortable with parents," and commented that her weaknesses included "faulty grammatical skills, lack of skill in organizing, planning, and implementing lesson plans, poor discipline, inflexibility, and resistance to criticism."

[Legal issue:] Did University establish common law defense of qualified privilege thereby precluding recovery for defamation by former education student?

[Lower court action:] Summary judgment in favor of University based on qualified privilege.

[Court of Appeals ruling:] Trial court judgment affirmed in favor of University.

[Rationale:] "Words falsely written which tend to injure or prejudice any person in her trade, profession or business are defamatory. . . . Whether a statement is defamatory is a question of law for the court. . . Only if the statement can be interpreted as having two meanings, one libelous and one not, should the case go to the jury. . . .

"Notwithstanding the possible defamatory nature of a communication, a communication may be protected by a qualified privilege if a need exists for full and unrestricted communication regarding matters on which the parties have a common interest or duty. . .

"Under the qualified privilege rule (or common interest rule), a communication is privileged if made in good faith on any subject matter in which the party making the communication has an interest or in reference to which he has a duty either public or private, whether legal, moral, or social, if made to a person having a corresponding interest or duty. . . . This privilege applies to communications concerning the qualifications of a school teacher. . . .

"IU has a responsibility in preparing and evaluating future schoolteachers. Lundy [the school principal] has a common interest to select the best possible teachers. The subject matter of the letter was information IU had a duty to report to school administrators. IU made a showing of qualified privilege in the trial court.

"The final question is whether IU has abused its qualified privilege. Once the existence of such a privilege is established, the burden is on the plaintiff to prove that it has been abused. . . . Qualified privilege may be lost if: a) there is a showing the communicator was primarily motivated by feelings of ill will, b) there is excessive publication of the defamatory statement, or c) the statement is made without belief or grounds for belief in its truth. . . .

"As discussed above, the record indicates Null [the University instructor] wrote the letter based on her experience as an educator and her personal observations and interactions with Olsson. While Olsson may dispute Null's ability to form an accurate opinion after only three classroom visits, she presented no material facts from which a trier of fact could reasonably infer reckless disregard for the truth, falsity of the letter, or malice.

"Olsson claims there was excessive publication of the letter. Olsson urges IU permitted prospective employers to see the letter. This assertion is based on the fact she gave the name of the school where she student taught when she applied for various positions. However, there is no evidence that anyone except Null, Lundy, and Superintendent Kain saw the letter. IU did not keep a copy of Null's letter. (R. 154). No potential employer has ever contacted Lundy with questions about Olsson's teaching ability. (R. 359). . . .

III. ASSAULT AND BATTERY

The common law tort of assault is an intentional act that causes a person to fear an imminent injury as a result of the act. A student, for example, may so frustrate a teacher that the teacher throws a textbook at the student. As the book sails toward the student, an assault occurs, assuming the student is able to convince the trier of fact (usually a jury) that a reasonable observer in his position would have feared imminent injury. If the object thrown had been a small piece of chalk, there may be no assault. Or if the student were asleep as the book approached him, there would be no assault because there would have been no fear of imminent injury.

The tort of battery, on the other hand, requires an intentional act that results in an impact on the person that causes an injury. An angry coach who throws an athlete to the asphalt causing a head bruise would commit battery, but there would be no battery if the coach tosses him on the three-foot thick foam in the high jump landing pit without a resulting injury.

Corporal punishment of a student may lead to a civil charge of assault and battery, but public policy considerations when combined with facts indicating that reasonable actions were taken usually result in a finding of no liability.

In the case of *Indiana State Personnel Board v. Jackson*, 192 N.E.2d 740 (Ind. 1963), the Indiana Supreme Court upheld the corporal punishment of a 14-year-old female student by a male teacher who, after attempts to reason with her failed and she continued her abusive language, struck her, without undue force, on the buttocks two times with his belt in the classroom and two or three times in his office in front of witnesses. Said the court at 743-744 (emphasis added):

> [T]he law of Indiana **clearly accords to the public school teacher in proper cases the same right over a child in his or her school as is possessed by the parent**, and this includes the right to administer corporal punishment when it is appropriate. The law is well settled in this state that **the teacher stands in loco parentis to the child**, and his authority in this respect is no more subject to question than is the authority of the parent. The teacher's authority and the kind and quantum of punishment employed to meet a given offense is measured by the same rules, standards and requirements as fixed and established for parents. . . .

> It is undisputed that appellee in lightly disciplining the fourteen year old child acted in a kindly manner and without anger, and it is difficult to see how appellee could otherwise have handled the difficult situation with which he was confronted, than he did in this case.

School personnel may also have to use physical force against students to protect themselves or other persons from harm, and such force may cause injury. In such cases, courts generally find no liability if the teacher's or administrator's actions are reasonable in light of the total set of circumstances, including the age, sex, and size of the aggressor, as well as any objects that are used as weapons by him/her in the attempt to harm the employee or other person. For example, in the prior example of a teacher throwing a textbook at a student, if it were done to protect another student who was about to be battered with a chair, the force applied to prevent the harm would most likely be deemed reasonable under the circumstances.

A. Individual Employee Liability

Under the common law, the master is deemed liable for the negligent acts of its servants ("respondeat superior", i.e., the superior must respond). When the master is a governmental entity, state tort claims acts have been passed to declare under what circumstances liability falls upon the governmental entity and when it falls upon the employee personally.

Also, state legislatures, when delegating legal power to local school boards, often include specific authority with respect to providing a legal defense to school employees and holding them harmless for costs and damages resulting from their actions performed within the scope of employment.

For example, Indiana's "School Powers Act" at IC 20-25-5-4(17) grants the following specific power to school boards (emphasis added):

> To defend any member of the governing body or any employee of the school corporation **in any suit arising out of the performance of his duties for or employment** with, the school corporation, **provided the governing body by resolution determined that such action was taken**

in good faith. To save any such member or employee harmless from any liability, cost, or damage in connection therewith, including but not limited to the payment of any legal fees, **except where such liability, cost, or damage is predicated on or arises out of the bad faith of such member or employee, or is a claim or judgment based on his malfeasance in office or employment**.

The Indiana Tort Claims Act at I.C. 34-13-3-5 speaks to tort claims filed against school board member and school employees as follows (emphasis added): Section 5:

(a) Civil actions relating to acts taken by a board, a committee, a commission, an authority, or another instrumentality of a governmental entity **may be brought only against the board**, the committee, the commission, the authority, or the other instrumentality of a governmental entity. **A member of a board,** a committee, a commission, an authority, or another instrumentality of a governmental entity **may not be named as a party in a civil suit that concerns the acts taken by a board,** a committee, a commission, an authority, or another instrumentality of a governmental entity **where the member was acting within the scope of the member's employment**. For the purposes of this subsection, a member of a board, a committee, a commission, an authority, or another instrumentality of a governmental entity is acting within the scope of the member's employment when the member acts as a member of the board, committee, commission, authority, or other instrumentality.

(b) **A judgment rendered with respect to or a settlement made by a governmental entity bars an action by the claimant against an employee, including a member of a board**, a committee, a commission, an authority, or another instrumentality of a governmental entity, whose conduct gave rise to the claim resulting in that judgment or settlement. **A lawsuit alleging that an employee acted within the scope of the employee's employment bars an action by the claimant against the employee personally. However, if the governmental entity answers that the employee acted outside the scope of the employee's employment, the plaintiff may amend the complaint and sue the employee personally**. . .

(c) **A lawsuit filed against an employee personally must allege that an act or omission of the employee that causes a loss is:**
    (1) criminal;
    (2) clearly outside the scope of the employee's employment;
    (3) malicious;
    (4) willful and wanton; or
    (5) calculated to benefit the employee personally.

The complaint must contain a reasonable factual basis supporting the allegations.

In order to defend a public school employee (or school board member), Indiana's School Powers Act requires the school board to adopt a resolution finding that the employees acted in good faith, and the statute permits the board to hold the employee harmless provided that the employee's action did not arise out of bad faith or malfeasance.

Secondly, Indiana's Tort Claims Act makes it clear that if the lawsuit alleges that the employee acted within the scope of employment, it prevents the plaintiff from recovering against the employee personally. However, if the governing body's answer to the suit states that the employee acted outside the scope of employment, the plaintiff is given the opportunity to amend the complaint and sue the employee personally. However, if the employee is sued personally, the plaintiff must allege (and prove) that the employee's act or omission was either criminal, *clearly* outside the scope of employment, malicious, willful and wanton, or designed to benefit the employee personally.

IV. PARENTAL LIABILITY FOR INJURIOUS ACTS OF CHILD

Although it is rare under the common law for a parent to be found liable in negligence for the injurious act of the parent's child in the school setting, a case from Wisconsin demonstrates how it may occur.

In *Nieuwendorp v. American Family Insurance*, 529 N.W.2d 594 (Wis. 1995), a teacher was injured by the actions of a fourth-grade child with attention deficit hyperactive disorder (ADHD) when he grabbed her hair causing her to fall and suffer a herniated disk in her neck. The Wisconsin Supreme Court upheld the jury's finding of negligence due to the parents' decision to stop administering medication to control the ADHD condition without informing themselves of the consequences of the action and without telling school officials of what they had done.

By statute, Indiana has made a parent having custody of a child who still lives with the parent automatically liable for intentional or reckless harm caused by the child, but only for damages up to $5,000. I.C. 34-31-4-1 reads:

> Sec. 1. Except as provided in section 2 of this chapter [where parent encourages child's involvement in a criminal gang], a parent is liable for not more than five thousand dollars ($5,000) in actual damages arising from harm to a person or damage to property knowingly, intentionally, or recklessly caused by the parent's child if: (1) the parent has custody of the child; and (2) the child is living with the parent.

Because the parent liability statute only makes parents responsible for harm to persons or damage to property caused by the *knowing*, *intentional*, or *reckless* acts of their children, a simple *negligent* act of the child would not be covered. For example, if the child accidentally backs into a teacher causing a fall that breaks the teacher's arm, the parent would not be liable.

V. CONSTITUIONAL TORTS – STATE-CREATED DANGER

A number of federal circuit courts have been faced with the issue of whether the state (in the form of local school districts) may be found liable in tort under the federal Constitution's Fourteenth Amendment Due Process Clause for the denial of life, liberty or property when a student suffers injury or death while under the supervision of school personnel. When the courts failed to find a constitutional legal duty of care, students' lawyers developed the theory of a state-created danger wherein a violation of due process would occur where school officials affirmatively acted to create the danger that caused the harm.

Although some courts have been willing to recognize the state-created danger concept, plaintiffs' counsel have not been very successful in proving that school personnel *affirmatively acted* so as to create the danger. For example, in a case where a student was sexually assaulted by other students and the court complaint stated that an administrator had learned of a prior situation involving the assaulters but failed to take action, the court determined that the administrator's failure to intervene was not an affirmative act that created the danger that caused the injury to the student. *D.R. v. Middle Bucks Area Vocational Dist.*, 972 F.2d 1364 (3d Cir. 1992).

In a school-shooting case where the student's mother alleged that school officials had prior knowledge that the student who shot her son had a gun on school grounds and had threatened him with it, the court found that foreseeability of harm cannot create the affirmative duty to protect under the Constitution, and that the plaintiff failed to show where school personnel affirmatively acted to create the danger. *Graham v. Independent Sch. Dist.*, 22 F.3d 991 (10th Cir. 1994).

In a situation where a trespasser in a school building shot and killed a student, the complaint was dismissed without a trial because it failed to allege the three required elements in order to state a claim under the state-created danger theory. The court stated the necessary elements as follows:

> [T]he environment created by the state actors must be dangerous; they must know it is dangerous; and, to be liable, they must have used their authority to create an opportunity that would not otherwise have existed for the third party's crime to occur.

Johnson v. Dallas Indep. Sch. Dist., 38 F.3d 198, 201 (5th Cir. 1994).

SCENARIOS
STATE AND APPLY THE RELEVANT LEGAL RULE(S) TO THE FACTS.

1. School Board policy expressly stated that teachers shall not take a child home for any reason except with the express consent of the principal. Board policy gave clear direction and authority to principals to set the time when parents must have picked up their children from after school events or have the local sheriff's department do so for a substantial fee. Principal properly informed all parents to get their children from the middle school dance no later than 10:00 p.m. When Child is still there at 10:00, Teacher, who had chaperoned dance, followed Principal's protocol by calling Parent, but could not reach Parent at phone number listed on dance permission slip. Because Teacher lived near Child's house, Teacher decided to take Child home rather than calling Principal to get consent or calling sheriff and waiting for deputy to arrive. Teacher drove off road into ditch trying to answer cell phone, causing Child broken bones.

> Analyze each of the following subsections:

> a. Parent on Child's behalf sued School District for injuries suffered by Child.

> b. Parent on Child's behalf sued Teacher, individually, and not School District.

> c. If Child, a 14-year-year-old, well-built, six foot male of normal intelligence, falsified Parent's signature on permission slip to attend dance, talked Teacher into taking him home, and while Teacher parked car on side of road to answer cell phone, Teacher allowed Child to leave car to relieve himself, Child broke leg falling into ditch and Parent on behalf of Child sued Teacher, individually, and School District.

2. Teacher, who resigned from School District A at the end of the first semester, applied to teach in School District B at the start of the following school year. Because Teacher could coach and had graduated from B's high school and because the previous teacher-coach at B resigned one day before the start of school, B hired him after a brief interview and accepted his statement that he could not get along with A's principal and quit.

> Analyze each of the following subsections:

> a. The following spring Teacher violated the criminal code by having illegal sexual relations with an underage female student at School B. B had not obtained Teacher's criminal background history, which would have revealed that he had been arrested for sexual battery three year's before while in college, but the charge had been dropped. Had School B contacted School A at the time of hire, B would have learned that he resigned from A rather than being dismissed for sexual harassment of a student. Parent on behalf of underage female student sued School District B.

> b. Ignoring the facts in subsection a, assume that School B contacted Principal of School A, who truthfully told B that Teacher had resigned at the end of the first semester the prior school year to take graduate courses toward his administrative license and that Teacher was well liked by students and an excellent teacher. Principal of A did not tell School B that Teacher had resigned following a charge of sexual harassment and that as part of a settlement agreement, School A agreed that

in exchange for his resignation School A would only state to potential employers the three facts were revealed to B. Parent on behalf of daughter sued Teacher for having had sexual relations with daughter.

c. Ignoring the facts in subsections a and b, assume that Principal of School A, a middle school, at the request of School B, e-mailed the following statement to B before Teacher is hired: "I did not like Teacher's lazy manner and nonchalant attitude from the very beginning interview, but I was forced to hire him because he was to be the high school girl's coach and was a relative of a board member. He is a pervert in my opinion. In the first semester, he had a sexual harassment complaint made against him by a 15-year-old member of the girl's team that he coaches. Since this was at the high school, I did not investigate it, but learned by the grapevine that he was guilty as sin and got the player pregnant. Since he resigned at the end of the semester and before the end of the basketball season, it proves he was guilty of sexual relations with an under-age girl. This guy should be strung up by you know what!" Teacher, who did not get the job at School B, sued School A and its Principal when some six months later, the girl recanted her story and admitted it was a lie.

Chapter 3

School Employee Constitutional Rights

This chapter focuses on the fundamental constitutional rights of public school employees contained in the First and Fourth Amendments of the United States Constitution, which are speech, religion, and freedom from unreasonable searches and seizures. The right of privacy, although not expressly stated in a particular amendment, has been found by the Supreme Court and will be addressed. The Fourteenth Amendment right to due process of law is covered in the chapter on teacher termination and the right of equal protection in the discrimination chapter.

I. FREEDOM OF SPEECH

Freedom of expression under the First Amendment, which is made applicable to state and local governmental entities by the Fourteenth Amendment, is a fundamental right granted to all persons. However, no right is absolute. So, when it comes to public school employee speech, the courts will balance the interests of the employee to speak on matters of public (as opposed to personal) concern against the school employer's significant interest in maintaining an efficient operation.

School employee speech is not always free, even when it concerns a public matter. Employees, although speaking on such public issues as school board elections and student medication policies, have lost free-speech claims because the school met its burden of proving an overriding interest when the speech disrupted the efficient operation of its system.

A. Balancing Test

CASE
Pickering v. Board of Education, 391 U.S. 563 (1968)
(emphasis added)

Appellant Marvin L. Pickering, a teacher in Township High School District 205, Will County, Illinois, was dismissed from his position by the appellee Board of Education for sending a letter to a local newspaper in connection with a recently proposed tax increase that was critical of the way in which the Board and the district superintendent of schools had handled past proposals to raise new revenue for the schools.

Appellant's dismissal resulted from a determination by the Board, after a full hearing, that the publication of the letter was "detrimental to the efficient operation and administration of the schools of the district" and hence, under the relevant Illinois statute, Ill. Rev. Stat., c. 122, 10-22.4 (1963), that "interests of the school require[d] [his dismissal]." . . . .

For the reasons detailed below we agree that appellant's rights to freedom of speech were violated and we reverse.

[Facts:] In February of 1961 the appellee Board of Education asked the voters of the school district to approve a bond issue to raise $4,875,000 to erect two new schools. The proposal was defeated. Then, in December of 1961, the Board submitted another bond proposal to the voters, which called for the raising of $5,500,000 to build two new schools. This second proposal passed and the schools were built with the money raised by the bond sales. In May of 1964 a proposed increase in the tax rate to be used for educational purposes was submitted to the voters by the Board and was defeated. Finally, on September 19, 1964, a second proposal to increase the tax rate was submitted by the Board and was likewise defeated. It was in connection with this last proposal of the School Board that appellant wrote the letter to the editor (which we reproduce in an Appendix to this opinion) that resulted in his dismissal. . . .

The letter constituted, basically, an attack on the School Board's handling of the 1961 bond issue proposals and its subsequent allocation of financial resources between the schools' educational and athletic programs. It also charged the superintendent of schools with attempting to prevent teachers in the district from opposing or criticizing the proposed bond issue.

The Board dismissed Pickering for writing and publishing the letter. Pursuant to Illinois law, the Board was then required to hold a hearing on the dismissal. At the hearing the Board charged that numerous statements in the letter were false and that the publication of the statements unjustifiably impugned the "motives, honesty, integrity, truthfulness, responsibility and competence" of both the Board and the school administration. The Board also charged that the false statements damaged the professional reputations of its members and of the school administrators, would be disruptive of faculty discipline, and would tend to foment "controversy, conflict and dissension" among teachers, administrators, the Board of Education, and the residents of the district.

Testimony was introduced from a variety of witnesses on the truth or falsity of the particular statements in the letter with which the Board took issue. The Board found the statements to be false as charged. No evidence was introduced at any point in the proceedings as to the effect of the publication of the letter on the community as a whole or on the administration of the school system in particular, and no specific findings along these lines were made. . . .

[The Legal Standard:] . . . The problem . . . is to arrive at a **balance between the interests of the teacher, as a citizen, in commenting upon matters of public concern and the interest of the State, as an employer, in promoting the efficiency of the public services it performs through its employees**. . . .

[Rationale:] An examination of the statements in appellant's letter objected to by the Board reveals that they, like the letter as a whole, consist essentially of criticism of the Board's allocation of school funds between educational and athletic programs, and of both the Board's and the superintendent's methods of informing, or preventing the informing of, the district's taxpayers of the real reasons why additional tax revenues were being sought for the schools. **The statements are in no way directed towards any person with whom appellant would normally be in contact in the course of his daily work as a teacher. Thus no question of maintaining either discipline by immediate superiors or harmony among coworkers is presented here. Appellant's employment relationships with the Board and, to a somewhat lesser extent, with the superintendent are not the kind of close working relationships for which it can persuasively be claimed that personal loyalty and confidence are necessary to their proper functioning.** Accordingly, to the extent that the Board's position here can be taken to suggest that even comments on matters of public concern that are substantially correct, such as statements (1)-(4) of appellant's letter. . . may furnish grounds for dismissal if they are sufficiently critical in tone, we unequivocally reject it.

We next consider the statements in appellant's letter, which we agree to be false. The Board's original charges included allegations that the publication of the letter damaged the professional reputations of the Board and the superintendent and would foment controversy and conflict among the Board, teachers, administrators, and the residents of the district. However, no evidence to support these allegations was introduced at the hearing. So far as the record reveals, Pickering's letter was greeted by everyone but its main target, the Board, with massive apathy and total disbelief. . . .

In addition, the fact that particular illustrations of the Board's claimed undesirable emphasis on athletic programs are false would not normally have any necessary impact on the actual operation of the schools, beyond its tendency to anger the Board. For example, Pickering's letter was written after the defeat at the polls of the second proposed tax increase. It could, therefore, have had no effect on the ability of the school district to raise necessary revenue, since there was no showing that there was any proposal to increase taxes pending when the letter was written.

More importantly, **the question whether a school system requires additional funds is a matter of legitimate public concern** on which the judgment of the school administration, including the School Board, cannot, in a society that leaves such questions to popular vote, be taken as conclusive. **On such a question, free and open debate is vital to informed decision-making by the electorate**. Teachers are, as a class, the members of a community most likely to have informed and definite opinions as to how funds allotted to the operation of the schools should be spent. Accordingly, it is essential that they be able to speak out freely on such questions without fear of retaliatory dismissal.

In addition, the amounts expended on athletics, which Pickering reported erroneously, were matters of public record on which his position as a teacher in the district did not qualify him to speak with any greater authority than any other taxpayer. The Board could easily have rebutted appellant's errors by publishing the accurate figures itself, either via a letter to the same newspaper or otherwise. **We are thus not presented with a situation in which a teacher has carelessly made false statements about matters so closely related to the day-to-day operations of the schools that any harmful impact on the public would be difficult to counter because of the teacher's presumed greater access to the real facts.** Accordingly, we have no occasion to consider at this time whether under such circumstances a school board could reasonably require that a teacher make substantial efforts to verify the accuracy of his charges before publishing them.

What we do have before us is a case in which a teacher has made erroneous public statements upon issues then currently the subject of public attention, which are critical of his ultimate employer, but which are neither shown nor can be presumed to have in any way either impeded the teacher's proper performance of his daily duties in the classroom or to have interfered with the

regular operation of the schools generally. In these circumstances **we conclude that the interest of the school administration in limiting teachers' opportunities to contribute to public debate is not significantly greater than its interest in limiting a similar contribution by any member of the general public.**

The **public interest in having free and unhindered debate on matters of public importance - the core value of the Free Speech Clause of the First Amendment - is so great** that it has been held that a State cannot authorize the recovery of damages by a public official for defamatory statements directed at him except when such statements are shown to have been made either with knowledge of their falsity or with reckless disregard for their truth or falsity. *New York Times Co. v. Sulliv. . .*

The Ruling: In sum, we hold that, in a case such as this, **absent proof of false statements knowingly or recklessly made by him, a teacher's exercise of his right to speak on issues of public importance may not furnish the basis for his dismissal from public employment**. Since no such showing has been made in this case regarding appellant's letter. . . his dismissal for writing it cannot be upheld and the judgment of the Illinois Supreme Court must, accordingly, be reversed and the case remanded for further proceedings not inconsistent with this opinion.

It is so ordered.

Notes:

1. The Supreme Court, in a later non-school case, *Connick v. Meyers*, 461 U.S. 138 (1983), established the following three sub-tests to assist in determining whether the principle test of proof of public concern is met by the public employee: **form, content**, and **context**. As applied to *Pickering*, for example, the form of the speech was a letter to the editor of a newspaper, the content dealt with criticism of the school board and superintendent regarding expenditures of public funds, especially for athletic facilities, and the context was a bond-issue election for increasing taxes.

2. In *Connick*, the Supreme Court upheld the dismissal of an assistant district attorney who circulated an intra-office questionnaire (form) during the work day when she learned that she might be transferred to an undesirable position (context). Because a majority of the questions dealt with matters that concerned her personally, e.g., how the District Attorney managed the staff, and only one with a matter of public interest, e.g., expectation of employees to work in election campaigns (content), the Court found the expression to be one of personal, rather than public, concern.

3. The Supreme Court has also recognized that a school employee's expression on a matter of public concern does not have to be made to or in the public to be protected, i.e., the speech can be made in private. See *Givhan v. Western Line Consol. Sch. Dist*, 439 U.S. 410 (1979), where a teacher was dismissed when she complained privately to her principal on a number of occasions about the school's employment policies being racially discriminatory.

4. In regard to the *Pickering* balancing test, the Eighth Circuit expressed the need to look at the following factors in *Roberts v. Van Buren Public Schools*, 773 F.3d 949, 954 (8th Cir. 1985):

    (1) the need for harmony in the office or work place;

    (2) whether the government's responsibilities require a close working relationship to exist between the plaintiff and co-workers when the speech in question has caused or could cause the relationship to deteriorate;

    (3) the time, manner, and place of the speech;

    (4) the context in which the disputer arose;

    (5) the degree of public interest in the speech; and

    (6) whether the speech impeded the employee's ability to perform his or her duties.

B. *Mt. Healthy Test*

Nine years after deciding Pickering, the Supreme Court was faced with the concern that a school employee, whose job was thought to be in jeopardy, could improve his legal position by speaking on an issue of public concern. As a result, the Court added to the Pickering balancing test by (1) requiring the employee to prove that the speech was a substantial or motivating factor in the employer's resulting action and (2) allowing the school employer to attempt to prove that it would have taken the same job action regardless of the employee's speech.

CASE
Mt. Healthy City Sch. Dist. v. Doyle, 429 U.S. 274 (1977)
(emphasis added)

Respondent Doyle sued petitioner Mt. Healthy Board of Education in the United States District Court for the Southern District of Ohio. Doyle claimed that the Board's refusal to renew his contract in 1971 violated his rights under the First and Fourteenth Amendments to the United States Constitution. . . .

[Facts:] Doyle was first employed by the Board in 1966. He worked under one-year contracts for the first three years, and under a two-year contract from 1969 to 1971. In 1969 he was elected president of the Teachers' Association, in which position he worked to expand the subjects of direct negotiation between the Association and the Board of Education. During Doyle's one-year term as president of the Association, and during the succeeding year when he served on its executive committee, there was apparently some tension in relations between the Board and the Association.

Beginning early in 1970, Doyle was involved in several incidents not directly connected with his role in the Teachers' Association. In one instance, he engaged in an argument with another teacher, which culminated in the other teacher's slapping him. Doyle subsequently refused to accept an apology and insisted upon some punishment for the other teacher. His persistence in the matter resulted in the suspension of both teachers for one day, which was followed by a walkout by a number of other teachers, which in turn resulted in the lifting of the suspensions.

On other occasions, Doyle got into an argument with employees of the school cafeteria over the amount of spaghetti, which had been served him; referred to students, in connection with a disciplinary complaint, as "sons of bitches"; and made an obscene gesture to two girls in connection with their failure to obey commands made in his capacity as cafeteria supervisor. Chronologically the last in the series of incidents which respondent was involved in during his employment by the Board was a telephone call by him to a local radio station. It was the Board's consideration of this incident, which the court below found to be a violation of the First and Fourteenth Amendments.

In February 1971, the principal circulated to various teachers a memorandum relating to teacher dress and appearance, which was apparently prompted by the view of some in the administration that there was a relationship between teacher appearance and public support for bond issues. Doyle's response to the receipt of the memorandum - on a subject which he apparently understood was to be settled by joint teacher-administration action - was to convey the substance of the memorandum to a disc jockey at WSAI, a Cincinnati radio station, who promptly announced the adoption of the dress code as a news item. Doyle subsequently apologized to the principal, conceding that he should have made some prior communication of his criticism to the school administration.

Approximately one month later the superintendent made his customary annual recommendations to the Board as to the rehiring of nontenured teachers. He recommended that Doyle not be rehired. The same recommendation was made with respect to nine other teachers in the district, and in all instances, including Doyle's, the recommendation was adopted by the Board. Shortly after being notified of this decision, respondent requested a statement of reasons for the Board's actions. He received a statement citing "a notable lack of tact in handling professional matters which leaves much doubt as to your sincerity in establishing good school relationships." That general statement was followed by references to the radio station incident and to the obscene-gesture incident.

[District Court Considerations:] The District Court found that all of these incidents had in fact occurred. It concluded that respondent Doyle's telephone call to the radio station was "clearly protected by the First Amendment," and that because it had played a "substantial part" in the decision of the Board not to renew Doyle's employment, he was entitled to reinstatement with back pay. . . .

. . . The District Court did not expressly state what test it was applying in determining that the incident in question involved conduct protected by the First Amendment, but simply held that the communication to the radio station was such conduct. The Court of Appeals affirmed. . . .

That question of whether speech of a government employee is constitutionally protected expression necessarily entails striking "a balance between the interests of the teacher, as a citizen, in commenting upon matters of public concern and the interest of the State, as an employer, in promoting the efficiency

of the public services it performs through its employees." *Pickering v. Board of Education*, 391 U.S. 563, 568 (1968).

There is no suggestion by the Board that Doyle violated any established policy, or that its reaction to his communication to the radio station was anything more than an ad hoc response to Doyle's action in making the memorandum public. We therefore accept the District Court's finding that the communication was protected by the First and Fourteenth Amendments. We are not, however, entirely in agreement with that court's manner of reasoning from this finding to the conclusion that Doyle is entitled to reinstatement with back pay.

The District Court made the following "conclusions" on this aspect of the case:

> "1) If a non-permissible reason, e. g., exercise of First Amendment rights, played a substantial part in the decision not to renew - even in the face of other permissible grounds - the decision may not stand (citations omitted).

> "2) A non-permissible reason did play a substantial part. That is clear from the letter of the Superintendent immediately following the Board's decision, which stated two reasons - the one, the conversation with the radio station clearly protected by the First Amendment. A court may not engage in any limitation of First Amendment rights based on `tact' - that is not to say that the `tactfulness' is irrelevant to other issues in this case." . . .

At the same time, though, it stated that

> "[i]n fact, as this Court sees it and finds, both the Board and the Superintendent were faced with a situation in which there did exist in fact reason . . . independent of any First Amendment rights or exercise thereof, to not extend tenure." . . .

Since respondent Doyle had no tenure, and there was therefore not even a state-law requirement of "cause" or "reason" before a decision could be made not to renew his employment, it is not clear what the District Court meant by this latter statement. **Clearly the Board legally could have dismissed respondent had the radio station incident never come to its attention**. One plausible meaning of the court's statement is that the Board and the Superintendent not only could, but in fact would have reached that decision had not the constitutionally protected incident of the telephone call to the radio station occurred.

We are thus brought to the issue whether, even if that were the case, the fact that the protected conduct played a "substantial part" in the actual decision not to renew would necessarily amount to a constitutional violation justifying remedial action. We think that it would not.

[Rationale] A rule of causation which focuses **solely** on whether protected conduct played a part, "substantial" or otherwise, in a decision not to rehire, **could place an employee in a better position as a result of the exercise of constitutionally protected conduct than he would have occupied had he done nothing**.

The difficulty with the rule enunciated by the District Court is that it would require reinstatement in cases where a dramatic and perhaps abrasive incident is inevitably on the minds of those responsible for the decision to rehire, and does indeed play a part in that decision - even if the same decision would have been reached had the incident not occurred. **The constitutional principle at stake is sufficiently vindicated if such an employee is placed in no worse a position than if he had not engaged in the conduct. A borderline or marginal candidate should not have the employment question resolved against him because of constitutionally protected conduct. But that same candidate ought not to be able, by engaging in such conduct, to prevent his employer from assessing his performance record and reaching a decision not to rehire on the basis of that record, simply because the protected conduct makes the employer more certain of the correctness of its decision.**

This is especially true where, as the District Court observed was the case here, the current decision to rehire will accord "tenure." The long-term consequences of an award of tenure are of great moment both to the employee and to the employer. They are too significant for us to hold that the Board in this case would be precluded, because it considered constitutionally protected conduct in deciding not to rehire Doyle, from attempting to prove to a trier of fact that quite apart from such conduct Doyle's record was such that he would not have been rehired in any event. . . .

Initially, in this case, the burden was properly placed upon respondent to show that his conduct was constitutionally protected, and that this conduct was a "substantial factor" - or, to put it in other words, that it was a "motivating factor" in the Board's decision not to rehire him. Respondent having carried that burden, however, **the District Court should have gone on to determine whether the Board had shown by a preponderance of the evidence that it would have reached the same decision as to respondent's re-employment even in the absence of the protected conduct.**

We cannot tell from the District Court opinion and conclusions, nor from the opinion of the Court of Appeals affirming the judgment of the District Court, what conclusion those courts would have reached had they applied this test. The judgment of the Court of Appeals is therefore vacated, and the case remanded for further proceedings consistent with this opinion.

So ordered.

Notes:

1. The legal standard to be applied in school employee speech cases where the expression occurs in a forum independent of a school-sponsored speech forum (such as the classroom), may be summarized as follows:

2. The employee has the burden of proving (1) that the expression was on a matter of public (as opposed to personal) concern, where the court will look to the form, content, and context of the expression to aid it in determining this outcome), and

2. The employee has the burden of proving (1) that the expression was on a matter of public (as opposed to personal) concern, where the court will look to the form, content, and context of the expression to aid it in determining this outcome), and (2) that the expression was a substantial or motivating factor in the school's action taken.

3. Upon such proof by the employee, the burden shifts to the school district to prove *either* (1) that the employee's expression seriously impacted the efficient operation of the school, *or* (2) the school would have taken the same action against the employee regardless of having made the expression.

C. Application of Pickering and Mt. Healthy

The following are some examples of how this standard was applied in several situations.

C1. The Case of the Campaigning Superintendent

Kinsey v. Salado Indep. Sch. Dist., 950 F.2d 988 (5th Cir. 1992), is a case that demonstrates how divided individual judges became as to the legal tension between exercising political speech and the resulting negative impact on efficient school operations. This case led to the non-renewal of the superintendent's contract after his campaigning for three incumbent members resulted in their defeat and the formation of a new board majority. A divided Fifth Circuit, *en banc*, reversed its divided three-judge panel and ruled for the school district. The federal district court had originally upheld the school board's non-renewal of the superintendent's contract.

Despite the superintendent's exercise of speech on a matter of public concern during the election process, the majority of the *en banc* court struck the balance in favor of the school district due to the essential need for a close working relationship between the board of education and its chief executive. In support of such need, the court noted that "one of Kinsey's primary duties was to advise the Board," as well as meet with it during executive sessions and give his opinions and recommendations in order to guide its decisions; that he handled the district's finances, was custodian of confidential records, sealed bids, working papers on proposed rules, policies, and student records; and that he was required to advise the board on these and other confidential records.

C2. The Case of the Nurse's Critique of Medication Policy

In *Johnsen v. Ind. Sch. Dist. No. 3 of Tulsa County*, 891 F.2d 1485 (10[th]Cir. 1989), a school nurse's contract was not renewed due to disruption caused by numerous instances, both within the school and in the public, over several months time, concerning her criticisms of the medication policy that in her announced view, resulted in nurses "indiscriminately" administering drugs to students. Because the court characterized her multiple speeches as a "concerted, cohesive campaign on a single subject," it considered them as a whole, rather than weighing each one separately. It cited *Connick v. Meyers*, above, in Note 1 following the *Pickering* case above, where the Supreme Court considered the entire office questionnaire in applying the balance of interests test.

The court ruled that there was no infringement of her First Amendment rights and concluded that her speech "was needlessly disruptive of the school district's health service programs." In finding a disruptive impact on the efficient operation of the school district, the court cited plaintiff's false statement about the indiscriminate administration of drugs having a detrimental impact on school operations, the discord she created at monthly nurses' meetings that made them unproductive, the extreme disruption she caused by threatening to report nurses to the nursing board which resulted in them believing that their licenses could be jeopardized for illegally dispensing medication, and the unnecessary disruption she caused by contacting outside agencies before utilizing the school district's internal complaint mechanism when there was no reason to believe that the internal process would not be sufficient.

C3. The Cases of the Demoted Principal

In *Sharp v. Lindsey*, 285 F.3d 479 (6th Cir. 2002), the principal, whose stricter student dress code was rejected by the superintendent, wrote a letter to members of his dress code committee and performed a skit before the teachers on the opening day of school in which he criticized the superintendent's decision. As a result, the principal, who was demoted to the position of math tutor, but paid his administrator's salary under his contract, filed suit claiming a violation of his freedom of expression.

Although the court recognized that the principal's speech may not have been protected because it was more a matter of a personal employee grievance against his supervisor than one of public concern, it assumed that the speech was of public concern. The court then applied the *Pickering* balancing test and focused on whether the school's interest in the efficient operation of the educational system by a smooth, non-disruptive relationship between its superintendent and principal outweighed the principal's interest in speaking on a matter of public concern. In ruling for the school district, the court at 486-487 stated:

> The fostering of a good working relationship between the principal and his newly-appointed boss was hardly helped . . . by [the principal's] failure to speak with him privately before trying to put the superintendent in a bad light before the dress code committee and the teaching staff. A different superintendent might not have considered [the principal's] conduct insubordinate, but Dr. Lindsey obviously did – and we cannot say that he abused his discretion in concluding that the interest of a smoothly functioning administrative team would best be served by the reassignment of [the principal]. In our judgment, the interests of a tension-free superintendent/principal relationship outweighed [the principal's] interest in trying to make himself look good at the expense of Dr. Lindsey and the board.

In *Vargas-Harrison v. Racine Unified Sch. Dist.*, 272 F.3d 964 (7th Cir. 2001), a principal was demoted to an assistant principal's position after she spoke out against the direction of her superiors. The District's Curriculum and Instruction Committee was considering grant proposals regarding the reading program and she had been directed to cooperate with teacher union representatives and modify her proposed plan (which would have cut some teaching positions) because the district was attempting to improve relations with the union. In public meeting before the Committee, she criticized the current plan, presented her alternative plan, and said that it was "time to let the principal do the job and stop the union running the school."

The Seventh Circuit ruled for the school district, and instead of applying the more complex and fact-specific *Pickering* balancing test, applied what it termed the "policy-making corollary to the *Pickering* analysis." *Id.* at 972. Under the simpler test, if the plaintiff is deemed a policy-making employee, the court need only consider the question of whether the speech demonstrated a lack of loyalty or allegiance to his or her superiors. Said the court at 973:

> . . . in certain instances, 'the government employer's need for political allegiance from its policymaking employee outweighs the employee's freedom of expression to such a degree' that the fact-specific *Pickering* inquiry is not required . . . In such a situation, the friction between a politically adverse policy-maker and superior poses such a potential disruption to the efficient functioning of government that a fact-specific inquiry is unnecessary. . .

Similarly,

> . . . the policy-maker analysis applies to situations where a policy-making employee engages in speech critical of his superior's work-related policies. . . When the policy-maker's speech creates a conflict with the policy stance of his superiors, the effects on government are acute.

In the opinion of the court, a policy-making employee "is one whose position 'authorizes, either directly or indirectly, meaningful input into government decision making on issues where there is room for principled disagreement on goals or their implementation.'" *Id.* at 972. It found that as principal, she was the highest ranking employee at her school where she exercised discretion over its organizational structure, assisted in the selection, supervision, and evaluation of the faculty, and led the development of curriculum and instruction. The court also determined that she had meaningful input into governmental decision-making and emphasized that she did not have to have control over decision-making, only meaningful input.

II. ACADEMIC FREEDOM

Teacher expression that occurs in the public school classroom does not enjoy the degree of freedom that it does in an open forum such as a newspaper. Although the Supreme Court has recognized the importance of academic freedom at the higher education level, e.g., "the First Amendment . . . does not tolerate laws that cast a pall of orthodoxy over the classroom" and "The classroom is peculiarly the 'marketplace of ideas.'", *Keyishian v. Board of Regents*, 385 U.S. 589, 603. The Court has recognized that the K-12 public education environment is different, e.g., "[N]owhere [have we] suggested that students, teachers, or anyone else has an absolute constitutional right to use all parts of a school building or its immediate environs for . . . unlimited expressive purposes." *Grayned v. City of Rockford*, 408 U.S. 104, 117-118 (1972), *Perry Education Assoc. v. Perry Local Educators Assoc.* 460 U.S. 37, 44 (1983).

The Court in *Perry Education Assoc.* stated at 46:

Public property, which is not by tradition or designation a forum for public communication, is governed by different standards. We have recognized that the "First Amendment does not guarantee access to property simply because it is owned or controlled by the government." . . . In addition to time, place, and manner regulations, the State may reserve the forum for its intended purposes, communicative or otherwise, as long as the regulation on speech is reasonable and not an effort to suppress expression merely because public officials oppose the speaker's view.

Following the Supreme Court's decision in *Hazlewood School District v. Kuhlmeier*, 484 U.S. 260 (1988), where the Court recognized that student expression is limited when made in a school-sponsored speech forum such as the classroom, newspaper and assembly, federal courts began to apply the more restrictive *Hazlewood* standard to teacher expression that is made within such forums. Therefore, as long as the action taken against a teacher due to expression within its speech activities is "reasonably related to legitimate pedagogical concerns," *Id.* at 273, the school district will be upheld.

A case that demonstrates a school district's right to determine the content of its curricular material and message over a teacher's ability to express his disagreement within the school's academic forum is *Downs v. L.A. Unified Sch. Dist.*, 228 F.3d 1003 (9th Cir. 2001). In *Downs*, the school district's board of education designated June as Gay and Lesbian Awareness Month during which posters would be displayed for the purpose of eliminating hate and creating a safe school environment. Teacher Downs responded by posting materials that expressed his views against homosexuality. The Ninth Circuit in upholding the district's removal of his materials stated at 1013-1016:

We conclude that when a public high school is the speaker, its control of its own speech is not subject to the constraints of constitutional safeguards and forum analysis, but instead is measured by practical considerations applicable to any individual's choice of how to convey oneself: among other things, content, timing, and purpose. Simply because the government opens its mouth to speak does not give every outside individual or group a First Amendment right to play ventriloquist. As applied here, the First Amendment allows LAUSD [the school district] to decide that Downs may not speak as its representative. This power is certainly so if his message is one with which the district disagrees. . . .

When the government is formulating and conveying its message, "it may take legitimate and appropriate steps to ensure that its message is neither garbled nor distorted" by its individual messengers. . . .

. . . our decision is consistent with cases holding that school teachers have no First Amendment right to influence curriculum as they so choose. See, e.g., *Edwards*, 156 F.3d at 491-92 (holding that professor has no First Amendment right to compel university to allow him to teach class from religious perspective); *Boring v. Buncombe County Bd. of Educ.*, 136 F.3d 364, 370-71 (4th Cir. 1998) (*en banc*) (teacher's choice of play not constitutionally-protected speech); *Bradley v. Pittsburgh Bd. of Educ.*, 910 F.2d 1172, 1176 (3d Cir. 1990) (holding that teacher has no First Amendment right to employ classroom teaching methodology of choice); *Kirkland v. Northside Indep. Sch. Dist.*, 890 F.2d 794, 795 (5th Cir. 1989) (teacher's choice of supplemental reading list not constitutionally-protected speech). . . .

Our holding, however, does not prevent Downs from propounding his own opinion on the morality of homosexuality. Subject to any applicable forum analysis, he may do so on the sidewalks, in the parks, through the chat-rooms, at his dinner table, and in countless other locations. . . He may not do so, however, when he is speaking as the government, unless the government allows him to be its voice. . . .

The same ability to control teacher expression that occurs within the school-sponsored speech forum applies to religious expression. Due to the need to be neutral toward religion and avoid its endorsement due to the First Amendment's prohibition against the establishment of religion, schools have a legitimate concern in directing teachers to refrain from expression that could be interpreted by students to promote or endorse religious thinking or practices.

For example, in the case of *Peloza v. Capistrano Unified Sch. Dist.*, 37 F.3d 517 (9th Cir. 1994), the court upheld the school district when it prohibited the teacher from articulating his views on creationism and other religious matters during instructional time. Said the court at 522 (emphasis added):

> While at the high school, whether he is in or outside of it during the contract time, Peloza is not just any ordinary citizen. He is a teacher. He is one of those especially respected persons chosen to teach in the high school's classroom. He is clothed with the mantle of one who imparts knowledge and wisdom. His expressions of opinion are all the more believable because he is a teacher. The likelihood of high school students equating his views with those of the school is substantial. **To permit him to discuss his religious beliefs with students during school time on school grounds would violate the Establishment Clause of the First Amendment.** . . .

III. FREE EXERCISE OF RELIGION

The First Amendment's grant of free exercise of religion at times runs headlong into the public school's First Amendment obligation not to establish religion. At other times, the issue is whether the employee's free exercise rights are outweighed by the school's legitimate interest in implementing its curriculum. On occasion, the issue is whether the school has appropriately made accommodation to the employee's right to freely exercise religious rights.

This area has not been clearly determined by the judiciary, which has decided cases in both directions, and suffers due not only to a lack of cases, but also from some being brought under the religious clauses of state constitutions.

In constitutional cases involving the wearing of religious dress, the courts are split. In *Cooper v. Eugene Sch. Dist. No. 4J*, 723 P.2d 298 (Or. 1986), the Oregon Supreme Court upheld the revocation of a special education teacher's license after she became a Sikh and refused to cease wearing white clothes and a white turban associated with her faith, even after being warned about the state laws prohibiting teachers from wearing religious dress and requiring their suspension from teaching and revocation of licenses. The court stated at 308 and 313, respectively:

> The courts' tolerance of overt religious symbolism in public schools has differed over time and perhaps with the religious composition of different communities. Looking beyond the specific facts of the cases, however, the decisions generally have been that more than a teacher's religious dress is needed to show a forbidden sectarian influence in the classroom, but that a rule against such religious dress is permissible to avoid the appearance of sectarian influence, favoritism, or official approval in the public school. . .
>
> The religious influence on children while in the public school that . . . [the Oregon laws] seek to prevent is not mere knowledge that a teacher is an adherent of a particular religion. Their concern is that the teacher's appearance in religious garb may leave a conscious or unconscious impression among young people and their parents that the school endorses the particular religious commitment of the person whom it has assigned the public role of a teacher. This is what makes the otherwise privileged display of a teacher's religious commitment by her dress incompatible with the atmosphere of religious neutrality. . . .

The Mississippi Supreme Court went the opposite direction of Oregon's in the case of *Mississippi Employment Security Commission v. McGlothin*, 556 So.2d 324 (Miss. 1990) when it ruled that a teacher who was dismissed for refusing to remove her religious head dress was entitled to unemployment benefits because it violated her right to free exercise of religion. Citing the Supreme Court case of *Wisconsin v. Yoder*, 406 U.S. 20 (1972), which upheld the right of members of the Amish faith to withdraw their children from school after completion of the eighth grade, the Mississippi court noted that "one may not be forced to forsake religious expression or practice . . . unless the state has a compelling interest which overcomes the religious right and pursues this interest by the least restrictive means." 556 So.2d at 329.

In *Palmer v. Board of Education of the City of Chicago*, 603 F.2d 1271 (7th Cir. 1979), where the school dismissed a teacher who was a member of the Jehovah Witness faith because she refused to teach the school's required curriculum in the instruction of patriotic material, such as the Pledge of Allegiance, the Seventh Circuit upheld the school, finding that its interest in educating the children was compelling. The court noted at 1273 that "the First Amendment was not a teacher license for uncontrolled expression at variance with established curricular content," and stated at 1274 (emphasis added):

> Parents have a vital interest in what their children are taught. Their representatives have in general prescribed a curriculum. **There is a compelling state interest in the choice and adherence to a suitable curriculum for the benefit of our young citizens and society. It cannot be left to individual teachers to teach what they please.** Plaintiff's right to her own religious views and practices remains unfettered, but she has no constitutional right to require others to submit to her views and to forego a portion of their education they would otherwise enjoy. . . .

IV. FREEDOM FROM UNREASONABLE SEARCH AND SEIZURE

The Fourth Amendment prohibits public boards of education, as well as their individual board members and administrators, from violating the right of their employees to be free from unreasonable searches and seizures of their persons and property. The Supreme Court in a public hospital case relied heavily on its prior public school student search case, *New Jersey v. T.L.O., 469 U.S. 325 (1985)* and considered whether the search of a doctor's personal affects violated his Fourth Amendment rights.

CASE
O'Connor v. Ortega, 480 U.S. 709 (1987)
(emphasis added)

[Issue:] This suit under 42 U.S.C. 1983 presents two issues concerning the Fourth Amendment rights of public employees. First, we must determine whether the respondent, a public employee, had a **reasonable expectation of privacy** in his office, desk, and file cabinets at his place of work. Second, we must address the **appropriate Fourth Amendment standard for a search conducted by a public employer in areas in which a public employee is found to have a reasonable expectation of privacy**.

[Facts:] Dr. Magno Ortega, a physician and psychiatrist, held the position of Chief of Professional Education at Napa State Hospital (Hospital) for 17 years, until his dismissal from that position in 1981. As Chief of Professional Education, Dr. Ortega had primary responsibility for training young physicians in psychiatric residency programs.

In July 1981, Hospital officials. . . became concerned about possible improprieties in Dr. Ortega's management of the residency program. In particular, the Hospital officials were concerned with Dr. Ortega's acquisition of an Apple II computer for use in the residency program. The officials thought that Dr. Ortega might have misled Dr. O'Connor into believing that the computer had been donated, when in fact the computer had been financed by the possibly coerced contributions of residents. Additionally, the Hospital officials were concerned with charges that Dr. Ortega had sexually harassed two female Hospital employees, and had taken inappropriate disciplinary action against a resident. . .

The resulting search of Dr. Ortega's office was quite thorough. The investigators entered the office a number of times and seized several items from Dr. Ortega's desk and file cabinets, including a Valentine's Day card, a photograph, and a book of poetry all sent to Dr. Ortega by a former resident physician. . . The investigators did not otherwise separate Dr. Ortega's property from state property because, as one investigator testified, "[t]rying to sort State from non-State, it was too much to do, so I gave it up and boxed it up." . . . Thus, no formal inventory of the property in the office was ever made. Instead, all the papers in Dr. Ortega's office were merely placed in boxes, and put in storage for Dr. Ortega to retrieve. . . .

[Legal Standards on Expectation of Privacy:] The strictures of the Fourth Amendment, applied to the States through the Fourteenth Amendment, have been applied to the conduct of governmental officials in various civil activities. *New Jersey v. T. L. O.*, 469 U.S. 325 (1985). Thus, we have held in the past that the Fourth Amendment governs the conduct of school officials, . . .

The Fourth Amendment protects the "right of the people to be secure in their persons, houses, papers, and effects, against unreasonable searches and seizures. . . ." Our cases establish that Dr. Ortega's Fourth Amendment rights are implicated only if the conduct of the Hospital officials at issue in this case infringed "an expectation of privacy that society is prepared to consider reasonable." . . .

Because the reasonableness of an expectation of privacy, as well as the appropriate standard for a search, is understood to differ according to context, it is essential first to delineate the boundaries of the workplace context. **The workplace includes those areas and items that are related to work and are generally within the employer's control.** At a hospital, for example, the **hallways, cafeteria, offices, desks, and file cabinets, among other areas, are all part of the workplace**. These areas remain part of the workplace context even if the employee has placed personal items in them, such as a photograph placed in a desk or a letter posted on an employee bulletin board.

Not everything that passes through the confines of the business address can be considered part of the workplace context, however. An employee may bring closed luggage to the office prior to leaving on a trip, or a handbag or briefcase each workday. While whatever expectation of privacy the employee has in the existence and the outward appearance of the luggage is affected by its presence in the workplace, the employee's expectation of privacy in the contents of the luggage is not affected in the same way. **The appropriate standard for a workplace search does not necessarily apply to a piece of closed personal luggage, a handbag, or a briefcase that happens to be within the employer's business address**. . . .

. . . **Individuals do not lose Fourth Amendment rights merely because they work for the government instead of a private employer.** The operational realities of the workplace, however, may make some employees' expectations of privacy unreasonable when an intrusion is by a supervisor rather than a law enforcement official. **Public employees' expectations of privacy in their offices, desks, and file cabinets, like similar expectations of employees in the private sector, may be reduced by virtue of actual office practices and procedures, or by legitimate regulation. . . . The employee's expectation of privacy must be assessed in the context of the employment relation**.

An office is seldom a private enclave free from entry by supervisors, other employees, and business and personal invitees. Instead, in many cases offices are continually entered by fellow employees and other visitors during the workday for conferences, consultations, and other work-related visits. Simply put, it is the nature of government offices that others - such as fellow employees, supervisors, consensual visitors, and the general public - may have frequent access to an individual's office. . . Given the great variety of work environments in the public sector, the question whether an employee has a reasonable expectation of privacy must be addressed on a case-by-case basis.

[Application of Standards to the Facts:] . . . But regardless of any legitimate right of access the Hospital staff may have had to the office as such, we recognize that the undisputed evidence suggests that Dr. Ortega had a reasonable expectation of privacy in his desk and file cabinets. The undisputed evidence discloses that Dr. Ortega did not share his desk or file cabinets with any other employees. Dr. Ortega had occupied the office for 17 years and he kept materials in his office, which included personal correspondence, medical files, correspondence from private patients unconnected to the Hospital, personal financial records, teaching aids and notes, and personal gifts and mementos. . . The files on physicians in residency training were kept outside Dr. Ortega's office. . . Indeed, the only items found by the investigators were apparently personal items because, with the exception of the items seized for use in the administrative hearings, all the papers and effects found in the office were simply placed in boxes and made available to Dr. Ortega. . . Finally, we note that there was no evidence that the Hospital had established any reasonable regulation or policy discouraging employees such as Dr. Ortega from storing personal papers and effects in their desks or file cabinets, . . . although the absence of such a policy does not create an expectation of privacy where it would not otherwise exist.

On the basis of this undisputed evidence, we accept the conclusion of the Court of Appeals that Dr. Ortega had a reasonable expectation of privacy at least in his desk and file cabinets. . . .

[Standards on Reasonableness of the Search:] . . . [A]s we have stated in *T. L. O.*, "[t]o hold that the Fourth Amendment applies to searches conducted by [public employers] is only to begin the inquiry into the standards governing such searches. . . . **[W]hat is reasonable depends on the context within which a search takes place**." *New Jersey v. T. L. O.*, . . . Thus, we must determine the appropriate standard of reasonableness applicable to the search. A determination of the standard of reasonableness applicable to a particular class of searches requires "**balanc[ing] the nature and quality of the intrusion on the individual's Fourth Amendment interests against the importance of the governmental interests alleged to justify the intrusion.**" . . .

In the case of searches conducted by a public employer, **we must balance the invasion of the employees' legitimate expectations of privacy against the government's need for supervision, control, and the efficient operation of the workplace. . . .**

The legitimate privacy interests of public employees in the private objects they bring to the workplace may be substantial. Against these privacy interests,

however, must be balanced the realities of the workplace, which strongly suggest that a warrant requirement would be unworkable. . . .

The **governmental interest** justifying work-related intrusions by public employers **is the efficient and proper operation of the workplace.** . . . Indeed, it is difficult to give the concept of probable cause, rooted as it is in the criminal investigatory context, much meaning when the purpose of a search is to retrieve a file for work-related reasons. Similarly, the concept of probable cause has little meaning for a routine inventory conducted by public employers for the purpose of securing state property. . . **To ensure the efficient and proper operation of the agency, therefore, public employers must be given wide latitude to enter employee offices for work-related, noninvestigatory reasons**.

We come to a similar conclusion for searches conducted pursuant to an investigation of work-related employee misconduct. Even when employers conduct an investigation, they have an interest substantially different from "the normal need for law enforcement." . . . **Public employers have an interest in ensuring that their agencies operate in an effective and efficient manner**, and the work of these agencies inevitably suffers from the inefficiency, incompetence, mismanagement, or other work-related malfeasance of its employees. Indeed, in many cases, public employees are entrusted with tremendous responsibility, and the consequences of their misconduct or incompetence to both the agency and the public interest can be severe. . . **In our view, therefore, a probable cause requirement for searches of the type at issue here would impose intolerable burdens on public employers.** . . .**In sum, we conclude that the "special needs, beyond the normal need for law enforcement make the . . . probable-cause requirement impracticable," . . . for legitimate work-related, noninvestigatory intrusions as well as investigations of work-related misconduct.** A standard of reasonableness will neither unduly burden the efforts of government employers to ensure the efficient and proper operation of the workplace, nor authorize arbitrary intrusions upon the privacy of public employees. **We hold, therefore, that public employer intrusions on the constitutionally protected privacy interests of government employees for noninvestigatory, work-related purposes, as well as for investigations of work-related misconduct, should be judged by the standard of reasonableness under all the circumstances.** Under this reasonableness standard, **both the inception and the scope of the intrusion must be reasonable**:

"Determining the reasonableness of any search involves a twofold inquiry: **first, one must consider `whether the . . . action was justified at its inception,'** *Terry v. Ohio*, . . . **second, one must determine whether the search as actually conducted `was reasonably related in scope to the circumstances which justified the interference in the first place,'** . . ." *New Jersey v. T. L. O.*, . . .

Ordinarily, a search of an employee's office by a supervisor will be "justified at its inception" when there are reasonable grounds for suspecting that the search will turn up evidence that the employee is guilty of work-related misconduct, or that the search is necessary for a noninvestigatory work-related purpose such as to retrieve a needed file. Because petitioners had an "individualized suspicion" of misconduct by Dr. Ortega, we need not decide whether individualized suspicion is an essential element of the standard of reasonableness that we adopt today. See *New Jersey v. T. L. O.* . . . The search will be permissible in its scope when "the measures adopted are reasonably related to the objectives of the search and not excessively intrusive in light of . . . the nature of the [misconduct]." . . . .

On remand, therefore, the District Court must determine the justification for the search and seizure, and evaluate the reasonableness of both the inception of the search and its scope.

Accordingly, the judgment of the Court of Appeals is reversed, and the case is remanded to that court for further proceedings consistent with this opinion.

It is so ordered.

Seventeen years after the search of Dr. Ortega's office occurred, and eleven years after the Supreme Court's remand for a trial, the Ninth Circuit at 146 F.3d 1149, (1998) ruled in his favor, stating that "[b]ecause no reasonable official in the defendants' position would have believed that a search based on the skeletal and stale allegations of Dr. Ortega's sexual misconduct was permissible under the Fourth Amendment or that any such search could be conducted in the absence of a reasonable suspicion that particular evidence would be discovered, the district court did not err in granting relief to Dr. Ortega. . . ."

In terms of the expectation of privacy issue and based on the Supreme Court's *Ortega* decision, school officials, in order to remove any doubt, should inform school employees of what areas of the workplace in which teachers may store or keep personal items or information are deemed accessible by the employer at any time. Such areas would include school-furnished desks, storage and filing cabinets, and computers. However, an employee's purse or personally-owned laptop computer that is placed in the school's filing cabinet would retain an expectation of privacy, thus requiring school officials to have reasonable suspicion to believe that such objects contain material or information that violates school rules in order to search or seize.

A. Suspicionless Searches

In the case of *Knox County Education Assoc. v. Knox County Board of Education*, 158 F.3d 361 (6th Cir. 1998), the court upheld a policy that permitted drug and alcohol testing of employees who applied for, were transferred to, or were promoted to, "safety sensitive" positions, including teaching positions, even though there was no reasonable suspicion to believe that an individual used or was under the influence of such substances. The Policy defined "safety sensitive" positions as those positions "where a single mistake by such employee can create an immediate threat of serious harm to students and fellow employees." Principals, assistant principals, teachers, traveling teachers, teacher aides, substitute teachers, school secretaries and school bus drivers were listed as "safety sensitive" employees.

In its analysis of suspicionless drug and alcohol testing, the court stated at 373 (emphasis added):

> As a general rule, in order to be reasonable, a search must be undertaken pursuant to a warrant issued upon a showing of probable cause. . . That is, a valid search must ordinarily be based on an "individualized suspicion of wrongdoing." *Chandler*, 117 S.Ct. at 1301.

However, in *Chandler* the Court clarified how suspicionless testing -- presumably inherently suspect because by definition it is not accompanied by individualized suspicion -- can comport with the Fourth Amendment:

> **But particularized exceptions to the main rule are sometimes warranted based on "special needs, beyond the normal need for law enforcement.**"
> . . . When such "special needs"-- concerns other than crime detection-- are alleged in justification of a Fourth Amendment intrusion, courts must undertake a context-specific inquiry, examining closely the competing private and public interests advanced by the parties. See *Von Raab*, 489 U.S. at 665-666 . . . As *Skinner* stated: **"In limited circumstances, where the privacy interests implicated by the search are minimal, and where an important governmental interest furthered by the intrusion would be placed in jeopardy by a requirement of individualized suspicion, a search may be reasonable despite the absence of such suspicion."** 489 U.S. at 624. . . *Chandler*, 117 S.Ct. at 1301.

Thus, where a Fourth Amendment intrusion serves special needs, **"it is necessary to balance the individual's privacy expectations against the Government's interests to determine whether it is impractical to require a warrant or some level of individualized suspicion in the particular context."** *Von Raab*, 109 S.Ct. at 1390. Quite simply, then, in evaluating the constitutionality of the Board's drug testing Policy here, we must balance the government's (or public's) interest in testing against the individual's privacy interest.

After an extensive analysis of the school employer and employee interests, the *Knox County* court stated at 384 (emphasis added):

> . . . [W]e believe that the privacy interest for the employees not to be tested is significantly diminished by the level of regulation of their jobs and by the nature of the work itself. The ultimate inquiry before the Court is whether the search at issue here -- the one-time, suspicionless testing of people hired to serve in teaching and administrative positions -- is reasonable. On balance, the public interest in attempting to ensure that school teachers perform their jobs unimpaired is evident, considering their unique *in loco parentis* obligations and their immense influence over students. **These public interests clearly outweigh the privacy interests of the teacher not to be tested because the drug- testing regime adopted by Knox County is circumscribed, narrowly-tailored, and not overly intrusive, either in its monitoring procedures or in its disclosure requirements**. This is particularly so because it is a one-time test, with advance notice and with

no random testing component, and because the school system in which the employees work is heavily regulated, particularly as to drug usage.

The *Knox County* case was heavily relied upon by a Kentucky federal district court in *Crager v. Board of Educ. of Knott County, Kentucky*, 313 F.Supp.2d 690 (E.D.Ky. 2004), where the court upheld a random suspicionless drug testing policy for all employees in "safety-sensitive" positions, including teachers.

V. RIGHT OF PRIVACY

The Supreme Court in the case of *Roe v. Wade*, 413 U.S. 150 (1973) at 152-153 stated the constitutional basis for the right of privacy, even though there is no specific mention of the right, as follows (emphasis added):

The Constitution does not explicitly mention any right of privacy. In a line of decisions, however, going back perhaps as far as *Union Pacific R. Co. v. Botsford*, . . . (1891), the Court has recognized that a right of personal privacy, or a guarantee of certain areas or zones of privacy, does exist under the Constitution. In varying contexts, the Court or individual Justices have, indeed, found at least the roots of that right in the First Amendment, *Stanley v. Georgia*, . . . (1969); in the Fourth and Fifth Amendments, *Terry v. Ohio*, . . . (1968), *Katz v. United States*, . . . (1967), *Boyd v. United States*, . . . (1886), . . . ; in the penumbras of the Bill of Rights, *Griswold v. Connecticut*, . . . ; in the Ninth Amendment, *id.*, at 486 (Goldberg, J., concurring); or in the concept of liberty guaranteed by the first section of the Fourteenth Amendment, see *Meyer v. Nebraska*, . . . (1923). These decisions make it clear that only personal rights that can be deemed "fundamental" or "implicit in the concept of ordered liberty," *Palko v. Connecticut*, . . . (1937), are included in this guarantee of personal privacy. They also make it clear that **the right has some extension to activities relating to marriage**, *Loving v. Virginia*, . . . (1967); **procreation**, *Skinner v. Oklahoma*, . . . (1942); **contraception**, *Eisenstadt v. Baird*, . . . (WHITE, J., concurring in result); **family relationships**, *Prince v. Massachusetts*. . . (1944); and **child rearing and education**, *Pierce v. Society of Sisters*, . . . (1925), *Meyer v. Nebraska*, . . . [(1923)].

Examples of cases which examine teachers' rights of privacy:

The Fifth Circuit in *Dike v. School Board of Orange County, Fla.*, 650 F.2d 783 (5th Cir. 1981) considered a case brought by a kindergarten teacher who desired to breastfeed her baby at school during her duty-free lunch time. She had done so for three months when the principal directed her to stop based on a school board directive against teachers bringing their children to school. She complied, but the child became allergic to feeding formula and when it stopped nursing from a bottle filled with breast milk, the teacher was forced to take unpaid leave for the rest of the school term to feed her child at home. When she sued, the district court dismissed her complaint as frivolous. The Fifth Circuit, however, based on her constitutional right of privacy, reversed and remanded the case for a trial to determine if the school's reasons for the denial were sufficiently compelling to outweigh her privacy interest. Said the court 785-787:

> The Constitution protects from undue state interference citizens' freedom of personal choice in some areas of marriage and family life. These protected interests have been described as rights of personal privacy or as "fundamental" personal liberties. . .

> Among these protected liberties are individual decisions respecting marriage, procreation, contraception, abortion, and family relationships. The Supreme Court has long recognized that parents' interest in nurturing and rearing their children deserves special protection against state interference.

> Breastfeeding is the most elemental form of parental care. It is a communion between mother and child that, like marriage, is "intimate to the degree of being sacred". . . In light of the spectrum of interests that the Supreme Court has held specially protected we conclude that the Constitution protects from excessive state interference a woman's decision respecting breastfeeding her child.

In the case of *Daury v. Smith*, 842 F.2d 9 (1st Cir. 1988), the court upheld a Massachusetts' school district's directive that its former principal and then grade leader see a psychiatrist before returning from an agreed leave of absence. Daury based his suit on an alleged invasion of his constitutional right of privacy where he argued that the psychiatric examination "forced him to reveal information about his marriage, family history, and other personal relationships" despite the school's promise to keep the report confidential. *Id.* at 13. Said the First Circuit at 13-14:

> That a person has a constitutional right to privacy is now well established...Such right includes "the individual interest in avoiding disclosure of personal matters."...
> . . . The privacy right, however, must often give way to considerations of public interest. . . .

> In *Lyons v. Sullivan*, 602 F.2d 7 (1st Cir.) . . . (1979), we held that a matter of public concern overrode the right of privacy. Lyons, a public school teacher, filed an unusual complaint in a medical malpractice action, which led the school superintendent to question his mental stability. The superintendent required Lyons to place himself in the care of a psychiatrist as a condition to his continued employment. Lyons refused to see the psychiatrist and resigned. He then filed suit . . . We found that the superintendent had a reasonable basis for questioning Lyons' mental condition, and that there was no constitutional infirmity in the course of conduct pursued. . .

> As *Lyons* implicitly recognizes, there is a legitimate public interest in providing a safe and healthy educational environment. A school committee, therefore, may justifiably compel a teacher or administrator to submit to a psychiatric examination as a condition of continued employment if the

committee has reason to believe that the teacher or administrator may be jeopardizing the welfare of students under his or her supervision.

For a tough lesson on what happened when the school board discharged a female teacher who became pregnant and raised her child as a single mother, see the case of *Eckmann v. Board of Education of Hawthorn Sch. Dist. No. 17*, 636 F.Supp. 1214 (N.D.Ill. 1986). Upon the school board's motion for a judgment notwithstanding the verdict, the court upheld the judgment and determined there was sufficient evidence that the jury could find that her unwed pregnancy was a substantial or motivating factor in her discharge and that the board's proffered reasons for dismissal were pretextual. The court did reduce the jury's award or $2,000,000 in compensatory damages to $750,000, but upheld the punitive damage award against six individual board members in the amount of $250,000, $25,000, $10,000, $500,000, $25,000, and $500,000, respectively.

Although not describing the teacher's right to bear and raise a child as that of privacy, the court at 1217 quoted the Supreme Court case of *Griswold v. Connecticut*, 381 U.S. 479, 484 (1965) and described the right as "fundamental" and "implicit in the concept of ordered liberty." Such right, according to the *Eckmann* court at 1218 included "*assorted freedoms against state intrusion into family life and intimate personal decisions*." (Court's emphasis.) The court further stated at 1218 (emphasis in bold added):

> In *Loving v. Virginia* 388 U.S. 1 . . .(1967), the Supreme Court held that the freedom to decide whom "to marry, or not marry . . . resides with the individual and cannot be infringed by the state." **In other words, it is improper for the state to interfere with a person's decision to marry, or as it relates to this case,** *not* **to marry**.

The Supreme Court later stated that:

> **If the right of privacy means anything, it is the right of the** *individual*, **married or single, to be free from unwarranted governmental intrusion into matters so fundamentally affecting a person as the decision whether to bear or beget a child**.

Eisenstadt v. Baird, 405 U.S. 438 . . . (1972) (emphasis in original). . . Under the overwhelming weight of authority, it is beyond question that plaintiff had a substantive due process right to conceive and raise her child out of wedlock without unwarranted state (School Board) intrusion.

Had the school board in *Eisenstadt* produced substantial evidence that the teacher's behavior constituted immorality and had a direct and sufficiently negative impact on her fitness to teach, the jury could have determined that the board prevailed by the greater weight of the evidence and, hence, its dismissal action would have been warranted. These cases will necessarily entail a balancing of the interests of both the teacher and the public school and will be decided based on how the evidence of each side is weighed by the jury.

SCENARIOS
STATE AND APPLY THE RELEVANT LEGAL RULE(S) TO THE FACTS.

1. A non-tenured elementary school special education teacher envisioned herself as a "CEO want-to-be," ordered her two teaching assistants around constantly, criticizing them frequently for the slightest mistakes, hounded other teachers who evidenced any disrespect for disabled children, and on the playground and lunch room often yelled at and lectured normal children if she thought they were disrespecting disabled students. As a result, Principal had documented her professional shortcomings in her evaluation and placed her on "probationary status," which required her to make substantial improvements or be recommended for contract nonrenewal.

During all this time, Teacher became upset at what in her perception was Principal's less than 100 percent support of children with disabilities. Although Principal complied with statute and regulations for educating children with disabilities, in Teacher's opinion, Principal only believed in financing the compact car version of special education services when Teachers believed a full-sized sedan was needed. Teacher began writing letters to influential community leaders, school board members, the editorial page of the local newspaper, and parents of disabled children calling for "more sensitive leadership" from Principal and stating that he "needed to get his head out of the sand, join the 21st century, or retire." The result was that the teaching staff at Principal's school began taking sides, arguments over the Principal's philosophy regarding the extent of the education of the disabled broke out at staff meetings, teachers stopped talking to one another, and parents were so divided that the Parents Organization had to cancel its spring fundraiser.

Principal decided to recommend that Teacher's contract not be renewed, and the school board, properly following state statute, dismissed Teacher on a 3-2 vote. Teacher filed suit in federal district court claiming that the dismissal was a violation of her constitutional rights.

2. Teacher was a 23-year-old single male who became enamored with an 18-year-old single female senior student who likewise found him attractive. Although an emotional bond developed between the two, Teacher made it clear that there could be no dating or physical involvement until after she graduated. The school board policy expressly prohibited teachers from becoming romantically involved with students and went even further by preventing such involvement for one year after the student's graduation.

When Teacher and the student, following her graduation, found themselves inextricably in love, he consulted a constitutional-specialist attorney and filed suit in federal court against his school employer's policy prohibition against his being able to date and develop the relationship with the former student within a year of her graduation.

3. Teacher was a 52-year-old female middle school teacher who had been rumored by students to be intoxicated during the school day on three occasions over the span of a school year. Each time it was properly investigated, but when no odor of alcohol could be detected or other indicators observed, no action was taken other than oral warnings to be careful on how she was perceived by the students. When at the start of the following school year two reliable students reported that her breath smelled of alcohol when she arrived in

the morning, Teacher indicated to Principal, who definitely could detect the odor of alcohol, that she had a bad cold and had taken over-the-counter medicine that morning.

When Teacher went on lunch duty and her room was empty, Principal opened her unlocked desk drawers but found nothing out of the ordinary. He then checked her filing cabinet but found it locked. The only key was given to Teacher and that is where she kept test papers as well as her purse. The custodian was called to the room and directed to drill out the lock, and upon opening the cabinet, Principal found a half-empty bottle of an alcohol-based cold medicine, but not her purse. He then had her come to his office where he directed her to give him her purse, opened it, and discovered three small bottles of bourbon, two of which were empty. Based thereon, Teacher was suspended with pay pending contract dismissal proceedings. Teacher sued in federal court for an order to ban the evidence found in the filing cabinet and her purse from being introduced at the school board dismissal hearing.

CHAPTER 4

TERMINATION OF EMPLOYMENT

When public school officials deem it necessary to terminate a person's employment, attention must be given to whether the employment relationship is "at will" or by contract. If by contract (which may be oral or written), consideration must be given to what process is due the person, either by the terms of the contract itself, school board policy, state statute, and/or the Fourteenth Amendment Due Process Clause.

If the person was hired on an "at will" basis without a contract and without a statement that the employment was for a specific period of time, it generally means under common law principles that either the employee or the employer may terminate the relationship at any time for any reason (so long as the employer's reason does not violate any anti-discrimination statute, or if the employer is the government, does not violate protected constitutional rights such as freedom of speech and equal protection of the law). Caution must be given, however, because some state statutes or local school board policies or bargaining agreements may place procedural barriers in the way of the usual common law ability to immediately terminate non-contract, or "at-will" employees.

I. CONTRACTS

The common law components required to create an enforceable contract, oral or written, consist of an offer, acceptance of the offer, consideration, competent parties, legality of subject matter, and proper form if required by law. The offer may include the prospective employee signing a written document that expresses the terms of the employment agreement or it may be the oral or written expression of the willingness to be employed under agreed-upon terms. Acceptance of the offer may be evidenced by the school board's formal approval at an official meeting. Also, if state law requires it, acceptance would include the actual signing of a written document by the board members.

Consideration is basically the exchange of something of value. The employee agrees to exchange his or her work effort for the employer's promise of wages in most instances.

As to an employee, a competent party is one who has reached the age of majority and has the mental capability to understand what is being agreed to. Where state law requires that the person possess a license or permit to engage in the particular work, one is deemed competent only if that requirement is met. Under the case of *Sartori v. Switzerland County*, 442 N.E.2d 702 (Ind.App. 1982), failure to meet the license requirement for a teacher or to obtain a limited or emergency permit to teach meant that a "regular teacher contract" approved and signed by the school board and a farmer who possessed no license or permit to teach vocational agriculture was void and unenforceable from the beginning and could be nullified by the board at any time without recourse by the farmer.

Legality of subject matter means that under state or federal law it is lawful for the parties to make the agreement. A "friendly wager" between friends over the outcome of a sporting event, for example, is technically illegal in most, if not all, states, and, therefore, would not be enforceable in court. Similarly, a "contract" to kidnap someone would be unenforceable.

Where state law requires the particular transaction to be made in writing or on a prescribed form, such as teacher and real estate contracts, all agreements not so complying would be void, even though the parties had complied with all the other components of common law contracts.

II. FOURTEENTH AMENDMENT DUE PROCESS

Whether or not public school officials must afford due process of law under the Fourteenth Amendment when they seek to terminate a person's employment depends on whether that particular employee possesses a property or liberty interest. Absent proof that the state, via statute or regulation, or the local public school board, via policy or practice, has acted to create a cognizable property interest, or whether during the termination process the board has caused a sufficiently negative impact to the employee's liberty interest, no constitutional process must be given.

A. What Is Property?

The following cases are examples of cases which considered the property interests of teachers to retain their positions of employment.

CASE
Board of Regents v. Roth, 408 U.S. 564 (1972)

(emphasis added)

[Facts:] Wisconsin State University at Oshkosh contracted with Roth to be employed as an assistant professor for the 1968-1969 academic-year, and pursuant to state statute notified him by the following February 1 that he would not receive a contract for the next academic year.

[Supreme Court ruling:] The Supreme Court in ruling that Roth did not have a property interest in being re-employed and, therefore, was not entitled to the reasons for non-continuance and a hearing under the Fourteenth Amendment Due Process Clause, stated at 577-578 (emphasis added):

[Rationale:] Certain attributes of "property" interests protected by procedural due process emerge from these decisions. To have a property interest in a benefit, a person clearly must have more than an abstract need or desire for it. He must have more than a unilateral expectation of it. He must, instead, have a **legitimate claim of entitlement** to it. It is a purpose of the ancient institution of property to protect those claims upon which people rely in their daily lives, reliance that must not be arbitrarily undermined. It is a purpose of the constitutional right to a hearing to provide an opportunity for a person to vindicate those claims.

Property interests, of course, are not created by the Constitution. Rather, **they are created and their dimensions are defined by existing rules or understandings that stem from an independent source such as state law - rules or understandings that secure certain benefits and that support claims of entitlement to those benefits.** . . .

. . . the respondent's [Roth's] "property" interest in employment at Wisconsin State University-Oshkosh was created and defined by the terms of his appointment. Those terms secured his interest in employment up to June 30, 1969. But the important fact in this case is that they specifically provided that the respondent's employment was to terminate on June 30. They did not provide for contract renewal absent "sufficient cause." Indeed, they made no provision for renewal whatsoever.

Thus, the terms of the respondent's appointment secured absolutely no interest in re-employment for the next year. They supported absolutely no possible claim of entitlement to re-employment. Nor, significantly, was there any state statute or University rule or policy that secured his interest in re-employment or that created any legitimate claim to it. In these circumstances, the respondent surely had an abstract concern in being rehired, but he did not have a property interest sufficient to require the University authorities to give him a hearing when they declined to renew his contract of employment.

CASE
On the same day it ruled in the *Roth* case, the Supreme Court decided
Perry v. Sindermann, 408 U.S. 593 (1972)

(emphasis added)

[Facts:] This case was brought by Sindermann, who after teaching as a professor at Odessa Junior College in Texas under four successive one-year contracts, was summarily dismissed without receiving any reasons and a hearing. The only statement issued by the Board of Regents was a press release stating allegations of insubordination that included defiance of his superiors by going to legislative committee meetings when college administrators had clearly denied him permission to leave his classes for that reason. In agreeing with the Circuit Court of Appeals that the case should be remanded to the district court for a trial, the Supreme Court stated at 599-604 (emphasis added):

The respondent's lack of formal contractual or tenure security in continued employment at Odessa Junior College. . . is highly relevant to his procedural due process claim. But it may not be entirely dispositive.

[Court ruling:] We have held today in *Board of Regents v. Roth*, . . . that the Constitution does not require opportunity for a hearing before the nonrenewal of a nontenured teacher's contract, unless he can show that the decision not to rehire him somehow deprived him of an interest in "liberty" or that he had a "property" interest in continued employment, despite the lack of tenure or a formal contract.

Similarly, the respondent here [Sindermann] has yet to show that he has been deprived of an interest that could invoke procedural due process protection. As in *Roth*, the mere showing that he was not rehired in one particular job, without more, did not amount to a showing of a loss of liberty. Nor did it amount to a showing of a loss of property.

But the respondent's allegations . . . do raise a genuine issue as to his interest in continued employment at Odessa Junior College. He alleged that this interest, though not secured by a formal contractual tenure provision, was secured by a no less binding understanding fostered by the college administration. In particular, the respondent alleged that **the college had a de facto tenure program, and that he had tenure under that program**. He claimed that he and others legitimately relied upon an unusual provision that had been in the college's official Faculty Guide for many years:

"Teacher Tenure: Odessa College has no tenure system. The Administration of the College **wishes the faculty member to feel that he has permanent tenure as long as his teaching services are satisfactory and as long as he displays a cooperative attitude toward his co-workers and his superiors, and as long as he is happy in his work**."

[Rationale:] . . . We have made clear in *Roth,* . . . "property" interests subject to procedural due process protection are not limited by a few rigid, technical forms. Rather, "property" denotes a broad range of interests that are secured by "existing rules or understandings." . . . **A person's interest in a benefit is a "property" interest for due process purposes if there are such rules or mutually explicit understandings that support his claim of entitlement** to the benefit and that he may invoke at a hearing. . . .

In this case, **the respondent has alleged the existence of rules and understandings, promulgated and fostered by state officials that may justify his legitimate claim of entitlement to continued employment** absent "sufficient cause." **We disagree with the Court of Appeals insofar as it held that a mere subjective "expectancy" is protected by procedural due process,** but we **agree that the respondent must be given an opportunity to prove the legitimacy of his claim of such entitlement in light of "the policies and practices of the institution."** . . . Proof of such a property interest would not, of course, entitle him to reinstatement. But such proof would obligate college officials to grant a hearing at his request, where he could be informed of the grounds for his nonretention and challenge their sufficiency.

B.   *What Is Liberty?*

The following cases discuss the legal standard by which courts can determine an individual teacher's liberty interests.

CASE

In the *Roth* case, above, the Court stated at 572 -575

(emphasis added)

[Rationale:] "While this Court has not attempted to define with exactness the liberty . . . guaranteed [by the Fourteenth Amendment], the term has received much consideration and some of the included things have been definitely stated. Without doubt, it denotes not merely **freedom from bodily restraint** but also **the right of the individual to contract, to engage in any of the common occupations of life, to acquire useful knowledge, to marry, establish a home and bring up children, to worship God according to the dictates of his own conscience, and generally to enjoy those privileges long recognized . . . as essential to the orderly pursuit of happiness by free men**." *Meyer v. Nebraska,* . . . In a Constitution for a free people, there can be no doubt that the meaning of "liberty" must be broad indeed.

There might be cases in which a State refused to re-employ a person under such circumstances that interests in liberty would be implicated. But this is not such a case.

The State, in declining to rehire the respondent [Roth], did not make any charge against him that might **seriously damage his standing and associations in his community**. It did not base the nonrenewal of his contract on a charge, for example, that he had been guilty of dishonesty, or immorality. Had it done so, this would be a different case. For **"[w]here a person's good name, reputation, honor, or integrity is at stake because of what the government is doing to him, notice and an opportunity to be heard are essential."** . . . In such a case, due process would accord an opportunity to refute the charge before University officials. In the present case, however, there is no suggestion whatever that the respondent's "good name, reputation, honor, or integrity" is at stake.

Similarly, there is no suggestion that the State, in declining to re-employ the respondent, **imposed on him a stigma or other disability that foreclosed his freedom to take advantage of other employment opportunities**. The State, for example, did not invoke any regulations to bar the respondent from all other public employment in state universities. Had it done so, this, again, would be a different case. . . . In the present case, however, this principle does not come into play. .

Hence, on the record before us, all that clearly appears is that the respondent was not rehired for one year at one university. **It stretches the concept too far to suggest that a person is deprived of "liberty" when he simply is not rehired in one job but remains as free as before to seek another**.

C. *What Process Is Due?*

[Case:] The Supreme Court in *Cleveland Board of Education v. Loudermill*, 470 U.S. 532 (1985) considered the extent of due process required when it is determined that a property (or liberty) interest exists and state statute (or local regulation) does not set forth any procedure to be followed. The Court stated at 542-546 (emphasis added):

> **[Rationale:]** An essential principle of due process is that a deprivation of life, liberty, or property "be preceded by **notice and opportunity for hearing appropriate to the nature of the case.**" . . . We have described "the root requirement" of the Due Process Clause as being "that an individual be given an opportunity for a hearing before he is deprived of any significant property interest." . . . This principle requires "**some kind of a hearing" prior to the discharge of an employee who has a constitutionally protected property interest in his employment**. *Board of Regents v. Roth*, . . . *Perry v. Sindermann*. . . .
>
> The need for **some form of pretermination hearing**, recognized in these cases, is evident from a **balancing of the competing interests at stake**. These are the **private interest in retaining employment**, the **governmental interest in the expeditious removal of unsatisfactory employees and the avoidance of administrative burdens**, and the **risk of an erroneous termination**. . . .
>
> The foregoing considerations indicate that the **pretermination "hearing," though necessary, need not be elaborate**. We have pointed out that "[t]he formality and procedural requisites for the hearing can vary, depending upon the importance of the interests involved and the

nature of the subsequent proceedings." . . . **In general, "something less" than a full evidentiary hearing is sufficient prior to adverse administrative action.** *Mathews v. Eldridge.* . . .

Here, the pretermination hearing need not definitively resolve the propriety of the discharge. **It should be an initial check against mistaken decisions - essentially, a determination of whether there are reasonable grounds to believe that the charges against the employee are true and support the proposed action.**

The **essential requirements of due process. . . are notice and an opportunity to respond.** The opportunity to present reasons, either in person or in writing, why proposed action should not be taken is a fundamental due process requirement. . . . **The tenured public employee is entitled to oral or written notice of the charges against him, an explanation of the employer's evidence, and an opportunity to present his side of the story.** . . . To require more than this prior to termination would intrude to an unwarranted extent on the government's interest in quickly removing an unsatisfactory employee. . . .

D. What is Notice?

To be fair in the constitutional due process sense, the party facing denial of a property (or liberty) interest at the hands of a governmental body is entitled to notice, which includes not only a statement of the reasons for the government's actions, but also notice of the right to a hearing. In a case of alleged non-receipt of a notice of hearing, *Osborn v. Review Board of the Indiana Employment Security Division*, 381 N.E.2d 495 (Ind.App. 1978), the court ruled that the plaintiff, who sought unemployment compensation but did not receive the written notice of a hearing that was sent by regular mail, was not deprived of due process rights. The court stated at 500 (emphasis added):

Whether or not due process is afforded depends not on the particular hardship which may befall a person under exceptional circumstances. The issue, rather, is whether "this system of jurisprudence, with its provisions for safeguarding the rights of litigants, is due process of law.". . . **The Due Process Clause does not require the state to erect an ideal system for the administration of justice which is impervious to malfunctions.** Consequently, **the failure in fact of a person to receive notice does not necessarily indicate a deprivation of due process.** *Miedreich v. Lauenstein* [232 U.S. 236 (1914)]; *see United States v. Smith* (1968), 3d Cir., 398 F.2d 173 (service by regular mail may be sufficient due process even though addressee claims non-receipt).

A reasonable period of time must be given between receipt of notice and the hearing date, but what is reasonable will depend upon the particular facts. If the employee does not object or request a continuance based on a lack of time to prepare, courts will most likely uphold the school. If there is an objection, then the hearing body or officer will have to consider and decide whether or not to set another hearing date. The analysis is the same regarding the adequacy of the reasons given for the dismissal.

E. What is a Hearing?

Due process only requires the offer of an opportunity for a hearing. Such offer should contain a provision requiring the employee to request the hearing within a certain period of time or else be deemed to have waived the right to it. Courts will uphold such a waiver if it is shown that the employee had actual knowledge of the deadline, but failed to respond on time. Similarly, if a hearing date is set and the employee does not attend, waiver by the employee's actions in failing to show will likely be upheld.

At the hearing, public school officials have the burden of proving the asserted grounds for termination of employment. Although hearsay evidence is admissible because a school dismissal proceeding is an administrative hearing and not a court trial, a number of courts have ruled that a teacher's contract may not be terminated based on hearsay evidence alone.

However, in a school bus driver dismissal proceeding where the driver was alleged to have committed sexual acts against female students, the Seventh Circuit found no violation of constitutional due process when the school presented the students' hearsay testimony via affidavits that had the students' names blocked out. *Green v. Board of School Commissioners*, 716 F.2d 1191 (7th Cir. 1983).

The employee must be permitted to present evidence and likely has the right to cross examine the school's witnesses and be represented by counsel, or at least to consult with counsel. Case law in each federal circuit and state appellate courts needs to be reviewed on the issues of the right to cross examination and to counsel. The Supreme Court in *Loudermill*, above, stated that the hearing "need not be elaborate" and that "something less than a full evidentiary hearing is sufficient." It cited its prior case of *Mathews v. Eldridge*, 424 U.S. 319 (1976), which stated at 334-335 (emphasis added):

> More precisely, our prior decisions indicate that identification of the specific dictates of due process generally requires consideration of three distinct factors: **First, the private interest that will be affected** by the official action; **second, the risk of an erroneous deprivation** of such interest through the procedures used, and the probable value, if any, of additional or substitute procedural safeguards; and **finally, the Government's interest**, including the function involved and the fiscal and administrative burdens that the additional or substitute procedural requirement would entail.

As a matter of preventing a lawsuit, it is advisable to permit the employee to cross examine school witnesses and be represented by counsel. But in certain situations, school officials may choose to evaluate these issues in light of *Mathews* and *Loudermill*, and decide against permitting the employee to use counsel at a hearing and to cross examine witnesses.

F. *Impartiality of Hearing Body*

Constitutional due process is based on the premise of fairness, and the need for an impartial decision-maker in an employee dismissal hearing is paramount in meeting the fairness test.

[Case:] The Supreme Court in the case of *Hortonville Joint Sch. Dist. No. 1 v. Hortonville Ed. Assoc.*, 426 U.S. 482 (1976), considered whether a school board could fairly be the hearing body in the dismissal of its teachers who had participated in an illegal strike. In ruling that the hearing was fair, the Court stated at 491-492 (emphasis added):

> **[Rationale:]** [T]he teachers did not show, and the Wisconsin courts did not find, that the Board members had **the kind of personal or financial stake in the decision that might create a conflict of interest**, and there is nothing in the record to support **charges of personal animosity**. The Wisconsin Supreme Court was careful "not to suggest . . . that the board members were anything but dedicated public servants, trying to provide the district with quality education . . . within its limited budget." . . .
>
> **Mere familiarity with the facts of a case** gained by an agency in the performance of its statutory role **does not, however, disqualify a decision maker**. . . . **Nor is a decision maker disqualified simply because he has taken a position, even in public, on a policy issue related to the dispute**, **in the absence of a showing that he is not "capable of judging a particular controversy fairly on the basis of its own circumstances."** . . .

[Supreme Court Ruling:] The *Hortonville* Court concluded by saying at 496-497 (emphasis added):

> . . . A showing that the Board was "involved" in the events preceding this decision, in light of the important interest in leaving with the Board the power given by the state legislature, is not enough to overcome the **presumption of honesty and integrity in policymakers with decision-making power**. . . . Accordingly, we hold that the Due Process Clause of the Fourteenth Amendment did not guarantee respondents that the decision to terminate their employment would be made or reviewed by a body other than the School Board.

Note: The key aspects of *Hortonville* are that school board members (1) are not disqualified merely because they are familiar with the facts of the case or have taken a position before the hearing takes place, and (2) are given the legal "presumption of honesty and integrity" in their official role as decision makers, which can only be successfully rebutted upon a showing of a board member's actual "personal or financial stake in the outcome" or "personal animosity" toward the employee.

An example of a finding of such personal animosity is found in a different case.

[Case:] The case of *Valley v. Rapides Parish School Board*, 702 F.3d 1221 (5th Cir. 1997) where the court ruled that a majority of the board members violated the discharged superintendent's due process right to a fair and impartial hearing.

[Facts:] The court determined that two board members first became personally biased against the superintendent due to her participation in an investigation of the two members "abusive" use of the school's WATS telephone line, and that one of the two was further upset when she refused to go along with him when he desired to hire staff members in contradiction of a federal court order.

[Court Findings:] The *Valley* court also found that a third board member had made "'prehearing statements in public and to the media that promised a firing for [Superintendent] Betty Cox, [that] when coupled with open hostility to compliance with the court order concerning hiring recommendations that had been obeyed by Mrs. Cox, presented more than adequate proof of partiality.'" The court noted that "[s]pecifically, . . . a reporter for KRRV Radio, testified . . . that [the member] stated to her on November 17, 1995 that the November 29, 1995 school board hearing was "D-Day" for Cox and that 'she would be fired,'" and that "Cox testified about how on occasion [the member] would call 'irate' and 'screaming' wanting to know why Cox recommended a person for a position over a person he recommended for the position, even though he was aware of the court's order prohibiting such acts."

As to the fourth board member, the court found the existence of personal animosity against the superintendent after "Cox uncovered [the member's] practice of self dealing prior to his election to the School Board. . . [wherein he] bought equipment from a company he owned to service a nonprofit organization which he was on its board of directors and which provided services for the Rapides Parish school system . . . [that resulted in a] federal investigation. . .--initiated by Cox--. . .[causing his] forced resignation from his position as a member of the board of directors of the nonprofit organization. . . ."

III. TEACHER CONTRACT TERMINATION UNDER STATE STATUTE

Most state legislatures have established a system for the contractual employment of teachers and the termination of their contracts based on specific causes and procedures delineated in statute. Generally, the initial employment of teachers is year to year for a period of time during which the school employer has greater latitude with regard to the procedure and grounds for termination if the teacher's performance is deemed unsatisfactory at the conclusion of the contact year. Usually, after a teacher has completed a state-prescribed number of years of successful performance, the teacher becomes "tenured," which means the right to a continuing contract from year to year unless the school employer terminates the contract for the prescribed cause(s) by using the required procedure, including a hearing.

A. Non-Tenured Teachers

During the period of employment when teachers serve in a non-tenured capacity, they are contracted a year at a time with no right to automatically continue employment for another year. With no right of continuation, there is no "legitimate claim of entitlement" (*Roth* and *Sindermann* cases) to another contract and, hence, no property right under the Fourteenth Amendment that would require the school to offer constitutional due process before the expiration date of the contract. However, during the term of the contract, the teacher has a legitimate claim of entitlement to be employed for one school-year, and, as a result, constitutional due process, via notice and a hearing, would have to be offered if the termination is to be effective before the end of the contracted school-year.

Some states require some form of procedure less than constitutional due process when schools non-renew the contract of non-tenured teachers at year's end, which may include having to provide reasons and a "conference" wherein the principal and the teacher provide information to the school board supporting the respective position of each regarding the contract non-renewal.

B. Tenured Teachers

"Tenure" systems differ from state to state, but once the teacher qualifies, the teacher not only has a "legitimate claim of entitlement" to continued employment under the Fourteenth Amendment Due Process Clause, but also under the applicable state's tenure statute. A state's tenure law will set forth both the legal grounds for terminating a teacher's tenure status and the requisite procedures that conclude with a hearing and a determination by a designated hearing officer (such as an administrative law judge or referee) or body (such as a school board). When the determination is to terminate a teacher's tenure, state law, either by statute or constitution, will establish the teacher's method of appeal. States may provide for an administrative review prior to engaging the judicial system, while others permit direct access to a local court. When considering a teacher's appeal of tenure termination, courts apply a process referred to as "judicial review," wherein the sufficiency of the process and evidence will be judged along with the fairness of the proceeding and the conclusion reached.

The first case under the next section involving teacher immorality, *Fiscus v. Board of School Trustees*, is representative of how an appellate court applies judicial review standards.

C. Causes for Termination of Tenure

Each state's statutory tenure system states the causes or grounds for which a school district may terminate a teacher's tenure. Three of these will be discussed below, but others include neglect of duty, other good and just cause, and decrease in the number of teaching positions.

C1. Immorality

Most state tenure statutes do not define the term "immorality," and, therefore, it is left up to the judiciary of each state to determine its meaning. In addition to requiring the school board (or other officer) to find the existence of immorality, courts also require a determination that there was a factual nexus between the immoral conduct and the teacher's ability or fitness to perform his or her duties.

CASE

Fiscus v. Board of School Trustees of Central School
Dist. of Greene County, 509 N.E.2d 1137 (Ind.App. 1987)
(emphasis added)

Appellant, Alayne Fiscus (Fiscus), was a permanent teacher formerly employed by the Central School District of Greene County (School District). Fiscus appeals the judgment of the Monroe Superior Court, which upheld the Board of School Trustees of the Central School District of Greene County (School Board) in its decision to cancel her contract on the basis of immorality. We affirm.

[Facts:] Fiscus had been employed by the School District as a permanent teacher under an indefinite contract, and she taught art, physical education, and library skills in the elementary school. As far as the transcript shows, she had an unblemished record in her 12 years of experience. **Fiscus was accused of immorality because of the single utterance of an obscenity during a 5th-grade art class**, whereupon she was suspended pending a hearing.

At the hearing, held before the School Board with School District Superintendent Knoll acting as the prosecutor, the following evidence was presented. Out of a class of 24 children, six, aged either 10 or 11 years, testified they had heard the obscene remark. At the hearing, all six were asked the same leading question: "Did you hear Mrs. Fiscus say, 'Fuck you'?"

M.B., the center of this controversy, in answer to the question responded, "Uh-huh." . . . M.B. stated that he had asked Fiscus what grade he had received on an Easter cross art project. Fiscus responded with the obscene phrase, followed by "C-.". . . . M.B. had never heard Fiscus use profane or obscene language before. M.B. admitted he did not like Fiscus because she erroneously blamed him for "stuff", and often assigned him extra work as punishment. . . . M.B. had specifically looked at the clock when Fiscus uttered the remark because he anticipated that it would be relevant in an investigation. M.B.'s mother testified that Fiscus previously had given M.B. a "D" in physical education. When she learned of Fiscus's remark, she complained to the principal, Sandra Headley, and demanded that something be done. M.B.'s mother also stated that the incident had had a terrible effect on her son: when he sees Fiscus or a vehicle resembling her truck, he panics; he had suffered from diarrhea; and he had lost weight. M.B.'s mother did admit that her son talks too much, characterizing him as a "blabbermouth," and she related that he had once accused Fiscus of falling asleep during a physical education class.

. . . Like M.B., S.B. responded affirmatively to the leading question. However, he stated that the remark was not made in answer to a question, nor was it directed to anyone in particular; Fiscus just stood in the middle of the class and blurted

S.B. also did not care for Fiscus because she "always got on us for doing nothing."

. . . Another student, A.C., heard the obscene word, but said that Fiscus said nothing either before or after it. He testified that during the remainder of the class the students whispered among themselves concerning the incident. A.C. also related that earlier in the school year he had been in the company of two classmates, C.B. and J.B., while they wrote the identical phrase with their fingers in the dust on Fiscus's truck. A.C. denied participating in this activity.

In her testimony, Headley stated that C.B. and J.B. had been paddled for this and had been compelled to write Fiscus a note of apology. It is apparent that the entire class was aware of the truck-writing episode. E.G. also answered affirmatively to the leading question, but stated he did not hear M.B. ask Fiscus a question. D.R. testified he heard the entire conversation. A.D., who also corroborated M.B., was also a witness to the truck-writing episode, but he too denied participating. . . .

Headley testified she had known Fiscus for seven years and had never heard her use obscene language, either publicly or privately. Other long-time acquaintances of Fiscus testified in a similar vein. In her testimony Fiscus vehemently denied the charges, and added that immediately prior to the alleged conversation she had threatened to send M.B. either out into the hall or to Headley's office if he did not get quiet and get into his seat.

On May 23, 1984, the School Board, having found that Fiscus uttered the remark, canceled her indefinite contract on the basis of immorality. In its Findings of Fact and Conclusions of Law the School Board determined that:

"4. This profanity in the classroom is a detriment to the school and is an inappropriate model to the students.

5. The teacher's effectiveness in teaching is damaged by her use of the profanity.

6. Conduct of the teacher in use of profanity under these circumstances violates the standard of conduct expected of a teacher in the elementary school and considering the age, the in-class use of language in direct response to a student inquiry, profanity served no educational purpose and damaged the students and the teacher's effectiveness." . . .

[Trial Court Ruling:] The trial court entered its judgment on July 21, 1986. It found that the pertinent statutory procedures had been followed by the School District, that sufficient evidence existed to show that Fiscus had uttered the remark, that the School Board had not abused its discretion in limiting Fiscus to three character witnesses, and that, since Fiscus never asked the School District for assistance in compelling the attendance of students at the hearing, there was no violation of due process. Although the trial court had "reservations concerning the utilized process and the end result," it concluded it was "compelled by legal principles to uphold the [School Board's] decision." . . . .

Issue I: *Factual Finding* [Judicial Review Component]

Fiscus claims the School Board's finding that she uttered the remark is not supported by substantial evidence.

A **trial court's review** of an administrative decision is **limited to a determination of whether the board's action was arbitrary, capricious, an abuse of discretion, not in accordance with the law, or unsupported by substantial evidence**. In determining whether an administrative decision is supported by substantial evidence, the trial court must examine the whole record to determine whether the board's decision lacks a reasonably sound basis of evidentiary support. . . . Like the trial court, **our duty is to review the administrative proceedings to see that the board's decision is supported by substantial evidence, that it is not arbitrary and capricious, and that the board has complied with all relevant rules of law and procedure**. . . . **Judicial review of an administrative body's determination does not include a review of the weight and effect of the evidence** upon which the administrative decision is based. . . .

We have recited with specificity the evidence that was presented at the school board hearing. The School Board chose to believe that a mature grade-school teacher with 12 years of experience and an unblemished record would stand in the middle of her 5th-grade art class and mindlessly utter a barracks-room obscenity in response to a student's question concerning his grade. The possible motives of the students to prevaricate, such as discontent with grades, scoldings, the writing of the obscenity on Fiscus's truck, and the resulting punishment of their friends, did not dissuade the School Board.

While we, like the trial court, have grave misgivings regarding the justice of this matter, we acknowledge that we were not present at the proceedings. Again, **under our standard of review we may not weigh the evidence nor adjudge the credibility of the witnesses**, even if we might have drawn a different conclusion. . . The issue is simply whether the School Board believed the students or the teacher. It believed the students, and we hold the evidence is sufficient.

Issue II: *Immorality*

Fiscus contends the single utterance of the phrase cannot constitute immorality and justify the cancellation of her indefinite contract. . . .

Fiscus's contract was canceled solely on the basis of immorality. . . . The School Board defined immorality as conduct that "violates the exemplary standards to which teachers are held and/or when it offends the moral standards of the community and impedes the teacher's effectiveness in the school." . . . .

To date, no Indiana case has provided a definitional standard of what constitutes immorality by a teacher, but a definition provided by the Pennsylvania Supreme Court has been oft-cited.

In *Horosko v. Mount Pleasant Township School District* (1939), 335 Pa. 369, 372, 6 A.2d 866, 868, *cert. denied,* 308 U.S. 553. . . (1939), the court defined **immorality as "not essentially confined to a deviation from sex morality; it may be such a course of conduct as offends the morals of the community and is a bad example to the youth whose ideals a teacher is supposed to foster and to elevate**." Obviously, disputes arising under such a general concept, which is subject to varying interpretations based on shifting social attitudes, must be resolved on the facts and circumstances of each case. . . .

Although we have found no Indiana cases upholding the cancellation of a teacher's contract because of the in-school use of offensive language, courts of other jurisdictions have done so: *see Palo Verde Unified School District of Riverside County v. Hensey* (1970), 9 Cal.App.3d 967, 88 Cal. Rptr. 570 (teacher's use of vulgar language and gestures); *Pyle v. Washington County School Board* (1970), Fla.App., 238 So.2d 121 (teacher made sexually suggestive remarks to students); *Celestine v. Lafayette Parish School Board* (1973), La.App., 284 So.2d 650 (teacher had two students write vulgar word 1,000 times as punishment for saying it); *Resetar v. State Board of Education* (1979), 284 Md. 537, 399 A.2d 225 (teacher's use of racial epithet); *Clarke, supra* (teacher's use of racial epithet); *Bovino v. Board of School Directors* (1977), 32 Pa.Commonwealth 105, 377 A.2d 1284 (teacher called female student a "slut" and a "prostitute"); *Pryse v. Yakima School District No. 7* (1981), 30 Wash.App. 16, 632 P.2d 60 (teacher made sexually suggestive remarks to students). *But see Mailloux v. Kiley* (D.C.Mass.1971), 323 F.Supp. 1387; *Central York School District v. Ehrhart* (1978), 36 Pa.Commonwealth 278, 387 A.2d 1006 (no teacher immorality found where use of vulgar language was for educational purposes).

Given the above holdings, and the facts that the phrase was uttered during class but not for educational purposes, we do not believe the School Board abused its discretion in concluding that Fiscus's conduct constituted immorality.

Issue III: *Severity of Penalty*

Fiscus argues that, even if she concedes that she uttered the remark and it constitutes immorality, the penalty, cancellation of her indefinite contract, is so severe as to be an abuse of discretion.

In *New Albany v. Whiteman* (1968), the supreme court held that a court, absent a finding supported by evidence of an arbitrary and capricious ruling by an administrative board, may not modify or otherwise change the punishment meted out by the administrative board. To do so would be to substitute the court's judgment for that of the administrative body. Having held that the School Board's ruling was neither arbitrary nor capricious, we can not now invade its discretion regarding the penalty.

For the above reasons, the judgment of the trial court is in all things affirmed.

The following is an example of a case which considers a standard of immorality for public school employees.

CASE

Bertolini v. Whitehall City School District Bd. of Ed.,
744 N.E.2d 1245(Ohio App.3d 2000) (emphasis added)

Joseph L. Bertolini, appellant, appeals a judgment of the Franklin County Court of Common Pleas, Civil Division. The trial court affirmed a decision of the Whitehall City School District Board of Education, appellee, terminating appellant as associate superintendent for Whitehall City Schools. We reverse and remand.

[Facts:] In May 1997, appellant was hired by the Whitehall City School District Board of Education ("board") to be the associate superintendent for Whitehall City Schools ("Whitehall"). Appellant previously held the position of superintendent of the Leetonia School District ("Leetonia"). While working at Leetonia, appellant became acquainted with Patti Woods, who was also employed by Leetonia. Even though appellant and Woods were married to other individuals, from July 1997 to November 1997, the two began a sexual relationship. After the board hired appellant, Woods applied for the position of secretary to appellant. She was interviewed by several individuals but was not interviewed by appellant. The individuals responsible for hiring determined that Woods was overqualified to be a secretary, so she was offered the position of EMIS coordinator with Whitehall. As EMIS coordinator, Woods' supervisor was Donald Moore. Moore's supervisor was appellant. Woods moved to Columbus, but her husband remained in Columbiana County. Woods and her husband later divorced. . . .

Appellant's performance as an associate superintendent was later evaluated by Dr. Crawford. The results of Dr. Crawford's evaluation were expressed in a letter to appellant dated January 5, 1998, which stated: "Let me begin by stating how pleased I am to have you as a member of our administrative team. You certainly join our district with much expertise in the area of school administration. Some of your administrative skills that have impressed me the most at this point are:

"- Your knowledge of how to handle potential, volatile situations, particularly in processing complaints from parents and/or staff members. You have always addressed these situations in a very professional, very appropriate, and very fair manner. In the future, I hope you will continue to handle all situations as successfully as you have up to this point. . . .

"I would hope that you accept this evaluation as nothing less than a report of outstanding performance as associate superintendent of the Whitehall City Schools. Thank you for all your hard work and efforts." . . . .

Even though their romantic relationship ended in November 1997, appellant continued to stay in contact with Woods by sending her e-mail messages through Whitehall's computer system. . . . Woods added that she found the e-mails ``[o]ffensive, agitating'' because she was ``trying to get as far away from any type of personal relationship.'' . . . When asked at the hearing before the referee whether appellant's e-mails were causing her ``problems at work," Woods answered ``[n]o."

On February 21, 1998, Woods met with Dr. Crawford and told him about her relationship with appellant. Woods provided copies of e-mail messages from appellant and played phone messages from her home answering machine left by appellant. A letter dated February 21, 1998, from Dr. Crawford to appellant stated:

"Sexual harassment complaints have been issued against you by EMIS secretary, Patti Woods. You are hereby notified that you are suspended with pay, pending the investigation of these complaints. . . "

In June 1998, a referee held hearings in which evidence was presented by the parties concerning whether appellant's termination was proper. The referee, in a fourteen-page opinion that included forty-six findings of fact and six conclusions of law, recommended that appellant ``be paid his full salary for the full period of suspension * * * [and] that the charges and the record of the hearing be physically expunged from the minutes of the board." On October 14, 1998, the board rejected the referee's recommendations and voted to terminate appellant's contract ``for the grounds of gross inefficiency, immorality, willful and persistent violation of reasonable regulations of the Board and for other good and just cause, as of February 21, 1998." The board accepted most of the referee's findings of fact but rejected or modified some of the referee's key factual determinations.

On November 6, 1998, appellant filed a complaint with the Franklin County Court of Common Pleas . . .

[Trial Court Ruling/Rationale:] On November 4, 1999, the trial court held that the ``totality of the circumstances in this case and the aggregate of Appellant's conduct constitute serious enough matters to justify the termination for immorality and other good and just cause." Appellant appeals this decision . . .

The trial court found that appellant's termination was proper because appellant's conduct was (1) immoral and (2) constituted willful and persistent violation of Whitehall's policies. We will discuss each of the bases the trial court relied upon in its opinion in the order they have been presented. . .

The trial court upheld the board's decision to terminate appellant's contract, in part, based upon the finding that appellant's actions constituted serious immorality and were supported by a preponderance of the evidence. . .

The court also held that since appellant and Woods were both married when the affair began, "[h]is actions were clearly immoral."

[Appellate Court's Rationale/Ruling:] **While an adulterous affair may be considered immoral, in ``order to constitute `immorality' * * * as it relates to the termination of a teacher's contract, the conduct complained of must be hostile to the school community and cannot be some private act which has no impact on the teacher's professional duties."** . . . Therefore, **an adulterous affair by a teacher without evidence to establish that it created hostility in the (school) community or that it had a serious impact on the teacher's professional duties is not a valid reason for termination.**[1]

A review of the record shows that many individuals testified concerning the effectiveness of appellant as an associate superintendent. As noted by the trial court, on January 5, 1998, Dr. Crawford wrote a ``glowing evaluation'' of appellant's performance as an associate superintendent. Dr. Crawford stated in his evaluation that ``I would hope that you accept this evaluation as nothing less than a report of outstanding performance as associate superintendent of the Whitehall City Schools.'' . . . Additionally, **a review of all of the evidence presented against appellant shows that insufficient evidence was presented to establish that appellant's relationship with Woods was hostile to the community or that it had a serious impact on either of their professional duties.** . . .

A review of the referee's findings of fact shows that no facts were cited by the referee to support a finding that appellant's actions had a negative impact on the school community. Even if evidence was shown that appellant's colleagues had a ``negative perception'' of him because of the ``rumors of an affair,'' this is not sufficient evidence to justify his termination. . . .

Accordingly, after a complete review of the record, which includes the exhibits introduced at appellant's hearing, the transcripts of that hearing, the findings of fact and conclusions of law of the referee, and the board's resolution to terminate appellant's contract, we find that the trial court abused its discretion in holding that ``[a]ppellant's conduct constituted serious enough matters to justify the termination for immorality and other good and just cause.'' **We agree with the referee's detailed analysis of the evidence and conclusions that the board ``failed to prove by a preponderance of the evidence that [appellant] was guilty of immorality''** . . .

We note that the present case should also be viewed against other cases involving teachers and supervisors who appeal their contract terminations pursuant to R.C. 3319.16. A review of cases in which the appellate court affirmed a school board's decision to terminate a school employee shows that the teacher's behavior had or could have had a serious effect on the school system. For example, many of the cases involved inappropriate sexual relations between faculty and students.[2] Other cases involved instances in which a teacher had been convicted of a serious criminal offense.[3] . . . In the present case, appellant's actions did not involve any students. Appellant was not convicted of a criminal offense, and his actions were not harmful to any students. . . . Judgment reversed and cause remanded.

Footnotes:

1. We also note that the court in *Florian* stated that in order to constitute immorality, the conduct could not be a private act with no impact on the teacher's professional duties. This would seem to indicate that showing that a private act has had some impact on a teacher's professional duties would be sufficient to justify a termination. However, when considering the procedural protections afforded by R.C. 3319.16, **we believe that the evidence must instead show that the private act had a serious impact on the teacher's professional duties**. For example, evidence that a teacher is guilty of a simple traffic violation while not within the scope of his or her employment should not be sufficient evidence of an ``immoral'' private act to justify a termination of the teacher's contract. However, a teacher who engaged in a high speed chase down a major city street in an attempt to avoid apprehension from police while detaining a fifteen-year-old in his automobile against his will can constitute immorality and other good and just cause for the teacher's contract to be terminated. . . .

2. In *Strohm*, the teacher had sexual activity with female students enrolled in the school district and provided alcohol to minor females enrolled in the school district. . . .

3. In *Sayers* . . . . unreported 1994 WL 676869 the teacher was a physical education teacher who was fired after a criminal conviction for a sex offense. In *Stelzer* . . . . a teacher was fired after being convicted of a felony relating to the continued receipt of stolen property over a five-year period. . . .

C2. *Insubordination*

The elements of insubordination as most commonly defined in state teacher tenure statutes include a willful or intentional act that is done in defiance of state school laws or of local school regulations or administrative directives. Absent a showing of proof that the teacher more likely than not had knowledge of the prohibited conduct, but deliberately did it anyway, a school would not succeed in dismissal for insubordination. (However, neglect of duty or incompetence may be shown.)

A teacher who willfully participates in a work stoppage, "slow down," calling in sick in concert with other teachers, or any other action that would be deemed a strike under state law prohibiting strikes could be proven insubordinate. Similarly, knowing defiance of a school board policy or administrative directive prohibiting the showing of films that are "R" or "PG" rated would constitute insubordination. However, a principal's statement to a teacher that "it is advisable" not to show a "PG" film would most likely not qualify as a directive.

When interpreting whether insubordination has occurred, courts will not only look for evidence that the teacher knew and, therefore, willfully violated a regulation or directive, but will also require a showing that the rule was both (1) clear and (2) reasonable. In the case of *Werblo v. Bd. of Sch. Trustees of Hamiltion Heights Sch. Corp.*, 519 N.E.2d 185 (Ind.App. 1988), the court ruled against the school that had terminated a tenured teacher for insubordination. The facts indicated that the principal gave the teacher an oral directive that she accompany all her students to a school convocation containing religious content after she requested an exemption for herself and those students who desired to review a videotape of "Romeo and Juliet" in preparation for an examination. When the principal later the same day made a public address announcement that "excused from attendance all persons who objected to the convocation for religious or other reasons," the teacher and sixteen students followed the principal's requirement that those not attending the convocation report to the office and then went to the library to review the tape. In reversing the teacher's dismissal, the Werblo court found that the general announcement allowing "all persons" to decide against going to the convocation "muddied the scope" of the principal's prior direct order to the teacher to attend, created an ambiguity, and, thus, there was no clear directive. The court also found that the directive to attend was unreasonable because the "school's endorsement and promotion of the convocation appears to violate the establishment clause of the First Amendment."

C3. *Incompetency*

Due to the variety of teacher conduct that could come within the meaning of incompetency as a cause for dismissing a tenured teacher, state legislatures rarely attempt to define it in statute, but, rather, like the ground of immorality, leave it to the courts. In the case of *Harrison-Washington Community Sch. Corp. v. Bales*, 450 N.E.2d 559 (Ind.App. 1983), a dismissed tenured teacher failed in his attempt to argue that incompetency meant that the school had to prove "the onset of mental disease or serious physical impairment which prohibits continued performance by the teacher." The court relied on a 1909 Indiana case that ruled that to be considered incompetent, a teacher must merely be shown to have been "wanting in practical efficiency and discipline."

In the following case regarding the dismissal of a teacher who deliberately failed to answer questions posed by his superintendent that related to his fitness to teach, it will be seen that the Pennsylvania courts have given an expansive definition of incompetency, including what would constitute insubordination in most, if not all, states.

CASE
Beilan v. Board of Public Education, Sch. Dist. of Philadelphia, 357 U.S. 399
(1958) (emphasis added)

[Legal Question:] The question before us is whether the Board of Public Education . . . violated the Due Process Clause of the Fourteenth Amendment to the Constitution of the United States when the Board, purporting to act under the Pennsylvania Public School Code, discharged a public school teacher on the ground of "incompetency," evidenced by the teacher's refusal of his Superintendent's request to confirm or refute information as to the teacher's loyalty and his activities in certain allegedly subversive organizations. For the reasons hereafter stated, we hold that it did not.

[Facts:] On June 25, 1952, Herman A. Beilan, the petitioner, who had been a teacher for about 22 years in the Philadelphia Public School System, presented himself at his Superintendent's office in response to the latter's request. The Superintendent said he had information which reflected adversely on petitioner's loyalty and he wanted to determine its truth or falsity. In response to petitioner's suggestion that the Superintendent do the questioning, the latter said he would ask one question and petitioner could then determine whether he would answer it and others of that type. The Superintendent, accordingly, asked petitioner whether or not he had been the Press Director of the Professional Section of the Communist Political Association in 1944. Petitioner asked permission to consult counsel before answering and the Superintendent granted his request.

On October 14, 1952, in response to a similar request, petitioner again presented himself at the Superintendent's office. Petitioner stated that he had consulted counsel and that he declined to answer the question as to his activities in 1944. He announced he would also decline to answer any other "questions similar to it," "questions of this type," or "questions about political and religious beliefs . . . ." The Superintendent warned petitioner that this "was a very serious and a very important matter and that failure to answer the questions might lead to his dismissal." **The Superintendent made it clear that he was investigating "a real question of fitness for [petitioner] to be a teacher or to continue in the teaching work."** . . .

The only question before us is whether the Federal Constitution prohibits petitioner's discharge for statutory "incompetency" based on his refusal to answer the Superintendent's questions.

[Rationale:] By engaging in teaching in the public schools, petitioner did not give up his right to freedom of belief, speech or association. He did, however, **undertake obligations of frankness, candor and cooperation in answering inquiries made of him by his employing Board examining into his fitness to serve it as a public school teacher.**

"A teacher works in a sensitive area in a schoolroom. There he shapes the attitude of young minds towards the society in which they live. In this, the state has a vital concern. It must preserve the integrity of the schools. **That the school authorities have the right and the duty to screen the officials, teachers, and employees as to their fitness to maintain the integrity of the schools as a part of ordered society, cannot be doubted.**" *Adler v. Board of Education*, 342 U.S. 485, 493.

As this Court stated in *Garner v. Board of Public Works*, . . . "We think that a municipal employer is not disabled because it is an agency of the State from inquiring of its employees as to matters that may prove relevant to their fitness and suitability for the public service."

The question asked of petitioner by his Superintendent was relevant to the issue of petitioner's fitness and suitability to serve as a teacher. Petitioner is not in a position to challenge his dismissal merely because of the remoteness in time of the 1944 activities. It was apparent from the circumstances of the two interviews that the Superintendent had other questions to ask. Petitioner's refusal to answer was not based on the remoteness of his 1944 activities. He made it clear that he would not answer any question of the same type as the one asked. Petitioner blocked from the beginning any inquiry into his Communist activities, however relevant to his present loyalty. **The Board based its dismissal upon petitioner's refusal to answer any inquiry about his relevant activities - not upon those activities themselves**. It took care to charge petitioner with incompetency, and not with disloyalty. **It found him insubordinate and lacking in frankness and candor** - it made no finding as to his loyalty.

We find no requirement in the Federal Constitution that a teacher's classroom conduct be the sole basis for determining his fitness. Fitness for teaching depends on a broad range of factors. The Pennsylvania tenure provision specifies several disqualifying grounds, including immorality, intemperance, cruelty, mental derangement and persistent and willful violation of the school laws, as well as "incompetency." However, the Pennsylvania statute, unlike those of many other States, contains no catch-all phrase, such as "conduct unbecoming a teacher," to cover disqualifying conduct not included within the more specific provisions. Consequently, the Pennsylvania courts have given "incompetency" a broad interpretation. This was made clear in *Horosko v. Mt. Pleasant School District,* 335 Pa. 369, 371, 374-375, 6 A. 2d 866, 868, 869-870:

"If the fact be that she 'now commands neither the respect nor the good will of the community' and if the record shows that effect to be the result of her conduct within the clause quoted, it will be conclusive evidence of incompetency. **It has always been the recognized duty of the teacher to conduct himself in such way as to command the respect and good will of the community**, though one result of the choice of a teacher's vocation may be to deprive him of the same freedom of action enjoyed by persons in other vocations. **Educators have always regarded the example set by the teacher as of great importance**. . . .

"The term 'incompetency' has a 'common and approved usage'. The context does not limit the meaning of the word to lack of substantive knowledge of the subjects to be taught. Common and approved usage give a much wider meaning. For example, in 31 C. J., with reference to a number of supporting decisions, it is defined: 'A relative term without technical meaning. It may be employed as meaning disqualification; inability; incapacity; lack of ability, legal qualifications, or fitness to discharge the required duty.' . . .

In the *Horosko* case, a teacher was discharged for "incompetency" because of her after-hours activity in her husband's beer garden, serving as a bartender and waitress, occasionally drinking beer, shaking dice with the customers for drinks and playing the pinball machine. . . .

[Supreme Court Ruling:] In the instant case, the Pennsylvania Supreme Court has held that "incompetency" includes petitioner's "deliberate and insubordinate refusal to answer the questions of his administrative superior in a vitally important matter pertaining to his fitness." . . . This interpretation is not inconsistent with the Federal Constitution.

Petitioner **complains that he was denied due process because he was not sufficiently warned** of the consequences of his refusal to answer his Superintendent. The record, however, shows that the Superintendent, in his second interview, **specifically warned petitioner that his refusal to answer "was a very serious and a very important matter and that failure to answer the questions might lead to his dismissal." That was sufficient warning to petitioner that his refusal to answer might jeopardize his employment**. Furthermore, at petitioner's request, his Superintendent gave him ample opportunity to consult counsel. There was no element of surprise. . . .

Inasmuch as petitioner's dismissal did not violate the Federal Constitution, the judgment of the Supreme Court of Pennsylvania is Affirmed.

SCENARIOS
STATE AND APPLY THE RELEVANT LEGAL RULE(S) TO THE FACTS.

1. Aide graduated from college, received his State teacher's license, was unsuccessful at finding an elementary teaching job due to a lack of openings at the time, but accepted an instructional aide position. Consider each of the following situations separately:

a. School Board passed a motion "to employ Aide as an instructional aide; salary to be paid every two weeks based on an annual rate of $13,000." Without a written contract and based only Board's motion, Aide began work, but was so overly enthusiastic that he took on the role of teacher, interfered with proper instruction, upset the teacher and students, and after ten weeks School Board voted to dismiss him immediately. Aide was unable to find other employment and sued in federal court to recover his salary for the remainder of the school year.

b. Board's motion to employ Aide read as in (1) above. Aide was highly successful in his position, and since there were no teacher openings, he was rehired at progressively higher annual rates for an additional five successive years. The employee handbook stated that "each non-teacher employee, while not having tenure, is a highly valued member of School's educational family who should consider him/herself similar to tenured teachers as long as his/her work is satisfactory." At the end of Aide's sixth successful year, dark financial clouds form over School and Board suddenly, and without Aide's prior knowledge, voted not to re-employ him (as well as other aides) based on the Superintendent's statement that there were not sufficient funds for these positions to meet the increases in teacher pay due to the bargaining agreement.

Aide sued in federal court for reinstatement and back pay after he was unable to find other education-related employment in the area.

c. Board's motion to employ Aide read as in (1) above. Although very popular with the children and parents, Aide was mediocre at best in the performance of his job and very disorganized. In the spring of his first year, he was put in charge of collecting fund-raising revenues from the sale of 2,000 candy bars at $1.00 each. Due to his sloppiness, he was unable to account for some $500 in cash that was turned in to him by the students. (All 2,000 bars were sold.) Using this as a way to get around his enormous popularity, Board voted to dismiss him at the end of the year without any prior notice and without any explanation to him or the public as to the reason.

Aide and the parents were incensed and signed up to speak at the next board meeting. After several parents had spoken very positively about Aide (and most unkindly about the mentality of the Board for dismissing him), Board President, feeling the pressure from the crowd, nervously blurted out that "If the parents knew that Aide had stolen $500 from the fundraiser they would be more understanding of the Board." Aide was next to speak, denied the accusation that he has stolen the money, and demanded that he be given a hearing where School would have to prove he stole it. Board President briefly consulted with School Attorney, announced that the matter was closed, and adjourned the meeting.

Aide sued in federal district court.

2.   Teacher taught in a small town of 2000 citizens where he had earned tenure. He lived in a house on Main Street and Second Street, a block from the town square, and was divorced. Sue, a 25-year-old friend of Teacher's married daughter moved into his house at the start of the school year, supposedly because there was no other housing available for her. Teacher and Sue were seen when he took her to and picked her up from work every day, twice a week having dinner and drinks at the local tavern, sitting close to one another on his porch swing in the evenings drinking wine, attending home football games, and twice leaving together from his house Friday after work and returning Sunday night.

Their actions created considerable community, parent, school staff, and student comments about their relationship, including "being in love" and "living in sin;" so much in fact, that School Board in October, following proper statutory due process, including a hearing, cancelled his teaching contract, effective immediately, for immorality.

School's evidence was presented via eye witnesses, including parents, to the above-stated actions as well as the testimony of Neighbor, who lived next door to Teacher. Neighbor testified that on three different occasions when she took her dog out for his evening walk around 10 o'clock, she had observed, from her property about 15 feet from Teacher's house, candlelight flickering through the shear curtains of his bedroom, two shadows moving around the room, and Teacher's and Sue's voices and laughter. Teacher testified that he had known Sue for 20 years, treated her as his daughter, rented space to her in his house, visited his daughter with Sue in Chicago on the two weekends in question, and had never had sexual relations with her.

School Board determined that Teacher's conduct constituted "immorality" under State's Teacher Contract Termination Law, which did not define the term. Teacher sued in the county court to reverse the School Board's dismissal action.

3.   Principal authorized Teacher to use the school's 15 passenger van to drive his class of 14 second graders to the zoo on a field trip during the school day. Principal orally directed Teacher that due to the disturbance caused by his returning 15 minutes late from last year's trip, wherein the student's missed their buses and parents became very upset, he had to leave the zoo "in plenty of time" to be sure to get back before the buses left the school at 2:30. The normal driving time from zoo to school is 30 minutes. Teacher said that he understood. At the zoo, he got enchanted with the polar bears, forgot the time, and did not leave until 2:05. He informed Principal by cell phone that he had left late, should get there by 2:35, and asked her to hold the buses. Principal directed him to "drive as fast as necessary" to get there by 2:30 because she was not going to delay the buses. He refused

to go over the speed limit, arrived at 2:35 after the buses had departed, and, as a result, the same negative response from parents as last year occurred. Principal recommended, and the School Board acted (following proper statutory due process, including a hearing) to cancel his tenured teacher's contract based on insubordination for willfully refusing to obey the two directives. Teacher admitted at the dismissal hearing he had driven 80 miles per hour on the interstate where the speed limit was 70, he could have made it on time.

Principal filed suit in county court to reverse his dismissal.

CHAPTER
5

EMPLOYMENT
DISCRIMINATION

———————————————

In making employment decisions, public schools are bound not only by the Equal Protection Clause of the Fourteenth Amendment, but also by a host of federal, state, and local legislation prohibiting discrimination based on race, national origin, alienage, gender, disability, religion, and age. This chapter will address the legal standards that courts have adopted and applied in judging whether a claimed act of discrimination against an employer is valid.

I. FOURTEENTH AMENDMENT EQUAL PROTECTION

The Fourteenth Amendment to the federal Constitution requires that no state shall "deny to any person within its jurisdiction, the equal protection of the laws." The courts have been called upon to interpret and apply the Equal Protection Clause to numerous classifications that states and their subdivisions have created, intentionally or unintentionally, including race, alienage, and gender.

A. *Facially Evident Discrimination*

The following summary is the legal standard adopted by the Supreme Court in equal protection cases that applies where the government's discrimination against a class of persons is *evident on its face*:

First, it is necessary to determine the category of judicial scrutiny that will be applied to the plaintiff's class:

(1) High (strict) scrutiny -- *suspect class or fundamental right discrimination*;
(2) Medium scrutiny -- *gender or children of illegal aliens discrimination*; or
(3) Low scrutiny -- *all other forms of discrimination.*

Second, the government must prove the following with respect to each scrutiny category:

(1) High -- *compelling interest*;
(2) Medium -- *substantial relationship to an important objective/goal*; or
(3) Low -- *rational relationship to a legitimate objective/goal.*

Suspect classes have been determined to be race, alienage, and national origin/ancestry. Fundamental right classifications involve infringement upon the exercise of rights guaranteed in the Constitution, such as speech and religion.

If, for example, a public school would refuse to employ persons who are members of a certain national group or who originate from a particular ancestry, it would constitute suspect class discrimination for which the school would have to prove that it had a *compelling reason* for denying employment. Similarly, if persons of a particular faith or religion were not hired due to such faith, a compelling governmental interest would have to be proven in order to outweigh the persons' fundamental right to practice religion as they chose. Government employers would likely not be able to justify discrimination falling within the high or strict scrutiny category.

In a situation where a public school refused to grant a paternity leave to a male teacher while having granted numerous maternity leaves to females in order for them to care for their infants, the discrimination would be based upon gender, which comes within the medium scrutiny category where the employer would have to prove that its denial of the same benefit to males bears a *substantial relationship to an important goal or interest.*

All forms of facially evident discrimination that are not part of the high or medium scrutiny classifications are part of the low judicial scrutiny category where the courts only require the government employer prove that it has a *rational basis* for its discriminatory actions. For example, if a school would require that its teachers earn so many credit hours of graduate work every three years or face dismissal or a salary freeze, it would only need to show that such requirements bear a *rational relationship to a legitimate goal*.

B. Non-Facially Evident Discrimination

In those situations where the government's discriminatory action or practice is not evident on its face, and, in fact, appears neutral, but has a substantially negative or burdensome impact on a particular protected group, such as passing an examination, courts apply a legal standard requiring that a plaintiff suing under the Equal Protection Clause prove that the government *intentionally* intended to discriminate based on the group's status. This is a difficult burden in most instances, especially in the case of the use of an examination that is shown by the government to be a reliable and valid predictor of job performance. It would virtually mean proof that those who conceived of the examination did so for the express purpose of denying employment or promotion to persons of a specific national, ancestral, or racial group.

II. TITLE VII

Title VII of the Civil Rights Act of 1964, 20 U.S.C. sec. 2000e *et seq.*, prohibits discrimination by public and private employers who employ at least fifteen persons. Prohibited under Title VII is discrimination due to race, color, national origin, religion, and gender in all aspects of employment from hiring through firing, including retaliation for having filed a Title VII complaint with the Equal Employment Opportunity Commission (EEOC) or in federal or state court. The statute does allow an exception if the employer can demonstrate a bona fide occupational qualification (BFOQ) for having discriminated, but it only apples to the areas of national origin, religion, and gender, and the employer must show the business need for the BFOQ. A school would likely be able to prove a BFOQ in a situation where it seeks to employ guidance counselors of both genders so that students are better able to discuss personal issues with a counselor of the same gender. : A Montana school prevailed in this argument in the case of *Stone v. Belgrade Sch. Dist. No. 44*, 703 P.2d 136 (Mont. 1985).

Courts have established two analytical approaches in addressing Title VII claims - - disparate treatment and disparate impact. When an employee or applicant for employment asserts discrimination based on being treated in an unlike manner as those of a different race, color, etc., the disparate treatment legal standard will be applied. The disparate impact standard will be applied in those situations where the plaintiff complains that the employer used a neutral device, such as an examination or high school diploma requirement, which resulted in members of the plaintiff's protected group being denied employment, promotion, etc., in a disproportionate percentage to those who were employed or promoted.

A. Disparate Treatment

The Supreme Court in *McDonnel Douglas Corp. v. Green*, 411 U.S. 16 (1973) first developed the disparate treatment legal standard, which is composed of three parts.

First, an applicant for a position is required to prove a *"prima facie"* case of discrimination by showing that the person desiring a job belongs to one of the classes protected by Title VII, applied and was qualified for an existing opening, was denied, and the opening was not cancelled by the employer before being filled. Circuit courts have modified the *prima facie* standard in non-applicant situations such as dismissal, demotion, transfer, or reprimand. The Eighth Circuit, for example, stated that "the plaintiff must establish a factual presumption of intentional discrimination . . . that required evidence (either direct or circumstantial) that: (1) she was a member of a protected group, (2) she was meeting the legitimate expectations of her employer, (3) she suffered an adverse employment action, and (4) there are facts that permit an inference of discrimination." *Cherry v. Ritenour Sch. Dist.*, 361 F.3d 474, 478 (8th Cir. 2004).

Second, if the plaintiff meets the *prima facie* test requirement, the burden shifts to the employer to articulate a legitimate, non-discriminatory reason why the plaintiff was not chosen (or in the case of termination, why the job was lost).

Third, if the employer passes this relatively easy test, the ultimate burden of proof shifts back to the applicant or employee to demonstrate that the reason(s) given by the employer were pretextual, or a false cover for illegal discrimination.

CASE
Cherry v. Ritenour Sch. Dist., 361 F.3d 474 (8th Cir. 2004).

[**Facts:**] Cherry, an African American school counselor, whose contract was not renewed after her second year of employment, alleged racial discrimination. Her principal and assistant principal, both Caucasian, had identified problems with her work performance and in the fall of the second year began consulting with her and providing improvement plans, which continued into the spring semester. Concerns expressed included keeping her door closed, unwillingness to assist during after school hours, lack of organization, failure to utilize existing computer programs, and failure to be a team player in her work with the administration.

The counselor furnished evidence of being treated rudely by the principal when he twice interrupted a meeting between her and a parent and contended that she was more harshly criticized and treated differently due to her race. In support of her abilities she produced a letter from the school psychologist saying that she was dedicated and a hard worker.

[**Legal standard:**] In applying the *McDonnel Douglas* burden-shifting standard, the *Cherry* court examined if she had met the initial requirement of proving a *prima facie* case. Although the district court had found that she had failed to show the school's legitimate expectations, the Eighth Circuit assumed for purposes of the appeal that she had met this burden. It then determined that the school had articulated a legitimate non-discriminatory basis for her contract non-renewal (failure to improve in the areas for which she had been counseled).

[Issue:] The question for the court then came to whether Cherry met the ultimate burden of proving race discrimination by demonstrating that the school's articulated reason for her dismissal was a pretext for intentional discrimination. In setting out the legal parameters of the plaintiff's burden, the court stated at 479:

> ... [p]robably the most commonly employed method to demonstrate that an employer's explanation is pretextual is to show that similarly situated persons of a different race or sex received more favorable treatment. ... Specifically, the individuals used for comparison must have dealt with the same supervisor, have been subject to the same standards, and engaged in the same conduct without mitigating or distinguishing circumstances. ...

[Court ruling:] The court found that Cherry did not identify specific employees who were similarly situated to her who were more favorably treated. It noted that while she identified one Caucasian teacher and asserted there were others who kept their doors closed but did not receive improvement plans, she did not establish that these employees were otherwise comparable or similarly situated to her "in all relevant respects." *Id.* at 479. Lastly, the court stated that her "assertions that African American parents, students, and two former secretaries had declared that [the principal] discriminated against them or their children are not on point and are otherwise wholly insufficient." *Id.*

B. Disparate Impact

CASE
Griggs v. Duke Power Co., 401 U.S. 424 (1971) (emphasis added)

The objective of Congress in the enactment of Title VII is plain from the language of the statute. It was to achieve equality of employment opportunities and remove barriers that have operated in the past to favor an identifiable group of white employees over other employees. **Under the Act, practices, procedures, or tests neutral on their face, and even neutral in terms of intent, cannot be maintained if they operate to "freeze" the status quo of prior discriminatory employment practices**.

The Court of Appeals' opinion, and the partial dissent, agreed that, on the record in the present case, "whites register far better on the Company's alternative requirements" than Negroes. . . . This consequence would appear to be directly traceable to race. Basic intelligence must have the means of articulation to manifest itself fairly in a testing process. Because they are Negroes, petitioners have long received inferior education in segregated schools and this Court expressly recognized these differences . . . . Congress did not intend by Title VII, however, to guarantee a job to every person regardless of qualifications. In short, the Act does not command that any person be hired simply because he was formerly the subject of discrimination, or because he is a member of a minority group. Discriminatory preference for any group, minority or majority, is precisely and only what Congress has proscribed. **What is required by Congress is the removal of artificial, arbitrary, and unnecessary barriers to employment when the barriers operate invidiously to discriminate on the basis of racial or other impermissible classification.**

. . . The Act proscribes not only overt discrimination, but also practices that are fair in form, but discriminatory in operation. **The touchstone is business necessity**. If an employment practice which operates to exclude Negroes cannot be shown to be **related to job performance**, the practice is prohibited.

On the record before us, **neither the high school completion requirement nor the general intelligence test is shown to bear a demonstrable relationship to successful performance of the jobs for which it was used**. . . . The facts of this case demonstrate the inadequacy of broad and general testing devices as well as the infirmity of using diplomas or degrees as fixed measures of capability. History is filled with examples of men and women who rendered highly effective performance without the conventional badges of accomplishment in terms of certificates, diplomas, or degrees. Diplomas and tests are useful servants, but Congress has mandated the commonsense proposition that they are not to become masters of reality. . . .

Nothing in the Act precludes the use of testing or measuring procedures; obviously they are useful. **What Congress has forbidden is giving these devices and mechanisms controlling force unless they are demonstrably a reasonable measure of job performance**. Congress has not commanded that the less qualified be preferred over the better qualified simply because of minority origins. Far from disparaging job qualifications as such, Congress has made such qualifications the controlling factor, so that race, religion, nationality, and sex become irrelevant. What Congress has commanded is that any tests used must measure the person for the job and not the person in the abstract. . . .

C. Gender Discrimination

C1. Pregnancy

In reaction to a Supreme Court ruling, *General Electric Co. v. Gilbert*, 429 U.S. 125 (1976), Congress amended Title VII in 1978 with the Pregnancy Discrimination Act (PDA), 42 U.S.C. section 2000e(k), which states that "[t]he terms ''because of sex" or ''on the basis of sex" include, but are not limited to, because of or on the basis of pregnancy, childbirth, or related medical conditions. . . ." The amendment was passed in order to express its clear intent that pregnancy and matters related thereto were covered by Title VII. As a later Supreme Court decision stated, "When Congress amended Title VII in 1978, it unambiguously expressed its disapproval of both the holding and the reasoning of the Court in the *Gilbert* decision." *Newport News Shipbuilding & Dry Dock Co. v. EEOC*, 462 U.S. 669, 678 (1983).

As a result of the PDA amendment of Title VII, employers must treat pregnancy as a medical condition, and if males are permitted medical leaves, so must females who are pregnant. As to granting of maternity leaves to females for staying home with the newborn child after the period of medical disability ceases (or childrearing leaves), Title VII would only require such if fathers of newborns had been given paternity leaves.

In a case where a teacher collective bargaining agreement granted a childrearing leave following the period of medical disability for up to one year from the child's birth only to the mother, the Third Circuit in *Schafer v. Board of Public Educ. of Sch. Dist. of Pittsburgh*, 903 F.3d 243 (3rd Cir. 1990), ruled that the Title VII was violated when the school district refused to give the same leave to a male teacher.

C2. Sexual Harassment

Although the term "sexual harassment" is not mentioned in Title VII, the Equal Employment Opportunity Commission (EEOC) has adopted the following regulation that prohibits both "*quid pro quo*" and hostile environment sexual harassment:

Sec. 1604.**11** Sexual harassment.

(a) Harassment on the basis of sex is a violation of section 703 of title VII. Unwelcome sexual advances, requests for sexual favors, and other verbal or physical conduct of a sexual nature constitute sexual harassment when (1) submission to such conduct is made either explicitly or implicitly a term or condition of an individual's employment, (2) submission to or rejection of such conduct by an individual is used as the basis for employment decisions affecting such individual, or (3) such conduct has the purpose or effect of unreasonably interfering with an individual's work performance or creating an intimidating, hostile, or offensive working environment. . .

CASE
Molnar v. Booth, 229 F.3d 593 (7th Cir. 2000) (emphasis added.):

This appeal comes to us from a jury's verdict in favor of plaintiff Lisetta Molnar on her sexual harassment claims against the East Chicago Community School Corporation (East Chicago) and Lloyd Booth, the principal of the junior high school where she taught. She based these claims on both Title VII and 42 U.S.C. sec.1983. In addition to modest awards of $500 each on the two theories, the jury awarded $25,000 in punitive damages against Booth and the court added $65,760 in attorneys' fees against both defendants. . . .

[Facts:] Molnar began working at Westside Junior High School, which was part of East Chicago, on August 22, 1994. She had been engaged to teach art classes as an intern, and she hoped to become qualified to be a full-fledged teacher at the end of her internship there. Booth was the principal of Westside.

On her first day of work, Booth ogled her and made appreciative noises. He took her into his office, closed the door, and put on music. He then suggested that he and Molnar had much in common and asked for her telephone number. During the same conversation, he told her that he could secure various benefits for her like a permanent art room--a "perk" that she, like other junior teachers, did not have--and supplies. She perceived all of this as a sexual advance, which made her uncomfortable.

For a time, Booth's unwelcome behavior continued. Over the next three to four weeks he called Molnar down to his office on a regular basis during the class period set aside for planning. He discussed "personal things." She thought she saw him staring at her from outside her classroom on several occasions. He showed her a music room and a wrestling room as potential art rooms. He invited her onto his boat. He talked about how difficult it was to meet people and have relationships and discussed the threat of AIDS with her. Once he pulled his pants tightly over his crotch, making Molnar think he was calling attention to that part of his body. Molnar felt intimidated by Booth, but she rejected all of his advances.

Her spurning of him had rather immediate repercussions. Booth took back the art supplies he had given her, and all talk of giving her an art room evaporated. At one point Molnar asked the Director of Secondary Education for East Chicago, Charles Carter, for help in getting a room. When Booth learned of the inquiry, he became angry and told Molnar not to go over his head again.

Matters became worse at the end of the school year. In May 1995, Booth gave the Indiana Professional Standards Board an evaluation of Molnar's internship that could have been understood as failing her. He specifically failed her in two categories, but, in a contradictory move, he also signed the back of the form. Standing alone, the signature on the back of the form would have meant that she could get her license. On the other hand, the negative evaluation on the face of the form meant that she could not. The effect of the inconsistent feedback from Booth meant, according to Molnar, that she was not in a position to receive the license.

The rest of the evidence supports her view that the failing evaluation was a serious matter. Molnar learned of it in October 1995 when union officials told her about it. She asked them to file a grievance on her behalf complaining both about Booth's sexually harassing conduct and his retaliation when she rejected him by failing her. Around the same time, Booth learned that she was protesting the evaluation, and he warned her, "you don't know what you're getting yourself into." . . .

1. Title VII

. . . In *Ellerth* and *Faragher*, the Supreme Court established the standards that govern the liability of an employer for sexually harassing behavior of a supervisor toward a subordinate employee. The Court abandoned the prior distinction, for vicarious liability purposes, between so-called quid pro quo harassment and hostile environment harassment, in favor of a test that distinguished between cases in which the **supervisor takes a tangible employment action against the subordinate** and those in which he does not. *Ellerth*, 524 U.S. at 760-65; *Faragher*, 524 U.S. at 807. The employer's liability in all kinds of cases is determined under agency principles, as the Supreme Court has developed them.

In general, employers bear vicarious liability for the harassment committed by a supervisor, in accordance with the following rules as summarized in *Faragher*:

> **An employer is subject to vicarious liability to a victimized employee for an actionable hostile environment created by a supervisor** with immediate (or successively higher) authority over the employee. **When no tangible employment action is taken, a defending employer may raise an affirmative defense to liability or damages**, subject to proof by a preponderance of the evidence. . . . **No affirmative defense is available, however, when the supervisor's harassment culminates in a tangible employment action**, such as **discharge, demotion, or undesirable reassignment**.

524 U.S. at 807-08.

Regardless of the vocabulary then in use, Molnar therefore had to have evidence in the record that, if believed by the jury, would have shown that she was suffering from sexual harassment. In addition, the question whether the harassment led to a tangible employment action was critical. If so, East Chicago was liable without more; if not, East Chicago was entitled in principle to the opportunity to show (1) that it exercised reasonable care to prevent and correct promptly any sexually harassing behavior, and (2) that Molnar unreasonably failed to take advantage of any preventive or corrective opportunities provided by her employer or to avoid harm otherwise. . . .

Though we consider it a close call, **we conclude that Molnar did show a "tangible employment action,"** as the Court signaled that term should be understood in *Ellerth*. Citing with approval the concept of "tangible employment action" used in this court's decision in *Crady v. Liberty Nat. Bank & Trust Co. of Ind.*, 993 F.2d 132, 136 (7th Cir. 1993), the Court highlighted **indicia such as "termination of employment, a demotion evidenced by a decrease in wage or salary, a less distinguished title, a material loss of benefits, significantly diminished material responsibilities, or other indices that might be unique to a particular situation."**
. . . .

To similar effect, in *Savino v. C.P. Hall Co.*, 199 F.3d 925 (7th Cir. 1999), we said that **"[a] tangible employment action has to cause a substantial detriment to the plaintiff's employment relationship."** Id. at 932 n.8.

The clearest tangible employment action shown in Molnar's evidence was Booth's confiscation of the art supplies he had given her--supplies the jury could have believed were necessary for her to be able to perform her assigned job. . . . This deprivation was not something the School Board ever fixed.

At least as a temporary matter, the negative evaluation Booth gave Molnar was also a tangible employment action; the jury could have believed that it spelled the end of a career for an intern. The mere fact that the evaluation was reversed more than six months later and Molnar's career put back on track does not diminish its importance during the time it lasted. To hold otherwise would mean that harassing supervisors could demote employees who rejected their advances with impunity, as long as they later reversed the demotion and restored the employees to their former positions. The short duration is naturally relevant to the degree of damage Molnar suffered from the evaluation, but the jury's verdict of $500 on this claim indicates strongly that the jury was aware of that fact too. . . . On the alternate hypothesis that Molnar did not show a tangible employment action, we find the same to be true in the present record. East Chicago does not dispute Molnar's assertion that it had **no policy specifically aimed at sexual harassment**. The only relevant policy East Chicago puts forward as a potential basis for an affirmative defense is the general policy it had barring discrimination on the basis of race, color, or sex. That policy was not a sexual harassment policy: it did not provide any guidance as to what employees should do in the face of sexual harassment--it did not even mention or define sexual harassment. . . . Like the City in *Faragher*, East Chicago thus **could never show that it had exercised reasonable care to prevent and correct promptly any harassing behavior**. It could not show that Molnar unreasonably failed to take advantage of corrective opportunities it provided, because it provided none. . . .

4. Punitive Damages Against Booth

Booth claims that the jury's award of $25,000 against him was excessive, because there was insufficient evidence for it to find that he had the requisite scienter to support punitive damages. . . .

The events here took place in 1994, long after the law of sexual harassment had become well established by the Supreme Court. The jury could have found that Booth (the relevant actor here, since we are considering only the sec. 1983 theory) **acted with malice or reckless indifference** toward Molnar, particularly after she rejected his advances. Booth also attacks the amount of the award, $25,000, as grossly excessive. We realize that this is a significant amount of money for an individual, but as a matter of law $25,000 is not so far out of line that it must be reduced. We upheld a similar punitive damages award in *Merriweather v. Family Dollar Stores of Indiana*, 103 F.3d 576, 581 (7th Cir. 1996), another sexual harassment case.

Assuming as we must that the jury believed Molnar's account and not Booth's, this award is not "monstrously excessive.". . .

The judgment of the district court is Affirmed.

In a case involving hostile environment sexual harassment where the female employee, a member of a committee reviewing job applications, alleged that a single incident constituted hostile environment sexual harassment, the Supreme Court in *Clark County Sch. Dist. v. Breeden*, 532 U.S. 268 (2001) ruled in favor of the employer. The facts indicated that while reviewing a psychological evaluation of an applicant, a male member of the committee, who was the plaintiff's supervisor, read aloud a comment that the applicant had made to a co-worker, "I hear making love to you is like making love to the Grand Canyon," and then asked what it meant. The other male on the committee said "I will tell you later," and both men chuckled.

The *Clark County* Court stated at 270-271:

Just three terms ago, we reiterated, what was plain from our previous decisions, that sexual harassment is actionable under Title VII only if it is "so 'severe or pervasive' as to 'alter the conditions of [the victim's] employment and create an abusive working environment.' " *Faragher* v. *Boca Raton,* 524 U.S. 775, 786 (1998) . . . . See also *Burlington Industries, Inc.* v. *Ellerth*, 524 U.S. 742, 752 (1998) (Only harassing conduct that is "severe or pervasive" can produce a "constructive alteratio[n] in the terms or conditions of employment"); *Oncale* v. *Sundowner Offshore Services, Inc.,* 523 U.S. 75, 81 (1998) (Title VII "forbids only behavior so objectively offensive as to alter the 'conditions' of the victim's employment"). Workplace conduct is not measured in isolation; instead, "whether an environment is sufficiently hostile or abusive" must be judged "by 'looking at all the circumstances,' including the 'frequency of the discriminatory conduct; its severity; whether it is physically threatening or humiliating, or a mere offensive utterance; and whether it unreasonably interferes with an employee's work performance.' " *Faragher* v. *Boca Raton*. . . Hence, "[a] recurring point in [our] opinions is that simple teasing, offhand comments, and isolated incidents (unless extremely serious) will not amount to discriminatory changes in the 'terms and conditions of employment.' " *Faragher* v. *Boca Raton*. . . .

C3. Religious Discrimination

Title VII's prohibition against religious discrimination does provide for an "undue hardship" affirmative defense, which places the burden on the employer to prove that it was unable to provide reasonable accommodation to the religious observance or practice of the employee without undue hardship. However, according to the Supreme Court's *Ansonia* decision, below, once the employer offers a reasonable accommodation, there is no duty to prove that the employee's requested accommodations would cause an undue hardship.

CASE

Ansonia Board of Education v. Philbrook, 479 U.S. 60 (1986) (emphasis added)

[Facts:] Petitioner Ansonia Board of Education has employed respondent Ronald Philbrook since 1962 to teach high school business and typing classes in Ansonia, Connecticut. In 1968, Philbrook was baptized into the Worldwide Church of God. The tenets of the church require members to refrain from secular employment during designated holy days, a practice that has caused respondent to miss approximately six schooldays each year. We are asked to determine **whether the employer's efforts to adjust respondent's work schedule in light of his belief fulfill its obligation under 701 (j) of the Civil Rights Act of 1964, 86 Stat. 103, 42 U.S.C. 2000e(j), to "reasonably accommodate to an employee's . . . religious observance or practice without undue hardship on the conduct of the employer's business."**

Since the 1967-1968 school year, the school board's collective-bargaining agreements with the Ansonia Federation of Teachers have granted to each teacher 18 days of leave per year for illness, cumulative to 150 and later to 180 days. Accumulated leave may be used for purposes other than illness as specified in the agreement. A teacher may accordingly use five days' leave for a death in the immediate family, one day for attendance at a wedding, three days per year for attendance as an official delegate to a national veterans' organization, and the like. . . . With the exception of the agreement covering the 1967-1968 school year, each contract has specifically provided three days' annual leave for observance of mandatory religious holidays, as defined in the contract. Unlike other categories for which leave is permitted, absences for religious holidays are not charged against the teacher's annual or accumulated leave.

The school board has also agreed that teachers may use up to three days of accumulated leave each school year for "necessary personal business." Recent contracts limited permissible personal leave to those uses not otherwise specified in the contract. This limitation dictated, for example, that an employee who wanted more than three leave days to attend the convention of a national veterans' organization could not use personal leave to gain extra days for that purpose. Likewise, an employee already absent three days for mandatory religious observances could not later use personal leave for "[a]ny religious activity," . . . or "[a]ny religious observance." . . . Since the 1978-1979 school year, teachers have been allowed to take one of the three personal days without prior approval; use of the remaining two days requires advance approval by the school principal.

The limitations on the use of personal business leave spawned this litigation. Until the 1976-1977 year, Philbrook observed mandatory holy days by using the three days granted in the contract and then taking unauthorized leave. His pay was reduced accordingly. In 1976, however, respondent stopped taking unauthorized leave for religious reasons, and began scheduling required hospital visits on church holy days. He also worked on several holy days. Dissatisfied with this arrangement, Philbrook repeatedly asked the school board to adopt one of two alternatives. His preferred alternative would allow use of personal business leave for religious observance, effectively giving him three additional days of paid leave for that purpose. Short of this arrangement, respondent suggested that he pay the cost of a substitute and receive full pay for additional days off for religious observances. Petitioner has consistently rejected both proposals.

[Issues:]   We granted certiorari to consider the important questions of federal law presented by the decision of the Court of Appeals. . . . **Specifically, we are asked to address whether the Court of Appeals erred in finding that Philbrook established a prima facie case of religious discrimination and in opining that an employer must accept the employee's preferred accommodation absent proof of undue hardship.** We find little support in the statute for the approach adopted by the Court of Appeals, but we agree that the ultimate issue of reasonable accommodation cannot be resolved without further factual inquiry. We accordingly affirm the judgment of the Court of Appeals remanding the case to the District Court for additional findings. As we noted in our only previous consideration of 701(j), its language was added to the 1972 amendments on the floor of the Senate with little discussion. *Trans World Airlines, Inc. v. Hardison*, 432 U.S. 63, 74, n.9 (1977). . . . In *Hardison*, supra, at 84, we determined that **an accommodation causes "undue hardship" whenever that accommodation results in "more than a de minimis cost" to the employer**. *Hardison* had been discharged because his religious beliefs would not allow him to work on Saturdays and claimed that this action violated the employer's duty to effect a reasonable accommodation of his beliefs. Because we concluded that each of the suggested accommodations would impose on the employer an undue hardship, we had no occasion to consider the bounds of a prima facie case in the religious accommodation context or whether an employer is required to choose from available accommodations the alternative preferred by the employee. The employer in *Hardison* simply argued that all conceivable accommodations would result in undue hardship, and we agreed. . . .

We find no basis in either the statute or its legislative history for requiring an employer to choose any particular reasonable accommodation. By its very terms the statute directs that any reasonable accommodation by the employer is sufficient to meet its accommodation obligation. The employer violates the statute unless it "demonstrates that [it] is unable to reasonably accommodate . . . an employee's . . . religious observance or practice without undue hardship on the conduct of the employer's business." 42 U.S.C. 2000e(j). **Thus, where the employer has already reasonably accommodated the employee's religious needs, the statutory inquiry is at an end.** The employer need not further show that each of the employee's alternative accommodations would result in undue hardship. As *Hardison* illustrates, the extent of undue hardship on the employer's business is at issue only where the employer claims that it is unable to offer any reasonable accommodation without such hardship. Once the Court of Appeals assumed that the school board had offered to Philbrook a reasonable alternative, it erred by requiring the Board to nonetheless demonstrate the hardship of Philbrook's alternatives.

[Court ruling:] . . . **We accordingly hold that an employer has met its obligation under 701(j) when it demonstrates that it has offered a reasonable accommodation to the employee.**

The remaining issue in the case is whether the school board's leave policy constitutes a reasonable accommodation of Philbrook's religious beliefs. . . . We think that the school board policy in this case, requiring respondent to take unpaid leave for holy day observance that exceeded the amount allowed by the collective-bargaining agreement, would generally be a reasonable one. In enacting 701(j), Congress was understandably motivated by a desire to assure the individual additional opportunity to observe religious practices, **but it did not impose a duty on the employer to accommodate at all costs.** .

. . The provision of unpaid leave eliminates the conflict between employment requirements and religious practices by allowing the individual to observe fully religious holy days and requires him only to give up compensation for a day that he did not in fact work. Generally speaking, "[t]he direct effect of [unpaid leave] is merely a loss of income for the period the employee is not at work; such an exclusion has no direct effect upon either employment opportunities or job status." . . .

But unpaid leave is not a reasonable accommodation when paid leave is provided for all purposes except religious ones. A provision for paid leave "that is part and parcel of the employment relationship may not be doled out in a discriminatory fashion, even if the employer would be free . . . not to provide the benefit at all." . . . **Such an arrangement would display a discrimination against religious practices that is the antithesis of reasonableness.** Whether the policy here violates this teaching turns on factual inquiry into past and present administration of the personal business leave provisions of the collective-bargaining agreement. . . . We do not think that the record is sufficiently clear on this point for us to make the necessary factual findings, and we therefore affirm the judgment of the Court of Appeals remanding the case to the District Court. The latter court on remand should make the necessary findings as to past and existing practice in the administration of the collective-bargaining agreements.

It is so ordered.

III. AGE DISCRIMINATION IN EMPLOYMENT ACT (ADEA)

The ADEA, 29 U.S.C section 621 *et seq.*, prohibits discrimination based on age by employers of twenty or more employees. It applies to all aspects of employment and protects employees of public and private employers once they reach the age of forty. There is no upper age limit when the protection ends. A public employer may assert the defense of "Eleventh Amendment immunity," in an ADEA suit, but must be able to prove that it is the state or an arm of the state in order to prevail. Whether public elementary or secondary schools would succeed depends to a large extent on how much "local control" is given by state statutes in the operation of their business affairs.

CASE
Hazen Paper Co. v. Biggins, 507 U.S. 604 (1993) (emphasis added)

. . . Respondent brought suit against petitioners in the United States District Court for the District of Massachusetts, alleging a violation of the ADEA. He claimed that age had been a determinative factor in petitioners' decision to fire him. Petitioners contested this claim, asserting instead that respondent had been fired for doing business with competitors of Hazen Paper. The case was tried before a jury, which rendered a verdict for respondent on his ADEA claim and also found violations of the Employee Retirement Income Security Act of 1974 (ERISA), 88 Stat. 895, 510, 29 U.S.C. 1140, and state law. On the ADEA count, the jury specifically found that petitioners "willfully" violated the statute. Under 7(b) of the ADEA, 29 U.S.C. 626(b), a "willful" violation gives rise to liquidated damages.

. . . In affirming the judgments of liability, the Court of Appeals relied heavily on the evidence that petitioners had fired respondent in order to prevent his pension benefits from vesting. That evidence, as construed most favorably to respondent by the court, showed that the Hazen Paper pension plan had a 10-year vesting period and that respondent would have reached the 10-year mark had he worked "a few more weeks" after being fired. . . .

The courts of appeals repeatedly have faced the question whether an employer violates the ADEA by acting on the basis of a factor, such as an employee's pension status or seniority that is empirically correlated with age. . . . **We now clarify that there is no disparate treatment under the ADEA when the factor motivating the employer is some feature other than the employee's age.**

. . . The disparate treatment theory is, of course, available under the ADEA, as the language of that statute makes clear. "It shall be unlawful for an employer . . . to fail or refuse to hire or to discharge any individual or otherwise discriminate against any individual with respect to his compensation, terms, conditions, or privileges of employment, because of such individual's age." 29 U.S.C. 623(a)(1) (emphasis added). . .

In a disparate treatment case, liability depends on whether the protected trait (under the ADEA, age) **actually motivated the employer's decision**. . . . Whatever the employer's decisionmaking process, a disparate treatment claim cannot succeed unless the **employee's protected trait actually played a role in that process and had a determinative influence on the outcome.**

. . . Thus, the ADEA commands that "employers are to evaluate [older] employees . . . on their merits, and not their age." *Western Air Lines, Inc. v. Criswell,* . . . (1985). **The employer cannot rely on age as a proxy for an employee's remaining characteristics, such as productivity, but must instead focus on those factors directly.**

. . . On average, an older employee has had more years in the workforce than a younger employee, and thus may well have accumulated more years of service with a particular employer. Yet an **employee's age is analytically distinct from his years of service.** An employee who is younger than 40, and therefore outside the class of older workers as defined by the ADEA, see 29 U.S.C. 631(a), may have worked for a particular employer his entire career, while an older worker may have been newly hired. **Because age and years of service are analytically distinct, an employer can take account of one while ignoring the other, and thus it is incorrect to say that a decision based on years of service is necessarily "age-based."**

. . . We therefore remand the case for the Court of Appeals to reconsider whether the jury had sufficient evidence to find an ADEA violation.

An example of this age discrimination standard applied to a school employee is described below:

A school wanting to dismiss an employee based on age, such as a school bus driver, does have the statutory defense of a bona fide occupational qualification (BFOQ), but the burden is heavy. In the case of *Western Airlines, Inc. v. Criswell*, 472 U.S. 400 (1985) that dealt with an age-60 mandatory retirement requirement for pilots, co-pilots, and flight engineers, the syllabus that summarizes the Court's decision states at 472 U.S. 401 (emphasis added):

. . . The ADEA's restrictive language, its legislative history, and the consistent interpretation of the administrative agencies charged with enforcing the statute establish that the BFOQ exception was meant to be an **extremely narrow exception to the general prohibition of age discrimination** contained in the ADEA. . . .

The relevant considerations for resolving a BFOQ defense to an age-based qualification purportedly justified by safety interests are whether the **job qualification is "reasonably necessary" to the overriding interest in public safety, and whether the employer is compelled to rely on age as a proxy for the safety-related job qualification validated in the first inquiry.** The latter showing may be made by the employer's establishing either (a) that it had **reasonable cause to believe that all or substantially all persons over the age qualification would be unable to perform safely the duties of the job,** or (b) that it is **highly impractical to deal with the older employees on an individualized basis.** . . .

IV. AMERICANS WITH DISABILITIES ACT (ADA)

The ADA, 42 U.S.C. section 12101 *et seq.*, prohibits disability discrimination by private and public employers of fifteen or more employees. The following are key provisions of the ADA (emphasis added):

42 U.S.C. Section 12102. Definitions

As used in this chapter: . . . .

(2) **Disability**

The term ''disability'' means, with respect to an individual -

    (A) **a physical or mental impairment that substantially limits one or more of the major life activities of such individual**;

    (B) **a record of such an impairment**; or

    (C) **being regarded as having such an impairment**. . . .

42 U.S.C. Section 12111. Definitions

As used in this subchapter: . . . .

(8) **Qualified individual with a disability**

The term ''qualified individual with a disability'' means **an individual with a disability who, with or without reasonable accommodation, can perform the essential functions of the employment position that such individual holds or desires.** . . .

(9) **Reasonable accommodation**

The term "reasonable accommodation" may include -

    (A) making existing facilities used by employees readily accessible to and usable by individuals with disabilities; and

    (B) job restructuring, part-time or modified work schedules, reassignment to a vacant position, acquisition or modification of equipment or devices, appropriate adjustment or modifications of examinations, training materials or policies, the provision of qualified readers or interpreters, and other similar accommodations for individuals with disabilities.

(10) **Undue hardship**

    (A) In general

    The term "undue hardship" means **an action requiring significant difficulty or expense, when considered in light of the factors set forth in subparagraph (B).**

    (B) Factors to be considered

    In determining whether an accommodation would impose an undue hardship on a covered entity, factors to be considered include

    (i) the nature and cost of the accommodation needed under this chapter;

    (ii) the overall financial resources of the facility or facilities involved in the provision of the reasonable accommodation; the number of persons employed at such facility; the effect on expenses and resources, or the impact otherwise of such accommodation upon the operation of the facility;

(iii) the overall financial resources of the covered entity; the overall size of the business of a covered entity with respect to the number of its employees; the number, type, and location of its facilities; and

(iv) the type of operation or operations of the covered entity, including the composition, structure, and functions of the workforce of such entity; the geographic separateness, administrative, or fiscal relationship of the facility or facilities in question to the covered entity.

42 U.S.C. Section 12112. Discrimination

(a) General rule

No covered entity shall discriminate against a **qualified individual with a disability** because of the disability of such individual in regard to job application procedures, the hiring, advancement, or discharge of employees, employee compensation, job training, and other terms, conditions, and privileges of employment.

(b) Construction

As used in subsection (a) of this section, the term ''**discriminate**'' includes -

. . . (5)(A) **not making reasonable accommodations to the known physical or mental limitations of an otherwise qualified individual with a disability** who is an applicant or employee, unless such covered entity can demonstrate that the accommodation would impose an undue hardship on the operation of the business of such covered entity; . . .

(d) **Medical examinations and inquiries**

(1) In general

The prohibition against discrimination as referred to in subsection (a) of this section shall include medical examinations and inquiries.

(2) Preemployment

(A) Prohibited examination or inquiry

Except as provided in paragraph (3), a covered entity shall not conduct a medical examination or make inquiries of a job applicant as to whether such applicant is an individual with a disability or as to the nature or severity of such disability.

(B) **Acceptable inquiry**

A covered entity may make preemployment inquiries into the ability of an applicant to perform job-related functions.

(3) Employment entrance examination

A covered entity may require a medical examination **after an offer of employment** has been made to a job applicant and prior to the commencement of the employment duties of such applicant, and may condition an offer of employment on the results of such examination, if -

(A) all entering employees are subjected to such an examination regardless of disability;

(B) information obtained regarding the medical condition or history of the applicant is collected and maintained on separate forms and in separate medical files and is treated as a confidential medical record . . . .

(4) Examination and inquiry

(A) Prohibited examinations and inquiries

A covered entity shall not require a medical examination and shall not make inquiries of an employee as to whether such employee is an individual with a disability or as to the nature or severity of the disability, **unless such examination or inquiry is shown to be job-related and consistent with business necessity**. . . .

42 U.S.C. Section 12114. Illegal use of drugs and alcohol

(a) **Qualified individual with a disability**

For purposes of this subchapter, the term **"qualified individual with a disability" shall not include any employee or applicant who is currently engaging in the illegal use of drugs, when the covered entity acts on the basis of such use.**

(b) Rules of construction

Nothing in subsection (a) of this section shall be construed to exclude as a qualified individual with a disability an individual who -

(1) **has successfully completed a supervised drug rehabilitation program and is no longer engaging in the illegal use of drugs**, or has otherwise been rehabilitated successfully and is no longer engaging in such use;

(2) **is participating in a supervised rehabilitation program and is no longer engaging in such use**; or

(3) is erroneously regarded as engaging in such use, but is not engaging in such use; except that it shall not be a violation of this chapter for a covered entity to adopt or administer reasonable policies or procedures, including but not limited to drug testing, designed to ensure that an individual described in paragraph (1) or (2) is no longer engaging in the illegal use of drugs. . . .

CASE

Toyota Manufacturing Co. v. Williams, 534 U.S. 184 (2002) (emphasis added)

Under the Americans with Disabilities Act of 1990 (ADA or Act), . . . a physical impairment that "substantially limits one or more ... major life activities" is a "disability." 42 U. S. C. §12102(2)(A) (1994 ed.). Respondent, claiming to be disabled because of her carpal tunnel syndrome and other related impairments, sued petitioner, her former employer, for failing to provide her with a reasonable accommodation as required by the ADA. See §12112(b)(5)(A).

[Lower Court Ruling:]   The District Court granted summary judgment to petitioner, finding that respondent's impairments did not substantially limit any of her major life activities. The Court of Appeals for the Sixth Circuit reversed, finding that the impairments substantially limited respondent in the major life activity of performing manual tasks, and therefore granting partial summary judgment to respondent on the issue of whether she was disabled under the ADA. We conclude that the Court of Appeals did not apply the proper standard in making this determination because it analyzed only a limited class of manual tasks and failed to ask **whether respondent's impairments prevented or restricted her from performing tasks that are of central importance to most people's daily lives.**

[Facts:]   Respondent began working at petitioner's automobile manufacturing plant in Georgetown, Kentucky, in August 1990. She was soon placed on an engine fabrication assembly line, where her duties included work with pneumatic tools. Use of these tools eventually caused pain in respondent's hands, wrists, and arms. She sought treatment at petitioner's in-house medical service, where she was diagnosed with bilateral carpal tunnel syndrome and bilateral tendonitis. Respondent consulted a personal physician who placed her on permanent work restrictions that precluded her from lifting more than 20 pounds or from "frequently lifting or carrying of objects weighing up to 10 pounds," engaging in "constant repetitive ... flexion or extension of [her] wrists or elbows," performing "overhead work," or using "vibratory or pneumatic tools." . . .

A short while after the shell body audit job was added to respondent's rotations, she began to experience pain in her neck and shoulders. Respondent again sought care at petitioner's in-house medical service, where she was diagnosed with myotendonitis bilateral periscapular, an inflammation of the muscles and tendons around both of her shoulder blades; myotendonitis and myositis bilateral forearms with nerve compression causing median nerve irritation; and thoracic outlet compression, a condition that causes pain in the nerves that lead to the upper extremities. Respondent requested that petitioner accommodate her medical conditions by allowing her to return to doing only her original two jobs in QCIO, which respondent claimed she could still perform without difficulty.

The parties disagree about what happened next. According to respondent, petitioner refused her request and forced her to continue working in the shell body audit job, which caused her even greater physical injury. According to petitioner, respondent simply began missing work on a regular basis. Regardless, it is clear that on December 6, 1996, the last day respondent worked at petitioner's plant, she was placed under a no-work-of-any-kind restriction by her treating physicians. On January 27, 1997, respondent received a letter from petitioner that terminated her employment, citing her poor attendance record. . . .

[Issue:] We granted certiorari. . . to consider the proper standard for assessing whether an individual is substantially limited in performing manual tasks. We now reverse the Court of Appeals' decision to grant partial summary judgment to respondent on the issue whether she was substantially limited in performing manual tasks at the time she sought an accommodation. . . .

The ADA requires covered entities, including private employers, to provide "reasonable accommodations to the known physical or mental limitations of an otherwise qualified individual with a disability who is an applicant or employee, unless such covered entity can demonstrate that the accommodation would impose an undue hardship." 42 U. S. C. §12112(b)(5)(A) (1994 ed.); see also §12111(2) . . . The Act defines a "qualified individual with a disability" as "an individual with a disability who, with or without reasonable accommodation, can perform the essential functions of the employment position that such individual holds or desires." §12111(8). In turn, a "disability" is:

(A) a physical or mental impairment that substantially limits one or more of the major life activities of such individual;

(B) a record of such an impairment; or

(C) being regarded as having such an impairment. §12102(2). . . .

Merely having an impairment does not make one disabled for purposes of the ADA. Claimants also need to demonstrate that the impairment **limits a major life activity**. . . The HEW Rehabilitation Act regulations provide a list of examples of "major life activities," that includes "walking, seeing, hearing," and, as relevant here, "performing manual tasks." 45 CFR §84.3(j)(2)(ii) (2001).

To qualify as disabled, a claimant must further show that the limitation on the major life activity is "substantia[l]." 42 U. S. C. §12102(2)(A). . . .

The relevant question, therefore, is whether the Sixth Circuit correctly analyzed whether these impairments substantially limited respondent in the major life activity of performing manual tasks. Answering this requires us to address an issue about which the EEOC regulations are silent: what a plaintiff must demonstrate to establish a substantial limitation in the specific major life activity of performing manual tasks.

Our consideration of this issue is guided first and foremost by the words of the disability definition itself. "[S]ubstantially" in the phrase "substantially limits" suggests "considerable" or "to a large degree." See Webster's Third New International Dictionary 2280 (1976) (defining "substantially" as "in a substantial manner" and "substantial" as "considerable in amount, value, or worth" and "being that specified to a large degree or in the main. . . The word "substantial" thus clearly precludes impairments that interfere in only a minor way with the performance of manual tasks from qualifying as disabilities. . . .

"Major" in the phrase "major life activities" means important. See Webster's, *supra*, at 1363 (defining "major" as "greater in dignity, rank, importance, or interest"). "Major life activities" thus refers to those activities that are of central importance to daily life. **In order for performing manual tasks to fit into this category--a category that includes such basic abilities as walking, seeing, and hearing--the manual tasks in question must be central to daily life.** If each of the tasks included in the major life activity of performing manual tasks does not independently qualify as a major life activity, then together they must do so.

That these terms need to be interpreted strictly to create a demanding standard for qualifying as disabled is confirmed by the first section of the ADA, which lays out the legislative findings and purposes that motivate the Act. See 42 U. S. C. §12101. When it enacted the ADA in 1990, Congress found that "some 43,000,000 Americans have one or more physical or mental disabilities." §12101(a)(1).

If Congress intended everyone with a physical impairment that precluded the performance of some isolated, unimportant, or particularly difficult manual task to qualify as disabled, the number of disabled Americans would surely have been much higher. Cf. *Sutton* v. *United Air Lines, Inc.,* . . . (finding that because more than 100 million people need corrective lenses to see properly, "[h]ad Congress intended to include all persons with corrected physical limitations among those covered by the Act, it undoubtedly would have cited a much higher number [than 43 million disabled persons in the findings").

We therefore hold that to be substantially limited in performing manual tasks, an individual must have an impairment that prevents or severely restricts the individual from doing activities that are of **central importance to most people's daily lives**. The impairment's impact must also be **permanent or long-term.** See 29 CFR §§1630.2(j)(2)(ii)-(iii) (2001). . . .

While the Court of Appeals in this case addressed the different major life activity of performing manual tasks, its analysis circumvented *Sutton* by focusing on respondent's inability to perform manual tasks associated only with her job. This was in error. **When addressing the major life activity of performing manual 3tasks, the central inquiry must be whether the claimant is unable to perform the variety of tasks central to most people's daily lives, not whether the claimant is unable to perform the tasks associated with her specific job.** Otherwise, *Sutton*'s restriction on claims of disability based on a substantial limitation in working will be rendered meaningless because an inability to perform a specific job always can be recast as an inability to perform a "class" of tasks associated with that specific job. . . .

Even more critically, the manual tasks unique to any particular job are not necessarily important parts of most people's lives. As a result, occupation-specific tasks may have only limited relevance to the manual task inquiry. In this case, "repetitive work with hands and arms extended at or above shoulder levels for extended periods of time," . . . the manual task on which the Court of Appeals relied, is not an important part of most people's daily lives. The court, therefore, should not have considered respondent's inability to do such manual work in her specialized assembly line job as sufficient proof that she was substantially limited in performing manual tasks. . .

In addition, according to respondent's deposition testimony, even after her condition worsened, she could still brush her teeth, wash her face, bathe, tend her flower garden, fix breakfast, do laundry, and pick up around the house. . . The record also indicates that her medical conditions caused her to avoid sweeping, to quit dancing, to occasionally seek help dressing, and to reduce how often she plays with her children, gardens, and drives long distances. . . But these changes in her life did not amount to such severe restrictions in the activities that are of central importance to most people's daily lives that they establish a manual-task disability as a matter of law. On this record, it was therefore inappropriate for the Court of Appeals to grant partial summary judgment to respondent on the issue whether she was substantially limited in performing manual tasks, and its decision to do so must be reversed. . . .

Accordingly, we reverse the Court of Appeals' judgment granting partial summary judgment to respondent and remand the case for further proceedings consistent with this opinion.

So ordered.

SCENARIOS
STATE AND APPLY THE RELEVANT LEGAL RULE(S) TO THE FACTS.

1. Teacher, a male, had just become the proud father of twin boys. His wife, a chemist, was going back to work when the babies were six-weeks old, so Teacher applied for a paternity leave for one year from the birth of his children. State statute required schools to give female teacher's, upon request, a one-year leave from the child's birth, but no such right was given the male teacher. The school, whose teacher bargaining agreement was silent on paternity leaves denied the request and Teacher sued in federal court.

2. High School, located in a very rural part of the state, advertised for an assistant principal for the upcoming school year. Of the ten applicants, one was African American with outstanding credentials and four-years successful experience as a dean of students in a racially mixed, large suburban middle school twenty miles from High School. Three applicants were interviewed—a white male, very popular teacher-coach at High School the past ten years who was two courses shy of earning his administrative license, a white female former graduate of High School who just had become licensed and had three years high school teaching experience in a neighboring school district, and African American who successfully taught and coached at a large suburban high school for ten years before earning his administrative license and becoming a dean.

High School hired the soon-to-be licensed White Male, but rather than signing him to an assistant principal contract, gave him one where he was termed "administrative assistant." When African American filed a complaint of racial discrimination with the Equal Employment Opportunity Commission, its investigation indicated that High School said it hired White Male because he was a known quantity who had been very well liked and respected as a teacher and coach, and that African American had not done well in his interview because he very verbal and overly opinionated on how High School could improve its educational delivery system and its methods of student discipline.

The EEOC investigation also indicated that in the past ten years with Principal at the helm, High School had had three other administrative openings, at least one qualified black applicant had applied each time, none had been interviewed, and white applicants with less experience had been employed. There was evidence that that one of the whites employed was very expressive of his views on how education should be handled. Only one African American teacher had been employed in that ten-year period even though there had been at least a dozen teaching applicants. The one hired was an elementary special education teacher who was employed only after three white applicants rejected offers. After attempts by EEOC to mediate a resolution of the complaint failed, African American filed suit in federal court.

CHAPTER

6

STUDENT DUE PROCESS AND DISCIPLINE

The Fourteenth Amendment to the United States Constitution prohibits public school boards as governmental bodies and school employees as governmental actors from denying a student's property and liberty rights without due process of law. The state-granted right to attend public schools (as well as a duty under compulsory attendance laws, unless students attend private schools that offer at least equivalent instruction) is deemed a property interest requiring due process when a student will be separated from school attendance. Similarly, due process is necessitated if the action of a governmental body or actor so negatively impacts a student's good name and reputation that it harms the liberty interest. (Each state's constitution has an equivalent version of the Fourteenth Amendment Due Process Clause although the language may not be exactly the same.)

The question of the extent of the process due a student generally depends upon the extent of the interference with the property or liberty interest. Generally, the greater the student's stake in the matter, the greater the process. For example, the process required for a two-day suspension from school need not be as great as a two-semester removal from attendance.

There are two components of constitutional due process – *procedural* and *substantive*. Procedural due process generally refers to the procedures that the school must go through before impacting property and liberty interests, and includes some form of notice of what the student did to violate a conduct code and some form of opportunity to be heard. Substantive due process goes to the question of the reasonableness and fairness of the school's interference with the property or liberty interest.

Access to federal and state courts by a student claiming denial of due process by a school board or governmental actor is granted by the Civil Rights Act of 1871, 42 U.S.C. section 1983, which states in relevant part:

Every person who, under color of any statute . . . of any State . . . subjects or causes to be subjected, any citizen . . . or other person . . . to the deprivation of any rights . . . secured by the Constitution and laws, shall be liable to the party injured. . . .

Should a court find a violation of a student's Fourteenth Amendment due process rights, federal statute at 42 U.S.C. Section 1988 provides that the court in its discretion may award reasonable attorney fees to the student's lawyer.

The following case enunciated the legal standard for determining the basic principles of the suspension process.

I. PROCEDURAL DUE PROCESS -- NOTICE AND HEARING

CASE
Goss v. Lopez, 419 U.S. 565 (1975) (emphasis added)

This appeal by various administrators of the Columbus, Ohio, Public School System (CPSS) challenges the judgment of a three-judge federal court, declaring that appellees - various high school students in the CPSS - were denied due process of law contrary to the command of the Fourteenth Amendment in that they were temporarily suspended from their high schools without a hearing either prior to suspension or within a reasonable time thereafter, and enjoining the administrators to remove all references to such suspensions from the students' records. Ohio law. . . provides for free education to all children between the ages of six and 21. Section 3313.66 of the Code empowers the principal of an Ohio public school to suspend a pupil for misconduct for up to 10 days or to expel him. . .

[Issues:] The nine named appellees, each of whom alleged that he or she had been suspended from public high school in Columbus for up to 10 days without a hearing pursuant to 3313.66, filed an action under 42 U.S.C. 1983 against the Columbus Board of Education and various administrators of the CPSS. The complaint sought a declaration that 3313.66 was unconstitutional in that it permitted public school administrators to deprive plaintiffs of their rights to an education without a hearing of any kind, in violation of the procedural due process component of the Fourteenth Amendment. It also sought to enjoin the public school officials from issuing future suspensions pursuant to 3313.66 and to require them to remove references to the past suspensions from the records of the students in question.

The proof below established that the suspensions arose out of a period of widespread student unrest in the CPSS during February and March 1971. Six of the named plaintiffs . . . were each suspended for 10 days on account of disruptive or disobedient conduct committed in the presence of the school administrator who ordered the suspension. . . None was given a hearing to determine the operative facts underlying the suspension, but each, together with his or her parents, was offered the opportunity to attend a conference, subsequent to the effective date of the suspension, to discuss the student's future.

[Facts:] . . . Dwight Lopez . . . [a student] at the Central High School . . . was suspended in connection with a disturbance in the lunchroom which involved some physical damage to school property. Lopez testified that at least 75 other students were suspended from his school on the same day. He also testified below that he was not a party to the destructive conduct but was instead an innocent bystander. Because no one from the school testified with regard to this incident, there is no evidence in the record indicating the official basis for concluding otherwise. Lopez never had a hearing. . . .

[Legal standards:] The Fourteenth Amendment forbids the State to deprive any person of life, liberty, or property without due process of law. **Protected interests in property are normally "not created by the Constitution. Rather, they are created and their dimensions are defined" by an independent source such as state statutes or rules entitling the citizen to certain benefits.** *Board of Regents v. Roth*, 408 U.S. 564, 577 (1972). . . .

Here, on the basis of state law, appellees plainly had legitimate claims of entitlement to a public education. Ohio Rev. Code Ann. . . . direct local authorities to provide a free education to all residents between five and 21 years of age, and a compulsory-attendance law requires attendance for a school year of not less than 32 weeks. . .

"The Fourteenth Amendment, as now applied to the States, protects the citizen against the State itself and all of its creatures - Boards of Education not excepted." *West Virginia Board of Education v. Barnette*, 319 U.S. 624, 637 (1943). **The authority possessed by the State to prescribe and enforce standards of conduct in its schools although concededly very broad, must be exercised consistently with constitutional safeguards.** Among other things, **the State is constrained to recognize a student's legitimate entitlement to a public education as a property interest** which is protected by the Due Process Clause and which may not be taken away for misconduct without adherence to the minimum procedures required by that Clause.

The Due Process Clause also **forbids arbitrary deprivations of liberty. "Where a person's good name, reputation, honor, or integrity is at stake because of what the government is doing to him," the minimal requirements of the Clause must be satisfied**. . . School authorities here suspended appellees from school for periods of up to 10 days based on charges of misconduct. **If sustained and recorded, those charges could seriously damage the students' standing with their fellow pupils and their teachers as well as interfere with later opportunities for higher education and employment.** . . .

A short suspension is, of course, a far milder deprivation than expulsion. But, "education is perhaps the most important function of state and local governments," *Brown v. Board of Education,* . . .(1954), and the total exclusion from the educational process for more than a trivial period, and certainly if the suspension is for 10 days, is a serious event in the life of the suspended child. Neither the property interest in educational benefits temporarily denied nor the liberty interest in reputation, which is also implicated, is so insubstantial that suspensions may constitutionally be imposed by any procedure the school chooses, no matter how arbitrary.

"Once it is determined that due process applies, the question remains what process is due." . . . **We turn to that question, fully realizing as our cases regularly do that** the interpretation and application of the Due Process Clause are intensely practical matters and that "[t]he very nature of due process negates any concept of inflexible procedures universally applicable to every imaginable situation." . . .

[Rationale:] There are certain bench marks to guide us, however. *Mullane v. Central Hanover Trust Co.,* . . . (1950), . . . said that "[m]any controversies have raged about the cryptic and abstract words of the Due Process Clause but there can be no doubt that **at a minimum they require that deprivation of life, liberty or property by adjudication be preceded by notice and opportunity for hearing appropriate to the nature of the case."** . . . **"The fundamental requisite of due process of law is the opportunity to be heard,"** *Grannis v. Ordean,* . . . (1914), **a right that "has little reality or worth unless one is informed that the matter is pending and can choose for himself whether to . . . contest".** . . . At the very minimum, therefore, **students facing suspension and the consequent interference with a protected property interest must be given some kind of notice and afforded some kind of hearing**. . .

It also appears from our cases that **the timing and content of the notice and the nature of the hearing will depend on appropriate accommodation of the competing interests involved.** . . **The student's interest is to avoid unfair or mistaken exclusion from the educational process**, with all of its unfortunate consequences. . . Disciplinarians, although proceeding in utmost good faith, frequently act on the reports and advice of others; and the controlling facts and the nature of the conduct under challenge are often disputed. The risk of error is not at all trivial, and it should be guarded against **if that may be done without prohibitive cost or interference with the educational process** . . .

We do not believe that school authorities must be totally free from notice and hearing requirements if their schools are to operate with acceptable efficiency. Students facing temporary suspension have interests qualifying for protection of the Due Process Clause, and **due process requires, in connection with a suspension of 10 days or less, that the student be given oral or written notice of the charges against**

him and, if he denies them, an explanation of the evidence the authorities have and an opportunity to present his side of the story. The Clause requires at least these rudimentary precautions against unfair or mistaken findings of misconduct and arbitrary exclusion from school.

There need be no delay between the time "notice" is given and the time of the hearing. In the great majority of cases the disciplinarian may informally discuss the alleged misconduct with the student minutes after it has occurred. **We hold only that, in being given an opportunity to explain his version of the facts at this discussion, the student first be told what he is accused of doing and what the basis of the accusation is**. . . Since the hearing may occur almost immediately following the misconduct, it follows that **as a general rule notice and hearing should precede removal of the student from school**. We agree with the District Court, however, that **there are recurring situations in which prior notice and hearing cannot be insisted upon. Students whose presence poses a continuing danger to persons or property or an ongoing threat of disrupting the academic process may be immediately removed from school. In such cases, the necessary notice and rudimentary hearing should follow as soon as practicable**. . . .

We stop short of construing the Due Process Clause to require, countrywide, that hearings in connection with short suspensions must afford the student the opportunity to secure counsel, to confront and cross-examine witnesses supporting the charge, or to call his own witnesses to verify his version of the incident. Brief disciplinary suspensions are almost countless. To impose in each such case even truncated trial-type procedures might well overwhelm administrative facilities in many places and, by diverting resources, cost more than it would save in educational effectiveness. Moreover, further formalizing the suspension process and escalating its formality and adversary nature may not only make it too costly as a regular disciplinary tool but also destroy its effectiveness as part of the teaching process.

On the other hand, requiring effective notice and informal hearing permitting the student to give his version of the events will provide a meaningful hedge against erroneous action. At least the disciplinarian will be alerted to the existence of disputes about facts and arguments about cause and effect. He may then determine himself to summon the accuser, permit cross-examination, and allow the student to present his own witnesses. In more difficult cases, he may permit counsel. In any event, his discretion will be more informed and we think the risk of error substantially reduced.

Requiring that there be at least an informal give-and-take between student and disciplinarian, preferably prior to the suspension, will add little to the fact-finding function where the disciplinarian himself has witnessed the conduct forming the basis for the charge. But things are not always as they seem to be, and the student will at least have the opportunity to characterize his conduct and put it in what he deems the proper context.

We should also make it clear that we have addressed ourselves solely to the short suspension, not exceeding 10 days. **Longer suspensions or expulsions for the remainder of the school term, or permanently, may require more formal procedures. Nor do we put aside the possibility that in unusual situations, although involving only a short suspension, something more than the rudimentary procedures will be required**.

[Court ruling:] The District Court found each of the suspensions involved here to have occurred without a hearing, either before or after the suspension, and that each suspension was therefore invalid and the statute unconstitutional insofar as it permits such suspensions without notice or hearing. Accordingly, the judgment is Affirmed.

A. Suspensions

As noted in *Goss v. Lopez*, suspension of a student from school for ten or less days involves notice and an informal hearing tailored to the particular circumstances, wherein the student orally receives a statement of his conduct and the rule violated, and then, if the accusation is denied, and without further delay, given an opportunity to respond by explaining the student's version of the events. Most states have enacted legislation that codifies the basic principles of the suspension process enunciated in *Goss* and sets the number of days constituting a suspension from school.

B. Expulsions

Removing a student for an act of misconduct for a period longer than a short-term suspension is regulated to various degrees by state legislatures. In most states it is called an expulsion and usually constitutes removal from school in excess of ten days.

Each state, by statute and/or administrative regulation, decides the definition of expulsion, the amount of notice and extent of the hearing that is required, the necessary steps in the due process procedure, and the length of time of removal from attendance. Some states, like Illinois, have short and general procedural requirements, and leave the implementation of student expulsions to local school officials under the legal standards of constitutional case law emanating from *Goss v. Lopez*, above.

Other states have detailed procedures that establish strict timelines to follow and rights to be given students including the right to review the evidence and know the names of witnesses before the expulsion hearing and the right to an attorney and to cross examine witnesses at the hearing (some states like Illinois and Indiana refer to the hearing as a "meeting"). For example, in 1971 Indiana established a complex and elaborate student due process code with extensive student rights, but in 1995 repealed it and adopted a hybrid code that kept part of the prior law and, yet, simplified the procedures and removed such statutory rights as having an attorney at the hearing and cross examining witnesses.

Regardless of a particular state's expulsion statute, courts are faced with the constitutional issue of the amount of process that is due before a school expels a student. In a case upholding a Wisconsin student's permanent expulsion from school for participating in a conspiracy to bring a gun to school to shoot other students (the planned act never happened), *Remer v. Burlington Area Sch. Dist.*, 286 F.3d 1007, 1010-1011 (7th Cir. 2002), the court stated (emphasis added):

> ...Having provided for the right to education, Wisconsin "may not withdraw that right on grounds of misconduct, absent fundamentally fair procedures to determine whether the misconduct has occurred." Goss v. Lopez, . . . To comport with due process, **expulsion procedures must provide the student with a meaningful opportunity to be heard**. *Linwood v. Bd. of Educ.*, 463 F.2d 763, 769-70 (7th Cir. 1972). **The proceedings need not, however, "take the form of a judicial or quasi-judicial trial."** Id. at 770. As long as the student is given notice of the charges against him, notice of the time of the hearing and a full opportunity to be heard, the expulsion procedures do not offend due process requirements. *Betts v. Bd. of Educ.*, 466 F.2d 629, 633 (7th Cir.1972).

C. Expulsion Procedural Due Process Considerations

Absent a given state's specific requirements regarding such procedural due process issues as pre-hearing review of the evidence and learning identity of witnesses before the hearing, introduction of hearsay, cross examining witnesses, and having an attorney present at the expulsion hearing, the school is required to follow the Fourteenth Amendment's Due Process Clause as interpreted by the courts.

In assessing the sufficiency of procedural due process in student expulsion cases, courts have applied the balancing-of-interests legal standard set by the United States Supreme Court in the non-school case of *Mathews v. Eldridge*, 424 U.S. 319 (1976). The *Mathews* Court stated at 334-335 (emphasis added):

> . . . These decisions underscore the truism that "'[d]ue process,' unlike some legal rules, is not a technical conception with a fixed content unrelated to time, place and circumstances." . . . **"[D]ue process is flexible and calls for such procedural protections as the particular situation demands."** *Morrissey v. Brewer*, . . . (1972). Accordingly, resolution of the issue whether the administrative procedures provided here are constitutionally sufficient **requires analysis of the governmental and private interests that are affected.** . . . More precisely, our prior decisions indicate that identification of the specific dictates of due process generally **requires consideration of three distinct factors**: **First, the private interest** that will be affected by the official action; **second, the risk of an erroneous deprivation** of such interest through the procedures used, and the probable value, if any, of additional or substitute procedural safeguards; and **finally, the Government's interest**, including the function involved and the fiscal and administrative burdens that the additional or substitute procedural requirement would entail. . . .

D. *Identity of Accusers and Cross Examination*

The case below is an example of a case involving sexual misconduct and the rationale for not identifying the names of students accusing the perpetrator.

In the case of *B.S. ex rel Schneider v. Board of School Trustees*, 255 F.Supp. 2d 891 (N.D.Ind. 2003), the court applied the *Mathews v. Eldridge* balancing test in upholding the expulsion of a student who alleged that his procedural due process rights were violated when school officials refused to permit him to review documents before the hearing, give him the names of his accusers, and allow him to cross examine them at the expulsion hearing. His expulsion was based on alleged sexual activity wherein the primary accuser's name was kept confidential and her written statement, made under oath, was presented at the hearing by the administrator who testified as to what the administrator was told by her. Said the court at 898-901 (emphasis added):

> As to the first *Mathews* factor, there is no dispute that B.S. has an important interest at stake in this case. . . . However, the second *Mathews* factor, the risk of an erroneous deprivation of that interest through the procedures employed, is very low and weighs in favor of the Defendants. . . **[T]he clear weight of authority holds that a student facing an expulsion hearing does not have the right to cross-examine witnesses or even learn their identities.** *See, e.g., Newsome* [*v. Batavia Local School Dist.*, 842 F.2d 920 (6th Cir. 1988)]. . . .
>
> This conclusion stems from the recognition that while the "value of cross-examination to the discovery of the truth cannot be overemphasized," in the school discipline context,
>
> [t]he value of cross-examining student witnesses . . . is somewhat muted by the fact that **the veracity of a student account of misconduct by another student is initially assessed by a school administrator . . . who has, or has available to him, a particularized knowledge of the student's trustworthiness**. . . . Consequently, the process of cross-examining the student witness may often be merely duplicative of the evaluation process undertaken by the investigating school administrator.
>
> *Newsome*, 842 F.2d at 924. . . . Thus, under the *Mathews* framework, the risk of an erroneous deprivation was very low.
>
> Turning to the third *Mathews* factor, we must weigh the value of providing B.S. with the names of undisclosed accusers, their statements, and possible cross-examination, against the burden that such practices would place on the school administration. . . As several courts have previously noted, **in light of the increasing challenges schools face in maintaining order and discipline, requiring schools to permit the confrontation of student witnesses or even to disclose their identities in expulsion hearings would be overly- burdensome and unrealistic. . .The purposes behind the administrative expulsion process, and the expulsion hearing itself, is to**

avoid the formalistic trappings and cost of adversarial litigation . . . (expulsion proceeding need not take the form of a "judicial or quasi-judicial trial"). It merely states the obvious to suggest that formalized disciplinary proceedings would increase cost and complexity. . . .

Furthermore, FWCS [the school defendant] **has a strong interest in protecting students who report classmate misconduct.** "Those students may be understandably reluctant to come forward with information if they are faced with the prospect of formal cross examination by the offending student or his attorney," . . . or the unsettling prospect of ostracism or even physical reprisals at the hands of their peers . . . ([w]ithout the cloak of anonymity, students who witness [misconduct] will be much less likely to notify school authorities. . . .

Thus, in balancing the various *Mathews* factors, the Defendant's interests in avoiding administrative burdens associated with more formalized expulsion proceedings and protecting student witnesses greatly outweigh the little value derived from providing B.S. with the names of his accusers, their written statements, and the opportunity to cross examine them. "The question presented here is not whether the hearing was ideal, or whether its procedure could have been better. Rather, in all cases, the inquiry is whether, under the particular circumstances presented, the hearing was fair, and accorded the individual with the essential elements of due process." . . . We conclude, based on the facts in this case, that the Defendants afforded B.S. with a full and fair opportunity to be heard. . . .

The case below discusses the rationale for non-violation of 14th amendment due process when the student facing expulsion is prevented from knowing the identity of the accusers.

The case of *Newsome v. Batavia Local Sch. Dist.*, 842 F.2d 290 (6th Cir. 1988), that involved the expulsion of a high school student for possession and attempted sale of marijuana, is often cited due to its assessment that constitutional due process is not violated when a student facing expulsion is prevented from knowing the identity of his/her accusers and from cross examining them. The court at 924-925 stated:

. . . The school administrator generally knows firsthand . . . the accusing student's disciplinary history, which can serve as a valuable gauge in evaluating the believability of the student's account. Additionally, the school administrator often knows, or can readily discover, whether the student witness and the accused have had an amicable relationship in the past. Consequently, the process of cross-examining the student witness may often be merely duplicative of the evaluation process undertaken by the investigating school administrator. . . .

Giving due weight to the important interest a student accused of serious misconduct has in his public education, we conclude that the necessity of protecting student witnesses from ostracism and reprisal outweighs the value to the truth-determining process of allowing the accused student to cross-examine his accusers.

The *Newsome* court also found that there is not a procedural due process right to cross examine the administrators who present evidence at the expulsion hearing, and stated at 925-926 (emphasis added):

We hold that the burden of cross-examination on the administration of school discipline outweighs the benefits to be derived from the process. . . . **School boards and administrations are not quasi-judicial** . . . To saddle them with the burden of overseeing the process of cross-examination (and the innumerable objections that are raised to the form and content of cross-examination) is to require of them that which they are ill-equipped to perform. The detriment that will accrue to the educational process in general by diverting school board members' and school administrators' attention from their primary responsibilities in overseeing the educational process to learning and applying the common law rules of evidence simply outweighs the marginal benefit that will accrue to the fact finding process by allowing cross-examination.

E. Waivers

The issue of the ability of the parent and student to waive statutory and constitutional due process rights was addressed in the case of Porter v. Ascension Parish School Board, 393 F. 3d 608 (5th Cir. 2004) (emphasis added) where the court stated at pages 623-625:

. . . Adam's third claim alleges that he was denied his procedural due process right to a hearing before being removed from EAHS. Students have a "legitimate entitlement to a public education as a property interest which is protected by the Due Process Clause and which may not be taken away for misconduct without adherence to the minimum procedures required by . . . [the Due Process] Clause."

At a minimum, "students facing suspension and the consequent interference with a protected property interest must be given some kind of notice and afforded some kind of hearing." Adam had no formal hearing before the Ascension Parish School Board before being removed from EAHS and transferred to the alternative school. But, Adam had admitted to school officials his responsibility for the drawing as well as his ownership of the box cutter. Whether a student "admitted the charges" leveled against him is "relevant in determining substantial prejudice or harm." This is so because one of the primary purposes of expulsion hearings is that of confirming whether the student threatened with expulsion actually committed the conduct for which he is being punished. Once a student has admitted his guilt, the need for a hearing is substantially lessened.

In addition to Adam's admission, his **mother signed a written waiver of his right to a hearing. A parent may waive her child's due process rights to notice and a hearing prior to expulsion, provided that the waiver is made voluntarily, knowingly and intelligently**. In the context of school disciplinary hearings, **a waiver has been considered effective when it was placed in writing after a student's parents consulted with an attorney, was signed after all potential repercussions and consequences had been rationally evaluated, and stated in several places that the student was entitled to a hearing**.

Mary LeBlanc signed a form waiving Adam's right to a hearing after discussing the matter with Ascension Parish School Board hearing officer Linda Lamendola. LeBlanc had been told by school officials that her son was entitled to a hearing. She was presented with a range of options and probable outcomes by Lamendola, including the option of pursuing a hearing, which Lamendola indicated had little chance of success, and the option of waiving her right to a hearing and enrolling her son immediately in the alternative school. After weighing the alternatives, LeBlanc made a rational decision to waive the hearing and enroll Adam in the alternative school. Based on this evidence in the record, Adam's contention that his mother's waiver was made involuntarily is without merit. . . .

F.   *Transfers to Alternative Programs Do Not Violate Due Process*

The following case sets the legal standard identifying that sending a student to an alternative program as a disciplinary measure does not violate the student's due process.

CASE

Nevares v. San Marcos Consol. Indep. Sch. Dist., 111 F. 3d 25
(5th Cir. 1997) (emphasis added)

The district court has declared a Texas statute unconstitutional because it does not expressly mandate that the school afford a proper hearing for a student charged with off-campus conduct punishable as a felony prior to transferring the student to an alternative education program. . .

[**Facts:**] High school student Timothy Nevares sued the San Marcos Independent School District challenging his transfer to the Rebound alternative education program and the constitutionality of Texas Educ. Code §37.006(a). . . .

Timothy Nevares, a 15 year old tenth grade student, was detained for aggravated assault on January 23, 1996 by the San Marcos police. He reportedly threw stones at a car and injured one of the passengers. On February 12, 1996, the school received the police report of Nevares' detention and the assistant principal took Nevares from class to question him. Nevares refused to make any statement at this meeting other than to tell the school authorities to contact his father and lawyer, saying they were getting the matter dismissed.

Thereafter, Nevares' father called the school principal, admitted that the act in question had occurred but maintained that his son's behavior had been in self-defense, and requested a meeting to discuss the situation before the school took any action. The principal explained that according to school regulations, once there was reason to believe an aggravated assault had been committed, Timothy would be reassigned to the alternative education program. When the principal confirmed with the juvenile authorities that the aggravated assault charge on Nevares was still pending, he decided to transfer Timothy to the Rebound program. Nevares promptly sued. ...

[Rationale:] The Supreme Court has held that the suspension from school without some kind of notice and hearing may violate property and liberty interests. [*Goss v. Lopez*] The state statute to which the Court pointed in *Goss* gave students the entitlement to a public education. Timothy Nevares is not being denied access to public education, not even temporarily. He was only to be transferred from one school program to another program with stricter discipline. This alternative program is maintained by Texas schools for those students whose violations of the law or the school's code of conduct fall short of triggering suspension or expulsion, but who for reasons of safety and order must be removed from the regular classroom.

Today it is generally recognized that students are being deprived of their education by lack of discipline in the schools. Not only does disorder interfere with learning school studies, it also defeats the charge to "inculcate the habits and manners of civility." *Veronia School District 479 v. Acton.*

We have previously held that no protected property interest is implicated in a school's denial to offer a student a particular curriculum. In *Arundar*, a high school student had claimed that her property right to education was implicated when she was denied enrollment in certain courses of study. We affirmed the district court's dismissal of the case and held that although state law could create a protected interest in a particular kind of education, for example by mandating special education for exceptional children, absent such a basis in state law, there was no cause of action. **This court has also rejected arguments that there is any protected interest in the separate components of the educational process, such as participation in interscholastic athletics.**

The Tenth Circuit has held that a student does not have a constitutional right to particular incidents of education such as sports or advanced placement classes or attending a particular school. [*Seamons v. Snow*, 84 F.3d 1226, 1234-1235 (10th Cir. 1996).] **A transfer to a different school for disciplinary reasons has also been held not to support the court's jurisdiction on constitutional**

grounds. [*Zamora v. Pomeroy,* 639 F.2d 662, 669-670 (10th Cir. 1981).]

We recognize the importance of trust and confidence between students and school administrators. For that reason the student and parents must be treated fairly and given the opportunity to explain why anticipated assignments may not be warranted. But that is for Texas and the local schools to do.

[Court ruling:] We would not aid matters by relegating the dispute to federal litigation. And because the United States Constitution has not been offended in the present dispute, we retire from it.

Judgment reversed. Case dismissed.

Note: Regarding regulation of conduct off school property, some states, like Texas, provide by statute that certain off-school conduct by students may lead to removal from the regular curriculum. Other states are silent, and when the issue of a school's ability to suspend, expel, or transfer a student to another program arise, courts generally uphold the school if the facts indicate that the off-school conduct interferes with school activities or purposes, such as drug sales to other students or showing disrespect to a school teacher or administrator. One state, Indiana, requires the off-school conduct to be both "unlawful" and to interfere with school purposes or functions, or indicate the need to remove the student in order to restore order or protect persons on school property.

II. SUBSTANTIVE DUE PROCESS

Although school officials may perfectly apply the procedural requirements of state code and state and federal constitutional due process, courts have established the doctrine of substantive due process wherein they examine if the discipline applied to the student is reasonable and fair in light of all the particular circumstances of the situation. Courts generally find for the school if there is evidence of a rational relationship between the punishment given and the misconduct of the student. An example of a lack of a rational basis would be in the situation where a school has a clear rule requiring obedience to a teacher's directive, the failure of which could lead to suspension or expulsion from school; but if a one-time disobedient act of a sixth-grader chewing bubble gum would lead to a year's expulsion from school for that reason alone, the court would likely find a substantive due process violation regardless of the procedural requirements having been followed.

A. Unreasonable Official Conduct That Shocks the Conscience

The following case discusses the legal standard for unreasonable official conduct that shocks the conscience.

CASE
Dunn v. Fairfield Comm. High Sch. Dist. No. 225, 158 F.3d 962
(7th Cir. 1998) (emphasis added)

[Facts:]   Shaun Dunn and Bill McCullough were both budding musicians who participated as guitar players in the high school band program at Fairfield Community High School. . . Fairfield prohibited its band members from departing from the planned musical program during band performances, and it specifically forbade guitar solos during the performances. In direct defiance of those rules and their teacher's explicit orders, Dunn and McCullough . . . played two unauthorized guitar pieces . . . at a band program. In due course, the discipline they received for this infraction caused them both to receive an "F" for the band course, and that "F" prevented McCullough from graduating with honors. . . .

There is little more to the underlying story than the facts we have just outlined. During the 1995-96 school year, Dunn and McCullough were students at Fairfield and were enrolled in the Band class. One class requirement was to perform at various school-wide events, including home basketball games. Fairfield's grading policy for the Band class assigned a certain number of points to the different components of the course. That policy was prepared by the band instructor, filed with the school principal, and disseminated to each student in the class. It read as follows:

[Grading Policy:]   . . .Your conduct at performances is expected to be of the highest standard. We want to look, sound and be professional at all times--anything less is unacceptable. Performance conduct that is not of the highest standard will be dealt with severely. Possible disciplinary actions range from loss of all points for the performance to lowering of the final grade to dismissal from the band. . . .

In the face of both these general warnings and more specific admonishments from both School Principal Rena Talbert and Band Director Charlotte McGill, Dunn and McCullough decided to play their unauthorized guitar songs at the . . . band performance during a home basketball game. As they were doing so, McGill was shouting at them to stop, but they ignored her. Dunn and McCullough both testified in their depositions that they realized the songs were verboten and that they expected some form of punishment. McCullough explained the action as a form of protest against the school's rumored decision to remove guitars from the band.

When punishment came, it was far more severe than either student had anticipated. It began . . . with McGill's decision not to award them any performance points for the . . . event. Matters did not stop there, however. McGill evidently referred the matter to Principal Talbert, who decided that Dunn and McCullough had been guilty of disrespect to faculty and staff, which was a Classification III, subparagraph A6 violation of school rules. (Fairfield classified student misconduct into three categories, with Classification I being the most serious and Classification III the least. A student committing a Classification III offense could be removed from class for either academic misconduct (e.g., failure to complete homework) or nonacademic misconduct (e.g., possession of tobacco products).) As a penalty, Talbert decided to remove the two students from Band class for the remainder of the school year and to prohibit them from attending any more home basketball games for that year.

Because of the way the grading policy operated for Band class, this proved to be an exceptionally severe penalty. The prohibition against attending class meant that Dunn and McCullough could not earn any class points for the rest of the year, nor could they earn performance points or evaluation points. Not surprisingly, the number of points they had earned up until the ill-fated . . . performance was not enough to carry the day for them, and so both received final grades of "F" for the course. Both students graduated, although as we noted above, the "F" in Band prevented McCullough from doing so with honors, and the briefs inform us that both are now attending the Atlanta Institute of Music and hope eventually to have a career in music. . . .

[Issue:] The students' complaint alleged that Fairfield had violated their constitutional rights in two ways: first, that it violated their "right to substantive due process . . . by imposing disciplinary measures unrelated to academic conduct and . . . outside the parameters and intent of the Illinois School Code and [Fairfield's] disciplinary policy," . . .

The fundamental flaw in their theory of the case arises from their failure to appreciate the difference between the procedural protections afforded by the Fourteenth Amendment against state deprivations and the far more limited substantive standards that Amendment imposes on state actors. If this had been a case (as it is not) in which Dunn and McCullough had complained that Fairfield threw them out of Band class and effectively condemned them to an "F" in the course without giving them some kind of notice and a hearing, we would delve into the nature of the property interest Illinois law creates in a public education. Assuming a protectible interest exists, . . . we would then assess Fairfield's procedures under the standard framework described in *Mathews v. Eldridge*, 424 U.S. 319 (1976).

But that is not the students' claim. Instead, they assert that the federal Constitution places substantive restrictions on the type of disciplinary measures public school districts may use for conceded violations of rules of student conduct. At some extreme, that is certainly true; the question here is where the outer boundaries lie. The students seem to think that federal constitutional protection is co-extensive with the right recognized under Illinois law to a free public education through the end of high school. The Supreme Court's recent decision in *County of Sacramento v. Lewis*, 118 S.Ct. 1708 (1998), definitively shows that they are wrong. . . .

The Supreme Court rejected the Lewis's' claim in an opinion that **emphasized once again how limited the scope of the substantive due process doctrine is**. . . In so doing, it relied on two independent grounds: first, . . . and second, that "in any event the allegations are insufficient to state a substantive due process violation through executive abuse of power." . . .

The touchstone of due process, the Court explained, **is "protection of the individual against arbitrary action of government,"** . . . whether the problem is the denial of fundamental procedural fairness or **the exercise of governmental power without any reasonable justification**. The criteria that govern what is fatally arbitrary in the latter cases depend upon whether legislation or a specific act of a governmental officer is at issue.

In *Lewis*, the focus was on the specific act of a governmental officer, and in those cases, the Court said that **"only the most egregious official conduct" is arbitrary in the constitutional sense**. . . At least since *Rochin v. California*, . . . (1952), **the Court has looked for an abuse of power that "shocks the conscience"**; it reaffirmed that benchmark in *Lewis*. Looked at from the opposite point of view, the Court reiterated that "the due process guarantee does not entail a body of constitutional law imposing liability whenever someone cloaked with state authority causes harm." . . .

One is tempted to say that if a police officer's "precipitate recklessness," which caused the deprivation of someone's life, was not sufficiently shocking to satisfy substantive due process standards, then it would be nearly absurd to say that a school principal's decision effectively to give two students an "F" in Band class did. It may be worth acknowledging that this in no way necessarily implies approval of the state official's action; we are certain that no member of the Supreme Court thought in hindsight that the police officer in Lewis had responded prudently to the young motorcycle speeders, and we may have similar doubts about the wisdom of the severity of Fairfield's sanctions against the rebel musicians here. . . .

The **substantive component of the clause**, the Court explained, **"provides heightened protection against governmental interference with certain fundamental rights and liberty interests,"** including things like the right to marry, to have children, to direct the education and upbringing of one's children, to marital privacy, to use contraception, to bodily integrity, and to choose an abortion. . . Once again, measured by that standard the school policy that the students attack comes nowhere close to a constitutional violation. **Although students may have some substantive due process rights while they are in school, . . . education itself is not a fundamental right**, see *San Antonio Indep. Schl. Dist. v. Rodriguez*, ___ (1973). That means that Fairfield's decision to stack the deck so that these students would fail Band must be sustained unless it is **wholly arbitrary**.

Here, however, Dunn and McCullough freely conceded that they had violated a school rule, that the rule was designed to preserve discipline in the classroom and to punish student insubordination, and that these were legitimate interests on the part of the school district. That alone is enough to show that their claim cannot possibly succeed. **The Constitution does not guarantee these or any other students the right not to receive an "F" in a course from which they were excluded because of misbehavior**. . . .

[Court ruling:] For these reasons, we Affirm the judgment of the district court.

Notes:

1. As indicated in the *Dunn* case, substantive due process is limited in scope and narrowly applied. The doctrine is designed to prevent the irrational, arbitrary application of governmental power and is generally satisfied if there is some evidence showing a rational basis for the government's action. However, some federal circuit courts now appear to be requiring a plaintiff to prove that the government's conduct is so unreasonable and arbitrary that it shocks the conscience.

2. Where a 10-year-old special education student alleged a violation of his substantive due process rights when a teacher on the mistaken belief that he had deliberately stuffed up a toilet made him clean it out with his bare hands, the court found that the teacher's actions were not sufficiently excessive to shock the conscience. In *Harris v. Robinson*, 273 F.2d 927, 930 (10th Cir. 2001) the court stated that "the substantive due process inquiry is 'whether the force applied caused injury so severe, was so disproportionate to the need presented, and was so inspired by malice or sadism rather than a merely careless or unwise excess of zeal that it amounted to a brutal and inhumane abuse of official power literally shocking to the conscience.'"

3. Where a teacher was alleged to have verbally harassed a seventh-grade student by frequently calling her "stupid," "retarded," and "dumb" in front of other students, the court, while commenting that the teacher's conduct was "singularly unprofessional," stated that the girl and her parents had "not raised a genuine issue of material fact on whether his behavior was sufficiently shocking to the conscience to state a substantive due process claim." *Costello v. Mitchell Public School Dist. 79*, 79 F.3d 916, 921 (8th Cir. 2001). Also see, *S.M. v. Lakeland Sch. Dist.*, 148 F.Supp. 2d 542 (M.D. Pa. 2001), where the court found that a fifth grade teacher's alleged repeated yelling at female student for her inability to solve a math problem at the chalk board, which caused her to flee the room crying and to develop hives and a nervous stomach, was not sufficiently conscience shocking to violate substantive due process.

4. In a case involving the expulsion of a student under a zero tolerance policy for possession of a knife, where the record showed he had no knowledge of the knife's presence in the glove compartment of his mother's car that he had driven to school, the court held, on substantive due process grounds, that summary judgment for the school could not stand and remanded to the trial court for a determination of what basis the school expelled him. *Seal v. Morgan*, 229 F.3d 567 (6thCir. 2000). The court in applying a rational basis, rather than a shocking to conscience, rationale, said at 575-576:

. . .[S]uspending or expelling a student for weapons possession, even if the student did not knowingly possess any weapon, would not be rationally related to any legitimate state interest. No student can use a weapon to injure another person, to disrupt school operations, or, for that matter, any other purpose if the student is totally unaware of its presence. Indeed, the entire concept of possession—in the sense of possession for which the state can legitimately prescribe and mete out punishment—ordinarily implies knowing or conscious possession. . . .

B. Corporal Punishment

The following case discusses questions regarding corporal punishment in the school.

CASE
Ingraham v. Wright, 430 U.S. 651 (1977) (emphasis added)

This case presents questions concerning the use of corporal punishment in public schools: First, whether the paddling of students as a means of maintaining school discipline constitutes cruel and unusual punishment in violation of the Eighth Amendment; and, second, to the extent that paddling is constitutionally permissible, whether the Due Process Clause of the Fourteenth Amendment requires prior notice and an opportunity to be heard. . . .

[**Facts:**] Petitioners' evidence may be summarized briefly. In the 1970-1971 school year many of the 237 schools in Dade County used corporal punishment as a means of maintaining discipline pursuant to Florida legislation and a local School Board regulation. The statute then in effect authorized limited corporal punishment by negative inference, proscribing punishment which was "degrading or unduly severe" or which was inflicted without prior consultation with the principal or the teacher in charge of the school. . . .

The authorized punishment consisted of paddling the recalcitrant student on the buttocks with a flat wooden paddle measuring less than two feet long, three to four inches wide, and about one-half inch thick. The normal punishment was limited to one to five "licks" or blows with the paddle and resulted in no apparent physical injury to the student.

School authorities viewed corporal punishment as a less drastic means of discipline than suspension or expulsion. Contrary to the procedural requirements of the statute and regulation, teachers often paddled students on their own authority without first consulting the principal.

Petitioners focused on Drew Junior High School, the school in which both Ingraham and Andrews were enrolled in the fall of 1970. . . Because he was slow to respond to his teacher's instructions, Ingraham was subjected to more than 20 licks with a paddle while being held over a table in the principal's office. The paddling was so severe that he suffered a hematoma requiring medical attention and keeping him out of school for several days. Andrews was paddled several times for minor infractions. On two occasions he was struck on his arms, once depriving him of the full use of his arm for a week. . . .

[**Issues:**] The Fourteenth Amendment prohibits any state deprivation of life, liberty, or property without due process of law. Application of this prohibition requires the familiar two-stage analysis: We must first ask whether the asserted individual interests are encompassed within the Fourteenth Amendment's protection of "life, liberty or property"; if protected interests are implicated, we then must decide what procedures constitute "due process of law." . . . Following that analysis here, **we** find that corporal punishment in public schools implicates a constitutionally protected liberty interest, but we hold that the traditional common-law remedies are fully adequate to afford due process. . . .

This constitutionally protected liberty interest is at stake in this case. There is, of course, a de minimus level of imposition with which the Constitution is not concerned. But at least where school authorities, acting under color of state law, deliberately decide to punish a child for misconduct by restraining the child and inflicting appreciable physical pain, we hold that Fourteenth Amendment liberty interests are implicated. . . .

Whether in this case the common-law remedies for excessive corporal punishment constitute due process of law must turn on an analysis of the competing interests at stake, viewed against the background of "history, reason, [and] the past course of decisions."

The analysis requires consideration of three distinct factors: "First, the private interest that will be affected . . .; second, the risk of an erroneous deprivation of such interest . . . and the probable value, if any, of additional or substitute procedural safeguards; and finally, the [state] interest, including the function involved and the fiscal and administrative burdens that the additional or substitute procedural requirement would entail." Mathews v. Eldridge, . . .

The concept that reasonable corporal punishment in school is justifiable continues to be recognized in the laws of most States . . . It represents "the balance struck by this country," . . . between the child's interest in personal security and the traditional view that some limited corporal punishment may be necessary in the course of a child's education. Under that longstanding accommodation of interests, there can be no deprivation of substantive rights as long as disciplinary corporal punishment is within the limits of the common-law privilege.

This is not to say that the child's interest in procedural safeguards is insubstantial. The school disciplinary process is not "a totally accurate, unerring process, never mistaken and never unfair. . . ." *Goss v. Lopez,* . . . In any deliberate infliction of corporal punishment on a child who is restrained for that purpose, there is some risk that the intrusion on the child's liberty will be unjustified and therefore unlawful. In these circumstances the child has a strong interest in procedural safeguards that minimize the risk of wrongful punishment and provide for the resolution of disputed questions of justification. . . .

[Rationale:] But even if the need for advance procedural safeguards were clear, **the question would remain whether the incremental benefit could justify the cost**. Acceptance of petitioners' claims would work a transformation in the law governing corporal punishment in Florida and most other States. Given the impracticability of formulating a rule of procedural due process that varies with the severity of the particular imposition, the prior hearing petitioners seek would have to precede any paddling, however moderate or trivial.

Such a universal constitutional requirement would significantly burden the use of corporal punishment as a disciplinary measure. Hearings – even informal hearings – require time, personnel, and a diversion of attention from normal school pursuits. School authorities may well choose to abandon corporal punishment rather than incur the burdens of complying with the procedural requirements. Teachers, properly concerned with maintaining authority in the classroom, may well prefer to rely on other disciplinary measures - which they may view as less effective - rather than confront the possible disruption that prior notice and a hearing may entail. Paradoxically, such an alteration of disciplinary policy is most likely to occur in the ordinary case where the contemplated punishment is well within the common-law privilege. . . .

"At some point the benefit of an additional safeguard to the individual affected . . . and to society in terms of increased assurance that the action is just, may be outweighed by the cost." *Mathews v. Eldridge* . . . We think that point has been reached in this case. In view of the low incidence of abuse, the openness of our schools, and the common-law safeguards that already exist, the risk of error that may result in violation of a schoolchild's substantive rights can only be regarded as minimal. Imposing additional administrative safeguards as a constitutional requirement might reduce that risk marginally, but would also entail a significant intrusion into an area of primary educational responsibility.

[Court conclusions:] We conclude that the Due Process Clause does not require notice and a hearing prior to the imposition of corporal punishment in the public schools, as that practice is authorized and limited by the common law.

Petitioners cannot prevail on either of the theories before us in this case. The Eighth Amendment's prohibition against cruel and unusual punishment is inapplicable to school paddling, and the Fourteenth Amendment's requirement of procedural due process is satisfied by Florida's preservation of common-law constraints and remedies. We therefore agree with the Court of Appeals that petitioners' evidence affords no basis for injunctive relief, and that petitioners cannot recover damages on the basis of any Eighth Amendment or procedural due process violation. Affirmed.

Notes: 1. The Sixth Circuit in the case of *Saylor v. Board of Education of Harlan County, Kentucky*, 118 F.3d 507, 514 (6thCir. 1997) found no violation of substantive due process and upheld the corporal punishment of an eighth grade boy who had received five swats on the buttocks with a paddle, and stated:

Substantive due process decisions cannot turn on whether ten licks as opposed to five licks would be excessive, for example; substantive due process, the court indicated, is concerned with violations of bodily security of an altogether different order of magnitude. *Id* . Nonetheless, said the court, some tortuous school punishments may be "so brutal, demeaning and harmful," so "literally outrageous," as to violate the student's Fourteenth Amendment rights - and in this connection, *Hall* declared, "the substantive due process inquiry . . . must be whether the force applied caused injury so severe, was so disproportionate to the need presented, and was so inspired by malice or sadism rather than a merely careless or unwise excess of zeal that it amounted to a brutal and inhumane abuse of official power literally shocking to the conscience." *Id.* [Quoting *Hall v. Tawney*, 621 F.2d 607, 613 (4th Cir. 1980).]

2. The Tenth Circuit in *Garcia by Garcia v. Miera*, 817 F.2d 650 (10thCir. 1987), overturned the trial court's summary judgment in favor of the school and ruled that the evidence of two brutal beatings of an elementary school girl (the first when she was nine years old and held upside down by her ankles and struck with a split paddle that drew blood and produced a permanent scar, and the second when she was 10 and paddled so severely that she suffered pain for three weeks) was sufficient to remand the case for a trial to consider whether the corporal punishment was so grossly excessive as to shock the conscience and subject the school administrators involved to liability for violation of substantive due process rights.

C. *Void-for-Vagueness Doctrine*

Student conduct rules are frequently attacked under the void-for-vagueness doctrine which is a component of both procedural and substantive due process. A basic criterion of procedural due process is adequate or fair notice to those affected by governmental regulations of what conduct is prohibited. The Supreme Court has stated that a regulation is void due to vagueness when it "forbids or requires the doing of an act in terms so vague that [persons] of common intelligence must necessarily guess at its meaning and differ as to its application. . . ." *Connally v. General Construction Co.*, 269 U.S. 385, 391. (1926). The substantive due process component involves whether the regulation is so vague that it permits governmental officials to enforce it in either an arbitrary or discriminatory manner. *Grayned v. City of Rockford*, 408 U.S. 104, 108 (1972).

In the case of *Stephenson v. Davenport Community Sch. Dist.*, 110 F.3d 1303 (8th Cir. 1997), the court invalidated, due to vagueness, a school rule which stated that "[g]ang related activities such as display of 'colors,' symbols, signals, etc., will not be tolerated on school grounds. Students in violation will be suspended from school and/or recommended to the Board for expulsion." Student Stephenson had a small cross tattooed between her thumb and index finger while an eighth grader and wore it for 30 months when the school adopted the gang-activity policy due to increased gang activity. The school, after consulting with law enforcement, considered the tattoo cross a gang symbol, and even though there was no evidence that she was involved in gang activity, it threatened her with expulsion if she did not have it removed or altered. She had it surgically removed, but the process left a permanent scar.

The *Stephenson* court, due to (1) lack of a sufficiently specific definition in common usage of the term "gang" and (2) the absence of definition by the school district stated that "the district regulation violates the central purposes of the vagueness doctrine because it fails to provide adequate notice regarding unacceptable conduct and fails to offer clear guidance for those who apply it. A person of common intelligence must necessarily guess at the undefined meaning of gang related activities." *Id.* at 1311.

D. Due Process in Relation to Grades and Course Credits

D1. Academic Sanctions

When a student does not meet academic standards and the teacher makes a rational academic judgment that a failing grade be received for the course, there is no question of any constitutional process being due. Since education is not deemed a fundamental right under the United States Constitution, public schools need only have a rational, non-arbitrary basis for their decisions that impact a student's academic performance when the student alleges a violation of property and liberty interests, either via procedural or substantive due process.

CASE
Board of Curators of University of Missouri v. Horowitz,
435 U.S. 78 (1978) (emphasis added)

Respondent, a student at the University of Missouri-Kansas City Medical School, was dismissed by petitioner officials of the school during her final year of study for failure to meet academic standards . . . We granted certiorari . . . to consider what procedures must be accorded to a student at a state educational institution whose dismissal may constitute a deprivation of "liberty" or "property" within the meaning of the Fourteenth Amendment. . . .

[Facts:] Each student's academic performance at the School is evaluated on a periodic basis by the Council on Evaluation, a body composed of both faculty and students, which can recommend various actions including probation and dismissal. The recommendations of the Council are reviewed by the Coordinating Committee, a body composed solely of faculty members, and must ultimately be approved by the Dean. Students are not typically allowed to appear before either the Council or the Coordinating Committee on the occasion of their review of the student's academic performance. . . .

The Council met again in mid-May to consider whether respondent should be allowed to remain in school beyond June of that year. Noting that the report on respondent's recent surgery rotation rated her performance as "low-satisfactory," the Council unanimously recommended that barring receipt of any reports that Miss Horowitz has improved radically, [she] not be allowed to re-enroll in the . . . School of Medicine. The Council delayed making its recommendation official until receiving reports on other rotations; when a report on respondent's emergency rotation also turned out to be negative, the Council unanimously reaffirmed its recommendation that respondent be dropped from the school. The Coordinating Committee and the Dean approved the recommendation and notified respondent, who appealed the decision in writing to the University's Provost for Health Sciences. The Provost sustained the school's actions after reviewing the record compiled during the earlier proceedings.

[Issue:] To be entitled to the procedural protections of the Fourteenth Amendment, respondent must in a case such as this demonstrate that her dismissal from the school deprived her of either a "liberty" or a "property" interest. Respondent has never alleged that she was deprived of a property interest. Because property interests are creatures of state law, *Perry v. Sindermann,* . . . (1972), respondent would have been required to show at trial that her seat at the Medical School was a "property" interest recognized by Missouri state law. Instead, respondent argued that her dismissal deprived her of "liberty" by substantially impairing her opportunities to continue her medical education or to return to employment in a medically related field. . . .

We need not decide, however, whether respondent's dismissal deprived her of a liberty interest in pursuing a medical career. Nor need we decide whether respondent's dismissal infringed any other interest constitutionally protected against deprivation without procedural due process. Assuming the existence of a liberty or property interest, respondent has been awarded at least as much due process as the Fourteenth Amendment requires. The school fully informed respondent of the faculty's dissatisfaction with her clinical progress and the danger that this posed to timely graduation and continued enrollment. The ultimate decision to dismiss respondent was careful and deliberate. These procedures were sufficient under the Due Process Clause of the Fourteenth Amendment. We agree with the District Court that respondent

> was afforded full procedural due process by the [school]. In fact, the Court is of the opinion, and so finds, that the school went beyond [constitutionally required] procedural due process by affording [respondent] the opportunity to be examined by seven independent physicians in order to be absolutely certain that their grading of the [respondent] in her medical skills was correct. . . .

[Rationale:] In *Goss v. Lopez,* . . . (1975), we held that due process requires, in connection with the suspension of a student from public school for disciplinary reasons, "that the student be given oral or written notice of the charges against him and, if he denies them, an explanation of the evidence the authorities have and an opportunity to present his side of the story." . . . But we have frequently emphasized that "[t]he very nature of due process negates any concept of inflexible procedures universally applicable to every imaginable situation." . . . **The need for flexibility is well illustrated by the significant difference between the failure of a student to meet academic standards and the violation by a student of valid rules of conduct. This difference calls for far less stringent procedural requirements in the case of an academic dismissal.**

Since the issue first arose 50 years ago, state and lower federal courts have recognized that there are distinct differences between decisions to suspend or dismiss a student for disciplinary purposes and similar actions taken for academic reasons which may call for hearings in connection with the former but not the latter. . . .

Reason, furthermore, clearly supports the perception of these decisions. A school is an academic institution, not a courtroom or administrative hearing room. . . .

Academic evaluations of a student, in contrast to disciplinary determinations, bear little resemblance to the judicial and administrative fact finding proceedings to which we have traditionally attached a full-hearing requirement. In *Goss*, the school's decision to suspend the students rested on factual conclusions that the individual students had participated in demonstrations that had disrupted classes, attacked a police officer, or caused physical damage to school property. The requirement of a hearing, where the student could present his side of the factual issue, could under such circumstances "provide a meaningful hedge against erroneous action." . . . The decision to dismiss respondent, by comparison, rested on the academic judgment of school officials that she did not have the necessary clinical ability to perform adequately as a medical doctor and was making insufficient progress toward that goal. Such a judgment is by its nature more subjective and evaluative than the typical factual questions presented in the average disciplinary decision. **Like the decision of an individual professor as to the proper grade for a student in his course, the determination whether to dismiss a student for academic reasons requires an expert evaluation of cumulative information and is not readily adapted to the procedural tools of judicial or administrative decision making.** . . .

In reversing the District Court on procedural due process grounds, the Court of Appeals expressly failed to "reach the substantive due process ground advanced by Horowitz." . . . Respondent urges that we remand the cause to the Court of Appeals for consideration of this additional claim. In this regard, a number of lower courts have implied in dictum that academic dismissals from state institutions can be enjoined if "shown to be clearly arbitrary or capricious." . . . Even assuming that the courts can review under such a standard an academic decision of a public educational institution, we agree with the District Court that no showing of arbitrariness or capriciousness has been made in this case. **Courts are particularly ill-equipped to evaluate academic performance.** The factors discussed in Part II with respect to procedural due process speak a fortiori here and warn against any such judicial intrusion into academic decision making.

[Court ruling:] The judgment of the Court of Appeals is therefore reversed.

Unlike the University of Missouri in the *Horowitz* case, public elementary and secondary schools do not dismiss students for merely failing to meet academic standards. However, students who are denied course credit under an attendance policy may challenge that the policy was disciplinary, rather than academic and, hence, the school failed to provide adequate due process.

The following case sets the standard for attendance policies, which are academic in nature, vs. those which are disciplinary.

Such was the situation in the case of *State ex rel. Yarber v. McHenry*, 915 S.W.2d 325 (Mo.banc, 1995) where the Missouri Supreme Court ruled that the school's attendance policy, which denied the student semester credits for excessive absenteeism, was disciplinary and that the school's failure to grant notice and hearing violated his due process rights. The policy was found disciplinary because it stated that should the student fail to make up the excessive absences (defined as those greater than six), he or she will "lose credit for that semester." Because Yarber had gained credit for the semester (apparently because his failure to attend two of the four make-up sessions came at the end of the semester), the court stated that the policy "**takes away previously earned credit as punishment for unsatisfactory attendance**." *Id.* at 329 (emphasis added).

Issues: The *Yarber* court recognized that the Connecticut Supreme Court had upheld a school's policy that it found to be academic rather than disciplinary in nature. However, *Yarber* distinguished the Connecticut school's policy from that of the Missouri school saying that under the former's attendance policy: "(1) the school *withheld* credit from the student for missing twenty-four class periods rather than taking away credit already earned; [and] (2) the attendance policy explicitly stated that its purpose was academic. . . ." *Id.* at 330 (court's emphasis).

The Connecticut case is *Campbell v. Board of Education of New Milford*, 475 A.2d 289 (Conn. 1984) where the court upheld an attendance policy that withheld course credit "from any student who, without receiving an administrative waiver, is absent from any year-long course for more than twenty-four class periods." *Id.* at 290. (The policy even permitted days of a disciplinary suspension to be counted toward the twenty-four day maximum.) Secondly, the policy called for a five-point grade reduction for each unexcused absence beyond the first, but a disciplinary suspension day could not be counted as an unexcused absence for purposes of lowering the grade. Lastly, the policy's stated purpose was that it was educational and not disciplinary.

Facts: In three of his classes, student Campbell had accumulated sufficient unexcused absences to have his grades lowered to failing and in a fourth class, although his grades were passing, he received no credit due to having thirty-eight absences. He charged a violation of his substantive due process rights claiming the policy interfered with the fundamental right to an education, the liberty interest in his academic reputation, and his property interest in grades reflecting academic achievement.

Court decision: The court found that that the policy was not disciplinary, that Campbell's right to an education was not fundamental under Connecticut's constitution, and that his claims would be judged under the "rational basis test." Said the court at 296:

In order to succeed on these claims, the plaintiff bears the heavy burden of proving that the challenged policy has no reasonable relationship to any legitimate state purpose . . . and that the plaintiff class has suffered a specific injury as a result of the policy's enforcement . . . The plaintiff has established neither the legal nor the factual predicate for meeting this burden of proof.

The *Yarber* and *Campbell* cases demonstrate the factually sensitive and complex nature of formulating student attendance policies. Generally speaking, the cases indicate that the purpose of such policy must clearly be academic rather than punitive. However, it is difficult to understand the distinction between *Yarber's* finding that due process must be afforded because it is "punishment" when the school "*takes away*" previously earned credit due to excessive absences and *Campbell's* conclusion that no violation exists under an "academic" policy that "*withholds*" course credit for such absences. Perhaps it means that course credit is taken away when the facts show that the absence in question came so late in the semester that the student would have passed. If this is so, then had Yarber's failure to make up his excessive absence occurred so early in the semester that he could not have passed if no further credit were given, there would not have been a taking away of credits already earned. The lesson for school administrators in applying attendance polices is that if there is any question as to whether or not to give due process when denying course credit (or taking it away), give it.

Case: The Michigan Court of Appeals in *Slocum v. Holton Board of Education*, 429 N.W. 2d 607 (Mich.App. 1988) did not expressly discuss the distinction between disciplinary and academic sanctions when a tenth grade student alleged that her substantive due process rights were violated when the school reduced each course grade during the grading period by one letter grade. Instead, the court found that she had no property interest in grades that she alleged were already "earned," and that no liberty interest in her good name and reputation had been violated. In the alternative, the court stated that even had she had a protected interest, no due process rights were violated because the school's attendance policy was "rationally related to a legitimate government purpose." (This alternative conclusion implies the court considered the policy academic in nature.)

Facts: The attendance policy in *Slocum* required students who had more than three excused absences in a grading period to attend an after school study session to make up the work missed. When Slocum only showed up for one of the five sessions that she was scheduled to attend, her grades were reduced by one letter grade pursuant to the policy. In concluding that Slocum had no property interest at stake in receiving a higher grade, the court stated at 611 (emphasis added):

> Lori had no more "earned" grades higher than what she received than someone else who did not complete the necessary requirements for a higher grade (e.g., not completing a class assignment, failing an examination or quiz, not participating in class discussions). . . [T]here is more to an education than correctly answering questions asked on an examination. **There are many factors, which may properly be considered in determining a student's course grade—attendance is one such factor.** To hold that Lori had a vested property interest in higher grades would be as absurd as holding that an employee has the right to a paycheck for which she has not worked . . . **The mere potential for, or expectancy of, Lori in receiving higher grades cannot create constitutional . . . entitlement** where none theretofore existed.

Issues: The *Slocum* court addressed the student's liberty interest claims at 611-612 (emphasis added):

> Plaintiff claims a protected liberty interest in Lori's good name, reputation, honor or integrity, which is derived from "the recognition by state law of her right to accurately reflective academic evaluations." Again, that argument merely begs the

question at hand since it presupposes that class attendance is not a proper measure of academic achievement. Assuming as one must, that an examination cannot cover every bit of information discussed in class, it would be reasonable to hold that where two students have identical examination scores the student who had created attendance also had greater knowledge (i.e., education) of the subject. Moreover, **reputation alone, apart from some more tangible interest such as employment, is not enough to invoke the due process clause of the United States Constitution**.

Essentially, the *Slocum* court found that no property or liberty interest arose under an attendance policy that was rationally related to academic performance because the student's deliberate non-attendance at the after school make-up-work sessions demonstrated a lack of effort in academic achievement which was appropriately measured by the lowering of grades. The *Slocum* case also presents a valid counter to the questionable result in the above-discussed *Yarber* case that found a policy "disciplinary" because it took away previously earned credits by denying semester credit for excessive absences.

D2. *Disciplinary Sanctions*

Many cases are clearly disciplinary in nature and result in a student receiving lower grades or being denied course credit due to a suspension from school or removal from class. In the case of *Smith v. School City of Hobart*, 811 F.Supp. 391 (N.D.Ind. 1993), a senior student was suspended five days from school for violating a discipline rule. The suspension policy called for a four percent grade reduction for each day of suspension which significantly lowered her nine-week grade. The court in finding the grade reduction policy arbitrary and in violation of substantive due process stated at 397 (emphasis added):

While the issue of reducing a student's grades as punishment for nonacademic conduct is not well-settled in this country . . . a general consensus can be reached as to what a student's grades should represent. A student's grade or credit should reflect the student's academic performance or achievement, including participation in class, and presence in class. **Reducing grades unrelated to academic conduct results in a skewed and inaccurate reflection of a student's academic performance**.

The *Smith* court further stated that **"[t]o warrant an academic sanction, a student's misconduct must be directly related to the student's academic performance**, and there is no indication in this record that such is the case." *Id.* at 399 (emphasis added).

At least one state court went in the opposite direction of the *Smith v. Hobart* case. In *New Braunfels Ind. Sch. Dist. v. Armke*, 658 S.W.2d 330 (Tex.App. 10 Dist. 1983), the Texas court upheld a policy that counted disciplinary suspension days as unexcused absences and reduced the six-week grades by three percent for each of the three days of the two students' suspension (as well as giving zeroes for course work missed during the suspension). According to the court at 337, the nine percent penalty reduction for that grading period had "no adverse impact on Appellees' property rights to a public education" and "neither did the evidence show that imposition of the scholastic penalties proposed will have any negative impact on the honor, reputation or name of either appellees."

The case of *Dunn v. Fairfield Comm. High Sch. Dist. No. 225*, 158 F.3d 962 (7th

Cir. 1998), presented earlier in this chapter, involved two students who received a semester grade of "F" after being removed from band class for refusing, as members of the pep band, to obey their teachers directive to stop playing their guitars during a basketball game. The Seventh Circuit in applying the "shocks the conscience" standard did not find a violation of the students' substantive due process rights, even though the failing grade meant a loss of credit for the course. In *Dunn*, the misconduct during a band performance had a direct relationship to the course being taught and the students' removal from class meant that they could not earn sufficient credits to pass the semester. The court stated at 966:

> That means that Fairfield's decision to stack the deck so that these students would fail Band must be sustained unless it is wholly arbitrary. Here, however, Dunn and McCullough freely conceded that they had violated a school rule, that the rule was designed to preserve discipline in the classroom and to punish student insubordination, and that these were legitimate interests on the part of the school district. That alone is enough to show that their claim cannot possibly succeed. The Constitution does not guarantee these or any other students the right not to receive an "F" in a course from which they were excluded because of misbehavior. . . .

In a disciplinary case where due to repeated tardies to a geometry class in violation of policy the student was removed, assigned to study hall, received no credit, and had the class deleted from the student's record, the court found no violation of procedural or substantive due process rights. *M.S. v. Eagle-Union Community School Corporation*, 717 N.E. 2d 1255 (Ind.App. 1999). The process afforded the student, although not precisely what was called for in the policy, was constitutionally sufficient in that M.S. received at least two notices of the tardiness problem and a conference with the assistant principal wherein the student had the "opportunity to present concerns about the tardy situation or the disciplinary process." Because the tardy policy was clearly linked to academic performance in the geometry classroom, the *M.S.* case appears to come within the rule stated in *Smith*, above, i.e., "[t]o warrant an academic sanction, a student's misconduct must be directly related to the student's academic performance . . ." 811 F.Supp. at 399.

In a case where a marching band student was removed from that class for deliberately disobeying his instructor's directive that he had to perform in a weekend competition, a New York federal district court ruled that no constitutional right was violated because he did not have a property right to participate in a single class offering. *Mazevski v. Horseheads Central School Dist.*, 950 F.Supp. 69 (W.D.N.Y. 1997), where the court stated at 72-73 (emphasis added):

> . . . **[B]ecause the property interest that exists is in the entire educational process, there is no constitutional right to any one specific curricular or extracurricular activity, meriting due process protections**. . . If the rule were otherwise, every disgruntled student (or, more likely, disgruntled parent) who believed she would not have been dropped from the pep squad, or who believed he should not have been benched for missing a team meeting, or who challenged his failure to be selected to take advance placement courses, could commence an action in federal court to challenge the decision of school administrators. This should not be. Discomfiture over

such schoolyard decisions does not warrant relief in federal court. To hold otherwise, is contrary to sound legal reasoning invites disruption of the educational process and has scant pedagogical value.

As to the issue of giving zeroes to a student for work missed during a disciplinary suspension from school, at least three state courts have upheld the practice. The Mississippi Supreme Court in *the Interest of T.H., III*, 681 So.2d 110 (Miss. 1996) ruled that an eleventh grader's 10-day suspension for alcohol consumption and the resulting zero grades for work missed during the suspension did not violate substantive due process rights. The school board policy clearly stated the rule (but wisely permitted grading period and semester final examinations to be made up for credit so that there would not be a substantial negative impact on the semester grade that would be a permanent part of a student's transcript). The *T.H.* court relied on its prior precedent where it stated at 115:

As a matter of state substantive due process rights, a school board's disciplinary rule or scheme is constitutionally enforceable where fairly viewed it furthers a substantial legitimate interest of the school district. The authority vested in school boards consistent with this constitutional limitation includes substantial discretion with respect to the administration of punishments to students who violate school rules.

The court concluded that the school had a substantial interest in deterring student misconduct with a rule that gives zeroes for work missed during the time of a suspension and stated that "[s]imply put, the no-credit provision is intended to deter general student disciplinary problems." *Id.* at 116.

In a case where a seventh grader received a three-day suspension for fighting and as a result given zeroes for grading-period final examinations that were missed, the Illinois Court of Appeals upheld the school district. *Donaldson v. Board of Education for Danville Sch. Dist. No. 18*, 424 N.E.2d 737 (Ill.App. 1981). The court stated at 738-739 (emphasis added):

School discipline is an area which courts enter with great hesitation and reluctance—and rightly so. School officials are trained and paid to determine what form of punishment best addresses a particular student's transgression. They are in a far better position than is a black-robed judge to decide what to do with a disobedient child at school. . . Because of their expertise and their closeness to the situation—and because we do not want them to fear court challenges to their every act—school officials are given wide discretion in their disciplinary actions.

Illinois courts have, therefore, said that a **decision to suspend or expel a student will be overturned only if it is arbitrary, unreasonable, capricious, or oppressive**. . . .

[The examinations] would not have been of the type that would have such a **substantial effect on Donaldson's ultimate grades** as to make the decision to suspend him during that time arbitrary. Also, we note that Donaldson is in the seventh grade. **He is not in high school, where grades are usually thought of as being more important and can affect a student's educational and employment prospects** after he leaves public school.

The third case to uphold giving zeroes for work missed during suspension days is *New Bruanfels Ind. Sch. Dist. v. Armke*, 658 S.W.2d 330 (Tex.App. 10 Dist. 1983), where the Texas court, as noted above, found that under the facts presented there was not a sufficiently adverse impact on the two high school senior students' grades and reputations for the court to find a violation of their constitutional property and liberty interests.

What can be learned from these three cases is that a policy or practice that gives zeroes on work missed during a disciplinary suspension from school will likely pass constitutional muster if the end result (i.e., the semester grade that becomes a permanent part of the student's record and that is computed into the overall grade point average for future employers or colleges to review) is not viewed by the reasonable person as arbitrary, oppressive, or shocking to the conscience.

SCENARIOS
STATE AND APPLY THE RELEVANT LEGAL RULE(S) TO THE FACTS.

1. Student, an above average ninth grader, was the son of parents who were both well educated and employed in professional capacities. When it was learned that Student had entered into a criminal conspiracy to bring firearms to school and kill students and teachers, but pulled out of the conspiracy the day before the planned event, he was immediately suspended from school pending the offer of a hearing to expel him permanently from school without any opportunity to ever return. Prior to the suspension, Principal took him to the office, told Student that his "deplorable criminal plot to kill and maim had backfired" and that he was "finished forever as a student at the school," and had the school security drive him home without giving Student a chance to speak.

When his parents received formal written notice that he had been suspended and that they could request a hearing on Principal's request to permanently expel and bar his attendance for having entering into the unfulfilled conspiracy, they requested the hearing and demanded, through their attorney, the following: list of names of all witnesses against him, the proposed testimony of each, all written statements made during the investigation, all other evidence discovered in the investigation, and the ability of the attorney to represent Student at the expulsion hearing and to cross examine all witnesses.

When School denied each one of the demands and set the date for the hearing, Parents, on child's behalf, filed suit in federal court for an injunction that would prevent the hearing from taking place until all of Student's attorney's demands were met. As part of the suit, Parents alleged that Student's suspension pending the expulsion hearing was illegal.

2. School's attendance policy read in relevant part:

The purpose of this policy is to maximize the time spent on classroom instruction. A tardy will be assessed each time the student is not at his/her desk ready to begin when the bell rings. Six tardies will equal one unexcused absence.

Class attendance is critical to learning. An unexcused absence is recognized as a lack of academic effort. Since grades are a measure of academic effort, students receiving an unexcused absence will have their nine-week grading period grades reduced by two percent for each such absence.

Any student who accumulates fifteen total absences, excused and/or unexcused, in a 90-day semester, will not be given credit for the course(s) affected, and will receive an NC (no credit) on his/her permanent record.

Any student who is suspended from school for violation of discipline rules will receive an unexcused absence for each day of the suspension.

Student was a senior with an evening job that caused him to oversleep and be frequently late for school in the mornings. In his second semester, first-period government class, successful completion of which is required for graduation, he accumulated 18 tardies (that equaled three unexcused absences thereby reducing his second nine-week grading period grade by six percentage points), missed ten days of excused absences due to documented illness, had a one-day suspension from school that reduced his second grading period grade by another two percent, and participated in "senior skip day" the last week of school that not only was his fifteenth absence in the semester, but was also as an unexcused absence that reduced his grade by another two percent. The effect of the grade reductions in the government class meant that he would have failed the semester by one percentage point, but because he missed 15 days of government classes, under the policy School decided rather than giving him an "F" grade, he would receive no credit for the class.

Although plenty of warning had been given to Student and his parents as he approached the 15 day maximum absence limit, Parents were irate because this meant he had to take summer school to pass government and to graduate, which meant that his induction into the military would be delayed. Parents, on child's behalf, sued in federal district court attacking the constitutionality of the policy and its application to Student.

CHAPTER
7

STUDENT SEARCH
AND SEIZURE

The Fourth Amendment to the United States Constitution guarantees the right to be free from unreasonable searches and seizures by governmental authorities. In the public school setting, the board of education as well as its administrators, teachers, and other employees may be challenged upon allegations that a particular search and/or seizure was unreasonable. The result of a Fourth Amendment lawsuit will be based on the application of legal standards established by the United States Supreme Court. This chapter will explore those standards and examine how they have been applied by federal and state courts to student searches and seizures.

I.   REASONABLE SUSPICION AND SCOPE

In the following case the court defines the standard and scope for reasonable suspicion in cases of student searches and seizures.

Case
T.L.O. v. New Jersey, 469 U.S. 325 (1985) (emphasis added)

We granted certiorari in this case to examine the appropriateness of the exclusionary rule as a remedy for searches carried out in violation of the Fourth Amendment by public school authorities. Our consideration of the proper application of the Fourth Amendment to the public schools, however, has led us to conclude that the search that gave rise to the case now before us did not violate the Fourth Amendment. **Accordingly, we here address only the questions of the proper standard for assessing the legality of searches conducted by public school officials and the application of that standard to the facts of this case.**

[**Facts:**] On March 7, 1980, a teacher at Piscataway High School in Middlesex County, N. J., discovered two girls smoking in a lavatory. One of the two girls was the respondent T. L. O., who at that time was a 14-year-old high school freshman. Because smoking in the lavatory was a violation of a school rule, the teacher took the two girls to the Principal's office, where they met with Assistant Vice Principal Theodore Choplick. In response to questioning by Mr. Choplick, T. L. O.'s companion admitted that she had violated the rule. T. L. O., however, denied that she had been smoking in the lavatory and claimed that she did not smoke at all.

Mr. Choplick asked T. L. O. to come into his private office and demanded to see her purse. Opening the purse, he found a pack of cigarettes, which he removed from the purse and held before T. L. O. as he accused her of having lied to him. As he reached into the purse for the cigarettes, Mr. Choplick also noticed a package of cigarette rolling papers. In his experience, possession of rolling papers by high school students was closely associated with the use of marihuana. Suspecting that a closer examination of the purse might yield further evidence of drug use, Mr. Choplick proceeded to search the purse thoroughly. The search revealed a small amount of marihuana, a pipe, a number of empty plastic bags, a substantial quantity of money in one-dollar bills, an index card that appeared to be a list of students who owed T. L. O. money, and two letters that implicated T. L. O. in marihuana dealing. . . .

[**Issues:**] In determining whether the search at issue in this case violated the Fourth Amendment, we are faced initially with the question whether that Amendment's prohibition on unreasonable searches and seizures applies to searches conducted by public school officials. We hold that it does. . . .

In carrying out searches and other disciplinary functions pursuant to such policies, **school officials act as representatives of the State**, not merely as surrogates for the parents, **and they cannot claim the parents' immunity from the strictures of the Fourth Amendment.**

[Rationale:] To hold that the Fourth Amendment applies to searches conducted by school authorities is only to begin the inquiry into the standards governing such searches. Although the underlying command of the Fourth Amendment is always that searches and seizures be reasonable, **what is reasonable depends on the context within which a search takes place.** The determination of the standard of reasonableness governing any specific class of searches requires "**balancing the need to search against the invasion which the search entails.**" . . . **On one side of the balance are arrayed the individual's legitimate expectations of privacy and personal security; on the other, the government's need for effective methods to deal with breaches of public order**. . . .

Of course, the Fourth Amendment does not protect subjective expectations of privacy that are unreasonable or otherwise "illegitimate." . . . To receive the protection of the Fourth Amendment, an expectation of privacy must be one that society is "prepared to recognize as legitimate." . . . The State of New Jersey has argued that because of the pervasive supervision to which children in the schools are necessarily subject, a child has virtually no legitimate expectation of privacy in articles of personal property "unnecessarily" carried into a school. This argument has two factual premises: (1) the fundamental incompatibility of expectations of privacy with the maintenance of a sound educational environment; and (2) the minimal interest of the child in bringing any items of personal property into the school. Both premises are severely flawed.

Although this Court may take notice of the difficulty of maintaining discipline in the public schools today, the situation is not so dire that students in the schools may claim no legitimate expectations of privacy. . . .

Nor does the State's suggestion that children have no legitimate need to bring personal property into the schools seem well anchored in reality. Students at a minimum must bring to school not only the supplies needed for their studies, but also keys, money, and the necessaries of personal hygiene and grooming. In addition, students may carry on their persons or in purses or wallets such nondisruptive, yet highly personal items, as photographs, letters, and diaries. Finally, students may have perfectly legitimate reasons to carry with them articles of property needed in connection with extracurricular or recreational activities. In short, schoolchildren may find it necessary to carry with them a variety of legitimate, noncontraband items, and there is no reason to conclude that they have necessarily waived all rights to privacy in such items merely by bringing them onto school grounds.

Against the child's interest in privacy must be set the substantial interest of teachers and administrators in maintaining discipline in the classroom and on school grounds. Maintaining order in the classroom has never been easy, but in recent years, school disorder has often taken particularly ugly forms: drug use and violent crime in the schools have become major social problems. . . . Even in schools that have been spared the most severe disciplinary problems, the preservation of order and a proper educational environment requires close supervision of schoolchildren, as well as the enforcement of rules against conduct that would be perfectly permissible if undertaken by an adult.

"Events calling for discipline are frequent occurrences and sometimes require immediate, effective action." . . . Accordingly, we have recognized that maintaining security and order in the schools requires a certain degree of flexibility in school disciplinary procedures, and we have respected the value of preserving the informality of the student-teacher relationship. . . .

How, then, should we strike the balance between the schoolchild's legitimate expectations of privacy and the school's equally legitimate need to maintain an environment in which learning can take place? **It is evident that the school setting requires some easing of the restrictions to which searches by public authorities are ordinarily subject.** The warrant requirement, in particular, is unsuited to the school environment: requiring a teacher to obtain a warrant before searching a child suspected of an infraction of school rules (or of the criminal law) would unduly interfere with the maintenance of the swift and informal disciplinary procedures needed in the schools. Just as we have in other cases dispensed with the warrant requirement when "the burden of obtaining a warrant is likely to frustrate the governmental purpose behind the search," . . . **we hold today that school officials need not obtain a warrant before searching a student who is under their authority.**

The school setting also requires some modification of the level of suspicion of illicit activity needed to justify a search. Ordinarily, a search - even one that may permissibly be carried out without a warrant - must be based upon "probable cause" to believe that a violation of the law has occurred. . . . However, "probable cause" is not an irreducible requirement of a valid search. The fundamental command of the Fourth Amendment is that searches and seizures be reasonable, and although "both the concept of probable cause and the requirement of a warrant bear on the reasonableness of a search, . . . in certain limited circumstances neither is required." . . . Where a careful balancing of governmental and private interests suggests that the public interest is best served by a Fourth Amendment standard of reasonableness that stops short of probable cause, we have not hesitated to adopt such a standard.

We join the majority of courts that have examined this issue in concluding that the accommodation of the privacy interests of schoolchildren with the substantial need of teachers and administrators for freedom to maintain order in the schools does not require strict adherence to the requirement that searches be based on probable cause to believe that the subject of the search has violated or is violating the law. Rather, **the legality of a search of a student should depend simply on the reasonableness, under all the circumstances, of the search. Determining the reasonableness of any search involves a twofold inquiry: first, one must consider "whether the . . . action was justified at its inception," . . .; second, one must determine whether the search as actually conducted "was reasonably related in scope to the circumstances which justified the interference in the**

first place," . . . Under ordinary circumstances, a search of a student by a teacher or other school official will be "justified at its inception" when there are **reasonable grounds for suspecting** that the search will turn up evidence that the student has violated or is violating either the law or the rules of the school. Such a search will be permissible in its scope when **the measures adopted are reasonably related to the objectives of the search and not excessively intrusive in light of the age and sex of the student and the nature of the infraction**. . . .

[Legal standards:]   There remains the question of the legality of the search in this case. We recognize that the "reasonable grounds" standard applied by the New Jersey Supreme Court in its consideration of this question is not substantially different from the standard that we have adopted today. Nonetheless, we believe that the New Jersey court's application of that standard to strike down the search of T. L. O.'s purse reflects a somewhat crabbed notion of reasonableness. Our review of the facts surrounding the search leads us to conclude that the search was in no sense unreasonable for Fourth Amendment purposes.

The incident that gave rise to this case actually involved two separate searches, with the first – the search for cigarettes – providing the suspicion that gave rise to the second – the search for marihuana. Although it is the fruits of the second search that are at issue here, the validity of the search for marihuana must depend on the reasonableness of the initial search for cigarettes, as there would have been no reason to suspect that T. L. O. possessed marihuana had the first search not taken place. Accordingly, it is to the search for cigarettes that we first turn our attention. . . .

T. L. O. had been accused of smoking, and had denied the accusation in the strongest possible terms when she stated that she did not smoke at all. Surely it cannot be said that under these circumstances, T. L. O.'s possession of cigarettes would be irrelevant to the charges against her or to her response to those charges. T. L. O.'s possession of cigarettes, once it was discovered, would both corroborate the report that she had been smoking and undermine the credibility of her defense to the charge of smoking. To be sure, the discovery of the cigarettes would not prove that T. L. O. had been smoking in the lavatory; nor would it, strictly speaking, necessarily be inconsistent with her claim that she did not smoke at all. **But it is universally recognized that evidence, to be relevant to an inquiry, need not conclusively prove the ultimate fact in issue, but only have "any tendency to make the existence of any fact that is of consequence to the determination of the action more probable or less probable than it would be without the evidence."** . . . The relevance of T. L. O.'s possession of cigarettes to the question whether she had been smoking and to the credibility of her denial that she smoked supplied the necessary "nexus" between the item searched for and the infraction under investigation. . . . Thus, if Mr. Choplick in fact had a reasonable suspicion that T. L. O. had cigarettes in her purse, the search was justified despite the fact that the cigarettes, if found, would constitute "mere evidence" of a violation. . . .

A teacher had reported that T. L. O. was smoking in the lavatory. Certainly this report gave Mr. Choplick reason to suspect that T. L. O. was carrying cigarettes with her; and if she did have cigarettes, her purse was the obvious place in which to find them. **Mr. Choplick's suspicion that there were cigarettes in the purse was not an "inchoate and unparticularized suspicion or `hunch,'"** ...; **rather, it was the sort of "common-sense conclusio[n] about human behavior" upon which "practical people" – including government officials – are entitled to rely.** ... Of course, even if the teacher's report were true, T. L. O. might not have had a pack of cigarettes with her; she might have borrowed a cigarette from someone else or have been sharing a cigarette with another student. **But the requirement of reasonable suspicion is not a requirement of absolute certainty: "sufficient probability, not certainty, is the touchstone of reasonableness under the Fourth Amendment.** ..."... Because the hypothesis that T. L. O. was carrying cigarettes in her purse was itself not unreasonable, it is irrelevant that other hypotheses were also consistent with the teacher's accusation. Accordingly, it cannot be said that Mr. Choplick acted unreasonably when he examined T. L. O.'s purse to see if it contained cigarettes.

Our conclusion that Mr. Choplick's decision to open T. L. O.'s purse was reasonable brings us to the question of the further search for marihuana once the pack of cigarettes was located. The suspicion upon which the search for marihuana was founded was provided when Mr. Choplick observed a package of rolling papers in the purse as he removed the pack of cigarettes. Although T. L. O. does not dispute the reasonableness of Mr. Choplick's belief that the rolling papers indicated the presence of marihuana, she does contend that the scope of the search Mr. Choplick conducted exceeded permissible bounds when he seized and read certain letters that implicated T. L. O. in drug dealing. This argument, too, is unpersuasive. The discovery of the rolling papers concededly gave rise to a reasonable suspicion that T. L. O. was carrying marihuana as well as cigarettes in her purse. This suspicion justified further exploration of T. L. O.'s purse, which turned up more evidence of drug-related activities: a pipe, a number of plastic bags of the type commonly used to store marihuana, a small quantity of marihuana, and a fairly substantial amount of money. **Under these circumstances, it was not unreasonable to extend the search to a separate zippered compartment of the purse; and when a search of that compartment revealed an index card containing a list of "people who owe me money" as well as two letters, the inference that T. L. O. was involved in marihuana trafficking was substantial enough to justify Mr. Choplick in examining the letters to determine whether they contained any further evidence.** In short, we cannot conclude that the search for marihuana was unreasonable in any respect.

[Court ruling:] Because the search resulting in the discovery of the evidence of marihuana dealing by T. L. O. was reasonable, the New Jersey Supreme Court's decision to exclude that evidence from T. L. O.'s juvenile delinquency proceedings on Fourth Amendment grounds was erroneous. Accordingly, the judgment of the Supreme Court of New Jersey is reversed.

The following case is an example of the application of the TLO reasonable suspicion and scope standard.

Case: *Bridgman v. New Trier High Sch. Dist. No. 203*, 128 F.3d 146 (7th Cir. 1997).

[Facts:] In this case the Seventh Circuit upheld the search of a ninth-grade male student for believed possession of marijuana even though none was found on his person and no evidence of consumption was indicated by a drug test secured by his parent. The initial search consisted of his outer jersey, hat, and shoes and socks, all of which he was required to remove, plus the contents of his pants pockets. The basis of the search resulted from the observation of his initial behavior by the school's Student Assistance Program Coordinator, a certified drug addiction counselor, who was conducting an after-school smoking cessation program. The student was giggling, acting unruly, and continued to be distracted and unruly after being told to calm down. The Coordinator noticed that his eyes were bloodshot, pupils dilated, and his writing on class work erratic. When confronted about being under the influence of drugs, he denied ever using such. The second alleged search occurred when the school nurse checked his pulse and blood pressure and found them to considerably higher than those listed on his freshman physical examination.

[Court ruling:] The *Bridgman* court found that there was sufficient evidence to justify the search at its inception and that the scope of the search was reasonable in light of all the circumstances. It noted that the student's "symptoms and [the Coordinator's use of the medical assessment as an investigative tool, indicate that her suspicions and further actions based upon the symptoms . . . were not unreasonable . . .[and] were sufficient to ground [her] suspicion, and the medical assessment was reasonably calculated to uncover further evidence of the suspected drug use." *Id.* at 1149.

The *T.L.O.* reasonable suspicion and scope standard was also applied in a Fourth Circuit case, *DesRoches by DesRoches v. Caprio*, 156 F.3d 571 (4th Cir. 1998), wherein the court upheld a high school dean's creative way to arrive at an individualized reasonable suspicion that a particular student possessed a stolen pair of tennis shoes in his backpack.

Case: *DesRoches by DesRoches v. Caprio,* 156 F3d 571 (4th Cir 1998)

[Facts:] Initially, it was a situation where anyone in the entire ninth grade art class could I have taken the shoes because they had been left on the owner's desk when the class left for lunch, but were missing when the class returned. The teacher had remained in the room and in an adjacent closet while cutting paper and had seen students whom she knew in the room during lunch. One of these students had seen a non-class member come into room, but the teacher had not. The dean's investigation consisted of talking to those art students who had been in the room and the teacher, but when no evidence was uncovered, decided that a search of the nineteen class members would be needed. He announced his intention to search and asked if anyone objected. Only DesRoches and another student objected, but the other student consented after being reminded that the school policy allowed a ten-day suspension for refusing to consent. DesRoches sat and watched as the other eighteen students consented to the search of their book bags and backpacks. He was then taken to the office where he refused the principal's request to search his backpack. After allowing him to call his parents in the hope that they would convince him to consent to the search, he still refused and was suspended for ten days as a result.

[Court ruling:] The court found that the school administrators had formulated reasonable, individualized suspicion on DesRoches during the course of the investigation, and because the proposed search of his backpack was reasonable, they did not violate the Fourth Amendment by suspending him from school for refusing to consent to the search. The court stated at 578:

. . . [O]nce the classroom and the other eighteen students had been searched, school officials had certainly developed individualized suspicion with respect to DesRoches and the unnamed non-classmember, not by way of any particular information suggesting that one of those two was the thief, but simply by the process of elimination. We therefore cannot fault school officials for renewing their request to search once individualized suspicion has arisen, or for suspending DesRoches when he refused consent to the search.

Notes: The *DesRoches* case signals two important concepts. First, school officials can develop reasonable, individualized suspicion on more than one individual from the same set of facts, and second that such suspicion can result from a process of elimination wherein willing class members consent to be searched knowing that they have nothing to hide.

What remains unclear, however, is at what number of students may an administrator conclude that there is reasonable suspicion for, in order to commence the search? Arguably, a required search of all nineteen students in the *DesRoches* case would have been unreasonable from the inception.

However, at least one federal district court ruled that a class-wide search of the desks, personal belongings, pockets, purses, shoes, and socks of every fifth grader for a reported stolen $26 of candy sale proceeds was reasonable based on *T.L.O.'s* reasonable suspicion/reasonable scope standard. The court in *Thomas v. Clayton County Bd. of Ed.*, 94 F.Supp.2d 1290 (N.D.Ga. 1999) determined that the teacher had reasonable suspicion "to conduct some kind of search," *Id.* at 1306, because a student had put an envelope containing the money on her desk just before it disappeared. It then found the above-described search reasonable in scope in light of the totality of circumstances and stated "the deterrence value of a search could arguably insure that other would-be thieves would think twice before purloining another student's valuable." *Id.* It further stated "a school that takes a casual attitude toward the theft of another student's candy money may well soon encounter disobedience of even more serious rules, as well as the erosion of order and a sense of well-being by students." *Id.* When the stolen money was not found, the class members were strip-searched.

The *Thomas* court found that this was unreasonable in scope and violated the students' Fourth Amendment rights.

Case

Porter v. Ascension Parish School Board, 393 F. 3d 608 (5th Cir. 2004)
(emphasis added)

Adam's second claim was that EAHS officials violated the Fourth Amendment by searching his book bag and his person immediately after he admitted that the drawing was his. Finding that the search was reasonable, the district court held that Adam had failed to raise a material fact issue regarding his Fourth Amendment claim. We agree that the search was reasonable under the circumstances, and therefore did not violate Adam's Fourth Amendment rights.

[Rationale:] Students have a constitutional right under the Fourth and Fourteenth Amendments to be free from unreasonable searches and seizures while on school premises. At the same time, the "accommodation of the privacy interests of schoolchildren with the substantial need of teachers and administrators for freedom to maintain order in the schools does not require strict adherence to the requirement that searches be based on probable cause"; rather, the legality of school searches depends upon the "reasonableness, under all the circumstances, of the search."

The action must be "justified at its inception" and must be "reasonably related in scope to the circumstances which justified the interference in the first place." Under ordinary circumstances, a search of a student by a teacher or other school official will be justified "at its inception" when there are reasonable grounds for suspecting that the search will turn up evidence that the student has violated or is violating either the law or the rules of the school. Such a search will be permissible in its scope when the measures adopted are reasonable related to the objectives of the search and not excessively intrusive in light of the age and sex of the student and the nature of the infraction.

Under the circumstances present at the time the search of Adam and his book bag was conducted, EAHS officials had reasonable grounds for suspecting that the search would produce evidence of an infraction of a school rule or policy. Specifically, the officials were in possession of a drawing depicting numerous violent acts being perpetrated against EAHS, its students, and staff. In addition, Adam had admitted that the drawing was his prior to the initiation of the search. Given that **school officials have a significant interest in deterring misconduct on the part of students, and the fact that Adam had admitted to drawing the sketch depicting large-scale acts of violence directed at EAHS, the decision to search Adam was appropriate under the circumstances**.

The search was also reasonable in scope and not overly intrusive under the circumstances. Following Adam's admission of responsibility for the drawing, EAHS officials searched his book bag, including textbooks and notebooks found in the bag, and Adam's person, including his wallet. Without question, searching a student's person and his book bag is a process invasive of personal privacy, requiring justification. Justification for the scope of the search was present in this case based on the facts supporting the initial decision to search.

[Court ruling:] Because the search of Adam by EAHS officials was reasonable at its inception, and was conducted in a reasonable manner when balanced against the school's interest in ensuring the safety and welfare of students, Adam's Fourth Amendment claim fails.

In footnote 58 of the *Porter* case, the court noted the following cases related to schools' substantial interest in a safe environment (emphasis added):

> In particular, the powerful interest of promoting school safety justified the scope of the search in this case. *See Vernonia Sch. Dist. 47J*, 515 U.S. at 661 (**when assessing scope of school searches, relevant inquiry is whether the interest being protected is "*important enough* to justify that particular search at hand**"); *Shade v. City of Farmington*, 309 F.3d 1054, 1059-62 (8th Cir. 2002) (**detention and pat-down of student after school employee reported seeing student with a knife was reasonable, even in light of fact that the knife had already been turned over by another student**); *Thompson v. Carthage Sch. Dist.*, 87 F.3d 979, 982-83 (6th Cir. 1996) (**finding that minimally invasive search of student's shoes and pockets was reasonable, even absent individualized suspicion, when school officials have independent grounds for believing that weapons had been brought to school on a particular day**); *Brousseau v. Town of Westerly*, 11 F. Supp. 2d 177, 182 (D.R.I. 1998) (**finding that searches by school officials for weapons and drugs are typically considered more compelling because the safety and welfare of students is implicated**).

Additionally, intrusions on the personal privacy interests of students have been upheld based on lower indices of individualized suspicion than is present in this case. *See Cuesta*, 285 F.3d at 968-70 (**arrest and strip search of student upheld as school officials had reasonable suspicion to believe that she was carrying weapons after connecting her to the distribution of a pamphlet filled with violent and racist content**); *Stockton*, 147 F. Supp. 2d at 646 (**finding that discovery of threatening letter on school property justified detention of a group of suspected students**); *Milligan*, 226 F.3d at 654-55 (**detention and questioning of students reasonable when school officials had reasonable suspicion that a fight was about to occur, even absent individualized suspicion that any one of them had engaged in or was about to engage in criminal behavior**).

II. UNREASONABLE SEARCHES

The following cases are examples of how the court applied the standard for student searches and defined which searches are unreasonable.

A. Blanket search and seizure policy

In the case of *Willis by Willis v. Anderson Community School Corp.*, 158 F.3d 415 (7th Cir. 1998), the school board had established a policy that required "a drug and alcohol test for any student who: possesses or uses tobacco products; is suspended for three or more days for fighting; is habitually truant; or violates any other school rule that results in at least a three-day suspension." The court in determining that a single fight by a freshman student was insufficient to form the basis of reasonable suspicion stated at 419 (emphasis added):

As the Supreme Court has acknowledged, articulating a precise definition of "reasonable suspicion" is impossible. See *Ornelas*, 517 U.S. at 695. The Court has made clear that **reasonable suspicion is a "commonsense, nontechnical conception that deal[s] with 'the factual and practical considerations of everyday life on which reasonable prudent men, not legal technicians, act.'"** *Id.* . . . With this definition in mind, we think a prudent person would reasonably conclude that while the Corporation's own statistics suggest some relationship between the use of illegal substances and fighting, the relationship is by no means conclusive. Indeed, it varies dramatically depending on how one analyzes the testing results-- by school, grade or whatever. (And, even more fundamentally, since it is unknown what percentage of the Corporation's general student population uses drugs or alcohol, it is also unknown whether-- at the Corporation's two high schools--students who fight are more likely than their peers to use illegal substances.)

Moreover, while the professional literature reports that fighting is an indication of substance abuse, it also describes fighting as normal for adolescents and advises that a clustering of disruptive behaviors is most indicative of unlawful substance use. As far as we know, of course, Willis was involved in only a single fight. The same can probably be said about some of the other students who have been suspended for fighting. We therefore cannot find that the Corporation's data is strong enough to conclusively establish reasonable suspicion of substance abuse when a student is suspended for fighting. . . .

B. Furtive Gesture

In what some have termed the "furtive gesture" case, the California Supreme Court ruled that an assistant principal lacked reasonable suspicion to search a 16-year-old student's calculator case when the student was stopped on campus because the administrator believed he was tardy for class and the student attempted to hide the case behind his back. When asked what he had in his hand the student said "Nothing." When the administrator looked to see what he was holding the student said, "You can't search me. You need a warrant for this." A search of the case produced marijuana, but the evidence could not be used in a juvenile delinquency proceeding due to the court's ruling that there was not reasonable suspicion to believe that under these circumstances the student possessed contraband. The case is *In Re William G.*, 709 P.2d 1287 (Cal. 1985).

C. Lack of reasonable suspicion

C1. In a case where the girls' swimming coach allegedly required a seventeen-year-old swimmer to take a pregnancy test upon noticing that her times were decreasing and hearing from others that she might be pregnant, the Third Circuit determined that such action constituted a search under the Fourth Amendment. *Gruenke v.Seip*, 225 F.3d 290 (3ʳᵈ Cir. 2000). Because the court concluded the search was unreasonable under this set of facts, the court reversed a summary judgment ruling that had given the coach qualified immunity from suit.

C2. Where an Oregon assistant principal was investigating a fight between a 16-year-old student and another, he took possession of the 16-year-old's jacket that had been lying on the ground. Because the jacket seemed heavier than it should have been, the administrator thought it might contain a weapon. When searched, the jacked produced not the weapon, but a small brass bong that smelled of marijuana and a small plastic bag of psilocybin mushrooms, a Schedule I drug. Applying the *T.L.O.* standard, the court determined that based only on the facts that the student was in a fight and that his jacket felt heavier than it should, the administrator lacked reasonable suspicion to begin the search of the pockets. Hence, the evidence had to be suppressed at the juvenile delinquency hearing. *State ex rel. Juvenile Dept. v. Finch*, 925 P.2d 913 (Or.App. 1996).

C3. Where a school security officer searched a 16-year-old's jacket pockets merely because she was late to class and found two partially smoked marijuana cigarettes, the evidence had to be suppressed because of a lack of reasonable suspicion. *D.I.R. v. State*, 683 N.E.2d 251 (Ind.App. 1997). Despite the fact that the search was performed by a school security officer, the court still applied the less stringent *T.L.O.* reasonable suspicion/ reasonable scope standard, but found that the only fact of the girl's being late to class did not create a reasonable suspicion that she possessed contraband and that "the further intrusion of reaching into D.I.R.'s pockets in light of her age, sex, and nature of the search was not justified under the circumstances." *Id.* at 253.

III. SUSPICIONLESS SEARCHES

In certain situations, courts have found that searches may be found reasonable even though school officials lacked a reasonable suspicion to believe that an individual student possessed or was under the influence of contraband. The dropping of the individualized reasonable suspicion requirement in such circumstances as random drug testing of athletes and other extracurricular activity participants and the use of metal detectors has been allowed due to the important, legitimate, and special need of public schools to protect children from such dominant social forces as drugs and weapons. Courts in these type of cases will apply the more generalized standard stated in *T.L.O.* – reasonableness under the totality of the circumstances.

A. *Suspicionless Urinalysis Testing of Athletes/Other Extracurricular Participants*

Case

Vernonia School Dist. 14J v. Acton, 515 U.S. 1646 (1995)
(footnotes omitted; emphasis added):

The Student Athlete Drug Policy adopted by School District 47J in the town of Vernonia, Oregon, authorizes random urinalysis drug testing of students who participate in the District's school athletics programs. We granted certiorari to decide whether this violates the Fourth and Fourteenth Amendments to the United States Constitution.

[Facts:] Petitioner Vernonia School District 47J (District) operates one high school and three grade schools in the logging community of Vernonia, Oregon. As elsewhere in small-town America, school sports play a prominent role in the town's life, and student athletes are admired in their schools and in the community.

Drugs had not been a major problem in Vernonia schools. In the mid-to-late 1980's, however, teachers and administrators observed a sharp increase in drug use. Students began to speak out about their attraction to the drug culture, and to boast that there was nothing the school could do about it. Along with more drugs came more disciplinary problems. Between 1988 and 1989 the number of disciplinary referrals in Vernonia schools rose to more than twice the number reported in the early 1980's, and several students were suspended. Students became increasingly rude during class; outbursts of profane language became common.

Not only were student athletes included among the drug users but, as the District Court found, athletes were the leaders of the drug culture. . . . This caused the District's administrators particular concern, since drug use increases the risk of sports-related injury. Expert testimony at the trial confirmed the deleterious effects of drugs on motivation, memory, judgment, reaction, coordination, and performance. The high school football and wrestling coach witnessed a severe sternum injury suffered by a wrestler, and various omissions of safety procedures and misexecutions by football players, all attributable in his belief to the effects of drug use. . . .

The school board approved the Policy for implementation in the fall of 1989. Its expressed purpose is to prevent student athletes from using drugs, to protect their health and safety, and to provide drug users with assistance programs.

The Policy applies to all students participating in interscholastic athletics. Students wishing to play sports must sign a form consenting to the testing and must obtain the written consent of their parents. Athletes are tested at the beginning of the season for their sport. In addition, once each week of the season the names of the athletes are placed in a "pool" from which a student, with the supervision of two adults, blindly draws the names of 10% of the athletes for random testing. Those selected are notified and tested that same day, if possible.

The student to be tested completes a specimen control form which bears an assigned number. Prescription medications that the student is taking must be identified by providing a copy of the prescription or a doctor's authorization. The student then enters an empty locker room accompanied by an adult monitor of the same sex. Each boy selected produces a sample at a urinal, remaining fully clothed with his back to the monitor, who stands approximately 12 to 15 feet behind the student. Monitors may (though do not always) watch the student while he produces the sample, and they listen for normal sounds of urination. Girls produce samples in an enclosed bathroom stall, so that they can be heard but not observed. After the sample is produced, it is given to the monitor, who checks it for temperature and tampering and then transfers it to a vial.

The samples are sent to an independent laboratory, which routinely tests them for amphetamines, cocaine, and marijuana. Other drugs, such as LSD, may be screened at the request of the District, but the identity of a particular student does not determine which drugs will be tested. The laboratory's procedures are 99.94% accurate. The District follows strict procedures regarding the chain of custody and access to test results. The laboratory does not know the identity of the students whose samples it tests. It is authorized to mail written test reports only to the superintendent and to provide test results to District personnel by telephone only after the requesting official recites a code confirming his authority. Only the superintendent, principals, vice-principals, and athletic directors have access to test results, and the results are not kept for more than one year.

If a sample tests positive, a second test is administered as soon as possible to confirm the result. If the second test is negative, no further action is taken. If the second test is positive, the athlete's parents are notified, and the school principal convenes a meeting with the student and his parents, at which the student is given the option of (1) participating for six weeks in an assistance program that includes weekly urinalysis, or (2) suffering suspension from athletics for the remainder of the current season and the next athletic season. The student is then retested prior to the start of the next athletic season for which he or she is eligible. The Policy states that a second offense results in automatic imposition of option (2); a third offense in suspension for the remainder of the current season and the next two athletic seasons.

In the fall of 1991, respondent James Acton, then a seventh-grader, signed up to play football at one of the District's grade schools. He was denied participation, however, because he and his parents refused to sign the testing consent forms. The Actons filed suit, seeking declaratory and injunctive relief from enforcement of the Policy on the grounds that it violated the Fourth and Fourteenth Amendments to the United States Constitution and Article I, 9, of the Oregon Constitution. . . .

[Rationale:] The Fourth Amendment to the United States Constitution provides that the Federal Government shall not violate "[t]he right of the people to be secure in their persons, houses, papers, and effects, against unreasonable searches and seizures, . . . " We have held that the Fourteenth Amendment extends this constitutional guarantee to searches and seizures by state officers, . . . including public school officials, *New Jersey v. T. L. O.* . . . In *Skinner v. Railway Labor Executives' Assn.,* . . . (1989), we held that state-compelled collection and testing of urine, such as that required by the Student Athlete Drug Policy, constitutes a "search" subject to the demands of the Fourth Amendment. . . .

As the text of the Fourth Amendment indicates**, the ultimate measure of the constitutionality of a governmental search is "reasonableness.**" At least in a case such as this, . . . whether a particular search meets the reasonableness standard **"is judged by balancing its intrusion on the individual's Fourth Amendment interests against its promotion of legitimate governmental interests**." . . . Where a search is undertaken by law enforcement officials to discover evidence of criminal wrongdoing, this Court has said that reasonableness generally requires the obtaining of a judicial warrant. . . . But a warrant is not required to establish the reasonableness of all government searches; and when a warrant is not required . . ., probable cause is not invariably required either. A search unsupported by probable cause can be constitutional, we have said, **"when special needs, beyond the normal need for law enforcement, make the warrant and probable-cause requirement impracticable**." . . .

We have found such "special needs" to exist in the public-school context. There, the warrant requirement "would unduly interfere with the maintenance of the swift and informal disciplinary procedures [that are] needed," and "strict adherence to the requirement that searches be based upon probable cause" would undercut "the substantial need of teachers and administrators for freedom to maintain order in the schools." *T. L. O.,* . . . The school search we approved in *T. L. O.*, while not based on probable cause, was based on **individualized suspicion of wrongdoing. As we explicitly acknowledged, however, "the Fourth Amendment imposes no irreducible requirement of such suspicion,"** . . . We have upheld **suspicionless searches and seizures** to conduct drug testing of railroad personnel involved in train accidents. . .; to conduct random drug testing of federal customs officers who carry arms or are involved in drug interdiction, . . .; and to maintain automobile checkpoints looking for illegal immigrants and contraband, . . . and drunk drivers, ...

[Issues:] The first factor to be considered is the **nature of the privacy interest upon which the search here at issue intrudes.** . . . **Central, in our view, to the present case is the fact that the subjects of the Policy are (1) children, who (2) have been committed to the temporary custody of the State as schoolmaster**.

Traditionally at common law, and still today, unemancipated minors lack some of the most fundamental rights of self-determination – including even the right of liberty in its narrow sense, i.e., the right to come and go at will. They are subject, even as to their physical freedom, to the control of their parents or guardians. . . .

Fourth Amendment rights, no less than First and Fourteenth Amendment rights, are different in public schools than elsewhere; **the "reasonableness" inquiry cannot**

disregard the schools' custodial and tutelary responsibility for children. For their own good and that of their classmates, public school children are routinely required to submit to various physical examinations, and to be vaccinated against various diseases. . . . Particularly with regard to medical examinations and procedures, therefore, "students within the school environment have a lesser expectation of privacy than members of the population generally." . . .

Legitimate privacy expectations are even less with regard to student athletes. School sports are not for the bashful. They require "suiting up" before each practice or event, and showering and changing afterwards. Public school locker rooms, the usual sites for these activities, are not notable for the privacy they afford. The locker rooms in Vernonia are typical: no individual dressing rooms are provided; shower heads are lined up along a wall, unseparated by any sort of partition or curtain; not even all the toilet stalls have doors. As the United States Court of Appeals for the Seventh Circuit has noted, there is "an element of `communal undress' inherent in athletic participation," *Schaill by Kross v. Tippecanoe County School Corp.*, 864 F.2d 1309, 1318 (1988).

There is an additional respect in which school athletes have a reduced expectation of privacy. By choosing to "go out for the team," **they voluntarily subject themselves to a degree of regulation even higher than that imposed on students generally**. In Vernonia's public schools, they must submit to a preseason physical exam (James testified that his included the giving of a urine sample, App. 17), they must acquire adequate insurance coverage or sign an insurance waiver, maintain a minimum grade point average, and comply with any "rules of conduct, dress, training hours and related matters as may be established for each sport by the head coach and athletic director with the principal's approval. . . . Somewhat like adults who choose to participate in a "closely regulated industry," **students who voluntarily participate in school athletics have reason to expect intrusions upon normal rights and privileges, including privacy**. . . .

Having considered the scope of the legitimate expectation of privacy at issue here, we turn next to the **character of the intrusion** that is complained of. We recognized in *Skinner* that collecting the samples for urinalysis intrudes upon "an excretory function traditionally shielded by great privacy." . . . We noted, however, that **the degree of intrusion depends upon the manner in which production of the urine sample is monitored**. . . . Under the District's Policy, male students produce samples at a urinal along a wall. They remain fully clothed and are only observed from behind, if at all. Female students produce samples in an enclosed stall, with a female monitor standing outside listening only for sounds of tampering. These conditions are nearly identical to those typically encountered in public restrooms, which men, women, and especially school children use daily. **Under such conditions, the privacy interests compromised by the process of obtaining the urine sample are in our view negligible.** The other **privacy-invasive aspect of urinalysis is**, of course, **the information it discloses concerning the state of the subject's body, and the materials he has ingested**. In this regard it is significant that the tests at issue here look only for drugs, and not for whether the student is, for example, epileptic, pregnant, or diabetic. . . . Moreover, the drugs for which the samples are screened are standard, and do not vary according to the identity of the student. And finally, the results of the tests are disclosed only to a limited class of school personnel who have a need to know; and they are not turned over to law enforcement authorities or used for any internal disciplinary function. . . .

[Court rulings:] The General Authorization Form that respondents refused to sign, which refusal was the basis for James's exclusion from the sports program, said only (in relevant part): "I . . . authorize the Vernonia School District to conduct a test on a urine specimen which I provide to test for drugs and/or alcohol use. I also authorize the release of information concerning the results of such a test to the Vernonia School District and to the parents and/or guardians of the student." . . . While the practice of the District seems to have been to have a school official take medication information from the student at the time of the test, . . . that practice is not set forth in, or required by, the Policy, which says simply: "Student athletes who . . . are or have been taking prescription medication must provide verification (either by a copy of the prescription or by doctor's authorization) prior to being tested." . . . It may well be that, if and when James was selected for random testing at a time that he was taking medication, the School District would have permitted him to provide the requested information in a confidential manner - for example, in a sealed envelope delivered to the testing lab. Nothing in the Policy contradicts that, and when respondents choose, in effect, to challenge the Policy on its face, we will not assume the worst. Accordingly, we reach the same conclusion as in Skinner: that the invasion of privacy was not significant.

Finally, we turn to consider the **nature and immediacy of the governmental concern** at issue here, and **the efficacy of this means for meeting it**. . . .

Rather, the phrase [compelling state interest] describes **an interest, which appears important enough to justify the particular search at hand, in light of other factors which show the search to be relatively intrusive upon a genuine expectation of privacy**. Whether that relatively high degree of government concern is necessary in this case or not, we think it is met.

That the nature of the concern is important - indeed, perhaps compelling can hardly be doubted. Deterring drug use by our Nation's schoolchildren is at least as important as enhancing efficient enforcement of the Nation's laws against the importation of drugs, which was the governmental concern in *Von Raab*, . . . or deterring drug use by engineers and trainmen, which was the governmental concern in *Skinner*, . . . School years are the time when the physical, psychological, and addictive effects of drugs are most severe. "Maturing nervous systems are more critically impaired by intoxicants than mature ones are; childhood losses in learning are lifelong and profound"; "children grow chemically dependent more quickly than adults, and their record of recovery is depressingly poor." . . . And of course the effects of a drug-infested school are visited not just upon the users, but upon the entire student body and faculty, as the educational process is disrupted. In the present case, moreover, **the necessity for the State to act is magnified by the fact that this evil is being visited not just upon individuals at large, but upon children for whom it has undertaken a special responsibility of care and direction**. Finally, it must not be lost sight of that this program is directed more narrowly to drug use by school athletes, where the risk of immediate physical harm to the drug user or those with whom he is playing his sport is particularly high. **Apart from psychological effects, which include impairment of judgment, slow reaction time, and a lessening of the perception of pain, the particular drugs screened by the District's Policy have been demonstrated to pose substantial physical risks to athletes**. Amphetamines produce an "artificially induced heart rate increase, [p]eripheral vasoconstriction, [b]lood pressure increase, and [m]asking of the normal fatigue response," making them a "very dangerous drug when used during exercise of any type." . . . Marijuana causes "[i]rregular blood pressure responses during changes in body position," "[r]eduction in the oxygen-carrying capacity of the blood," and "[i]nhibition of the normal sweating responses resulting in increased body temperature." Id., at 94. Cocaine produces "[v]asoconstriction[,] [e]levated blood pressure," and "[p]ossible coronary artery spasms and myocardial infarction." . . .

As for **the immediacy of the District's concerns**: We are not inclined to question – indeed, we could not possibly find clearly erroneous – the District Court's conclusion that "a large segment of the student body, particularly those involved in interscholastic athletics, was in a state of rebellion," that "[d]isciplinary actions had reached `epidemic proportions,'" and that "the rebellion was being fueled by alcohol and drug abuse as well as by the student's misperceptions about the drug culture." . . . That is an immediate crisis of greater proportions than existed in *Skinner*, where we upheld the Government's drug testing program based on findings of drug use by railroad employees nationwide, without proof that a problem existed on the particular railroads whose employees were subject to the test. . . . And of much greater proportions than existed in *Von Raab*, where there was no documented history of drug use by any customs officials. . . .

As to the **efficacy of this means for addressing the problem**: It seems to us self-evident that **a drug problem largely fueled by the "role model" effect of athletes' drug use, and of particular danger to athletes, is effectively addressed by making sure that athletes do not use drugs**. . . .

Taking into account all the factors we have considered above – **the decreased expectation of privacy, the relative unobtrusiveness of the search, and the severity of the need met by the search – we conclude Vernonia's Policy is reasonable and hence constitutional**.

We caution against the assumption that suspicionless drug testing will readily pass constitutional muster in other contexts. The most significant element in this case is the first we discussed: that the Policy was undertaken in furtherance

of the government's responsibilities, under a public school system, as guardian and tutor of children entrusted to its care. Just as when the government conducts a search in its capacity as employer (a warrantless search of an absent employee's desk to obtain an urgently needed file, for example), the relevant question is whether that intrusion upon privacy is one that a reasonable employer might engage in, . . ; so also **when the government acts as guardian and tutor the relevant question is whether the search is one that a reasonable guardian and tutor might undertake**. Given the findings of need made by the District Court, we conclude that in the present case it is. . . .

We therefore vacate the judgment, and remand the case to the Court of Appeals for further proceedings consistent with this opinion.

It is so ordered.

So that there would be no doubt as to the Supreme Court's expression of the importance and need of public schools to protect the safety and health of the students under its care and tutelage, just seven years after deciding *Vernonia*, it ruled in another suspicionless drug testing case involving athletes that a school need not have to prove identifiable drug use among the tested subjects and that it is sufficient, due to the significant governmental interest in deterring drug use, to show that drugs were being used by the general student body.

Case
Board of Education of Indep. Sch. Dist. No. 92 v. Earls, 536 U.S. 822, (2002).

In its discussion of the nature and immediacy of the Oklahoma school's need to adopt its suspicionless drug testing policy of students who participated in *all* extracurricular activities, not just athletics, the *Earls* court stated at pages 2567-2569 (emphasis added):

[**Rationale:**] This Court has already articulated in detail the importance of the governmental concern in preventing drug use by schoolchildren. . . . The drug abuse problem among our Nation's youth has hardly abated since *Vernonia* was decided in 1995. In fact, evidence suggests that it has only grown worse. As in *Vernonia*, "the necessity for the State to act is magnified by the fact that this evil is being visited not just upon individuals at large, but upon children for whom it has undertaken a special responsibility of care and direction." . . . The health and safety risks identified in *Vernonia* apply with equal force to Tecumseh's children. Indeed, the nationwide drug epidemic makes the war against drugs a pressing concern in every school. . . .

Likewise, the need to prevent and deter the substantial harm of childhood drug use provides the necessary immediacy for a school testing policy. Indeed, it would make little sense to require a school district to wait for a substantial portion of its students to begin using drugs before it was allowed to institute a drug testing program designed to deter drug use. . . .

Given the nationwide epidemic of drug use, and the evidence of increased drug use in Tecumseh schools, it was entirely reasonable for the School District to enact this particular drug testing policy. . . .

Respondents also argue that the testing of nonathletes does not implicate any safety concerns, and that safety is a "crucial factor" in applying the special needs framework. . . . They contend that there must be "surpassing safety interests," . . . or "extraordinary safety and national security hazards," . . . in order to override the usual protections of the Fourth Amendment. . . . Respondents are correct that safety factors into the special needs analysis, but **the safety interest furthered by drug testing is undoubtedly substantial for all children, athletes and nonathletes alike**. We know all too well that drug use carries a variety of health risks for children, including death from overdose. . . .

Finally, we find that testing students who participate in extracurricular activities is a reasonably effective means of addressing the School District's legitimate concerns in preventing, deterring, and detecting drug use. While in Vernonia there might have been a closer fit between the testing of athletes and the trial court's finding that the drug problem was "fueled by the 'role model effect of athletes' drug use," such a finding was not essential to the holding. . . . Vernonia did not require the school to test the group of students most likely to use drugs, but rather considered the constitutionality of the program in the context of the public school's custodial responsibilities. Evaluating the Policy in this context, we conclude that the drug testing of Tecumseh students who participate in extracurricular activities effectively serves the School District's interest in protecting the safety and health of its students. . . .

The *Earl's* rationale about the school's substantial interest in safety "for all children, athletes and nonathletes alike," although stated with reference to the particular policy that applied only to athletes and students participating in extracurricular activities, does appear to leave the conceptual door open for a potential winning argument that a school could suspicionlessly drug test students in the general school population if there is a strong enough factual basis to do so. Such a case is still around the proverbial corner.

Three years after the *Vernonia* decision, the Seventh Circuit was faced with the issue of the reasonableness of suspicionless urinalysis drug testing of students who chose to participate in all extracurricular activities, not just athletics.

In *Todd v. Rush County Schools,* 133 F.3d 894 (7ᵗʰ Cir. 1998), the court upheld the policy, stating at 486-487 (emphasis added):

As defendants explained, similar to the program in Vernonia, their program was **designed to deter drug use** and not to catch and punish users. The difference between the cited cases and the present one is that here the testing is also required of those engaging in other extracurricular activities. However, **we find that the reasoning compelling drug testing of athletes also applies to testing of students involved in extracurricular activities**. Certainly successful extracurricular activities require healthy students. While the testing in the present case includes alcohol and nicotine, that is insufficient to condemn it because those substances may also affect students' mental and physical condition.

[Rationale:] Additionally, while recognizing that extracurricular activities "are considered valuable to the school experience, and [that] participation may assist a student in getting into college," the district judge noted that **extracurricular activities, like athletics, "are a privilege at the High School"** . . . . [t]he Rush County Schools' drug testing program **applies only to students who have voluntarily chosen to participate** in an activity. As the district court also noted, students in other extracurricular activities, like athletes, "can take leadership roles in the school community and serve as an example to others" . . . . As this Court has reasoned, **"[p]articipation in interscholastic athletics is a benefit carrying with it enhanced prestige and status in the student community" and thus "[i]t is not unreasonable to couple these benefits with an obligation to undergo drug testing."** . . . Therefore it is appropriate to include students who participate in extracurricular activities in the drug testing.

[Court ruling:] **The linchpin of this drug-testing program is to protect the health of the students** involved. As we have stated, "[t]he plague of illicit drug use which currently threatens our nation's schools adds a major dimension to the difficulties the schools face in fulfilling their purpose--the education of our children. If the schools are to survive and prosper, school administrators must have reasonable means at their disposal to deter conduct which substantially disrupts the school environment." . . . We conclude that Rush County Schools' drug testing program is sufficiently similar to the programs in *Vernonia* and *Schaill* to pass muster under the Fourth and Fourteenth Amendments.

B. School Locker Suspicionless Searches

In the case of *State of Iowa v. Jones*, 666 N.W.2d 142 (Iowa 2003), school officials conducted an annual pre-winter break cleanout of lockers for the purpose of ensuring the health and safety of students and staff and to help maintain school supplies.

During the inspection, teachers observed for such items as trash, food, and overdue library books as the student went through his or her locker. The following day aides went through lockers that had not been inspected because the student did not show up, and in one, found a blue jacket, went through its pockets, and found what proved to be a bag of marijuana.

The court examined the question of whether the student had a legitimate expectation of privacy in the contents of the school locker and noted that the courts in the country are split on the issue. It noted that while some have found no such expectation, especially where a school or state regulation existed that clearly disclaimed a privacy right in the lockers, others have found a privacy expectation even where the school or the state had disclaimed such in its regulations. The court concluded that even though the school district's policy and state law clearly regulated school locker searches, the student had a legitimate expectation of privacy in the contents of the locker. However, in balancing the student's interest in privacy against the school's legitimate interest and duty in maintaining a proper educational environment, the court found the search reasonable under the totality of the circumstances.

The Wisconsin Supreme Court in the case of *Isaiah B. v. State of Wisconsin*, 500 N.W.2d 637 (Wis. 1993) upheld a suspicionless search of lockers when school officials became alarmed at the number of incidents involving reported gun possession at the high school and two incidents of gunfire on school premises over a weekend. The random search of the student's locker revealed a jacket that when taken from the locker felt extra heavy and when the pocket was opened exposed the handle of a revolver. A bag of cocaine was also discovered in the pocket. The court, unlike the Iowa Supreme Court, found that the published rules wherein the school expressed its retention of ownership and possessory control of the lockers resulted in the students having no expectation of privacy in the lockers. Hence, in the search at issue, the student's Fourth Amendment rights were not violated.

C. *Suspicionless Searches for Weapons*

The Eighth Circuit considered a case where a ninth grade student was expelled for possession of crack cocaine that was found in his coat pocket when school officials were looking for guns and knives, and reversed the district court that had found the search unreasonable and awarded $10,000 in damages for his wrongful expulsion.

Case
Thompson v. Carthage School District, 87 F.3d 979 (8th Cir. 1996).

[Facts:] The facts indicated that the school principal directed a search of the pockets and shoes and socks of all male students in grades six through twelve when a school bus driver reported fresh cuts in the seats of her bus. Once the search began, students told the principal that there was a gun at school that morning. After students removed their jackets, emptied their pockets, and removed their shoes and socks, a metal detector was used to check for any concealed weapons on the person of the students. If the detector alerted, a pat down was conducted. Even though the student in question passed the metal detector test, his coat pocket was searched and the crack cocaine discovered.

[Court Ruling:] The court followed the lead of *T.L.O.* and concluded that individualized reasonable suspicion is not always required in school searches and stated that the question "is whether the search was reasonable in all the circumstances," with the focus of the inquiry being "whether the search was justified at its inception [and] whether its scope was reasonably related to the circumstances justifying the search, and the extent of the privacy invasion." *Id.* at 982. Quoting from *T.L.O.*, the court stated that "[i]n a school setting, 'the relevant question is *whether the search is one that a reasonable guardian and tutor might make.*'" *Id.* (Emphasis added.)

Finding that the principal had two independent reasons for suspecting that weapons had been brought to school that morning, the court noted that although she had no grounds for suspecting a particular student, the search was reasonable at its inception because such weapons posed "a risk to student safety and school discipline that 'no reasonable guardian and tutor' could ignore." *Id.* at 983. Because the ordered search of shoes, socks, and pockets was minimally intrusive in light of all the circumstances, the scope of the search was found reasonable as well.

In another case involving a search of students for weapons, the supreme court sought to determine if the search was reasonable.

The Pennsylvania Supreme Court sought to determine if a "point of entry" search for weapons was reasonable. It upheld the search of all students without individualized suspicion as they entered a Philadelphia high school where they were directed to empty their pockets and place the contents along with their coats and backpacks on a table to be searched, and then subjected to a scanning of their person by a hand-held metal detector. *In Re F.B.*, 726 A.2d 361 (Pa. 1999). When the search produced a Swiss army knife with a three-inch blade, F.B. was arrested for a violation of state law.

In reviewing the students' privacy interest at stake, the court cited *T.L.O.* in stating that although students possess a legitimate expectation of privacy in their persons and belongings, such right is limited by "[t]he need to protect all students, to ensure school discipline, and protect school property." *Id.* at 365. In considering the scope of the intrusion, the court noted a prior decision of the court that found searches of lockers and personal affects of the students located therein as reasonable partially because the nature of the intrusion is less for a search of objects than it is for a person. But where the intrusion of the person is by a metal detector, the court noted that there is no physical intrusion and the "actual character of the intrusion suffered by the students during the search is no greater than that regularly experienced by millions of people as they pass through an airport." *Id.* at 366.

Notice to the students was the third element of the court's analysis, which it found to be satisfied by publication of the point of entry search policy and procedure in its manual which was mailed to students' homes and posted conspicuously throughout the building. The final analytical factor was the overall purpose to be achieved by the search and the immediate reasons for its implementation. The court found the purpose prong was met because "the primary object of the search, to remove weapons from students comports with the duty and responsibility of the school administrators to keep their charges save while in the school environment." *Id.* at 367. As to the immediacy prong, the court noted that the trial court had taken judicial notice of the accelerated violence rate in the Philadelphia school system and determined that an immediate need existed for the weapons search of all students when they entered the building. It stated that "[t]he Schools are simply not required to wait for a tragedy to occur within their walls to demonstrate that the need is immediate." *Id.*

D. School Trip Suspicionless Searches

The Washington Supreme Court in a case decided a few months prior to the Supreme Court's *T.L.O.* suspicionless search decision, *Kuehn v. Renton Sch. Dist.*, 694 P.2d 1078 (Wash. 1985), ruled that a suspicionless search of band students' luggage before the start of a concert tour was unreasonable and violated the Fourth Amendment, even though the participation in the trip was voluntary, the students and parents were given notice of the search, and the parents signed permission slips for their children to go on the trip. The court determined that the applicable legal rule not only required a reasonable belief of student contraband possession on the part of the searching school official, but also required that the official believe that the individual student who is searched possessed the prohibited item. The court stated that "[w]hen school officials search large groups of students solely for the purpose of deterring disruptive conduct and without any suspicion of each individual searched, the search does not meet the reasonable belief standard." *Id.* at 1079. If the Washington Supreme Court had had the benefit of the Supreme Court's *T.L.O.* decision, its *Kuehn* ruling may have been different.

Other courts after *T.L.O.* have ruled for the school in field trip related searches that lacked individualized reasonable suspicion at the inception of a search. For example, in *Desilets v. Clearview Regional Board of Education*, 627 A.2d 667 (N.J.Super.A.D. 1993), the court upheld a suspicionless search of all students' hand luggage before the bus left to take them on a field trip to a campground for a picnic. Parents were notified of the search in the permission slip that they signed and returned before their children were allowed on the trip. The *Desilets* court reviewed the Supreme Court's *T.L.O.* decision and quoted from footnote eight therein that stated, "We do not decide whether individualized suspicion is an essential element of the reasonableness standard we adopt for searches by school authorities. . . . the Fourth Amendment imposes no irreducible requirement of such suspicion. . . ." *Id.* at 669. The court in *Desilets* stated at 673:

> The deterrent effect of the board's search policy advances the legitimate interest of the school administrators in preventing students from taking contraband . . . on field trips. . . . [A]ll students . . . must submit to a search of their hand luggage. . . . Consequently, there is no stigma attached to the school search. Anxiety is eliminated by the prior warning that hand luggage will be searched, by the universality of the experience, and by the performance of the search in the open.

We are persuaded that the search was justified at its inception by the unique burdens placed on school personnel in the field trip context and that the search limited to hand luggage was reasonably related to the school's duty to provide discipline, supervision and control. . . .

A federal district court in New York upheld, ultimately on *in loco parentis* grounds, a school official's search of up to twenty hotel rooms of students on a school trip to Disney World after he smelled marijuana smoke in the hallway. *Rhodes v. Guarricino*, 54 F.Supp.2d 186 (S.D.N.Y. 1999). In one room he discovered marijuana in a safe and in another room a bottle of alcohol in a drawer. The offending students were sent home early and suspended from school for three days. In response to the plaintiffs' claim that the administrator lacked individualized suspicion on the particular students that were disciplined, the court stated at 193:

> Since *T.L.O.*, the Supreme Court has specifically held that individualized suspicion is not required for a search to be reasonable [citing *Vernonia*]. While we hold that the extent of suspicion and the scope of the search is clearly relevant to assessing the overall reasonableness of the search in question, the Supreme Court's analysis in *Vernonia* clearly demonstrates that [the school official's] search was reasonable, whether or not there was reason or not to suspect any particular plaintiffs.

E. Recognition of In Loco Parentis to Overnight School Trips

The Sixth Circuit upheld a Tennessee school on the issue of the reasonableness of the search when, during a band trip to Hawaii, its principal searched the female plaintiff's hotel room and an unoccupied adjacent room that was being reached by her and her roommates via an outside shared balcony and whose refrigerator contained alcohol. *Webb v. McCullough*, 828 F.2d 1151 (6th Cir. 1987). The plaintiff and roommates were sent home early and suspended from school. The issue did not involve a question of a lack of individualized reasonable suspicion, but rather whether the doctrine of *in loco parentis* would apply to uphold the reasonableness of the principal's search of the two rooms. The court, acknowledging that the Supreme Court in *T.L.O.* had rejected this doctrine as a source of general authority of school administrators over students, stated at 1157:

> However, *in loco parentis* retains vitality in appropriate circumstances. For instance, one who is *in loco parentis* to a child who is a member of a household acquires the immunity to negligence claims of a natural parent in many jurisdictions. . . .

> The trip to Hawaii was an appropriate circumstance for the operation of in loco parentis. The principal was acting as both a representative of the state and in loco parentis in his task of searching Webb's room. As the district court stated:

> > . . . More so than in an ordinary school situation, the school officials were standing *in loco parentis*. They were faced with the difficult task of supervising students in an unstructured environment far different from that present within the confines of the schoolhouse. In such a situation, it was incumbent upon the school personnel to

be especially vigilant and ready to deal with any violations of the
conduct guidelines which had been established for the trip. . . .

IV. STRIP SEARCHES

A building administrator's decision to strip search a student should be made only
after careful deliberation, and, preferably, with the benefit of legal counsel. Because of
the significant privacy interests involved with the maintenance of bodily integrity, not only
must there be a substantial amount of facts creating a reasonable suspicion that the private
areas of a student's body contains the object of the search, the countervailing interests of
the school district in proceeding with such a search must also be significant. For example,
a school's interest in a search for drugs or weapons that can cause immediate harm is much
higher than in a search for an alleged stolen ring or money.

The Seventh Circuit in the case of *Cornfield v. Consolidated Sch. Dist. No. 230*, 991
F.2d 1316 (7th Cir. 1993) was faced with the question of a strip search of a sixteen-year-old
student who was in a behavioral disorder program and believed to be "crotching" drugs.

On the day before the search, a teacher's aide had reported to Cornfield's teacher
and to the Dean of Students that Cornfield had an unusual bulge in his crotch area. Her
observation was corroborated by another aide and a teacher. The next day his teacher and
the Dean, both males, also observed the same phenomenon, took Cornfield to the office
to question him, where he became belligerent and shouted obscenities. After calling his
mother who refused to give consent to a search, they took him to the empty boys' locker
room, stood at least ten feet on either side of him, and directed him to remove his clothes
and put on a pair of gym shorts. He complied and no drugs or other contraband were
discovered on his person or in his clothes, which were also searched.

The court applied the traditional *T.L.O.* reasonable suspicion/reasonable scope
standard saying that at its inception "a search is warranted only if the student's conduct
creates a reasonable suspicion that a particular regulation or law has been violated, with the
search serving to produce evidence of that violation." *Id.* at 1320. Quoting from *T.L.O.*, the
court noted that in order for the scope of the search to be reasonable "the measures adopted
are reasonably related to the objectives of the search and are not excessively intrusive in
light of the age and sex of the student and the nature of the infraction." *Id.* The court
further warned that "a highly intrusive search in response to a minor infraction would . . .
not comport with the sliding scale advocated by the Supreme Court in *T.L.O.* . . Therefore,
as the intrusiveness of the search of a student intensifies, so too does the standard of Fourth
Amendment reasonableness." *Id.* at 1320-1321.

The court found that there was reasonable suspicion to believe that Cornfield was
"crotching" drugs. In addition to the unusable bulge observed by three staff members on
the first day and by the teacher and dean on the day of the search, the school's evidence
indicated that Cornfield had stated to the teacher that he had in the past been dealing in
drugs and that if he had been drug tested on a certain date, it would have shown positive for
marijuana. The facts also revealed that his bus driver had reported the smell of marijuana

where Cornfield had been sitting, a student had stated that he saw him smoke marijuana on the school bus while another student said he saw Cornfield in possession of drugs on school grounds, and that he had told an aide that he had "crotched" drugs during a police raid at his mother's house. Lastly, the teacher, who along with the Dean observed the bulge in his pants the day of the search, stated that he had observed Cornfield throughout the school year and this was the first time he had noticed an unusual bulge in his crotch area.

The court, in finding that reasonable scope prong of the *T.L.O.* legal standard had also been met, stated at 1323:

> As administered, two male school personnel performed the search and did so in the privacy of the boys' locker room. . . . As Cornfield changed, Spencer and Frye observed from a certain distance away to ensure Cornfield could not conceal any drugs or other contraband he was suspected of carrying. In addition, Spencer and Frye did not physically touch him or subject him to a body cavity search, nor did they have him suffer the indignity of standing naked before them but allowed him to put on a gym uniform while they searched his street clothes. Finally, the fact that [they] found no drugs or other contraband does not allow us to conclude retrospectively that the search was unreasonable in scope.

Another case also examines the legal standard for strip searches. In *State ex rel. Galford v. Mark Anthony B.*, 433 S.E.2d 41 (W.Va. 1993) a case involving the theft of $100 from a teacher's purse that had been placed under her desk, the West Virginia Supreme Court invalidated the strip search of a fourteen-year-old eighth grade boy even though the stolen money was found in the back of his underwear. The court applied the *T.L.O.* standard and found that the search was reasonable at its inception because the principal had reasonable grounds to suspect the student after he admitted to the school social worker that he had been alone in the teacher's room during the time relevant to the theft's occurrence.

The search consisted of the principal taking the boy to the restroom and looking in his pockets and socks, followed by having him lower his pants and first pulling his underwear open in the front, and then the back where the money was located. In finding that the strip search violated *T.L.O.*'s reasonable scope standard, the court discounted the two cases relied upon by the state that had upheld the reasonableness of student strip searches where the object of the search was drugs because in those cases the courts had reasoned that the scope of the search was not excessively intrusive when weighed against the school's substantial need to safeguard students from the dangers of drugs. However, where the object of the search was stolen money, the *Galford* court found the danger faced by the school was "relatively slight," and stated at 49 (emphasis added):

The appellant was suspected of stealing money. Such activity should never be condoned or encouraged in our schools. However, escalating the nature of the suspected infraction strictly in terms of the danger it presents to other students, it does not begin to approach the threat posed by the possession of weapons or drugs. Quite simply, the appellant's suspected conduct did not pose the type of **immediate danger to others** that might conceivably necessitate and justify a warrantless strip search. . . .

We conclude that in the absence of exigent circumstances which necessitate an immediate search in order to ensure the safety of other students, a warrantless strip search of a student conducted by a school official is presumed to be "excessively intrusive" and thus unreasonable in scope.

V. CANINE DRUG DETECTION

Is it a "search" within the meaning of the Fourth Amendment to use trained dogs to detect the presence of drugs on the persons of students? The Seventh Circuit has answered that is not a search, *Doe v. Renfrow*, 631 F.2d 91 (7th Cir. 1980), whereas the Fifth Circuit has ruled it a search, *Horton v. Goose Creek Indep. Sch. Dist.*, 690 F.2d 470 (5th Cir. 1982). The Supreme Court has not answered the question in the school context.

The Seventh Circuit in *Renfrow* affirmed, without discussion, the ruling of the northern Indiana federal district court at 475 F.Supp. 1012 (N.D.Ind. 1979), which found that under circumstances, where in the previous twenty days school officials at the junior high and high school had found thirteen students in possession or under the influence of illegal drugs or alcohol, the use of trained dogs to sniff the air around each student's desk "was an aid to the school administrator and as such its use is not considered a search." *Id.* at 1022. The district court's view of the school's utilization of canine detection of the odor of drugs in the air surrounding each student was that it amounted to an inspection. The court stated that "[a] reasonable right to inspection is necessary to the school's performance of its duty to provide an educational environment." *Id.*

On the other hand, the Fifth Circuit in *Horton* saw the use of dogs to sniff the persons of the students as a search. An important fact that was introduced into evidence in *Horton*, but not in *Renfrow*, was that the dogs actually touched the bodies of the students, which the Fifth Circuit found highly intrusive and constituted a search. The court stated that "society recognizes the interest in the integrity of one's person, and the fourth amendment applies with its fullest vigor against any intrusion on the human body." 690 F.2d at 478.

VI. POLICE INVOLVEMENT IN SEARCHES

In the previously discussed *Doe v. Renfrow* "dog sniff" case, the federal district court discussed, as follows, the legal impact of the presence of police as dog handlers when, as the court phrased it, the air surrounding the students' desks was sniffed:

> Acting alone, each school administrator could have unquestionably surveyed a classroom to prevent drug use. Because these administrators now acted with assistance from a uniformed officer does not change their function. The officers were merely **aiding in the inspection, at the request of the school administrators**. Their presence does not change the actions of the school official from that of supervision *in loco parentis* to that of an unwarranted search. . . .

475 F.Supp. 1012, 1020 (N.D.Ind. 1979) (emphasis added), affirmed, except for the immunity issue, 631 F.2d 91 (7th Cir. 1980).

The Illinois Supreme Court in the case of *People v. Dilworth*, 661 N.E.2d 310 (Ill. 1996) was faced with the issue of whether a school security officer, who had searched a student and seized crack cocaine, by being employed by the police and assigned full time as a staff member to the alternative school was required to have probable cause in order to begin a search. In reviewing numerous cases on the correct legal standard to apply to public school searches and seizures when law enforcement personnel are utilized, the court determined that the lower reasonable suspicion standard applied, and stated at 317 (emphasis added):

> Decisions . . . that involve police officers in school settings can generally be grouped into the following three categories: (1) those where school officials initiate a search or where police involvement is minimal, (2) those involving school police or liaison officers acting on their own authority, and (3) those where outside police officers initiate a search. Where school officials initiate the search or police involvement is minimal, most courts have held that the reasonable suspicion standard obtains. . . . The same is true in cases involving school police or liaison officers acting on their own authority. . . . However, **where outside police officers initiate the search or where school officials act at the behest of law enforcement agencies, the probable cause standard has been applied**.

VII. CONSENT TO SEARCH

In the case of *Anable v. Ford*, 653 F.Supp. 22 (W.D.Ark. 1985), the court was faced with the issue of whether Anable, a high school student, had freely and voluntarily consented to take a breathalyzer test, the results of which were positive for having alcohol in his system.

Based on numerous incidents of disruptive conduct at school one morning plus the observation of the superintendent that he and his stepbrother smelled of alcohol and the discovery of a soft drink bottle smelling of liquor found in the car in which they rode to school, Anable was told that he had three choices: withdraw from school, be expelled, or take a breathalyzer test. After initially refusing, he, with the approval of his mother, agreed to take the test and signed a written consent form.

The court first considered whether school officials under *T.L.O.* had reasonable suspicion to believe that Anable was under the influence of alcohol before they presented the three options to him, and concluded that they had a justifiable belief that he was sufficiently under such influence "as to alter his ability to function on a physical or mental task." *Id.* at 36.

The court then considered the consent issue and in finding that he had been repeatedly informed of the three choices stated at page 36 (emphasis added):

The dispositive reason, however, why the breathalyzer test poses no constitutional problem is that plaintiff **freely executed a valid consent** to the procedure. His mother had also given her consent. Anable's written consent states clearly "Mr. Green, I will take a breathalyzer test. You have my consent and my mother's consent."

Anable was not misled. He was told what the evidence was and that the official would expel him or allow him to withdraw. . . .

Finally, the court believes that the breathalyzer is not an exceptionally invasive procedure. Taking a student to the police station to blow into a breathalyzer machine is little more invasive in itself than taking a child to a five-and-dime store to blow up a balloon.

In the Michigan case which follows, the court set a standard for determining the validity of a student's waiver of rights. ***Fewless ex rel. Fewless v. Board of Education of Wayland Union Schools***, 208 F.Supp.2d 806 (W.D.Mich. 2002)

The court was faced with the school's defense that fourteen-year-old Fewless consented to a strip search that occurred after an assistant principal was informed by other students that Fewless had told them that he had evaded a previous search that day for marijuana in his pockets and gym bag by hiding it in his "butt crack." The school argued that after Fewless had denied the accusation, the school security officer informed him that three times that he did not have to consent, that he could leave, that that the strip search had to be freely and voluntarily given, and that Fewless gave consent by saying, "I have nothing to hide."

The court enunciated the components of the legal standard for consent at page 813 (emphasis added):

A search authorized by consent of the searched individual is constitutionally permissible, as long as the **consent was given both freely and voluntarily**. . . .

Voluntariness of a consent to a search should be **determined from the totality of the circumstances**, including both the characteristics of the searched party and the details of the interrogation. . . . First, the Court should examine the **characteristics of the**

searched individual, including age, intelligence, and education; whether the individual **understands the right to refuse to consent**; and whether the **individual understands his or her constitutional rights**. . . . Second, the Court should consider the **details of any detention, and the use of coercive or punishing conduct**. . . . Further, the Court is to consider **indications of more subtle forms of coercion** that might impact an individual's judgment.

The Sixth Circuit has held that there is a **presumption against the waiver of constitutional rights**. . . . When litigating the issue of consent, **the burden is on the defendants to demonstrate such a voluntary relinquishment of constitutional rights** by the plaintiff. . . . **Consent must be proved by clear and positive testimony and must be unequivocal, specific, and intelligently given, uncontaminated by any duress and coercion**. . . .

The court in concluding that valid consent had not been given and in ruling against the school stated at 815:

> Joseph Fewless was a vulnerable youth in a situation akin to police custody. Defendants knew of his vulnerability, youth, and behavioral conditions impacting his impulse control and decision making capacity. He was not provided an opportunity to speak to someone who was an advocate for him like a parent, counselor, or attorney. He never gave explicit, clear consent to be searched which is required for a constitutionally valid consent; at most, his statements and actions could be described as acquiescence. . . . "I have nothing to hide," without more, is not an expression of consent to be searched, particularly consent to be examined partially naked, as Joseph was. . . .

VIII. SEIZURES

The protections of the Fourth Amendment apply not only to student searches, which are the overwhelmingly litigated area, but also to the question of whether a student has been improperly "seized" by school officials.

In the case of *Wallace v. Batavia Sch. Dist. 101*, 69 F.3d 1010 (7th Cir. 1995), a sixteen-year-old female student alleged that her business teacher had violated the unreasonable seizure prong of the Fourth Amendment when he took hold of her arm at the elbow and moved her toward the door. The school argued that the teacher was justified in that his actions were reasonable in that he took hold of her after he had broken up a fight between her and another student and when she would not voluntarily follow his directive to remove herself from the room.

The court in ruling against the student noted that the Supreme Court in the *Vernonia* athlete suspicionless drug testing case had recognized "that students have a reduced liberty interest once inside the schoolhouse gate," and stated at 1014:

We thus hold that, in the context of a public school, a teacher or administrator who seizes a student does so in violation of the Fourth Amendment only when the restriction of liberty is unreasonable under the circumstances then existing and apparent. Therefore, in seeking to maintain order and discipline, a teacher or administrator is simply constrained to taking reasonable action to achieve those goals. Depending on the circumstances, reasonable action may certainly include the seizure of a student in the fact of provocative or disruptive behavior.

The Ninth Circuit set a standard for reasonable seizure in *Doe ex rel. Doe v. State of Hawaii Dept. of Educ.*, 334 F.3d 906 (9th Cir. 2003) in finding a Fourth Amendment seizure violation when an elementary school vice principal taped an eight-year-old boy's head to a tree for five minutes for refusing his directive to stand still against a wall in the office as time-out punishment for having participated in a fight. The court stated that "a seizure occurs when there is a restraint on liberty to the degree that a reasonable person would not feel free to leave. . . .", that a "seizure violates the Fourth Amendment if it is objectively unreasonable under the circumstances, and that in applying the Fourth Amendment in the school context, the reasonableness of the seizure must be considered in light of the educational objectives . . . trying to be achieved." *Id.* at 909.

The courts examined another case dealing with reasonable seizure in *Daniel S. v. Board of Educ. of York Community High Sch.*, 152 F.Supp.2d 949 (N.D.Ill. 2001), where the court denied the school's motion to dismiss when it was sued for an illegal Fourth Amendment seizure after the high school gym teacher ordered the seventeen-year-old plaintiff, along with another boy, to stand naked in the shower area after they had deliberately ripped apart their swimming suits upon entering the locker room. The teacher directed them to remove the remains of their swim suits and refused to hand them towels when they requested such. The teacher then left and the boys remained standing in such a state as the rest of their classmates dressed and left and as the next gym class entered the locker room, a total of some sixteen minutes. The court applied the *Wallace v. Batavia* legal standard, discussed above, denied the school's motion to dismiss, and noted that the "Defendants have failed to present any specific legal authority which states that seizure under these conditions is reasonable as a matter of law." *Id.* at 953.

SCENARIO

STATE AND APPLY THE RELEVANT LEGAL RULE(S) TO THE FACTS.

Student was a short, slightly-built thirteen-year-old seventh grader. Principal informed the teaching staff that based on a number of reports from other students he thought Student may be a drug dealer, and that the teachers should closely observe him, especially in the hallways, rest rooms, and cafeteria. One lunch period, within a span or ten minutes, Teacher observed Student entering and leaving the restroom three times, each time with a different student. On all three occasions, Student and the other student remained in the restroom for 15 seconds at most, and in Teacher's opinion "appeared nervous" when they left. Teacher reported these facts and his opinion to Principal. Another teacher had already reported to Principal on the same day that Student and another student, who was under suspicion for drug dealing, were having lunch together in an isolated corner of the cafeteria.

Based on this information, Principal had Student brought to his office and in the presence of the school security officer directed Student to empty his pockets, which produced some change and a bi-fold wallet. Principal opened the wallet and found three ten dollar bills, which were explained by Student to be birthday money when he turned thirteen last week. Principal then looked for and found a secret compartment in the wallet that produced five, thin plastic packages of a white powder. Student explained that the substance was baking powder and that he brought it to school as a practical joke to get a friend after school to believe it was cocaine. Immediately, Student was made to remove all of his clothing, including underwear, which produced a plastic packet from his underwear containing four "rocks" of a substance resembling crack cocaine. A laboratory test revealed that the powder was in fact baking powder, and the "rocks" were crack cocaine.

Following proper due process, Principal suspended Student from school pending expulsion proceedings for drug possession. Parents on behalf of Student responded by filing suit in federal district court to prevent the evidence from being presented at the expulsion hearing

CHAPTER 8

STUDENT EXPRESSION AND THE FIRST AMENDMENT

The First Amendment's guarantee of freedom of speech is applied to public school students in all the states through the Fourteenth Amendment. In an early student expression case, where the Supreme Court upheld the right of students to remain silent in the face of a state-compelled flag salute and recitation of the Pledge of Allegiance, the court in *West Virginia State Bd. of Educ. v. Barnette*, 319 U.S. 624, 624 (1943), stated:

> If there is any fixed star in our constitutional constellation, it is that no official, high or petty, can prescribe what shall be orthodox in politics, nationalism, religion, or other matters of opinion, or force citizens to confess by word or act their faith therein. If there are any circumstances which permit an exception, they do not now occur to us.

> We think the action of the local authorities in compelling the flag salute and pledge transcends constitutional limitations on their power, and invades the sphere of intellect and spirit which it is the purpose of the First Amendment to our Constitution to reserve from all official control.

I. CASES WHICH SET THE LEGAL STANDARD FOR STUDENT EXPRESSION: THE BLACK ARM BAND, LEWD SPEECH, AND SCHOOL PAPER CASES

A. The Tinker "Black Arm Band" Case

The first of three major student speech cases that followed *Barnette* was decided in 1969 in the case of *Tinker v. Des Moines Indep. Sch. Dist.*, 393 U.S.503, where the court fashioned a legal standard to be applied to protected personal expression (as opposed to expression occurring in school-sponsored speech activities such as the school paper). The *Tinker* standard requires officials to prove that the personal (as opposed to school-sponsored) speech in question created a substantial disruption of or material interference with school activities or purposes, or at least led to a reasonable forecast of such disruption or interference. In Tinker, the court ruled that the school's evidence failed to prove that black armbands worn by several students as a silent, symbolic protest of the Viet Nam war met the standard. The *Tinker* Court in a number of significant passages stated (emphasis added):

> The District Court concluded that the action of the school authorities was reasonable because it was based upon their fear of a disturbance from the wearing of the armbands. But, in our system, undifferentiated fear or apprehension of disturbance is not enough to overcome the right to freedom of expression. . .

> In order for the State in the person of school officials to justify prohibition of a particular expression of opinion, **it must be able to show that its action was caused by something more than a mere desire to avoid the discomfort and unpleasantness that always accompany an unpopular viewpoint**. . .

> . . . the action of the school authorities appears to have been based upon an urgent wish to avoid the controversy which might result from the expression, even by the silent symbol of armbands, of opposition to this Nation's part in the conflagration in Vietnam. . .

> It is also relevant that the school authorities did not purport to prohibit the wearing of all symbols of political or controversial significance. The record shows that students   in some of the schools wore buttons relating to national political campaigns, and some even wore the Iron Cross, traditionally a symbol of Nazism. The order prohibiting the   wearing   of   armbands did not extend to these. Instead, a particular symbol -- black armbands worn to exhibit opposition to this Nation's involvement in Vietnam -- was singled out for prohibition. **Clearly, the prohibition of expression of one particular opinion, at least without evidence that it is necessary to avoid material and substantial interference with schoolwork or discipline, is not constitutionally permissible.**

In our system, state-operated schools may not be enclaves of totalitarianism. **School officials do not possess absolute authority over their students.** Students in school, as well as out of school, are "persons" under our Constitution. **They are possessed of fundamental rights which the State must respect,** just as they themselves must respect their obligations to the State. In our system, students may not be regarded as closed-circuit recipients of only that which the State chooses to communicate. They may not be confined to the expression of those sentiments that are officially approved. **In the absence of a specific showing of constitutionally valid reasons to regulate their speech, students are entitled to freedom of expression of their views.** . .

A student's rights, therefore, do not embrace merely the classroom hours. **When he is in the cafeteria, or on the playing field, or on the campus during the authorized hours, he may express his opinions,** even on controversial subjects like the conflict in Vietnam, **if he does so without "materially and substantially interfer[ing] with the requirements of appropriate discipline in the operation of the school" and without colliding with the rights of others.** . . . .

B. The Fraser "Lewd Speech" Case

In 1986, the Supreme Court decided the second major student speech case in *Bethel Sch. Dist. v. Fraser*, 478 U.S. 675. The court was faced with the district and circuit courts having ruled in favor of student Fraser because, in applying the Tinker legal standard, both courts found that the school had not met its burden of proving that his sexually suggestive nomination speech had caused substantial disruption or material interference. The Supreme Court reversed the circuit court, ruled in favor of the school district, and established the legal standard that schools may discipline student expression that is lewd, vulgar, indecent or plainly offensive. The *Fraser* court stated (emphasis added):

The marked distinction between the political "message" of the armbands in Tinker and the sexual content of respondent's speech in this case seems to have been given little weight by the Court of Appeals. In upholding the students' right to engage in a nondisruptive, passive expression of a political viewpoint in Tinker, this Court was careful to note that the case did "not concern speech or action that intrudes upon the work of the schools or the rights of other students." . . . **The role and purpose of the American public school system** were well described by two historians, who stated:

[P]ublic education must prepare pupils for citizenship in the Republic. . . . **It must inculcate the habits and manners of civility as values in themselves** conducive to happiness and as indispensable to the practice of self-government in the community and the nation.

. . . **These fundamental values of "habits and manners of civility"**

essential to a democratic society must, of course, include tolerance of divergent political and religious views, even when the views expressed may be unpopular. But these "fundamental values" must also take into account consideration of the sensibilities of others, and, in the case of a school, the sensibilities of fellow students. **The undoubted freedom to advocate unpopular and controversial views in schools and classrooms must be balanced against the society's countervailing interest in teaching students the boundaries of socially appropriate behavior**. . .

The First Amendment guarantees wide freedom in matters of adult public discourse. A sharply divided Court upheld the right to express an antidraft viewpoint in a public place, albeit in terms highly offensive to most citizens. See *Cohen v. California*, 403 U.S. 15(1971). It does not follow, however, that, simply because the use of an offensive form of expression may not be prohibited to adults making what the speaker considers a political point, the same latitude must be permitted to children in a public school. In New Jersey v. T.L.O., 469 U.S. 325, 340-342, (1985), we reaffirmed that **the constitutional rights of students in public school are not automatically coextensive with the rights of adults in other settings.** As cogently expressed by Judge Newman, "the First Amendment gives a high school student the classroom right to wear Tinker's armband, but not Cohen's jacket." *Thomas v. Board of Education, Granville Central School Dist.*, 607 F.2d 1043, 1057 (CA2 1979) (opinion concurring in result). . . .

In the *Cohen v. California* case cited above, the Supreme Court upheld Cohen's right, *in a public place*, to wear a jacket in a courthouse that displayed the phrase, "F--- the draft."

C. *The Hazelwood "School Newspaper Censorship" Case*

The third Supreme Court student speech case, *Hazelwood Sch. Dist. v. Kuhlmeier*, 484 U.S. 260 (1988), upheld the school principal's deletion of two student-written articles from the newspaper that was part of the school's journalism curriculum. One article dealt with teen pregnancy and the other with divorce. The court set the legal standard to be used when evaluating student expression within a school-sponsored speech forum as that of a legitimate pedagogical concern. In a number of important passages, it stated, the *Hazlewood* court stated [emphasis added]:

We deal first with the question whether Spectrum may appropriately be characterized as a forum for public expression. **The public schools do not possess all of the attributes of streets, parks, and other traditional public forums** that "time out of mind, have been used for purposes of assembly, communicating thoughts between citizens, and discussing public questions." . . . Hence, **school facilities may be deemed to be public forums only if school authorities have "by policy or by practice" opened those facilities "for indiscriminate use by the general public,"** Perry Education

Assn. v. Perry Local Educators' Assn., 460 U.S. 37, 47 (1983), or by some segment of the public, such as student organizations. . . **If the facilities have instead been reserved for other intended purposes, "communicative or otherwise," then no public forum has been created, and school officials may impose reasonable restrictions on the speech of students, teachers, and other members of the school community. . . The government does not create a public forum by inaction or by permitting limited discourse, but only by intentionally opening a nontraditional forum for public discourse. . .**

The question whether the First Amendment requires a school to tolerate particular student speech -- the question that we addressed in Tinker -- is different from the question whether the First Amendment requires a school affirmatively to promote particular student speech. The former question addresses educators' ability to silence a student's personal expression that happens to occur on the school premises. **The latter question concerns educators' authority over school-sponsored publications, theatrical productions, and other expressive activities that students, parents, and members of the public might reasonably perceive to bear the imprimatur of the school. These activities may fairly be characterized as part of the school curriculum,** whether or not they occur in a traditional classroom setting, **so long as they are supervised by faculty members and designed to impart particular knowledge or skills to student participants and audiences.**

Educators are entitled to exercise greater control over this second form of student expression to assure that participants learn whatever lessons the activity is designed to teach, that readers or listeners are not exposed to material that may be inappropriate for their level of maturity, and that the views of the individual speaker are not erroneously attributed to the school. Hence, a school may, in its capacity as publisher of a school newspaper or producer of a school play, "disassociate itself," . . . not only from speech that would "substantially interfere with [its] work . . . or impinge upon the rights of other students," Tinker. . . but also from speech that is, for example, ungrammatical, poorly written, inadequately researched, biased or prejudiced, vulgar or profane, or unsuitable for immature audiences. . .

. . . we conclude that the standard articulated in Tinker for determining when a school may punish student expression need not also be the standard for determining when a school may refuse to lend its name and resources to the dissemination of student expression. Instead, **we hold that educators do not offend the First Amendment by exercising editorial control over the style and content of student speech in school-sponsored expressive activities, so long as their actions are reasonably related to legitimate pedagogical concerns. . . .**

Case
Henerey ex rel Henerey, 200 F.3d 1128 (8th Cir. 1999)
(emphasis added)

[Facts:] In March 1997, Henerey, then a sophomore at St. Charles High School, applied to run for junior class president in an upcoming student council election. Although candidacy was open to all members of the sophomore class, those seeking to run were required to meet with Mary Stodden, the student council advisor, and to sign a contract of obligation. Under the terms of the contract, candidates agreed to obey all school rules. After Henerey signed the contract, a member of the student council advised him that all campaign flyers and posters had to be approved by the administration prior to distribution.

The campaign officially began on April 7, 1997. Henerey obtained approval from the administration for his campaign slogan, "Adam Henerey, The Safe Choice." On the evening of April 7, Henerey was informed by Stodden that other candidates had complained that his posters had been posted over theirs and that references to other candidates were demeaning. Stodden then told Henerey that all materials needed to be approved by the administration.

On the morning of April 10, 1997, the day of the election, Henerey handed out in the school hallways some eleven condoms attached to stickers bearing his campaign slogan. He had given the administration no prior indication that he planned to distribute condoms or that his campaign would in any way involve sex-related topics.

As Ms. Stodden was counting the ballots, a student complained to her about Henerey's distribution of condoms. Ms. Stodden in turn relayed the complaint to Dr. Jerry Cook, the school principal, who determined that Henerey should be disqualified from the student election for his failure to comply with School Board Rule KJ-R, which required students to get prior approval from the school principal or assistant principal before distributing any materials. A subsequent count of the votes revealed that Henerey had received a majority of the votes for junior class president. . . [but the principal decided] to disqualify Henerey for his failure to comply with Rule KJ-R. . .

[Legal Background:] Although students do not "shed their constitutional rights to freedom of speech or expression at the schoolhouse gate," *Tinker v. Des Moines Indep. Community Sch. Dist.*, . . . **the Constitution does not compel "teachers, parents, and elected school officials to surrender control of the American public school system to public school students."** *Bethel Sch. Dist. No. 403 v. Fraser*, . . . (The constitutional rights of public school students "are not automatically coextensive with the rights of adults in other settings," *Fraser*, . . . , and a school need not tolerate speech that is inconsistent with its pedagogical mission, even though the government could not suppress that speech outside of the schoolhouse. See *Hazelwood Sch. Dist. v. Kuhlmeier* . . .; *Poling v. Murphy*, 872 F.2d 757, 762

(6th Cir. 1989 ("Limitations on speech that would be unconstitutional outside the schoolhouse are not necessarily unconstitutional within it."). Therefore, **courts must analyze First Amendment violations alleged by students "in light of the special characteristics of the school environment."** *Hazelwood* . . .

Purely individual speech by students constituting "personal expression that happens to occur on the school premises" is subject to a high degree of First Amendment protection. *Hazelwood*, . . . However, school officials may restrict even individual student expression that "materially and substantially interfere[s] with the requirements of appropriate discipline in the operation of the school," or that "would substantially interfere with the work of the school or impinge upon the rights of other students." *Tinker*. . .

When the expressive conduct at issue occurs in the context of a school-sponsored activity that is not also a public forum, the authority of schools to exercise control over the content of speech is at its greatest. . . In the absence of a public forum, school officials may limit a student's speech in a school-sponsored activity if the limitation is "reasonably related to legitimate pedagogical concerns." *Hazelwood* . . .

[Forum Analysis:] Henerey argues that the campaign for class president must be considered a forum for public expression. The nature of the forum affects the degree of protection the First Amendment affords to expressive activity, even within the public school setting. See, e.g., Hazelwood . . . (conducting forum analysis as first step in addressing student speech claim); Perry Educ. Ass'n v. Perry Local Educators' Ass'n, 460 U.S. 37, 44 (1983) ("The existence of a right of access to public property and the standard by which limitations upon such a right must be evaluated differ depending on the character of the property at issue."); Muller v. Jefferson Lighthouse Sch., 98 F.3d 1530, 1540 (7th Cir. 1996) (prior restraint of student speech not unconstitutional in nonpublic forum).

Although school facilities are traditionally deemed nonpublic fora, they may be designated public when school authorities have a policy or practice of opening them for indiscriminate use by the general public, or by some segment of the public such as student organizations. . . . "The government does not create a public forum by inaction or by permitting limited discourse, but only by intentionally opening a nontraditional forum for public discourse." Hazelwood . . .

Here, the District did not open the campaign to the public, and it obviously intended to control the speech associated with the student election. Only enrolled students were eligible for candidacy in the election, and those who sought an elected position were required to sign an agreement stating that they would obey school rules. In addition, all campaign materials had to be approved prior to their distribution or use. Thus, because there is no evidence that the school intended by "policy or practice" to relinquish its control over the election and designate it a forum for public expression . . . we conclude that the election was conducted within the context of a nonpublic forum.

[School-Sponsored or Independent (Personal) Speech:] The next question is whether Henerey's expression was school-sponsored speech or independent student speech. . . A school may exercise greater control over student speech uttered during participation in a school sponsored activity than that expressed during an independent activity because "students, parents, and members of the public might reasonably perceive [the school sponsored speech] to bear the imprimatur of the school." . . . Such control also "assure[s] that participants learn whatever lessons the activity is designed to teach, that readers or listeners are not exposed to material that may be inappropriate for their level of maturity, and that the views of the individual speaker are not erroneously attributed to the school." . . . Although to be considered "school-sponsored," expressive activities must be "curricular" in a broad sense, they need not "occur in a traditional classroom setting, so long as they are supervised by faculty members and designed to impart particular knowledge or skills to student participants and audiences." . . .

The election was supervised by a school administrator serving as the student council advisor, and it ran for a limited time period set by the school. It was operated under the auspices of the school administration, and any member of the public could reasonably have concluded that campaign materials were distributed with the implied approval of the school. Moreover, the election was conducted for the pedagogical purposes of allowing candidates to learn leadership skills and exposing the general student body to the democratic process. Accordingly, we agree with the district court that the election was a school-sponsored activity that was a part of the school's curriculum. . . . (there can be "no doubt" that a student election is a school-sponsored activity for First Amendment purposes). In this setting, the question becomes whether the District's decision to disqualify Henerey from the election was reasonably related to legitimate pedagogical concerns. See *Hazelwood* . . .

[Rule on Student Advertising:] We turn first to the District's contention that the sole basis for its decision to disqualify Henerey was his violation of school rules. The relevant portions of Rule KJR read as follows:

ADVERTISING IN THE SCHOOLS (Board Policy KJ-R)

> 1. Places
> The distribution of such items may take place in a location approved by principal of the school. . . .

> 3. Approval
> The approval must be obtained the previous day or earlier from the principal or assistant principal. (For materials not readily classifiable or approvable more than one school day should be allowed.) The approved articles will bear the official stamp of the school, "Approved for Distribution or Posting." . . .

> 5. Unacceptable Items
> Hate literature which attacks ethnic, religious or racial groups, other

irresponsible publications aimed at encouraging hostility and violence; pornography, obscenity and materials unsuitable for distribution in the schools is unacceptable as well as:

a. Materials judged libelous to specific individuals in or out of school

b. Materials designed for commercial purposes - to advertise or promote a product or service for sale or rent.

c. Materials which are designed to solicit funds unless approved by the superintendent or his assistant

d. Materials the principal is convinced would materially disrupt class work or involve substantial disorder or invasion of the rights of others

6. Acceptable Materials
All materials not proscribed in "Unacceptable items".

The District's position is that it disciplined Henerey simply because he had failed to comply with Rule KJ-R. The District contends that it acted reasonably because it has a legitimate interest in disciplining students who do not obey school rules, noting that despite repeated warnings, Henerey failed to obtain prior approval for his campaign materials. . .

[Issue of Unconstitutional Prior Restraint and Vagueness:] Henerey argues that Rule KJ-R is unconstitutional on its face as a prior restraint on speech and as unconstitutionally vague. **Generally, prior restraints are subject to the highest degree of scrutiny and are the form of regulation most difficult to sustain under the First Amendment. . . However, the prior restraint of speech within secondary schools is not per se unconstitutional.** See *Hazelwood. . .*; *Bystrom v. Fridley High Sch., Indep. Sch. Dist. No. 14*, 822 F.2d 747, 750 (8th Cir. 1987).

As to vagueness, Henerey argues that Rule KJ-R effectively gives the principal unfettered discretion to determine what materials are unacceptable. As we noted in Bystrom, however, "a high degree of generality is made necessary by the subject matter. The concepts involved (indecency, vulgarity, likelihood of material disruption) are general by their very nature." . . . The rule furthers several legitimate interests of public schools identified in Bystrom, including the interest in assuring that "school hours and school property are devoted primarily to education as embodied in the district's prescribed curriculum," and the interest in "preserv[ing] some trace of calm on school property." . . . More generally, Rule KJ-R appears to be "one expression of the 'legitimate and substantial community interest in promoting respect for authority and traditional values be they social, moral, or political.'" . . . (quoting *Board of Educ., Island Trees Union Free Sch. Dist. No. 26 v. Pico*, 457 U.S. 853, 864 (1982) . . . See, e.g., *Muller* . . . (upholding similar twenty-four-hour prescreening requirement in public school setting as a reasonable prior restraint). Accordingly, we do not find the rule unconstitutional on its face, and we agree with the district court that Dr. Cook's decision to disqualify Henerey for his failure to comply with the rule represented a reasonable response to that noncompliance. . .

[Independent (Personal) Speech Analysis:] Even assuming, for the purpose of argument, that Henerey's action in handing out the condoms constituted the expression of constitutionally protected speech and that Dr. Cook's action in disqualifying Henerey was motivated by a disagreement with the content of that speech, it does not follow that a First Amendment violation necessarily occurred. As the Sixth Circuit observed in a case involving a student council election, "[t]he universe of legitimate pedagogical concerns is by no means confined to the academic." *Poling* . . . Thus, for example, "schools must teach by example the shared values of a civilized social order." *Fraser* . . . These shared values include "discipline, courtesy, and respect for authority." . . . In addition, **a school must be able to take into account the emotional maturity of the intended audience** in determining whether to disseminate student speech on potentially sensitive topics, which might range from the existence of Santa Claus in an elementary school setting to the particulars of teenage sexual activity in a high school setting. A school must also retain the authority to refuse to sponsor student speech that might reasonably be perceived to advocate drug or alcohol use, irresponsible sex, or conduct otherwise inconsistent with "the shared values of a civilized social order," or to associate the school with any position other than neutrality on matters of political controversy. *Hazelwood* . . . (quoting *Fraser*) . . . . **As the Sixth Circuit put it, "[c]ivility is a legitimate pedagogical concern."** . . . **So, too, is compliance with school rules**. . . .

The distribution of condoms is qualitatively different from the handing out of candy or gum. The one can be read to signify approval or encouragement of teenage sexual activity. The other constitutes the traditional bestowing of a de minimis gratuity not associated with any social or political message. School districts have an interest in maintaining decorum and in preventing the creation of an environment in which learning might be impeded, an interest that was particularly strong in the present case because the condom distribution occurred within the context of a school-sponsored election. **Henerey's distribution of the condoms carried with it the implied imprimatur of the school**, see *Hazelwood* . . ., for the other students would most likely have assumed that Henerey had complied with Rule KJ-R and had secured approval or the distribution. **The District has a legitimate interest in divorcing its extracurricular programs from controversial and sensitive topics, such as teenage sex**, . . ., an interest that would be brought to naught were the school administration not allowed to discipline those whose conduct would necessarily embroil those extracurricular activities in the very topics from which they were to remain free.

Nor can there be any doubt that teenage sex is a controversial topic in the public schools. For example, parents have brought suit against school districts because their children were exposed to offensive or graphic materials without their consent. See, e.g., *Parents United for Better Schools, Inc. v. School Dist. of Philadelphia Bd. of Educ.*, 148 F.3d 260 (3d Cir. 1998); *Brown v. Hot, Sexy and Safer Productions, Inc.*, 68 F.3d 525 (1st Cir. 1995). At the very least, school districts have an interest in requiring prior notice from anyone proposing to introduce students to information or materials of an explicit sexual nature, notice that would enable school administrators to avoid or at least minimize the threat of costly confrontations by arranging accommodations for those with strong objections to such material. Thus, it was well within the District's rights to disqualify Henerey for his actions in distributing material that ran counter to the District's pedagogical concern and its educational mission.

[Conclusion:] "[T]he education of the Nation's youth is primarily the responsibility of parents, teachers, and state and local school officials, and not of federal judges." *Hazelwood* . . . "It is only when the decision to censor a school-sponsored . . . vehicle of student expression has no valid educational purpose that the First Amendment is so directly and sharply implicated as to require judicial intervention to protect students' constitutional rights." . . . That was not the case here, and thus we affirm the summary judgment.

The judgment is affirmed.

Student Henerey attempted to bring his condom campaign sticker within the category of personal expression protected by *Tinker*, which would cause school officials to have to meet the more rigorous burden of proving substantial disruption or material interference, or a reasonable forecast thereof. However, the court determined that *Hazelwood* applied since the student's election campaign expression occurred as part of a school-sponsored speech activity, and thus the school only needed to prove that its discipline was reasonably related to legitimate educational concerns.

II. APPLYING THE FREE SPEECH STANDARD: THE FOUR QUESTIONS

School administrators, in consultation with legal counsel, must ask four questions that make up the legal standard which courts will apply in First Amendment student speech cases.

A. First, ask if the attempted student communication is actually "speech."

Courts require the student to prove the existence of expression that was intended to communicate a specific message that a reasonable receiver would likely comprehend. See, for example, *Bivens v. Albuquerque Public Schools*, 899 F.Supp. 556 (D.N.M. 1995) where the court rejected the student's argument that the First Amendment protected the wearing of sagging pants in violation of the dress code as his expression of a "statement of his identity as a black youth" and "a way for him to express his link with black culture and the styles of black urban youth." Id. at 558.

The *Bivens* court relied on the flag-burning case of *Texas v. Johnson*, 491 U.S. 397 (1989), where the Supreme Court set a **two-part legal standard to determine if non-verbal** conduct constituted speech: <u>"First, the actor must intend to convey a particularized message, and second, there must be a great likelihood that the message would be understood by those who observe the conduct."</u> . . . An earlier court found that a male high school senior's action in attempting to bring another male to the senior dinner-dance as a political statement of his homosexual identity was a form of expression protected by the First Amendment. See *Fricke v. Lynch*, 491 F.Supp. 381 (D.R.I. 1980), which relied on the case of *Gay Students Organization v. Bonner*, 509 F.2d 652 (1st Cir. 1974) that ruled against the University of New Hampshire's refusal to permit the Organization to hold dances and other social events that the court found would communicate a sufficiently specific message.

B. The second question is whether the speech was protected.

Courts have held that inflammatory expression (so-called "fighting words") that could reasonably be seen as arousing the passions of the intended recipient falls into this category. Defamatory speech also comes within the unprotected category, as does speech that constitutes a true threat to the safety of persons or property. Since the *Fraser* case, courts have consistently <u>deemed lewd, vulgar, indecent or plainly offensive</u> speech as <u>unprotected</u>, "even when it is expressed outside the context of an official school program or event." See *Chandler v. McMinnville Sch. Dist.*, 978 F.2d 524, 529 (9th Cir. 1992), where the court determined that the wearing of "no Scabs" buttons by two students whose fathers were striking teachers was not *per se* plainly offensive to replacement teachers, and since the speech was protected, had to be judged by the more rigorous *Tinker* substantial disruption/material interference standard.

The Supreme Court in *Chaplinski v. State of New Hampshire*, 315 U.S. 568, 571-572 (1942) stated:

> . . . There are certain well-defined and narrowly limited classes of speech, the prevention and punishment of which has never been thought to raise any Constitutional problem. These include the lewd and obscene, the profane, the libelous, and the insulting or 'fighting' words-those which by their very utterance inflict injury or tend to incite an immediate breach of the peace. It has been well observed that such utterances are no essential part of any exposition of ideas, and are of such slight social value as a step to truth that any benefit that may be derived from them is clearly outweighed by the social interest in order and morality. Resort to epithets or personal abuse is not in any proper sense communication of information or opinion safeguarded by the Constitution.

C. The third question is whether the speech occurred in a school-sponsored speech forum, such as the school newspaper or classroom, where the expression could be reasonably viewed as bearing the imprimatur or approval of the school.

The less difficult to prove *Hazelwood* legitimate pedagogical concern standard applies if this is the case. (In the *Chandler* case, above, the court found that the "no Scabs" buttons, although worn in the classroom, expressed the personal opinion of the students "in a manner commonly used to convey silently an idea, message, or political opinion to the community" and "expressed a position on a local political issue that was diametrically opposed to the school district's decision to hire replacement teachers" so that a reasonable person could not have viewed the buttons as bearing the imprimatur of the school. 978 F.2d at 530.)

D. The fourth question is whether the speech caused, or could reasonably be foreseen to cause, substantial disruption to or material interference of school activities or purposes.

This is the *Tinker* standard and the most difficult to prove. (In the *Chandler* "no Scabs" case, the court reversed the district court, found that the buttons were not inherently disruptive, and remanded the case for a trial. The court did state, however, that "[s]ubsquent proof may show that the word "scab" can reasonably be viewed as insulting, and may show that the slogans were directed at the replacement teachers. Such evidence would bear upon the issue of whether the buttons might reasonably have led school officials to forecast substantial disruption to school activities." 978 F. 2d at 531.)

III. PREAPPROVAL OF WRITTEN COMMUNICATION (PRIOR RESTRAINT)

When school administrators, via policy or practice, require students to submit non-school sponsored writings for review and approval prior to distribution, they may be met with the accusation of illegal prior restraint. Although there is no school-related Supreme Court case on this point, some (but not all, such as the Eighth Circuit's *Henerey* case, above) federal circuit courts have found prior restraint policies violative of the First Amendment because they are overly broad and subject protected expression to prior review by school authorities. See, for example, *Burch v. Barker*, 961 F.2d 1149 (9th Cir. 1988) and *Scoville v. Board of Education*, 425 F.2d 10 (7th Cir. 1970).

Twenty-six years after its *Scoville* decision, the Seventh Circuit in a case involving a Wisconsin elementary school, *Muller v. Jefferson Lighthouse School*, 98 F.3d 1530 (7th Cir. 1996), upheld the school district's policy of requiring students to present outside material to the principal for review and approval. In the following selected passages, the *Muller* court questioned the application of *Tinker* to the elementary school level and applied a forum analysis (emphasis added):

> Key to the holding in *Hazelwood*, and ultimately to our holding here . . . was an initial determination of the type of forum at issue. When is a school a public forum? The Court answered that "school facilities may be deemed to be public forums only if school authorities have 'by policy or by practice' opened those facilities 'for indiscriminate use by the general public,' or by some segment of the public, such as student organizations.". . . A public forum is not created by default, only by design: " 'The government does

not create a public forum by inaction or by permitting limited discourse, but only by intentionally opening a nontraditional forum for public discourse.' " . . . Speech in nonpublic forums is subject to significantly greater regulation than speech in traditional public forums. . . Thus, where school facilities have been "reserved for other intended purposes, 'communicative or otherwise,' and no public forum has been created, "school officials may impose reasonable restrictions on the speech of students, teachers, and other members of the school community." . . . The Court's test now is whether the restrictions are "reasonably related to legitimate pedagogical concerns." *Hazelwood*. . . .

Age is a critical factor in student speech cases . . . If a high school can suppress speech to protect 14-year-olds from sexual innuendo at a voluntary school assembly (*Fraser*), and if it can delete entire pages from a school newspaper because they touch on "sensitive topics" (*Hazelwood*. . .) **it follows that a public elementary school can shield its five- through thirteen-year-olds from topics and viewpoints that could harm their emotional, moral, social, and intellectual development.** The "marketplace of ideas," an important theme in the high school student expression cases, is a less appropriate description of an elementary school, where children are just beginning to acquire the means of expression. . . . **Grammar schools are more about learning, including learning to sit still and be polite, than about robust debate**. . . . *Tinker* may still stand for the similar proposition that student political speech cannot be suppressed solely because it is political.

. . . In sum, since *Tinker*, students retain First Amendment rights, but "the nature of those rights is what is appropriate for children in school" where the government as educator discharges its "custodial and tutelary responsibility for children." . . . **Especially considering the important role age plays in student speech cases, . . . it is unlikely that Tinker and its progeny apply to public elementary (or preschool) students.** But because the Supreme Court has not directly decided this question, the following analysis will assume that grade schoolers partake in certain of the speech rights set out in the *Tinker* line of cases. . .

A. Forum Analysis

. . . Thus, we begin by analyzing what kind of forum this public elementary school is. . . The district court concluded that Jefferson Lighthouse Elementary School is a nonpublic forum subject to reasonable restrictions on speech. . . .

"[S]chool facilities may be deemed to be public forums only if school authorities have 'by policy or by practice' opened those facilities 'for indiscriminate use by the general public' [citation omitted] or by some segment of the public, such as student organizations." . . . Nothing in the record suggests Jefferson Lighthouse Elementary School has been opened to anyone for "indiscriminate use." . . .

Further, the potential "verbal cacophony" of a public forum. . . can be antithetical to the delicate "custodial and tutelary" environment of an elementary school. . . . The cultivation of the "habits and manners of civility" that *Fraser* held "essential to a democratic society," . . . can require a level of parent-like guidance that has no place in a public forum. Declaring the elementary school classroom, hallway, or playground forums for unfettered student communication would require either a severe incursion into the critical educational mission of the elementary school or a substantial contraction of the First Amendment protections afforded speech in a public forum. Perhaps both. But neither alteration is necessary on the facts before us. **In a public forum, the Christian can tell the Jew he is going to hell, or the Jew can tell the Christian he is not one of God's chosen, no matter how that may hurt. But it makes no sense to say that the overly zealous Christian or Jewish child in an elementary school can say the same thing to his classmate, no matter the impact. Racist and other hateful views can be expressed in a public forum. But an elementary school under its custodial responsibilities may restrict such speech that could crush a child's sense of self-worth.**

Even assuming *Tinker* expression rights apply to children in public elementary schools, an elementary school's nonpublic forum status remains, and we apply the most recent standard elaborated by the Supreme Court in *Hazelwood*, that of "reasonableness." **The test, therefore, is whether the restrictions on student expression are "reasonably related to legitimate pedagogical concerns."** . . . As the Supreme Court has stressed, **such "pedagogical concerns" include not only the structured transmission of a body of knowledge in an orderly environment, but also the inculcation of civility (including manners) and traditional moral, social, and political norms**. . .

B. Prior Restraint

. . . **Prior restraint of student speech in a nonpublic forum is constitutional if reasonable.** *Hazelwood* dealt with prior restraint by a high school principal of articles to be published in a student newspaper. Deeming the newspaper a nonpublic forum, the Supreme Court engaged in a rational basis analysis and upheld the prior restraint as reasonable. . .

Prior restraint in the public school context, and especially where elementary schools are concerned, can be an important tool in preserving a proper educational environment. It may be necessary at times to prevent obscenity from reaching young students. Grade school students are generally between the ages of five and fourteen. The Supreme Court's "First Amendment jurisprudence has acknowledged limitations on the otherwise absolute interest of the speaker in reaching an unlimited audience where the speech is sexually explicit and the audience may include children." *Fraser*. . . . Certainly racially and religiously bigoted materials can be intercepted before they damage children and the school environment. Educators have the discretion to decide that anything promoting hate or violence will not be allowed to contaminate the (nonpublic forum) atmosphere of a public school. **Where public school children are involved there is no practical way to protect students from materials that can disrupt the educational environment or even severely traumatize a child without some form of prior restraint.**

Of course, the leaflets Andrew sought to distribute were innocuous enough, but it could have been different. Obviously, school officials cannot know beforehand the nature of all literature which students, or those acting through them, seek to distribute; and post-hoc responses to a harmful distribution cannot always undo the damage. Children in public schools are a "captive audience" that "school authorities acting in loco parentis" may "protect." *Fraser* . . . . The challenged Code provisions aim to do that by permitting the principal to prescreen for "libelous or obscene language," incitement "to illegal acts," insults "to any group or individuals," or other materials that "will greatly disrupt or materially interfere with school procedures and intrude into school affairs or the lives of others." . . . There is nothing facially unreasonable about such restrictions. . . .

In a high school prior restraint of speech case, the Ninth Circuit invalidated a pre-distribution review policy that was applied to students when they distributed copies of their off-school-grounds paper, called *Bad Astra*, at school in violation of the policy. *Burch v. Barker*, 861 F.2d 1149 (9th Cir. 1988). The court relied heavily on *Tinker* and construed *Hazelwood* to apply only to school-sponsored speech activities that bear the imprimatur of the school. The *Burch* court noted that " communications, like *Bad Astra*, . . . are in no sense 'school-sponsored,'" and "are therefore not within the purview of the school's exercise of reasonable editorial control." The court thus applied the more stringent *Tinker* standard and stated that "student distribution of non-school-sponsored material . . . cannot be subjected to regulation on the basis of undifferentiated fears of possible disturbances or embarrassment to school officials. . . ."

In another high school prior restraint case, *Bystrom v. Fridley High Sch. Indep. Sch. Dist.*, 822 F.2d 747 (8th Cir. 1987), the court ruled that a prior restraint policy is not per se unconstitutional "merely because it asserts a right of prior review and restraint on the part of school authorities." In examining the particulars of the policy, which prohibited material that is obscene, libelous, pervasively indecent or vulgar, "advertises any product or service not permitted to minors by law," "invades the privacy of another person or endangers the health or safety of another person," and "presents a clear and present likelihood that . . . it will cause a material and substantial disruption of the orderly operation and discipline of the school or school activities. . . ." the court found all but the invasion of privacy portion sufficiently narrow and specific to pass constitutional muster. (The one failed because in the state of Minnesota, where the high school was located, there was no law prohibiting an invasion of privacy. Hence, that part of the policy was overbroad in that it prohibited protected expression.)

IV.   "HATE SPEECH" OR ANTI-HARASSMENT RESTRICTIONS

Some federal circuit courts have addressed school policies that prohibit student verbal and nonverbal expression intended to communicate an epithet or to harass others based on particular characteristics such as their race, religion, ancestry, disability, sexual orientation, dress, and looks. The first of two First Amendment issues frequently raised in such cases is whether the policy, in the words of *Tinker*, was based on an "undifferentiated fear or apprehension," (invalid) or a "reasonable forecast" (valid) of substantial disruption of or material interference with school activities or purposes. The second is whether the policy is so overbroad that it punishes speech that is protected by the First Amendment or is so vague that a student cannot reasonably determine what speech is prohibited.

In the case below, the Tenth Circuit did outline a standard under which "hate speech" or anti-harassment Restrictions could be imposed. ***West v. Derby Unified Sch. Dist.***, 206 F.3d 1358, 1361 (10th Cir. 2000).

The Tenth Circuit upheld the three-day suspension of a seventh grader for drawing a confederate flag on a piece of paper during math class in violation of "Racial Harassment and Intimidation" policy, which read in relevant part:

> District employees and student(s) shall not racially harass or intimidate another student(s) by name calling, using racial or derogatory slurs, wearing or possession of items depicting or implying racial hatred or prejudice. District employees and students shall not at school, on school property or at school activities wear or have in their possession any written material, either printed or in their own handwriting, that is racially divisive or creates ill will or hatred. (Examples: clothing, articles, material, publications or any item that denotes Ku Klux Klan, Aryan Nation-White Supremacy, Black Power, Confederate flags or articles, Neo-Nazi or any other "hate" group. This list is not intended to be all inclusive). Violations of this policy shall result in disciplinary action by school authorities. For students there will be a three day out-of-school suspension for the first offense with a required parent conference prior to readmittance. . . .

Because the policy originated due to serious confrontations between white and black students after which the school formed a 350-person community-wide committee to study the problems and recommend a policy to help resolve them, the *West* court found the existence of a reasonable forecast of substantial disruption. Secondly, the court found that the policy was narrowly drafted to address the specific problem of racial harassment, which existed at the school, and it determined that the language was sufficiently clear to be understood by the students.

A. Regulation of Harassing Speech

When the Supreme Court in the 1969 *Tinker* black armband silent political expression case noted that "this case does not concern speech or action that intrudes upon . . . the rights of other students" (393 U.S. 503 at 508), it laid a vague hint that schools in future cases may be able to justify restriction of student personal speech that collides with rights possessed by others. What was not answered are questions facing schools decades later: Do students have a "right" not to be offended, subjected to hate messages, harassed, or belittled by others due to such characteristics as race, gender, sexual orientation, religion, weight, etc.?

In 1986 the Supreme Court indicated in the *Fraser* lewd speech case that schools could regulate speech that was "offensive" and "plainly offensive," 478 U.S. 675, 683. In the following paragraph at 478 U.S. 681, it seemed to send a message to future generations that schools could restrict language that offended the "personal sensibilities" of other students:

> These fundamental values of "habits and manners of civility" essential to a democratic society must, of course, include tolerance of divergent political and religious views, even when the views expressed may be unpopular. But these "fundamental values" must also take into account consideration of the sensibilities of others, and, in the case of a school, the sensibilities of fellow students. The undoubted freedom to advocate unpopular and controversial views in schools and classrooms must be balanced against the society's countervailing interest in teaching students the boundaries of socially appropriate behavior. Even the most heated political discourse in a democratic society requires consideration for the personal sensibilities of the other participants and audiences.

B. The Anti-Harassment Policy Case

Federal circuit courts, however, have the role of interpreting all relevant Supreme Court cases, not just the language of one, such as in *Fraser*, above.

For example, the Third Circuit in the case of *Saxe v. State College Area Sch. Dist.*, 240 F.3d 200 (3rd Cir. 2001) invalidated a carefully and thoughtfully drafted "Anti-Harassment Policy." Prohibited forms of harassment were race, sex, color, religion, national origin, disability, and "other" that included characteristics such as "clothing, physical appearance, social skills, peer group, intellect, educational program, hobbies or values, etc." *Id.* at 203.

Plaintiff Saxe, a member of the Pennsylvania State Board of Education, and legal guardian of two children attending the defendant School District stated in his complaint that he and his children were Christians whose "religion teaches that homosexuality is a sin . . . [and] believe that they have a right to speak out about the sinful nature and harmful effects of homosexuality . . . [and] feel compelled by their religion to speak out on other topics, especially moral issues." *Id.*

Saxe alleged that the Anti-Harassment Policy placed the children in fear of punishment for speaking out about their beliefs and sought to have the Policy found unconstitutionally vague and overbroad. Because the court found it overbroad, it did not consider the issue of vagueness.

The court found that the Policy was much broader than such types of harassment prohibited by federal law under Title VI (race) and Title IX (sex). It sought to prohibit disparaging expression against another student's "values, which "strikes at the heart of moral and political discourse--the lifeblood of constitutional self-government (and democratic education) and the core concern of the First Amendment." *Id.* at 210. It also found that the Policy extended to speech that merely had the "purpose" of harassing another and, hence, "by focusing on the speaker's motive rather than the effect of speech on the learning environment, appears to sweep in those simple acts of teasing and name calling. . . ." *Id.* at 210-211.

The court then considered if the School District's rationale for the Anti-Harassment Policy was justified under the Supreme Court's *Tinker* substantial disruption/material interference standard and stated that the District "fails to provide any particularized reason as to why it anticipates substantial disruption for the broad swath of student speech prohibited under the Policy. The Policy, then, appears to cover substantially more speech than could be prohibited under Tinker's substantial disruption test. . . ." *Id.* at 217.

The Saxe case demonstrates the intricate complexities involved in First Amendment student speech analysis and teaches that in attempting to prohibit offensive or harassing expression, schools must have concrete evidence of at least a reasonable forecast of substantial disruption or material interference with the rights of others as to each specific type expression prohibited.

C. The "Straight Pride" Sweatshirt Case

In the case of *Chambers v. Babbitt*, 145 F.Supp. 1068 (D.Minn. 2001), the federal district court granted a preliminary injunction in favor of student Chambers against his principal after Chambers had been prohibited from again wearing his sweatshirt containing the message "Straight Pride" on the front and symbol of a man and woman holding hands on the back.

The high school's dress code stated that "[s]tudents may not wear items with unacceptable writing or graphic depiction's which offend anyone or distract from the educational experience. . . ." [Emphasis added.] On the day Chambers wore the shirt, another student reported to the assistant principal that he and a group of students were upset by it. The next day he was directed not to wear it again because of the offense taken by other students and the principal's safety concerns for Chambers and other students.

The court cited the Supreme Court's admonition in *Tinker* that in order to suppress student expression there must be a reasonable belief based on facts that "might reasonably have led school authorities to forecast substantial disruption of or material interference with school activities." Id. at 1071, quoting *Tinker*, 393 U.S. 503, 514. It concluded that the principal's evidence was insufficient to meet this standard and rejected the argument that a racial incident had any connection to Chamber's sweatshirt message and that a debate wherein students "took sides" at a religious club meeting regarding Christianity and homosexuality qualified as reasonable forecast of substantial disruption. Said the court at 1073:

> Maintaining a school community of tolerance includes the tolerance of such viewpoints as expressed by "Straight Pride." While the sentiment behind the "Straight Pride message appears to be one of intolerance, the responsibility remains with the school and its community to maintain an environment open to diversity and to educate and support its students as they confront ideas different from their own. The Court does not disregard the laudable intention of Principal Babbitt to create a positive social and learning environment by his decision, however the constitutional implications . . . are equally important and must prevail under the circumstances.

V. REASONABLE TIME, PLACE, AND MANNER RESTRICTIONS

School officials may find that student distribution of written material at school is analogous to the content of the following Supreme Court statement: "A nuisance may be merely a right thing in the wrong place, like a pig in the parlor instead of the barnyard." *Board of Education of Educ. v. Pico*, 457 U.S. 857, 920 (1982), Rehnquist, J. in dissent, (quoting *Village of Euclid v. Ambler Realty Co.*, 272 U.S. 365, 388 (1926)).

The Supreme Court has recognized that public universities, which traditionally have areas that are open forums for student speech purposes, may limit expression in such forums provided that the restraints are reasonable as to the time, place and manner of occurrence. See *Widmar v. Vincent*, 454 U.S. 263, 268-269 (1981), stating that a public university may "impose reasonable regulations compatible with [its educational] mission upon the use of its campus and facilities." In a public school labor relations case involving the issue of a minority teachers union's access to the school's internal mail delivery system, *Perry Educational Association v. Perry Local Educators' Association*, 460 U.S.37, 45 (1983), the Supreme Court stated:

> The State may also enforce regulations of the time, place, and manner of expression which are content-neutral, are narrowly tailored to serve a significant government interest, and leave open ample alternative channels of communication. . . .

Federal circuit courts have upheld public schools that set reasonable limits as to the time, place and manner that students may distribute literature on school grounds. In *Muller v. Jefferson Lighthouse School*, 98 F.3d 1530, 1543 (7th Cir. 1996), the court stated:

> The establishment of an appropriate time, place, and manner for a student to

distribute fliers, even where the quantities are small, is therefore appropriate. The Mullers disagree, arguing that "[s]tudents obviously should not be prohibited from passing a love note to   another student, giving that student a birthday card, or giving another directions to his or her home." But the simple response is that it depends on the time, place, and manner of the distribution. The school may reasonably prohibit distribution of love notes or birthday cards during math class; math class is for learning math, not for passing love notes or birthday cards. Prohibiting handbilling in the hallway between classes is also reasonable to avoid congestion, confusion, and tardiness, to say nothing of the inevitable clutter caused when the recipient indiscriminately discards the handout. See *Hemry by Hemry v. School Bd. of Colorado Springs*, 760 F. Supp. 856 (D. Colo. 1991). When, where, and how children can distribute literature in a school is for educators, not judges, to decide "provided [such choices] are not arbitrary or whimsical." *Hedges*, 9 F.3d at 1302; see also id. at 1301 (place restrictions proper given nature of school and function of principal). Here the Code requires the student and principal to determine "cooperatively" an appropriate time and place for the distribution. This permits flexibility so that the unique needs of the school and the student can be accommodated. There is nothing apriori unreasonable about that. . . .

Also note *Hedges v. Wauconda Comm. Unit. Sch. Dist.*, 9 F.3d 1295 (7th Cir. 1993), where the court upheld a policy that required student distribution of more than ten copies of any material to occur during half-hour periods before and after school at a table near the school's main entrance, and *Eisner v. Stamford Bd. of Educ.*, 440 F.2d 803 (2d Cir. 1971), where the court upheld the school board's delineation of places in school buildings where students could distribute expressive material.

VI. EXPRESSION OFF SCHOOL GROUNDS – THE INTERNET

Student use of the Internet from their home computers to communicate negative opinions about school authority figures or threatening comments toward school personnel and other students has led to a growing number of First Amendment suits when the student was disciplined. In one of the first reported Internet cases, *Beussink v. Woodland R-IV Sch. Dist.*, 30 F.Supp. 2d 1175 (E.D. Mo. 1998), student Beussink obtained a preliminary injunction after he was suspended from school for creating a home webpage wherein he used vulgar language to express critical opinions of his teachers and principal.

There was no evidence that Beussink created or accessed his home webpage from the school, or that he gave other students his website while at school. Although other students, and a teacher, accessed the site from school, they did so as a result of his former girlfriend giving the address to others at school. Citing Tinker's requirement of at least a reasonable forecast of substantial disruption or material interference, the court stated at 1179:

Principal Poorman testified . . . that he made the determination to discipline Beussink immediately upon seeing the homepage. He was upset that the message had found its way into his school's classrooms. Principal Poorman's testimony does not indicate that he disciplined Beussink based on a fear of disruption or interference with school discipline (reasonable or otherwise.) Principal Poorman's own testimony indicates he disciplined Beussink because he was upset by the content of the homepage. Disliking or being upset by the content of a student's speech is not an acceptable justification for limiting student speech under Tinker.

Two other early home Internet expression cases went against the principal, *Emmett v. Kent Sch. Dist. No. 415*, 92 F.Supp. 2d 1088 (W.D. Wash. 2000) and *Killion v. Franklin Regional Sch. Dist.*, 136 F.Supp.2d 446 (W.D.Pa. 2001). In *Emmett*, the 3.95 G.P.A. student with no prior disciplinary history and co-captain of the basketball team, created two mock obituaries of his friends and invited visitors to his home webpage to vote on who should "die" next so that they could have their "obituaries" printed. Due to a local television carrying the story and characterizing it as a "hit list," even though student Emmett did not use the term, he was suspended the next day for intimidation, harassment, and disruption of the educational process. Emmett won a preliminary injunction with the court stating at 1090:

> The defendant argues, persuasively, that school administrators are in an acutely difficult position after recent school shootings in Colorado, Oregon, and other places. Web sites can be an early indication of a student's violent inclinations, and can spread those beliefs quickly to like-minded or susceptible people. The defendant, however, has presented no evidence that mock obituaries and voting on this web site were intended to threaten anyone, did actually threaten anyone, or manifested any violent tendencies whatsoever.

In the *Killion* case, student Paul prevailed after he was suspended for e-mailing friends from his home computer a "Top Ten" list containing disparaging comments about the school athletic director including the size of his genitalia. Paul did not send the e-mail, or bring a hard copy, to school. A friend, however, brought a copy and distributed it at school. The court found that the school failed to provide evidence of substantial disruption or material interference, or a reasonable forecast thereof, as required by *Tinker*. Secondly, the court refused to apply the Supreme Court's *Fraser* standard of lewd, vulgar, indecent, or plainly offensive speech because the student's Internet expression occurred off school property.

Of the early four reported Internet student speech cases, only one upheld the school's discipline, an expulsion of an eighth grader for the content of his home web page entitled "Teacher Sux." In *J.S. v. Bethlehem Area Sch. Dist.*, 757 A.2d 412 (Pa.Cmwlth. 2000), the student asked why his algebra teacher should die and requested twenty dollar contributions to pay for a hit man. Further, he created a diagram showing the teacher with her head cut off, blood dripping from her neck. The teacher suffered stress, anxiety, and headaches, was forced to take anti-depressants and a leave of absence for the remainder of the year, and took a medical leave the following year. In applying *Tinker's* standard and reviewing cases involving off-campus student speech, the court stated at 421-422:

. . . [I]t is evident that the courts have allowed school officials to discipline students for conduct occurring off of school premises where it is established that the conduct materially and substantially interferes with the educational process. . .

Regrettably, in this day and age where school violence is becoming more commonplace, school officials are justified in taking very seriously threats against faculty and other students. . . Given the contents of Student's web-site and the effect it had upon . . . Mrs. Fulmer and the school community, we conclude that the trial court properly determined that the School District did not violate Student's rights under the First Amendment.

VII. "THREATS" VERSUS "TRUE THREATS"

"If they ever make me carry a rifle the first man I want to get in my sights is L.B.J." This statement was made by an 18-year old man who was convicted of a felony under a 1917 federal law prohibiting the making of a threat against the President of the United States. The Supreme Court in the case of *Watts v. United States*, 394 U.S. 705,706 (1969), found that the statement was protected "political hyperbole" and not a true threat when viewed in the context of the statement being made at a public rally on the grounds of the Washington Monument.

Generally speaking, all schools have discipline policies that prohibit students from making "threats" against other students, school personnel, or visitors. The essential key for school administrators is determining if the alleged "threat" is a "true threat;" the latter being unprotected by the First Amendment speech clause and, thereby allowing the administrator to invoke appropriate discipline.

A case demonstrating the complexities of true threat issues is *Doe v. Pulaski County Special Sch. Dist.*, 306 F.3d 616 (8th Cir. 2002), which was an *en banc* ruling in favor of the school that reversed the earlier decision of the three-judge panel in favor of the student because the panel found that his letter to a former girlfriend did not contain true threats. 263 F.3d 833 (8th Cir. 2001).

The *en banc* court characterized the letters written during summer vacation by "J.M.," the boy who was expelled at the start of his eighth-grade year, as "violent, misogynic, and obscenity-laden rants expressing a desire to molest, rape, and murder K.G.", his former girlfriend who had broken up with him during the summer. 306 F.3d 616, 619.

The facts indicated that the boy had penned and signed the letters at home where one was found by a male friend, who was then allowed by the boy to read it. His friend, a week before the start of school, purloined one of the letters and gave it to the ex-girlfriend at school, who conveyed it to the principal, thus leading to the boy's expulsion for violating the rule against making terrorizing threats against others. Further evidence indicated that the boy had discussed the contents of letter with his former girlfriend in at least two telephone conversations.

The federal trial court concluded that the letter did not contain a true threat of violence because it had been written at home and was not intended to be delivered to his ex-girlfriend, the object of the threat. Hence, the expulsion was invalid because the speech was protected.

On appeal, the three-judge panel of the Eighth Circuit affirmed. In ruling for the boy who had written the letter, it applied the Ninth Circuit's legal standard of whether a reasonable speaker would realize that his/her statement(s) would be interpreted by the recipient as a serious expression of intent to injure.

In reversing the original panel's decision that the expelled boy did not foresee that his letter would be interpreted by the former girlfriend to be a serious statement of intent to injure her, the *en banc* court relied on existing Eighth Circuit case law that focused not on the what the speaker would foresee of the recipient's perception, but rather what the reasonable recipient would interpret. The court held that **"a true threat is a statement that a reasonable recipient would have interpreted as a serious expression of an intent to harm or cause injury to another."** *Id.* at 624. (Emphasis added.)

The court then found ample evidence that a reasonable recipient would have viewed the letter as containing serious statements of an intent to harm or cause injury. The expelled boy referred to her as a "bitch," "slut," "ass," and "whore" over 80 times, repeatedly expressed his desire to "sodomize, rape, and kill" her, and twice warned that she should not go to sleep because he would be waiting under her bed to kill her with a knife. *Id.* at 625.

Lastly, the court stated the second element of the true threat legal standard as "the speaker must have intentionally or knowingly communicated the statement in question to someone before he or she may be punished or disciplined for it. . ." *Id.* at 624. (Emphasis added.) The court added that "[t]he requirement is satisfied if the speaker communicates the statement to the object of the purported threat or to a third party." *Id.* The fact that the expelled boy allowed his friend to read the letter knowing that his friend was a friend of his ex-girlfriend and likely to tell her of its contents and that he talked to her about the contents of the letter satisfied the legal test that he intended or knew that the statements would reach her and, in fact, reached a third party.

Because the circuit courts are divided, as exemplified by Ninth's legal standard based on the reasonable speaker of the threat and the Eighth's standard based on the reasonable recipient thereof, both tests should be analyzed in the assessment of whether or not a "true threat" was made.

In ***Porter v. Ascension Parish School Board***, 393 F. 3d 608 (5th Cir. 2004), the court addressed the issue of true threats at pages 615-618:

> Given the unique facts of the present case, **we decline to find that Adam's drawing constitutes student speech on the school premises**. Adam's drawing was completed in his home, stored for two years, and never intended by him to be brought to campus. He took no action that would increase the chances that his drawing would find its way to school; he simply stored it in a closet where it remained until, by chance, it was unwittingly taken to Galvez Middle School by his brother. **This is not exactly speech on campus or even speech directed at the campus**.
>
> Our analysis today is not in conflict with this body of case law; rather, **the fact that Adam's drawing was composed off-campus and remained off-campus for two years until it was unintentionally taken to school**

by his younger brother takes the present case outside the scope of these precedents. *See Thomas v. Bd. of Educ., Granville Cent. Sch. Dist.*, 607 F.2d 1043, 1050-52 (2d. Cir. 1979) (**refusing to apply** *Tinker* **to student newspaper published and distributed offcampus**); *Klein v. Smith*, 635 F. Supp. 1440, 1441-42 (D. Me. 1986) (**enjoining suspension of student who made a vulgar gesture to a teacher while off-campus**); *see also Killion*, 136 F. Supp. 2d at 454 ("**Although there is limited case law on the issue, courts considering speech that occurs off school grounds have concluded [relying on Supreme Court decisions] that school official's authority over off-campus expression is much more limited than expression on school grounds.**"); Clay Calvert, *Off-Campus Speech, On-Campus Punishment: Censorship of the Emerging Internet Underground*, 7 B.U.J. SCI. & TECH. L. 243, 279 (2001) (**noting that** *Tinker* **is ill-suited to deal with off-campus student expression that is unintentionally brought on-campus by others**).

The third standard employed by the district court in analyzing Adam's drawing was developed to deal with speech constituting a "true threat." As a general rule, the First Amendment prohibits government actors from "dictating what we see or read or speak or hear." However, **the government can proscribe a true threat of violence without offending the First Amendment. Speech is a "true threat" and therefore unprotected if an objectively reasonable person would interpret the speech as a "serious expression of an intent to cause a present or future harm."** The protected status of the threatening speech is not determined by whether the speaker had the subjective intent to carry out the threat; rather, **to lose the protection of the First Amendment and be lawfully punished, the threat must be intentionally or knowingly** *communicated* **to either the object of the threat or a third person. Importantly, whether a speaker intended to communicate a potential threat is a threshold issue, and a finding of no intent to communicate obviates the need to assess whether the speech constitutes a "true threat."**

The Eighth Circuit's decision in *Doe v. Pulaski County Special School District* [306 F.3d 616 (8th Cir. 2002)] is an illustrative application of these principles to an alleged threat made by a student off-campus but carried on campus by another student. In *Doe*, a boy in junior high school drafted two letters to his former girlfriend containing "violent, misogynic and obscenity-laden rants" expressing a desire to assault and murder her. Months later, the boy's best friend discovered the letters, and after first objecting, the boy allowed his friend to read them. The friend later absconded with at least one of the letters and showed it to the girlfriend. In addition, the boy had discussed the violent letters with his former girlfriend in phone conversations, ultimately admitting that he penned the letters. After obtaining and reading one of the letters, the girlfriend reported the boy to school officials who recommended him for expulsion. The boy's parents filed suit, arguing infringement of his First Amendment rights. **The district court held that the letter was protected**

under the First Amendment, and did not constitute a true threat because the boy did not intend to deliver it to his girlfriend. Reversing the district court, **the Eighth Circuit found that a reasonable and objective recipient would regard the letter as a true threat.** In addition, the Eighth Circuit found that **the boy intentionally communicated the threat because he allowed his friend to read the letter knowing that his friend was also a close friend of his former girlfriend.** Furthermore, the boy discussed the letters with his girlfriend on the telephone on multiple occasions.

Unlike the court in *Doe*, **we need not decide whether Adam's drawing would constitute a true threat in the eyes of a reasonable and objective person because Adam did not intentionally or knowingly communicate his drawing in a way sufficient to remove it from the protection of the First Amendment.** While it is true that Adam showed his drawing to his mother, brother, and friend Kendall Goudeau, this communication was confined to his own home, and more than two years passed before the drawing serendipitously reached the EAHS campus. That the introduction of the drawing to EAHS was wholly accidental and unconnected with Adam's earlier display of the drawing to members of his household is undisputed. Private writings made and kept in one's home enjoy the protection of the First Amendment, as well as the Fourth. **For such writings to lose their First Amendment protection, something more than their accidental and unintentional exposure to public scrutiny must take place.**

Because Adam's drawing cannot be considered a true threat as it was not intentionally communicated, **the state was without authority to sanction him for the message it contained.** Although Adam has produced evidence that his drawing comprised the primary impetus for his expulsion from school, he has not established this as a matter of law. Consequently, a fact issue remains as to whether Adam's First Amendment rights were infringed by EAHS, and the district court erred in finding otherwise. . . .

In footnote 22 of the ***Porter*** case at pages 615-616, the court noted other cases involving off-campus speech that makes its way onto school property (emphasis added):

> We are aware of the difficulties posed by state regulation of student speech that takes place off-campus and is later brought on-campus either by the communicating student or others to whom the message was communicated. Refusing to differentiate between student speech taking place on-campus and speech taking place off-campus, a number of courts have applied the test in *Tinker* when analyzing off-campus speech brought onto the school campus. *See Boucher v. Sch. Bd. of Sch. Dist. of Greenfield*, 134 F.3d 821, 827-28 (7th Cir. 1998) (**student disciplined for an article printed in an underground newspaper that was distributed on school campus**); *Sullivan v. Houston Indep. Sch. Dist.*, 475 F.2d 1071, 1075-77 (5th Cir. 1973) (**student punished for authoring article printed in underground newspaper distributed off-campus, but near school grounds**); *LaVine*, 257 F.3d at 989 (**analyzing student poem composed off-campus and brought onto campus by the composing student under *Tinker***); *Killion v. Franklin Reg'l Sch. Dist.*, 136 F. Supp. 2d 446, 455 (W.D. Pa. 2001) (**student**

disciplined for composing degrading top-ten list distributed via e-mail to school friends, who then brought it onto campus; author had been disciplined before for bringing topten lists onto campus); *Emmett v. Kent Sch. Dist. No. 415*, 92 F. Supp. 2d 1088, 1090 (W.D. Wash. 2000) (applying *Tinker* to mock obituary website constructed offcampus); *Beussink v. Woodland R-IV Sch. Dist.*, 30 F. Supp. 2d 1175, 1180 (E.D. Mo. 1998) (student disciplined for article posted on personal internet site); *Bystrom v. Fridley High Sch.*, 686 F. Supp. 1387, 1392 (D. Minn. 1987) (student disciplined for writing article that appeared in an underground newspaper distributed on school campus).

In footnote 26 of the *Porter* case at pages 616-617, the court noted other cases involving the issue of true threats (emphasis added):

> *See Black*, 538 U.S. at 359 ("'True threats' encompass those statements where the speaker means to communicate a serious expression of an intent to commit an act of unlawful violence to a particular individual or group of individuals."); *Doe*, 306 F.3d at 624 ("In determining whether a statement amounts to an unprotected threat, there is no requirement that the speaker intended to carry out the threat, nor is there any requirement that the speaker was capable of carrying out the purported threat of violence. However, the speaker must have intentionally or knowingly communicated the statement in question to someone before he or she may be punished or disciplined for it." (citing *Planned Parenthood of the Columbia/Willamette, Inc. v. Am. Coalition of Life Activists*, 290 F.3d 1058, 1075 (9th Cir. 2002)); *see also United States v. Stevenson*, 126 F.3d 662, 664 (5th Cir. 1997) (finding that, for purpose of criminalizing speech as a threat under 18 U.S.C. § 115(a)(1)(B) and 18 U.S.C. § 871, the speaker need only "intentionally or knowingly [communicate] his threat") (quoting *United States v. Orozco-Santillan*, 903 F.2d 1262, 1265 (9th Cir. 1990)).

SCENARIOS
STATE AND APPLY THE RELEVANT LEGAL RULE(S) TO THE FACTS.

Upon the recommendation of his principal and superintendent, Teacher, the very popular, yet mysterious, first year female English instructor at Suburban High School (1200 students enrolled), received proper written notice that his teaching contract would be considered for nonrenewal at the next school board meeting, effective at the end of the school year, and that he would be afforded all statutory and constitutional due process. Teacher immediately requested the reasons as well as the public conference with School Board that was provided by State statute.

Student, editor of the school's newspaper, which was part of the English journalism course, was also senior class president and National Merit Scholar, and had been accepted to an Ivy League college on a full scholarship to major in English Literature. Upset that his favorite teacher was being considered for dismissal, Student lead the charge to convince School Board not to dismiss Teacher. The following steps (in chronological order) were taken by Student, with the following responses by Principal:

a. Getting his idea from students who prayed around the school's flagpole in September, lead a planned ten-minute Teacher support meeting of approximately 50 students around the flagpole the next morning, 25 minutes before the start of classes. It consisted of chanting the phrase "Re-hire Teacher," and is videotaped by a local television station from the city built and maintained sidewalk, which was told of the event by Student. Principal broke up the meeting after two minutes of chanting and told Student that he will be suspended if there are any more demonstrations, or if he contacted the media again over Teacher's dismissal. The television station showed 10 seconds of the demonstration along with a 30-second interview with Student (which it taped just after the demonstration was broken up) on the six and eleven o'clock news.

b. Distributed a copy of his home website address on the city built and maintained sidewalk in front of the school as students left school the afternoon of the day following the demonstration urging students to read his article about Principal's actions. The article called Principal "dictatorial, uncaring, and ignorant of the constitution," and fairly and accurately criticized him for stopping the flagpole meeting and threatening him with suspension if he further demonstrated or went to the media. The article also urged students to get their parents involved in contacting board members to rehire Teacher. Not only does Principal check the website article, so do dozens of students while in a computer class the next day. Principal responded by suspending Student for three days (following proper due process) for violating the school's student discipline code that prohibited (a) "showing disrespect to a staff member" by calling him a dictator and criticizing him in public and (b) "causing disruption to a school activity" by giving students access to his website that interrupted computer class.

c. Notified the television station which appeared, along with Student, at the school board meeting for the statutory public conference between Board and Teacher, watched as Board voted to nonrenew Teacher's contract, and during the "public input" portion at the end of the agenda, for no more than a minute, spoke calmly, but emphatically, against Board and Principal for their "shortsightedness and lack of thoughtfulness in dismissing the most enlightened teacher at Suburban High," and accused Principal of "gross unfairness and negligence' in recommending Teacher's dismissal. Lastly, he stated that "if the Board knew the true reason, for which Student had documented evidence, as to why Principal recommended Teacher's dismissal, the Board would be firing Principal instead of Teacher." Principal responded by issuing Student a 10-day suspension from school (following proper process) for a second violation of the "disrespect" rule for the name-calling at the public school board meeting and for deliberate disobedience of his directive not to involve the television station again, which violated the rule prohibiting insubordination against a staff member.

d. In the last issue of the school newspaper, drafted and published an editorial entitled "Principal: Sexual Harasser," wherein he fairly and responsibly criticized Principal for recommending Teacher's dismissal and clearly suggested, based on a legally-taped discussion between Teacher and Principal (a copy of which is in Student's possession) that the real reason for the firing was Teacher's rejection of "Principal's proposition to enter into a sexual relationship." A reasonable person listening to the tape would conclude that Principal was making an unwelcomed sexual proposition to Teacher. Square responded by initiating the process to expel Student for repeatedly violating the rule against disrespecting a staff member.

CHAPTER
9

STUDENT EQUALITY ISSUES

"Equal" may mean "unequal." That is to say, if a school district treats every student equally, it may cause an unequal consequence to the detriment of a given group of students. Should a school, for example, create an honors program to be composed of exactly the same number of male and female students (apparently equal), the end result may be that some females are excluded although they have better grades and test scores than some of their male counterparts, who are included (unequal), because a certain number of spaces have been guaranteed for males. Similarly, if students with a learning disability are given the very same "equal" instruction as non-disabled children, the end result may be "unequal" to the disabled learners.

The question, then, is: At what point is the unequal result of apparently equal treatment unlawful? This is where the Constitution, Congress, and the courts weigh in.

I. THE EQUAL PROTECTION CLAUSE

The Fourteenth Amendment to the federal Constitution requires that no state shall "deny to any person within its jurisdiction, the equal protection of the laws." The courts have been called upon to interpret and apply the Equal Protection Clause to numerous classifications that states and their school districts have created including race, alienage, gender, and school finance.

The legal standard adopted by the Supreme Court in equal protection cases applies where the government's discrimination against a class of persons is plainly evident, or obvious on its face, and generally can be summarized as follows:

First, determine the category of judicial scrutiny that will be applied to the plaintiff's class:

(1) High (strict) scrutiny -- *suspect class or fundamental right discrimination*;

(2) Medium scrutiny -- *gender or children of illegal aliens discrimination*; or

(3) Low scrutiny -- *all other forms of discrimination.*

Second, the government must prove the following with respect to each scrutiny category:

(1) High -- *compelling interest*;

(2) Medium -- *substantial relationship to an important objective/goal*; or

(3) Low -- *rational relationship to a legitimate objective/goal.*

Suspect classes have been determined to be race, alienage, and national origin/ancestry. Fundamental right classifications involve infringement upon the exercise of rights guaranteed in the Constitution, such as speech and religion.

In an alienage discrimination case, *Graham v. Richardson*, 403 U.S. 365 (1971), the Supreme Court invalidated an Arizona statute that conditioned receipt of certain federal welfare benefits on either being a U.S. citizen or an alien having resided in the U.S. for at least 15 years, and stated at 371-372, (emphasis added):

> Under traditional equal protection principles, a State retains broad discretion to classify as long as its classification has a reasonable basis. . . This is so in "the area of economics and social welfare." . . . **But the Court's decisions have established that classifications based on alienage, like those based on nationality or race, are inherently suspect and subject to close judicial scrutiny.** Aliens as a class are a prime example of a "discrete and insular" minority . . . for whom such heightened judicial solicitude is appropriate. . . .

An example of this heightened judicial solicitude was shown in the national origin/ancestry case discussed below.

In a national origin/ancestry case (which the court also referenced as including race), *Korematsu v. United States*, 323 U.S. 214 (1944), the Supreme Court found a compelling governmental interest (which is extremely rare) under the strict scrutiny test due to suspect-class discrimination, and ruled for the government against a Japanese-American citizen who did not submit himself for relocation as required when this country went to war with Japan. Said the Court at 223-24:

> It is said that we are dealing here with the case of imprisonment of a citizen in a concentration camp solely because of his ancestry, without evidence or inquiry concerning his loyalty and good disposition towards the United States. . .

> To cast this case into outlines of racial prejudice, without reference to the real military dangers which were presented, merely confuses the issue. Korematsu was not excluded from the Military Area because of hostility to him or his race. He was excluded because we are at war with the Japanese Empire, because the properly constituted military authorities feared an invasion of our West Coast and felt constrained to take proper security measures, because they decided that the military urgency of the situation demanded that all citizens of Japanese ancestry be segregated from the West Coast temporarily, and finally, because Congress, reposing its confidence in this time of war in our military leaders-as inevitably it must-determined that they should have the power to do just this. There was evidence of disloyalty on the part of some, the military authorities considered that the need for action was great, and time was short. We cannot-by availing ourselves of the calm perspective of hindsight-now say that at that time these actions were unjustified.

A. *Equal Protection and Race*

In the landmark case of *Brown v. Board of Education*, 347 U.S. 483 (1954), the Supreme Court applied the equal protection clause to the racial segregation practices of schools in four states and rejected the doctrine of "separate but equal." Relevant portions of the case follow (emphasis added):

> These cases come to us from the States of Kansas, South Carolina, Virginia, and Delaware. They are premised on different facts and different local conditions, but a common legal question justifies their consideration together in this consolidated opinion.

> In each of the cases, minors of the Negro race, through their legal representatives, seek the aid of the courts in obtaining admission to the public schools of their community on a nonsegregated basis. In each instance, they had been denied admission to schools attended by white children under laws requiring or permitting segregation according to race. This segregation was alleged to deprive the plaintiffs of the equal protection of the laws under the Fourteenth Amendment. . . .

> In the first cases in this Court construing the Fourteenth Amendment, decided

shortly after its adoption, the Court interpreted it as proscribing all state-imposed discriminations against the Negro race. The doctrine of "separate but equal" did not make its appearance in this Court until 1896 in the case of *Plessy v. Ferguson* . . . involving not education but transportation. American courts have since labored with the doctrine for over half a century. . . .

In the instant cases, that question is directly presented. Here, . . . there are findings below that the Negro and white schools involved have been equalized, or are being equalized, with respect to buildings, curricula, qualifications and salaries of teachers, and other "tangible" factors. Our decision, therefore, cannot turn on merely a comparison of these tangible factors in the Negro and white schools involved in each of the cases. **We must look instead to the effect of segregation itself on public education.**

Today, education is perhaps the most important function of state and local governments. Compulsory school attendance laws and the great expenditures for education both demonstrate our recognition of the importance of education to our democratic society. It is required in the performance of our most basic public responsibilities, even service in the armed forces. It is the very foundation of good citizenship. Today it is a principal instrument in awakening the child to cultural values, in preparing him for later professional training, and in helping him to adjust normally to his environment. In these days, it is doubtful that any child may reasonably be expected to succeed in life if he is denied the opportunity of an education. Such an opportunity, where the state has undertaken to provide it, is a right which must be made available to all on equal terms.

We come then to the question presented: **Does segregation of children in public schools solely on the basis of race, even though the physical facilities and other "tangible" factors may be equal, deprive the children of the minority group of equal educational opportunities?** We believe that it does.

In *Sweatt v. Painter* . . . in finding that a segregated law school for Negroes could not provide them equal educational opportunities, this Court relied in large part on "those qualities which are incapable of objective measurement but which make for greatness in a law school." In *McLaurin v. Oklahoma State Regents* . . . the Court, in requiring that a Negro admitted to a white graduate school be treated like all other students, again resorted to intangible considerations: ". . . his ability to study, to engage in discussions and exchange views with other students, and, in general, to learn his profession." Such considerations apply with added force to children in grade and high schools. To separate them from others of similar age and qualifications solely because of their race generates a feeling of inferiority as to their status in the community that may affect their hearts and minds in a way unlikely ever to be undone. The effect of this separation on their educational opportunities was well stated by a finding in the Kansas case by a court which nevertheless felt compelled to rule against the Negro plaintiffs:

"Segregation of white and colored children in public schools has a detrimental effect upon the colored children. The impact is greater when it has the sanction of the law; for the policy of separating the races is usually interpreted as denoting the inferiority of the negro group. A sense of inferiority affects the motivation of a child to learn. Segregation with the sanction of law, therefore, has a tendency to [retard] the educational and mental development of negro children and to deprive them of some of the benefits they would receive in a racial[ly] integrated school system."

Whatever may have been the extent of psychological knowledge at the time of *Plessy v. Ferguson*, this finding is amply supported by modern authority. Any language in *Plessy v. Ferguson* contrary to this finding is rejected.

We conclude that in the field of public education the doctrine of "separate but equal" has no place. **Separate educational facilities are inherently unequal.** Therefore, we hold that the plaintiffs and others similarly situated for whom the actions have been brought are, by reason of the segregation complained of, deprived of the equal protection of the laws guaranteed by the Fourteenth Amendment. . . .

It is so ordered.

B. Equal Protection and Alienage

When the state of Texas passed legislation that resulted in the denial of public education to children of illegal aliens, the Supreme Court required the state to prove that its action was based on a **substantial state interest** and ruled that the Equal Protection Clause was violated. (The Court did not require the showing of a compelling state interest nor grant a suspect class status as it had to legal aliens in the *Graham v. Richardson* case, above, due to the illegal alien status of the plaintiff class.) The syllabus, which is a summary of the Supreme Court's ruling in the case of *Plyler v. Doe*, 457 U.S. 202 (1982) stated (emphasis added):

Held:
A Texas statute which withholds from local school districts any state funds for the education of children who were not "legally admitted" into the United States, and which authorizes local school districts to deny enrollment to such children, violates the Equal Protection Clause of the Fourteenth Amendment.

(a) The illegal aliens who are plaintiffs in these cases challenging the statute may claim the benefit of the Equal Protection Clause, which provides that no State shall "deny to any person within its jurisdiction the equal protection of the laws." Whatever his status under the immigration laws, **an alien is**

a "person" in any ordinary sense of that term. This Court's prior cases recognizing that illegal aliens are "persons" protected by the Due Process Clauses of the Fifth and Fourteenth Amendments, which Clauses do not include the phrase "within its jurisdiction," cannot be distinguished on the asserted ground that persons who have entered the country illegally are not "within the jurisdiction" of a State even if they are present within its boundaries and subject to its laws. Nor do the logic and history of the Fourteenth Amendment support such a construction. Instead, use of the phrase "within its jurisdiction" confirms the understanding that the Fourteenth Amendment's protection extends to anyone, citizen or stranger, who is subject to the laws of a State, and reaches into every corner of a State's territory.

(b) The discrimination contained in the Texas statute cannot be considered rational unless it furthers some substantial goal of the State. Although undocumented resident aliens cannot be treated as a "suspect class," and although education is not a "fundamental right," so as to require the State to justify the statutory classification by showing that it serves a compelling governmental interest, nevertheless the Texas statute imposes a lifetime hardship on a discrete class of children not accountable for their disabling status. These children can neither affect their parents' conduct nor their own undocumented status. The deprivation of public education is not like the deprivation of some other governmental benefit. Public education has a pivotal role in maintaining the fabric of our society and in sustaining our political and cultural heritage; the deprivation of education takes an inestimable toll on the social, economic, intellectual, and psychological well-being of the individual, and poses an obstacle to individual achievement. In determining the rationality of the Texas statute, its costs to the Nation and to the innocent children may properly be considered.

(c) The undocumented status of these children vel non does not establish a sufficient rational basis for denying them benefits that the State affords other residents. It is true that when faced with an equal protection challenge respecting a State's differential treatment of aliens, the courts must be attentive to congressional policy concerning aliens. But in the area of special constitutional sensitivity presented by these cases, and in the absence of any contrary indication fairly discernible in the legislative record, no national policy is perceived that might justify the State in denying these children an elementary education.

(d) **Texas' statutory classification cannot be sustained as furthering its interest in the "preservation of the state's limited resources for the education of its lawful residents."** While the State might have an interest in mitigating potentially harsh economic effects from an influx of illegal immigrants, the Texas statute does not offer an effective method of dealing with the problem. Even assuming that the net impact of illegal aliens on the economy is negative, charging tuition to undocumented children constitutes an ineffectual attempt to stem the tide of illegal immigration, at least when compared with the alternative of prohibiting employment of illegal aliens. Nor is there any merit to the suggestion that undocumented children are appropriately singled out for exclusion because of the special burdens they impose on the State's ability to provide high-quality public education. The record does not show that exclusion of undocumented children is likely to improve the overall quality of education in the State. Neither is there any merit to the claim that undocumented children are appropriately singled out because their unlawful presence within the United States renders them less likely than other children to remain within the State's boundaries and to put their education to productive social or political use within the State.

C. Equal Protection and Gender

The following case in Virginia set the standard for protecting the interests of students to be able to receive equal educational opportunities regardless of gender.

In ruling against the State of Virginia's creation of a male-only military school, the Supreme Court determined that the State failed in its burden of proving that it had an **important governmental objective** for its denial of females to the school and that the discriminatory tactics that it used were **substantially related to the obtaining of that objective**. In finding a violation of the Equal Protection Clause, the syllabus from the case of *United States v. Virginia*, 518 U.S. 515 (1996), stated (emphasis added):

Virginia Military Institute (VMI) is the sole single-sex school among Virginia's public institutions of higher learning. VMI's distinctive mission is to produce "citizen-soldiers," men prepared for leadership in civilian life and in military service. Using an "adversative method" of training not available elsewhere in Virginia, VMI endeavors to instill physical and mental discipline in its cadets and impart to them a strong moral code. . . The United States sued Virginia and VMI, alleging that VMI's exclusively male admission policy violated the Fourteenth Amendment's Equal Protection Clause. . . .

Held:
1. **Parties who seek to defend gender-based government action must demonstrate an "exceedingly persuasive justification" for that action.** . . Neither federal nor state government acts compatibly with equal protection when a law or official policy denies to women, simply because they are women, full citizenship stature-equal opportunity to aspire, achieve, participate in and contribute to society based on their individual talents and capacities. To meet the burden of justification, a State must show "at least that the [challenged] classification serves **important governmental objectives and that the discriminatory means employed are substantially related to the achievement of those objectives**." . . . The justification must be genuine, not hypothesized or invented post hoc in response to litigation. And it must not rely on overbroad generalizations about the different talents, capacities,

or preferences of males and females. . . . **The heightened review standard applicable to sex-based classifications does not make sex a proscribed classification, but it does mean that categorization by sex may not be used to create or perpetuate the legal, social, and economic inferiority of women.**

2. **Virginia's categorical exclusion of women from the educational opportunities VMI provides denies equal protection to women.** . . .

(a) Virginia contends that single-sex education yields important educational benefits and that provision of an option for such education fosters diversity in educational approaches. Benign justifications proffered in defense of categorical exclusions, however, must describe actual state purposes, not rationalizations for actions in fact differently grounded. Virginia has not shown that VMI was established, or has been maintained, with a view to diversifying, by its categorical exclusion of women, educational opportunities within the State. **A purpose genuinely to advance an array of educational options is not served by VMI's historic and constant plan to afford a unique educational benefit only to males. However well this plan serves Virginia's sons, it makes no provision whatever for her daughters.**

(b) Virginia also argues that VMI's adversative method of training provides educational benefits that cannot be made available, unmodified, to women, and that alterations to accommodate women would necessarily be so drastic as to destroy VMI's program. It is uncontested that women's admission to VMI would require accommodations, primarily in arranging housing assignments and physical training programs for female cadets. It is also undisputed, however, that neither the goal of producing citizen soldiers, VMI's raison d'etre, nor VMI's implementing methodology is inherently unsuitable to women. . . . Courts, however, must take "a hard look" at generalizations or tendencies of the kind Virginia pressed, for state actors controlling gates to opportunity have no warrant to exclude qualified individuals based on "fixed notions concerning the roles and abilities of males and females." . . . The notion that admission of women would downgrade VMI's stature, destroy the adversative system and, with it, even the school, is a judgment hardly proved, a prediction hardly different from other "self-fulfilling prophec[ies], . . . once routinely used to deny rights or opportunities. Women's successful entry into the federal military academies, and their participation in the Nation's military forces, indicate that Virginia's fears for VMI's future may not be solidly grounded. **The State's justification for excluding all women from "citizen-soldier" training for which some are qualified, in any event, does not rank as "exceedingly persuasive."**

3. **The remedy proffered by Virginia-maintain VMI as a male-only college and create VWIL as a separate program for women-does not cure the constitutional violation.**

(a) A remedial decree must closely fit the constitutional violation; it must be shaped to place persons unconstitutionally denied an opportunity or advantage in the position they would have occupied in the absence of discrimination. . . The constitutional violation in this case is the categorical exclusion of women, in disregard of their individual merit, from an extraordinary educational opportunity afforded men. Virginia chose to leave untouched VMI's exclusionary policy, and proposed for women only a separate program, different in kind from VMI and unequal in tangible and intangible facilities. VWIL affords women no opportunity to experience the rigorous military training for which VMI is famed. Kept away from the pressures, hazards, and psychological bonding characteristic of VMI's adversative training, VWIL students will not know the feeling of tremendous accomplishment commonly experienced by VMI's successful cadets. Virginia maintains that methodological differences are justified by the important differences between men and women in learning and developmental needs, but generalizations about "the way women are," estimates of what is appropriate for most women, no longer justify denying opportunity to women whose talent and capacity place them outside the average description. In myriad respects other than military training, VWIL does not qualify as VMI's equal. The VWIL program is a pale shadow of VMI in terms of the range of curricular choices and faculty stature, funding, prestige, alumni support and influence. **Virginia has not shown substantial equality in the separate educational opportunities the State supports at VWIL and VMI**.

(b) The Fourth Circuit failed to inquire whether the proposed remedy placed women denied the VMI advantage in the position they would have occupied in the absence of discrimination, . . . and considered instead whether the State could provide, with fidelity to equal protection, separate and unequal educational programs for men and women. In declaring the substantially different and significantly unequal VWIL program satisfactory, the appeals court displaced the exacting standard developed by this Court with a deferential standard, and added an inquiry of its own invention, the "substantive comparability" test. The Fourth Circuit plainly erred in exposing Virginia's VWIL plan to such a deferential analysis, **for "all gender based classifications today" warrant "heightened scrutiny."** . . . Women seeking and fit for a VMI-quality education cannot be offered anything less, under the State's obligation to afford them genuinely equal protection.

D. *Equal Protection, Gender, and Athletics*

The following cases discuss legal standards that have been determined regarding equal protection in athletics regardless of gender. Although the Supreme Court has not considered an equal protection case where an athlete has alleged sex discrimination under the Fourteenth Amendment, there have been numerous cases at the federal trial and circuit court levels, with mixed results. As a general rule, however, females mostly prevail when they sue to participate in traditionally male non-contact athletic programs, but the opposite is true when males attempt to play on female teams.

The courts are most divided when females attempt to use the Constitution to participate in male contact sports. An illustrative case where a freshman female wrestler prevailed in obtaining a preliminary injunction to permit her to try out for the team is *Adams v. Baker*, 919 F.Supp. 1496 (D.Kan. 1996). The court stated at 1504, (emphasis added):

> In this case the defendants identified several rationales behind the decision to prohibit girls from wrestling at Valley Center High School. The reasons given were safety, fear of sexual harassment litigation, potential disruption of the school setting, student and parent objections based on moral beliefs, and a variety of inconveniences.
>
> **The court concludes that the last two rationales do not constitute "important governmental objectives" in this case.** The school district certainly does not consider itself subject to every parental complaint or whim. Furthermore, it is not the duty of the school to shield students from every situation that they may find objectionable or embarrassing due to their own prejudices. The defendants also identified potential problems with coaching techniques, availability of locker room facilities and other inconveniences. However, **the district's interest in avoiding such trivial problems is hardly an important governmental objective.** . .
>
> The court agrees that **student safety is an important governmental objective**. . . However, **the district's policy of prohibiting females from wrestling is not substantially related to that objective**. The defendant's only evidence that plaintiff's safety is at greater risk because of her gender is based on generalized assumptions about the differences between males and females regarding physical strength. . . The evidence shows that some females are stronger than some males. The school can take into account differences of size, strength, and experience without assuming those qualities based on gender. Furthermore, there was evidence presented of injuries boys have sustained while wrestling, and it is certainly improper to subject boys to greater danger than girls. . .
>
> Likewise, **a school district has an interest in avoiding sexual harassment litigation.** However, **prohibiting female participation in activities is not substantially related to that goal**. The evidence before this court stated the obvious, that wrestling is an athletic activity and not a sexual activity. There is no reason to suspect that girls who seek to join the wrestling team would be likely to mistake the contact, which is inherent in the sport, for sexual misconduct. A school district best avoids sexual harassment litigation by acting to prevent sexual harassment rather than excluding females from participating in activities.
>
> Finally, **the court concludes that the defendant's actions are not**

substantially related to the goal of avoiding disruption of the school setting. According to the defense witnesses' testimony, there was no such disruption when plaintiff wrestled last year. Furthermore, the only evidence of potential disruption this year is the suggestion that some boys may quit the wrestling team if the plaintiff is allowed to participate, which the court concludes does not really constitute disruption of the school setting at all. A gender-based classification simply is not necessary to keep Valley Center High School running smoothly. . . .

E. *Equal Protection and School Finance*

The Supreme Court in the case of *San Antonio Indep. Sch. Dist. v. Rodriquez*, 411 U.S. 1 (1973), ruled that since the State of Texas proved that its system of school finance was **rationally related to a legitimate state purpose** (low judicial scrutiny test), there was no violation of the Equal Protection Clause. The Court rejected the federal trial court's finding that wealth (or a lack thereof) constituted a "suspect class" and that education was a "fundamental right" under the federal Constitution (which would have meant application of the "strict scrutiny" test wherein the state would have to prove a compelling justification for the financial disparities in financing its schools). The syllabus to *Rodriquez* stated (emphasis in bold added):

> The financing of public elementary and secondary schools in Texas is a product of state and local participation. Almost half of the revenues are derived from a largely state-funded program designed to provide a basic minimum educational offering in every school. Each district supplements state aid through an ad valorem tax on property within its jurisdiction. Appellees brought this class action on behalf of schoolchildren said to be members of poor families who reside in school districts having a low property tax base, making the claim that the Texas system's reliance on local property taxation favors the more affluent and violates equal protection requirements because of substantial interdistrict disparities in per-pupil expenditures resulting primarily from differences in the value of assessable property among the districts. The District Court, finding that wealth is a "suspect" classification and that education is a "fundamental" right, concluded that the system could be upheld only upon a showing, which appellants failed to make, that there was a compelling state interest for the system. The court also concluded that appellants failed even to demonstrate a reasonable or rational basis for the State's system.

> Held:

> 1. This is not a proper case in which to examine a State's laws under standards of strict judicial scrutiny, since that test is reserved for cases involving laws that operate to the disadvantage of suspect classes or interfere with the exercise of fundamental rights and liberties explicitly

or implicitly protected by the Constitution.

(a) The Texas system does not disadvantage any suspect class. It has not been shown to discriminate against any definable class of "poor" people or to occasion discriminations depending on the relative wealth of the families in any district. And, insofar as the financing system disadvantages those who, disregarding their individual income characteristics, reside in comparatively poor school districts, the resulting class cannot be said to be suspect.

(b) Nor does the Texas school-financing system impermissibly interfere with the exercise of a "fundamental" right or liberty. Though education is one of the most important services performed by the State, it is not within the limited category of rights recognized by this Court as guaranteed by the Constitution. Even if some identifiable quantum of education is arguably entitled to constitutional protection to make meaningful the exercise of other constitutional rights, here there is no showing that the Texas system fails to provide the basic minimal skills necessary for that purpose.

(c) Moreover, this is an inappropriate case in which to invoke strict scrutiny since it involves the most delicate and difficult questions of local taxation, fiscal planning, educational policy, and federalism, considerations counseling a more restrained form of review.

2. The Texas system does not violate the Equal Protection Clause of the Fourteenth Amendment. Though concededly imperfect, **the system bears a rational relationship to a legitimate state purpose**. While assuring a basic education for every child in the State, it permits and encourages participation in and significant control of each district's schools at the local level.

Because the *Rodriquez* court found that education was not a fundamental right and poverty was not a suspect class under the federal Constitution, it applied the low scrutiny "rational basis" test and determined that the disparity in financing Texas schools was justified by a showing that the scheme was rationally related to the legitimate state goal of affording a "basic education for every child." After the 1973 *Rodriquez* case, school finance litigation shifted to each state where the courts therein either had to decide whether education was a fundamental right under that state's version of the Equal Protection Clause or interpret the particular education language relating to the establishment of the school system.

For, example, the Illinois Supreme Court determined that education was not a fundamental right under the Illinois constitution and found that differences in school funding met the low scrutiny, rational basis standard. *Committee for Educational Rights v. Edgar*, 672 N.E.2d 1178 (Ill. 1996). On the other hand, the Kentucky Supreme Court in

Rose v. Council for Better Education, 790 S.W.2d 186 (Ky. 1989), found education to be a fundamental right, but decided that an equal protection analysis was not needed because the state failed to operate an "efficient" education system under its constitution.

II. ACTS OF CONGRESS

In addition to the Constitution's Equal Protection Clause, Congress has enacted a wide body of legislation addressed at granting students equal rights based on race, gender, disability, and native language.

A. Title VI: Racial, Color, and National Origin Equality

In 1964, Congress passed the wide-sweeping Civil Rights Act to prohibit various forms of discrimination in both the private and public sectors. It is codified at Title 42 of the United States Code. "Title VI" of the Act is codified at 42 U.S.C. Section 2000d *et seq.*, with section 2000d stating:

> No person in the United States shall, on the ground of race, color, or national origin, be excluded from participation in, be denied the benefits of, or be subjected to discrimination under any program or activity receiving Federal financial assistance.

> Title VI establishes an administrative structure for reporting, investigating, and resolving charges of discrimination by recipients of federal funds. Such recipients are both public and private schools that receive any type of federal assistance. Only after attempts to obtain voluntary compliance to cease acts believed to violate Title VI would the administrative process begin to withdraw federal support. The regulations adopted pursuant to Title VI are found at 34 C.F.R. section 100 *et seq.*

CASE
Lau v. Nichols, 414 U.S. 563 (1974) (emphasis added)

The San Francisco, California, school system was integrated in 1971 as a result of a federal court decree. . . The District Court found that there are 2,856 students of Chinese ancestry in the school system who do not speak English. Of those who have that language deficiency, about 1,000 are given supplemental courses in the English language. About 1,800, however, do not receive that instruction.

This class suit brought by non-English-speaking Chinese students against officials responsible for the operation of the San Francisco Unified School District seeks relief against the unequal educational opportunities. . . .

This is a public school system of California and 71 of the California Education Code states that "English shall be the basic language of instruction in all schools." That section permits a school district to determine "when and under what circumstances instruction may be given bilingually." That section also states as "the policy of the state" to insure "the mastery of English by all pupils in the schools." And bilingual instruction is authorized "to the extent that it does not interfere with the systematic, sequential, and regular instruction of all pupils in the English language."

Moreover, 8573 of the Education Code provides that no pupil shall receive a diploma of graduation from grade 12 who has not met the standards of proficiency in "English," as well as other prescribed subjects. Moreover, by 12101 of the Education Code (Supp. 1973) children between the ages of six and 16 years are (with exceptions not material here) "subject to compulsory full-time education."

Under these state-imposed standards there is no equality of treatment merely by providing students with the same facilities, textbooks, teachers, and curriculum; for students who do not understand English are effectively foreclosed from any meaningful education.

Basic English skills are at the very core of what these public schools teach. Imposition of a requirement that, before a child can effectively participate in the educational program, he must already have acquired those basic skills is to make a mockery of public education. **We know that those who do not understand English are certain to find their classroom experiences wholly incomprehensible and in no way meaningful. . . .**

The school district involved in this litigation receives large amounts of federal financial assistance. The Department of Health, Education, and Welfare (HEW) [presently the Department of Education], which has authority to promulgate regulations prohibiting discrimination in federally assisted school systems, 42 U.S.C. 2000d-1, in 1968 issued one guideline that "[s]chool systems are responsible for assuring that students of a particular race, color, or national origin are not denied the opportunity to obtain the education generally obtained by other students in the system." 33 Fed. Reg. 4956. In 1970 HEW made the guidelines more specific, requiring school districts that were federally funded "to rectify the language deficiency in order to open" the instruction to students who had "linguistic deficiencies," 35 Fed. Reg. 11595. . . .

 Discrimination is barred which has that effect even though no purposeful design is present: a recipient "may not . . . utilize criteria or methods of administration which have the effect of subjecting individuals to discrimination" or have "the effect of defeating or substantially impairing accomplishment of the objectives of the program as respect individuals of a particular race, color, or national origin." . . .

It seems obvious that the Chinese-speaking minority receive fewer benefits than the English-speaking majority from respondents' school system which denies them a meaningful opportunity to participate in the educational program - all earmarks of the discrimination banned by the regulations. . . .

Respondent school district contractually agreed to "comply with title VI of the Civil Rights Act of 1964 . . . and all requirements imposed by or pursuant to the Regulation" of HEW (45 CFR pt. 80) which are "issued pursuant to that title . . ."

and also immediately to "take any measures necessary to effectuate this agreement." The Federal Government has power to fix the terms on which its money allotments to the States shall be disbursed. . . Whatever may be the limits of that power. . . they have not been reached here. Senator Humphrey, during the floor debates on the Civil Rights Act of 1964, said:

"Simple justice requires that public funds, to which all taxpayers of all races contribute, not be spent in any fashion which encourages, entrenches, subsidizes, or results in racial discrimination."

We accordingly reverse the judgment of the Court of Appeals and remand the case for the fashioning of appropriate relief.

Reversed and remanded.

B. Title IX: Gender Equality

In the Education Amendments of 1972, Congress passed Title IX to prohibit gender discrimination by institutions receiving federal funds, 20 U.S.C. Section 1681-1688, with regulations at 34 C.F.R. section 106.1 *et seq.* (2003). The Office of Civil Rights ("OCR") of the Department of Education enforces Title IX by investigating complaints, attempting to gain voluntary compliance by consent agreements, and holding hearings, if needed, before withholding federal funds from an educational entity found in violation. A person allegedly aggrieved may also file suit directly in federal court to enforce Title IX.

C. Title IX and Athletics

The regulations governing athletics at 34 C.F.R. Section 106.41 state in relevant part (emphasis added):

(a) General. No person shall, on the basis of sex, be excluded from participation in, be denied the benefits of, be treated differently from another person or otherwise be discriminated against in any interscholastic, intercollegiate, club or intramural athletics offered by a recipient, and no recipient shall provide any such athletics separately on such basis.

(b) **Separate teams.** Notwithstanding the requirements of paragraph (a) of this section, a recipient **may operate or sponsor separate teams** for members of each **sex where selection for such teams is *based upon competitive skill or the activity involved is a contact sport*. However, where a recipient operates or sponsors a team in a particular sport for members of one sex but operates or sponsors no such team for members of the other sex, *and athletic opportunities for members of that sex have previously been limited*, members of the excluded sex must be allowed to try-out for the team offered unless the sport involved is a contact sport. For the purposes of this part, contact sports include boxing, wrestling, rugby, ice hockey, football, basketball and other sports the purpose or major activity of which involves bodily contact.**

(c) Equal opportunity. A recipient which operates or sponsors interscholastic, intercollegiate, club or intramural athletics shall provide equal athletic opportunity for members of both sexes. In determining whether equal opportunities are available the Director will consider, among other factors:

(1) Whether the selection of sports and levels of competition effectively accommodate the interests and abilities of members of both sexes;

(2) The provision of equipment and supplies;

(3) Scheduling of games and practice time;

(4) Travel and per diem allowance;

(5) Opportunity to receive coaching and academic tutoring;

(6) Assignment and compensation of coaches and tutors;

(7) Provision of locker rooms, practice and competitive facilities;

(8) Provision of medical and training facilities and services;

(9) Provision of housing and dining facilities and services;

(10) Publicity.

Unequal aggregate expenditures for members of each sex or unequal expenditures for male and female teams if a recipient operates or sponsors separate teams will not constitute noncompliance with this section, but the Assistant Secretary may consider the failure to provide necessary funds for teams for one sex in assessing equality of opportunity for members of each sex. . . .

In the case of *Mercer v. Duke University*, 190 F.3d 643 (4ᵗʰ Cir. 1999), the court was required to interpret subsections (a) and (b) of these regulations when the University was sued under Title IX by a female football place kicker who had made the team the prior year and then was cut at the start of the next year. In ruling that she stated a claim under Title IX and was entitled to a trial, the court stated at pages 646-648 (emphasis added):

> Subsections (a) and (b) of section 106.41 stand in a symbiotic relationship to one another. Subsection (a) establishes a baseline prohibition against sex discrimination in intercollegiate athletics, tracking almost identically the language in the parallel statutory provision prohibiting discrimination by federally funded educational institutions. In addition to generally barring discrimination on the basis of sex in intercollegiate athletics, subsection (a) specifically prohibits any covered institution from "provid[ing] any such athletics separately on such basis."
>
> **Standing alone, then, subsection (a) would require covered institutions to integrate all of their sports teams.** In order to avoid such a result

-which would have radically altered the face of intercollegiate athletics -HEW provided an **explicit exception to the rule of subsection (a) in the first sentence of subsection (b), allowing covered institutions to "operate or sponsor separate teams for members of each sex where selection for such teams is based upon competitive skill or the activity involved is a contact sport."** By its terms, this sentence permits covered institutions to operate separate teams for men and women in many sports, including contact sports such as football, rather than integrating those teams.

The first sentence of subsection (b), however, **leaves unanswered the question of what, if any, restrictions apply to sports in which a covered institution operates a team for one sex, but operates no corresponding team for the other sex.** HEW addressed this question in the second sentence of subsection (b).

This second sentence is applicable only when **two predicate criteria are met: first, that the institution in question "operates or sponsors a team in a particular sport for members of one sex but operates or sponsors no such team for members of the other sex," and second, that "athletic opportunities for members of that sex have previously been limited."** In this case, appellees do not dispute that athletic opportunities for women at Duke have previously been limited, and thus we assume that the second condition has been met. Further, we assume, without deciding, that Duke operated its football team "for members of one sex" -that is, for only men-but did not operate a separate team "for members of the other sex," and therefore that the first condition has also been satisfied. Thus, insofar as the present appeal is concerned, we consider the predicate conditions to application of the sentence to have been met. . .

We therefore construe the second sentence of subsection (b) as providing that in non-contact sports, but not in contact sports, covered institutions must allow members of an excluded sex to try out for single-sex teams. Once an institution has allowed a member of one sex to try out for a team operated by the institution for the other sex in a contact sport, subsection (b) is simply no longer applicable, and the institution is subject to the general anti-discrimination provision of subsection (a). . .

Accordingly, **because appellant has alleged that Duke allowed her to try out for its football team (and actually made her a member of the team), then discriminated against her and ultimately excluded her from participation in the sport on the basis of her sex, we conclude that she has stated a claim under the applicable regulation, and therefore under Title IX.** We take to heart appellees' cautionary observation that, in so holding, we thereby become "the first Court in United States history to recognize such a cause of action." . . . Where, as here, however, the university invites women into what appellees characterize as the "traditionally all-male bastion of collegiate football," . . . , we are convinced that this reading of the regulation is the only one permissible under law. . . .

D. Title IX and Sexual Harassment

The Supreme Court in *Franklin v. Gwinnett County Public Schools*, 503 U.S. 60 (1992), ruled that Title IX applied to sexual harassment against students at schools receiving federal assistance and that the federal court had the authority to award damages in such an action. The Court stated at page 75:

> . . . Unquestionably, Title IX placed on the Gwinnett County Schools the duty not to discriminate on the basis of sex, and "when a supervisor sexually harasses a subordinate because of the subordinate's sex, that supervisor `discriminate[s]' on the basis of sex." *Meritor Savings Bank, FSB v. Vinson*, 477 U.S. 57, 64 (1986). We believe the same rule should apply when a teacher sexually harasses and abuses a student. Congress surely did not intend for federal monies to be expended to support the intentional actions it sought by statute to proscribe. . . .

Six years after the *Franklin* case, the Supreme Court clarified what had to happen before a school would be found liable for sexual harassment of its students by employees. In the case of *Gebser v. Lago Vista Indep. Sch. Dist.*, 524 U.S. 274, 118 S.Ct. 1989 (1998), the Court determined that a school would face Title IX damages only when a school official who had the authority to take corrective action had actual knowledge of the harassment and then acted with deliberate indifference. Said the Court at 118 S.Ct 1999:

> Consequently, in cases like this one that do not involve official policy of the recipient entity, we hold that a damages remedy will not lie under Title IX unless an official who at a minimum has authority to address the alleged discrimination and to institute corrective measures on the recipient's behalf has actual knowledge of discrimination in the recipient's programs and fails adequately to respond.

> We think, moreover, that the response must amount to deliberate indifference to discrimination. The administrative enforcement scheme presupposes that an official who is advised of a Title IX violation refuses to take action to bring the recipient into compliance. The premise, in other words, is an official decision by the recipient not to remedy the violation.

In a student to student sexual harassment case a year after *Gebser*, the Supreme Court in *Davis v. Monroe County Bd. of Ed.*, 525 U.S. 629, 119 S.Ct. 1661 (1999), established a similar standard with an important addition. To recover damages under Title IX, the allegedly harassed student must prove that (1) a school official knew of the offensive conduct and acted with deliberate indifference to it, and (2) the harassment was sufficiently severe, pervasive, and objectively offensive to cause the student's educational experience to be undermined so as to effectively deny equal access to school resources. The *Davis* Court at 119 S.Ct. 1675 stated (emphasis added):

> The most obvious example of student-on-student sexual harassment capable of triggering a damages claim would thus involve the overt, physical deprivation of access to school resources. Consider, for example, a case in which male students physically threaten their female peers every day, successfully preventing the female students from using a particular school resource--an athletic field or a computer lab, for instance. District administrators are well aware of the daily ritual, yet they deliberately ignore requests for aid from the female students wishing to use the resource. The district's knowing refusal to take any action in response to such behavior would fly in the face of Title IX's core principles, and such deliberate indifference may appropriately be subject to claims for monetary damages. It is not necessary, however, to show physical exclusion to demonstrate that students have been deprived by the actions of another student or students of an educational opportunity on the basis of sex. Rather, **a plaintiff must establish sexual harassment of students that is so severe, pervasive, and objectively offensive, and that so undermines and detracts from the victims' educational experience, that the victim-students are effectively denied equal access to an institution's resources and opportunities**. . . .
>
> **Whether gender-oriented conduct rises to the level of actionable "harassment" thus "depends on a constellation of surrounding circumstances, expectations, and relationships,"** . . . , **including, but not limited to, the ages of the harasser and the victim and the number of individuals involved**, see OCR Title IX Guidelines 12041-12042. Courts, moreover, must bear in mind that schools are unlike the adult workplace and that children may regularly interact in a manner that would be unacceptable among adults. . . Indeed, at least early on, students are still learning how to interact appropriately with their peers. It is thus understandable that, in the school setting, students often engage in insults, banter, teasing, shoving, pushing, and gender-specific conduct that is upsetting to the students subjected to it. **Damages are not available for simple acts of teasing and name-calling among school children, however, even where these comments target differences in gender.** Rather, in the context of student-on-student harassment, damages are available only where the behavior is so severe, pervasive, and objectively offensive that it denies its victims the equal access to education that Title IX is designed to protect.

E. *Title IX and Pregnancy/Marriage*

The regulations regarding a student's "parental, family, or marital status" are found at 34 C.F.R. Section 106.40, which read in relevant part (emphasis added):

(a) Status generally. A recipient shall not apply any rule concerning a student's actual or potential parental, family, or marital status which treats students differently on the basis of sex

(b) Pregnancy and related conditions.

(1) A recipient shall not discriminate against any student, or exclude any student from its education program or activity, **including any class or extracurricular activity**, on the basis of such student's **pregnancy, childbirth, false pregnancy, termination of pregnancy or recovery there from,** unless the student requests voluntarily to participate in a separate portion of the program or activity of the recipient.

(2) A recipient **may require such a student to obtain the certification of physician that the student is physically and emotionally able to continue participation so long as such a certification is required of all students for other physical or emotional conditions** requiring the attention of a physician. . . .

SCENARIOS
STATE AND APPLY THE RELEVANT LEGAL RULE(S) TO THE FACTS.

1. Urban School District had comprehensive data over a ten-year period demonstrating that male students had academic performance levels relative equal to that of female students during the first six grades, but beginning at grade seven, the males began experiencing a serious decline that continued to get worse through high school. In an attempt to counter this academic decline and after seeking input from national experts, Urban School began segregating, on the basis of gender, classes in math, science, English, foreign language, and social studies in grades seven through twelve.

Suit was filed by parents of both male and female students contending a violation of the federal constitution in that learning is more than just academics and that segregating the genders in this manner was inherently unequal and detrimental to the full education of each child. (Title IX was not utilized due to expressions of a Congressional intent in the No Child Left Behind Act that gender segregated classes were statutorily valid.)

2. Had Urban School District, based on unquestionable data of academic decline by African American male students starting at the seventh grade level, decided to create academically strengthened classes in the above-listed subjects for this group and pull them from the general student population for such classes, what would be the legal issue and how would the court likely consider and apply the relevant legal standard?

3. Sixteen-year-old Female Student, a clearly gifted soccer player with the speed, agility, and strength of at least two thirds of the male players, requested to try out for the male high school team, but was denied and told that she had to play on the female soccer team. Because soccer is classified as a contact sport under Title IX regulations and since there was a female team, Parents filed suit under the constitution rather than Title IX contending that the denial limited the full enhancement of her skills and as well as soccer scholarship opportunities to major universities.

4. Cheerleader in both football and basketball disclosed to her coach at the start of the football season that she was pregnant, but had gotten written medical clearance from her physician to participate normally for the next four weeks, and then modify her routines as needed as the pregnancy progressed. Coach did not say that she was removed from the cheerleading squad, but stated that once her pregnancy became visible, she could no longer wear the uniform and cheer for the team in front of the crowd. It was generally known that male athletes who had fathered children had been allowed to participate on their teams without interruption. If suit were filed, what would be the legal issue and how would a court likely consider and apply the relevant legal standard?

CHAPTER
10

STUDENTS WITH DISABILITIES

I. REHABILITATION ACT OF 1973 ("SECTION 504")

Prior to national legislation, the rights of disabled children had been established on a piecemeal basis by some state legislatures and by the judicial system under the equal protection clause of the Fourteenth Amendment. Congress first entered the picture by passage of Section 504 of the Rehabilitation Act of 1973, which prohibited recipients of federal funding from discriminating against an "otherwise qualified individual with a disability . . . solely by reason of her or his disability. . . ." 29 U.S.C. section 794a (2003). The regulations at 34 C.F.R. section 104 *et seq.* (2003) state in relevant part (emphasis added):

Sec. 104.4 Discrimination prohibited.

(a) General. No qualified handicapped person shall, on the basis of handicap, be excluded from participation in, and be denied the benefits of, or otherwise be subjected to discrimination under any program or activity which receives Federal financial assistance. . . .

Sec. 104.3 Definitions. . . .

(j) **Handicapped person—**

    (1) **Handicapped persons** means any person who

        (i) has a physical or mental impairment which substantially limits one or more major life activities,

        (ii) has a record of such an impairment, or

        (iii) is regarded as having such an impairment.

    (2) As used in paragraph (j)(1) of this section, the phrase:

        (i) **Physical or mental impairment** means

            (A) any physiological disorder or condition, cosmetic disfigurement, or anatomical loss affecting one or more of the following body systems: neurological; musculoskeletal; special sense organs; respiratory, including speech organs; cardiovascular; reproductive, digestive, genito-urinary; hemic and lymphatic; skin; and endocrine; or

            (B) any mental or psychological disorder, such as mental retardation, organic brain syndrome, emotional or mental illness, and specific learning disabilities.

        (ii) **Major life activities** means functions such as caring for one's self, performing manual tasks, walking, seeing, hearing, speaking, breathing, learning, and working.

        (iii) **Has a record of such an impairment** means has a history of, or has been misclassified as having, a mental or physical impairment that substantially limits one or more major life activities.

        (iv) **Is regarded as having an impairment** means

            (A) has a physical or mental impairment that does not substantially limit major life activities but that is treated by a recipient as constituting such a limitation;

            (B) has a physical or mental impairment that substantially limits major life activities only as a result of the attitudes of others toward such impairment; or

            (C) has none of the impairments defined in paragraph (j)(2)(i) of this section but is treated by a recipient as having such an impairment.

(l) **Qualified handicapped person** means: . . . .

(2) With respect to public preschool elementary, secondary, or adult educational services, a handicapped person

(i) of an age during which nonhandicapped persons are provided such services,

(ii) of any age during which it is mandatory under state law to provide such services to handicapped persons, or

(iii) to whom a state is required to provide a free appropriate public education under section 612 of the Education of the Handicapped Act; . . .

The following case explores the legal standard for handicapped students to participate in educational activities.

Case

Knapp v. Northwestern University, 101 F.3d 473 (7th Cir. 1996) (emphasis added)

[Issues:] Nicholas Knapp wants to play NCAA basketball for Northwestern University--so badly that he is willing to face an increased risk of death to do so. . . Usually, competent, intelligent adults are allowed to make such decisions. This is especially true when, as here, the individual's family approves of the decision and the individual and his parents are willing to sign liability waivers regarding the worst-case scenario should it occur.

Northwestern, however, refuses to allow Knapp to play on or even practice with its men's basketball team. . . .

The issue in this case boils down to whether the school--because of sec. 504 of the Rehabilitation Act of 1973, as amended, 29 U.S.C. sec. 794--will be forced to let Knapp don a purple uniform and take the floor as a member of Northwestern's basketball team. .

[Facts:] A few weeks into his senior year, Knapp suffered sudden cardiac death–meaning his heart stopped–during a pick-up basketball game. Paramedics used cardiopulmonary resuscitation, defibrillation (i.e., electric shocks), and injections of drugs to bring Knapp back to life. A few weeks later, doctors implanted an internal cardioverter-defibril-lator in Knapp's abdomen. The device detects heart arrhythmia and delivers a shock to convert the abnormal heart rhythm back to normal. In other words, if Knapp's heart stops again the device is supposed to restart it. . . .

[Rationale:] The Rehabilitation Act, which is the sole basis for Knapp's claim, ensures that **[n]o otherwise qualified individual with a disability in the United States**, as defined in section 7(8) [29 USCS sec. 706(8)], **shall, solely by reason of her or his disability, be excluded from the participation in, be denied the benefits of, or be subjected to discrimination under any program or activity receiving Federal financial assistance**. . . . 29 U.S.C. sec. 794(a). To prevail on his claim for discrimination under the Act, **Knapp must prove** that: (1) he is **disabled** as defined by the Act; (2) he is **otherwise qualified** for the position sought; (3) he has been **excluded** from the position **solely because of his disability**; and (4) the position exists as part of a program or activity receiving federal financial assistance. . . .

To show that he is disabled under the terms of the Act, **Knapp must prove** that he (i) has a **physical . . . impairment** which **substantially limits** one or more of [his] **major life activities**, (ii) has a record of such an impairment, or (iii) is regarded as having such an impairment. 29 U.S.C. sec. 706(8)(B). Knapp satisfies the first element of part (i) of this definition. A cardiovascular problem constitutes a physical impairment under sec. 706(8)(B). 34 C.F.R. sec. 104.3(j)(2)(i)(A); 45 C.F.R. sec. 84.3(j)(2)(i)(A).

Northwestern does not dispute this fact, but it instead zeros in on the second element of the disability definition: **whether playing intercollegiate basketball is part of a major life activity** and, if so, **whether its diagnosis of Knapp's cardiac condition substantially limits Knapp in that activity**.

. . . [The] regulations define "**major life activities**" as **basic functions of life** "such as caring for one's self, performing manual tasks, walking, seeing, hearing, speaking, breathing, learning, and working." . . .

We decline to define the major life activity of learning in such a way that the Act applies whenever someone wants to play intercollegiate athletics. A "major life activity," as defined in the regulations, is a basic function of life "such as caring for one's self, performing manual tasks, walking, seeing, hearing, speaking, breathing, learning, and working." . . . These are basic functions, not more specific ones such as being an astronaut, working as a firefighter, driving a race car, or learning by playing Big Ten basketball. . . .

Not every impairment that affects an individual's major life activities is a substantially limiting impairment. The key obviously is the extent to which the impairment restricts the major life activity. . . **An impairment that interferes with an individual's ability to perform a particular function, but does not significantly decrease that individual's ability to obtain a satisfactory education otherwise, does not substantially limit the major life activity of learning.** . . .

Because learning through playing intercollegiate basketball is only one part of the education available to Knapp at Northwestern, even under a subjective standard, Knapp's ability to learn is not substantially limited. Knapp's scholarship continues, allowing him access to all academic and-- except for intercollegiate basketball--all nonacademic ser- vices and activities available to other Northwestern students, in addition to all other services available to scholarship athletes. . . The Rehabilitation Act does not guarantee an individual the exact educational experience that he may desire, just a fair one. **Consequently, we hold that Knapp as a matter of law is not disabled within the meaning of the Rehabilitation Act.**

Even if we were inclined to find Knapp disabled under the Rehabilitation Act, he would still come up short because **we also hold as a matter of law that he is not, under the statute, "otherwise qualified" to play intercollegiate basketball at Northwestern.** A qualified disabled person, with respect to postsecondary education services, is a "person who meets the academic and technical standards requisite to admission or participation in the [school's] education program or activity." . . . .

[Precedents:] In *Mantolete*, the Ninth Circuit addressed the standard to apply in determining if an individual is otherwise physically qualified to perform an activity when the possibility of future injury exists:

[I]n some cases, a job requirement that screens out qualified handicapped individuals on the basis of possible future injury is necessary. However, **we hold that in order to exclude such individuals, there must be a showing of a reasonable probability of substantial harm.** Such a determination cannot be based merely on an employer's subjective evaluation or, except in cases of a most apparent nature, merely on medical reports. The question is whether, in light of the individual's work history and medical history, employment of that individual would pose a reasonable probability of substantial harm. . . .

In this case, the severity of the potential injury is as high as it could be–death. . . Although the doctors indicated that these numbers were merely estimates, all agreed that the risk to Knapp is higher than to the average male collegiate basketball player. . . .

Section 794 prohibits authorities from deciding without significant medical support that certain activities are too risky for a disabled person. Decisions of this sort cannot rest on paternalistic concerns. Knapp, who is an adult, is not in need of paternalistic decisions regarding his health, and his parents--more entitled to be paternalistic toward him than Northwestern--approve of his decision. . . But here, where Northwestern acted rationally and reasonably rather than paternalistically, no Rehabilitation Act violation has occurred. The Rehabilitation Act "is carefully structured to replace . . . reflexive actions to actual or perceived handicaps with actions based on reasoned and medically sound judgments. . .

[Court ruling:] For these reasons, the district court's grant of the permanent injunction and denial of Northwestern's motion for summary judgment are reversed and the case is remanded with instructions to enter summary judgment in favor of Northwestern.

REVERSED.

II. INDIVIDUALS WITH DISABILITES EDUCATION ACT (IDEA)

To set a national standard for educating children with disabilities, Congress passed Public Law 94-142 in 1975, entitled "Education for All Handicapped Children Act" (EAHCA), which has been re-named the "Individuals with Disabilities Education Act" (IDEA). The IDEA requires schools that receive federal financial assistance to provide disabled students between the ages of three and twenty two a free, appropriate public education ("FAPE") in the least restrictive environment ("LRE"), including the development of an individualized education program ("IEP") and educationally related non-medical services such as transportation and catheritization.

The underlying rationale for the Act and its basic purposes were described by the Supreme Court in the student-expulsion case of *Honig v. Doe*, 484 U.S. 305 (1998), wherein the Act's so-called "stay-put" provision was challenged by the state of California.

Case
Honig v. Doe, 484 U.S. 305 (1988) (emphasis added)

[Background:] As a condition of federal financial assistance, the Education of the Handicapped Act requires States to ensure a "free appropriate public education" for all disabled children within their jurisdictions. In aid of this goal, the Act establishes a comprehensive system of procedural safeguards designed to ensure parental participation in decisions concerning the education of their disabled children and to provide administrative and judicial review of any decisions with which those parents disagree. Among these safeguards is the so-called **"stay-put" provision, which directs that a disabled child "shall remain in [his or her] then current educational placement" pending completion of any review proceedings, unless the parents and state or local educational agencies otherwise agree.** 20 U.S.C. 1415(e)(3). **Today we must decide whether, in the face of this statutory proscription, state or local school authorities may nevertheless unilaterally exclude disabled children from the classroom for dangerous or disruptive conduct growing out of their disabilities.** . . .

In the Education of the Handicapped Act (EHA or the Act), . . . Congress sought "to assure that all handicapped children have available to them . . . a **free appropriate public education which emphasizes special education and related services designed to meet their unique needs,** [and] to assure that the rights of handicapped children and their parents or guardians are protected." 1400(c). When the law was passed in 1975, Congress had before it ample evidence that such legislative assurances were sorely needed: 21 years after this Court declared education to be "perhaps the most important function of state and local governments," Brown v. Board of Education, 347 U.S. 483, 493 (1954), congressional studies revealed that better than half of the Nation's 8 million disabled children were not receiving appropriate educational services. 1400(b)(3). Indeed, one out of every eight of these children was excluded from the public school system altogether, 1400(b)(4); many others were simply "warehoused" in special classes or were neglectfully shepherded through the system until they were old enough to drop out. . . Among the most poorly served of disabled students were emotionally disturbed children: Congressional statistics revealed that for the school year immediately preceding passage of the Act, the educational needs of 82 percent of all children with emotional disabilities went unmet. . . .

Although these educational failings resulted in part from funding constraints, Congress recognized that the problem reflected more than a lack of financial resources at the state and local levels. Two federal-court decisions, . . . demonstrated that many disabled children were excluded pursuant to state statutes or local rules and policies, typically without any consultation with, or even notice to, their parents. See *Mills v. Board of Education of District of Columbia*, 348 F. Supp. 866 (DC 1972); *Pennsylvania Assn. for Retarded Children v. Pennsylvania*, 334 F. Supp. 1257 (ED Pa. 1971), and 343 F. Supp. 279 (1972) (PARC). Indeed, by the time of the EHA's enactment, parents had brought legal challenges to similar exclusionary practices in 27 other States. . . .

In responding to these problems, Congress did not content itself with passage of a simple funding statute. Rather, **the EHA confers upon disabled students an enforceable substantive right to public education in participating States,** see Board of Education of Hendrick Hudson Central School Dist. v. Rowley, 458 U.S. 176 (1982), **and conditions federal financial assistance upon a State's compliance with the substantive and procedural goals of the Act.** Accordingly, States seeking to qualify for federal funds must develop policies assuring all disabled children the "right to a free appropriate public education," and must file with the Secretary of Education formal plans mapping out in detail the programs, procedures, and timetables under which they will effectuate these policies. 20 U.S.C. 1412(1), 1413(a). **Such plans must assure that, "to the maximum extent appropriate," States will "mainstream" disabled children, i. e., that they will educate them with children who are not disabled, and that they will segregate or otherwise remove such children from the regular classroom setting "only when the nature or severity of the handicap is such that education in regular classes . . . cannot be achieved satisfactorily."** 1412(5).

The primary vehicle for implementing these congressional goals is the "individualized educational program" (IEP), which the EHA mandates for each disabled child. Prepared at meetings between a representative of the local school district, the child's teacher, the parents or guardians, and, whenever appropriate, the disabled child, **the IEP sets out the child's present educational performance, establishes annual and short-term objectives for improvements in that performance, and describes the specially designed instruction and services that will enable the child to meet those objectives.** 1401(19). **The IEP must be reviewed and, where necessary, revised at least once a year** in order to ensure that local agencies tailor the statutorily required "free appropriate public education" to each child's unique needs. . . .

Envisioning the IEP as the centerpiece of the statute's education delivery system for disabled children, and aware that schools had all too often denied such children appropriate educations without in any way consulting their parents, Congress repeatedly emphasized throughout the Act the **importance and indeed the necessity of parental participation in both the development of the IEP and any subsequent assessments of its effectiveness.** . . . Accordingly, **the Act establishes various procedural safeguards that guarantee parents both an opportunity for meaningful input into all decisions affecting their child's education and the right to seek review of any decisions they think inappropriate. These safeguards include the right to examine all relevant records pertaining to the identification, evaluation, and educational placement of their child; prior written notice whenever the responsible educational agency proposes (or refuses) to change the child's placement or program; an opportunity to present complaints concerning any aspect of the local agency's provision of a free appropriate public education; and an opportunity for "an impartial due process hearing" with respect to any such complaints.** . . .

At the conclusion of any such hearing, both the parents and the local educational agency may seek further administrative review and, where that proves unsatisfactory, may file a civil action in any state or federal court. . . . In addition to reviewing the administrative record, courts are empowered to take additional evidence at the request of either party and to "grant such relief as [they] determine is appropriate." 1415(e)(2).

The "stay-put" provision at issue in this case governs the placement of a child while these often lengthy review procedures run their course. It directs that:

"During the pendency of any proceedings conducted pursuant to [1415], unless the State or local educational agency and the parents or guardian otherwise agree, the child shall remain in the then current educational placement of such child. . . ."

[Facts:] The present dispute grows out of the efforts of certain officials of the San Francisco Unified School District (SFUSD) to expel two emotionally disturbed children from school indefinitely for violent and disruptive conduct related to their disabilities. In November 1980, respondent John Doe assaulted another student at the Louise Lombard School, a developmental center for disabled children. Doe's April 1980 IEP identified him as a socially and physically awkward 17-year-old who experienced considerable difficulty controlling his impulses and anger. . . .

On November 6, 1980, Doe responded to the taunts of a fellow student in precisely the explosive manner anticipated by his IEP: he choked the student with sufficient force to leave abrasions on the child's neck, and kicked out a school window while being escorted to the principal's office afterwards. . .

In another case, respondent Jack Smith was identified as an emotionally disturbed child by the time he entered the second grade in 1976. School records prepared that year indicated that he was unable "to control verbal or physical outburst[s]" and exhibited a "[s]evere disturbance in relationships with peers and adults." . . .

School officials met twice with his grandparents in October 1980 to discuss returning him to a half-day program; although the grandparents agreed to the reduction, they apparently were never apprised of their right to challenge the decision through EHA procedures. The school officials also warned them that if the child continued his disruptive behavior – which included stealing, extorting money from fellow students, and making sexual comments to female classmates – they would seek to expel him. On November 14, they made good on this threat, suspending Smith for five days after he made further lewd comments. His principal referred the matter to the SPC, which recommended exclusion from SFUSD. As it did in John Doe's case, the Committee scheduled a hearing and extended the suspension indefinitely pending a final disposition in the matter. . . .

The language of 1415(e)(3) is unequivocal. It states plainly that during the pendency of any proceedings initiated under the Act, unless the state or local educational agency and the parents or guardian of a disabled child otherwise agree, "the child shall remain in the then current educational placement." . . . Faced with this clear directive, petitioner asks us to read a "dangerousness" exception into the stay-put provision on the basis of either of two essentially inconsistent assumptions: first, that Congress thought the residual authority of school officials to exclude dangerous students from the classroom too obvious for comment; or second, that Congress inadvertently failed to provide such authority and this Court must therefore remedy the oversight. Because we cannot accept either premise, we decline petitioner's invitation to rewrite the statute.

Petitioner's arguments proceed, he suggests, from a simple, commonsense proposition: Congress could not have intended the stay-put provision to be read literally, for such a construction leads to the clearly unintended, and untenable, result that school districts must return violent or dangerous students to school while the often lengthy EHA proceedings run their course. We think it clear, however, that Congress very much meant to strip schools of the unilateral authority they had traditionally employed to exclude disabled students, particularly emotionally disturbed students, from school. In so doing, Congress did not leave school administrators powerless to deal with dangerous students; it did, however, deny school officials their former right to "self-help," and directed that in the future the removal of disabled students could be accomplished only with the permission of the parents or, as a last resort, the courts.

As noted above, Congress passed the EHA after finding that school systems across the country had excluded one out of every eight disabled children from classes. . . .

Congress attacked such exclusionary practices in a variety of ways. It required participating States to educate all disabled children, regardless of the severity of their disabilities, . . . and included within the definition of "handicapped" those children with serious emotional disturbances. . . It further provided for meaningful parental participation in all aspects of a child's educational placement, and barred schools, through the stay-put provision, from changing that placement over the parent's objection until all review proceedings were completed. Recognizing that those proceedings might prove long and tedious, the Act's drafters did not intend 1415(e)(3) to operate inflexibly, . . . and they therefore allowed for interim placements where parents and school officials are able to agree on one. . . .

Our conclusion that 1415(e)(3) means what it says does not leave educators hamstrung. The Department of Education has observed that, "[w]hile the [child's] placement may not be changed [during any complaint proceeding], this does not preclude the agency from using its normal procedures for dealing with children who are endangering themselves or others." . . . Such procedures may include the use of study carrels, time-outs, detention, or the restriction of privileges. **More drastically, where a student poses an immediate threat to the safety of others, officials may temporarily suspend him or her for up to 10 schooldays.** This authority, which respondent in no way disputes, not only ensures that school administrators can protect the safety of others by promptly removing the most dangerous of students, it also provides a "cooling down" period during which officials can initiate IEP review and seek to persuade the child's parents to agree to an interim placement. **And in those cases in which the parents of a truly dangerous child adamantly refuse to permit any change in placement, the 10-day respite gives school officials an opportunity to invoke the aid of the courts under 1415(e)(2), which empowers courts to grant any appropriate relief.**

. . . While many of the EHA's procedural safeguards protect the rights of parents and children, schools can and do seek redress through the administrative review process, and we have no reason to believe that Congress meant to require schools alone to exhaust in all cases, no matter how exigent the circumstances. The burden in such cases, of course, rests with the school to demonstrate the futility or inadequacy of administrative review, but nothing in 1415(e)(2) suggests that schools are completely barred from attempting to make such a showing. **Nor do we think that 1415(e)(3) operates to limit the equitable powers of district courts such that they cannot, in appropriate cases, temporarily enjoin a dangerous disabled child from attending school.**

As the EHA's legislative history makes clear, one of the evils Congress sought to remedy was the unilateral exclusion of disabled children by schools, not courts, and one of the purposes of 1415(e)(3), therefore, was "to prevent school officials from removing a child from the regular public school classroom over the parents' objection pending completion of the review proceedings." . . . The stay-put provision in no way purports to limit or pre-empt the authority conferred on courts by 1415(e)(2), . . .; indeed, it says nothing whatever about judicial power.

[Court ruling:] In short, then, **we believe that school officials are entitled to seek injunctive relief under 1415(e)(2) in appropriate cases. In any such action, 1415(e)(3) effectively creates a presumption in favor of the child's current educational placement which school officials can overcome only by showing that maintaining the child in his or her current placement is substantially likely to result in injury either to himself or herself, or to others.** In the present case, we are satisfied that the **District Court**, in enjoining the state and local defendants from indefinitely suspending respondent or otherwise unilaterally altering his then current placement, **properly balanced respondent's interest in receiving a free appropriate public education in accordance with the procedures and requirements of the EHA against the interests of the state and local school officials in maintaining a safe learning environment for all their students.** . . .

III. IDEA REQUIREMENTS

A. *IDEA: FAPE and Extent of Education Required*

Case
Hendrick Hudson Dist. Bd. of Ed. v. Rowley, 458 U.S. 176 (1982)
(Court syllabus; emphasis added)

. . . Respondents – a child with only minimal residual hearing who had been furnished by school authorities with a special hearing aid for use in the classroom and who was to receive additional instruction from tutors, and the child's parents – filed suit in Federal District Court to review New York administrative proceedings that had upheld the school administrators' denial of the parents' request that the child also be provided a qualified sign-language interpreter in all of her academic classes. Entering judgment for respondents, the District Court found that although the child performed better than the average child in her class and was advancing easily from grade to grade, she was not performing as well academically as she would without her handicap. Because of this disparity between the child's achievement and her potential, the court held that she was not receiving a "free appropriate public education," which the court defined as "an opportunity to achieve [her] full potential commensurate with the opportunity provided to other children." The Court of Appeals affirmed.

Held:
1. **The Act's requirement of a "free appropriate public education" is satisfied when the State provides personalized instruction with sufficient support services to permit the handicapped child to benefit educationally from that instruction.** Such instruction and services must be provided at public expense, must meet the State's educational standards, must approximate grade levels used in the State's regular education, and must comport with the child's IEP, as formulated in accordance with the Act's requirements. **If the child is being educated in regular**

classrooms, as here, the IEP should be reasonably calculated to enable the child to achieve passing marks and advance from grade to grade. . . .

(a) This interpretation is supported by the definitions contained in the Act, as well as by   other provisions imposing procedural requirements and setting forth statutory findings and priorities for States to follow in extending educational services to handicapped children. **The Act's language contains no express substantive standard prescribing the level of education to be accorded handicapped children.** . . . .

(b) The Act's legislative history shows that Congress sought to make public education available to handicapped children, **but did not intend to impose upon the States any greater substantive educational standard than is necessary to make such access to public education meaningful. The Act's intent was more to open the door of public education to handicapped children by means of specialized educational services than to guarantee any particular substantive level of education once inside.** . . .

(c) While Congress sought to provide assistance to the States in carrying out their constitutional responsibilities to provide equal protection of the laws, it did not intend to achieve strict equality of opportunity or services for handicapped and nonhandicapped children, but rather sought primarily to identify and evaluate handicapped children, and to provide them with access to a free public education. **The Act does not require a State to maximize the potential of each handicapped child commensurate with the opportunity provided nonhandicapped children.** . . .

2. In suits brought under the Act's judicial-review provisions, **a court must first determine whether the State has complied with the statutory procedures, and must then determine whether the individualized program developed through such procedures is reasonably calculated to enable the child to receive educational benefits.** If these requirements are met, the State has complied with the obligations imposed by Congress and the courts can require no more. . . .

(a) Although the judicial-review provisions do not limit courts to ensuring that States have complied with the Act's procedural requirements, the Act's emphasis on procedural safeguards demonstrates the legislative conviction that adequate compliance with prescribed procedures will in most cases assure much, if not all, of what Congress wished in the way of substantive content in an IEP. . . .

(b) **The courts must be careful to avoid imposing their view of preferable educational methods upon the States.** Once a court determines that the Act's requirements have been met, questions of methodology are for resolution by the States. . .

3. Entrusting a child's education to state and local agencies does not leave the child without protection. As demonstrated by this case, parents and guardians will not lack ardor in seeking to ensure that handicapped children receive all of the benefits to which they are entitled by the Act. . . .

4. The Act does not require the provision of a sign-language interpreter here. Neither of the courts below found that there had been a failure to comply with the Act's procedures, and the findings of neither court will support a conclusion that the child's educational program failed to comply with the substantive requirements of the Act.

B. FAPE: Least Restrictive Environment; Unilateral Private Placement

Case

Board. of Education. of Lagrange Sch. Dist. No. 105 v. Ill. State Bd. of Ed., 81 F.3d 673 (7th Cir. 1999) (emphasis added)

LaGrange School District No. 105 appeals the district court's decision finding that it failed to offer Ryan B. ("Ryan") a free appropriate public education within the meaning of the Individuals With Disabilities Education Act, 20 U.S.C. sec. 1400 et seq. ("IDEA") and ordering reimbursement to Ryan's parents for the cost of his education in a private pre-school.

I. BACKGROUND

Children age three to twenty-one who are eligible for special education under IDEA are entitled to receive a free appropriate public education ("FAPE") from their home school district. Ryan was born on January 23, 1994 and has Down Syndrome. In 1996, when he was two, his parents placed him in a private pre-school with nondisabled children. When he turned three, his home school district, LaGrange School District No. 105 ("School District"), was asked to evaluate him and determine his eligibility for special education programs pursuant to IDEA. The School District does not have a program for disabled students. The School District convened a multi-disciplinary conference ("MDC") and prepared the statutorily required individualized education program ("IEP"), which, in January 1997, concluded that Ryan was eligible for special education and recommended placing him in a program limited to disabled students at Brook Park Elementary School, five miles from his home and in a different school district.

In February 1997, Ryan's parents rejected the Brook Park placement and requested the creation of a program within the School District that would include nondisabled students or access to similar programs in neighboring districts. A second IEP meeting was held and Ryan's parents again rejected the Brook Park program. On March 19, 1997, the School District offered to have the IEP team consider a state-funded "At-Risk" program, called Project IDEAL, within Ryan's district. This program is available to children who are primarily at risk of academic failure. After Ryan's parents visited Project IDEAL, they requested a due process hearing as provided for in IDEA. . . .

Under IDEA, disputes such as these are first handled administratively through a two-tiered process. The initial hearing is called the Level I Due Process Hearing. Appeal from that decision results in a second administrative hearing, the Level II. . . The Level II hearing officer ruled that neither the Brook Park placement nor the At-Risk program provided Ryan with a FAPE because neither placement satisfied IDEA's requirement that disabled children be educated in the "least restrictive environment." . . . The Level II officer also ordered the School District to pay for Ryan's private school.

The School District appealed. On cross motions for summary judgment, the district court ruled in Ryan's favor and held that the School District had failed to provide a FAPE and affirmed the award of private pre-school costs. The School District now appeals. . . .

II. DISCUSSION . . . .

B. Whether either program was a FAPE.

The central issue in this case is whether either program offered by the School District was a FAPE within the meaning of IDEA. The district court held that neither was because each failed to satisfy the least restrictive environment requirement and that private placement provided Ryan with optimal educational benefit. The School District argues that, in so holding, the district court misapplied the LRE requirement.

Under IDEA, **a FAPE is an educational program "specifically designed to meet the unique needs of the handicapped child, supported by such services as are necessary to permit the child to benefit from the instruction."** . . . IDEA explicitly provides that states receiving federal funds must:

establish procedures to insure that, **to the maximum extent appropriate, handicapped children . . . are educated with children who are not handicapped**, and that special education, separate schooling, or other removal of handicapped children from the regular education environment occurs only when the nature or severity of the handicap is such that education in regular classes with the use of supplementary aids and services cannot be achieved satisfactorily.

20 U.S.C. sec. 1412 (5)(B). This requirement is known as "**main streaming**," and, as we have held, this provision creates a strong preference in favor of it. . . In addition to the statutory presumption, IDEA's implementing regulations provide that disabled children are to be educated in the **least restrictive environment ("LRE")**. 34 C.F.R. sec. 300.550(b)(1). Just as the statute indicates, the regulations provide **that a child may be removed from a regular educational environment only when the nature or severity of that child's disability is such that education in regular classes with the use of supplementary aids and services cannot be achieved satisfactorily**. 34 C.F.R. sec. 300.550(b)(2).

According to 34 C.F.R. sec. 300.552, a child is to be educated in the school that he or she would otherwise attend if not disabled unless the IEP for that child requires some other placement. The commentary to this regulation provides:

Public agencies that do not operate programs for nondisabled children are not required to initiate such programs to satisfy the requirements regarding placement in the LRE embodied in Sections 300.550-556. For these public agencies, some alternative methods for meeting the requirements include

(1) Providing opportunities for participation (even part time) of preschool children with disabilities in other preschool programs operated by public agencies (such as Head Start);

(2) Placing children with disabilities in private school programs for nondisabled preschool children or private preschool programs that integrate children with disabilities and nondisabled children; and

(3) Locating classes for preschool children with disabilities in regular elementary schools.

In each case the public agency must ensure that each child's placement is in the LRE in which the unique needs of that child can be met, based on the child's IEP, and meets all of the other requirements of Sections 300.340-300.350 and Sections 300.550-300.556.

The district court concluded, as did the Level II hearing officer, that because neither placement offered by the School District satisfied the least restrictive environment requirement nor met Ryan's unique needs, the School District failed to provide Ryan with a FAPE. The School District argues this was error because each of its proposed programs met one of the alternatives stated in the commentary to 34 C.F.R. sec. 300.552.

Therefore, claims the School District, it met its obligation to provide Ryan with a FAPE. We will discuss each placement in turn.

1. Brook Park Placement.

The district court held that the Brook Park program did not satisfy the LRE requirement because the private placement demanded by Ryan's parents was less restrictive and better met his unique needs. The School District argues that the Brook Park placement was a FAPE because it met the third alternative provided by the LRE regulation.. . . .

[W]e agree with Ryan that the alternatives provided in the regulation do not absolve the School District of its duty to comply with the least restrictive environment requirement. Here, the Level II hearing officer concluded that the Brook Park placement was not the least restrictive environment for Ryan, in part **because the evidence presented at the hearing indicated that his disability and IEP did not prevent him from benefiting from a more inclusive setting**. The district court affirmed that conclusion, finding that the private preschool in which Ryan was able to interact with nondisabled children provided the least restrictive environment. Given the extremely deferential standard with which we review those determinations, . . .we conclude that the district court's decision was not in error. Therefore, we agree that the Brook Park placement is not a FAPE for Ryan within the meaning of IDEA because it does not provide the least restrictive environment in which his individual needs can be met.

2. Project IDEAL/At-Risk.

The School District argues that the Project IDEAL/At-Risk program is a FAPE because it is similar to Head Start, and thus meets the first alternative provided in the commentary to 34 C.F.R. sec. 300.552. According to the School District, Project IDEAL is like Head Start because both programs are designed for children who have language, cultural and economic disadvantages and both are targeted toward nondisabled children.

The district court did not err in holding that Project IDEAL was not a FAPE. The Level II hearing officer rejected the At-Risk placement because she found that there was no evidence introduced at the hearing that the School District ever evaluated this program with reference to Ryan's IEP. The district court agreed with the hearing officer, noting that the record below was bereft of any testimony suggesting that the At-Risk program was ever evaluated in light of Ryan's unique needs as IDEA and the regulations mandate. . . .

Thus, based on the limited evidence before it, the district court did not err in concluding that the At-Risk program offered by the School District was not sufficient to provide the least restrictive environment for Ryan, based on his unique needs.

C. Reimbursement.

The district court also ordered the School District to reimburse Ryan's parents for the costs of his private education. **The Supreme Court has held that parents may obtain reimbursement for private school tuition if the placement offered by the school district is inappropriate, the private placement selected by the parents is appropriate and equitable considerations support the parents' claim.** Florence County Sch. Dist. Four v. Carter, 510 U.S. 7, 15 (1993). . . .

III. CONCLUSION

For the foregoing reasons, we conclude that neither program offered by the School District provided Ryan with a free appropriate public education and that the district court did not abuse its discretion in ordering reimbursement to Ryan's parents for the cost of his private preschool. Therefore, we Affirm the judgment of the district court.

C. IDEA: Public School Instruction at Private School

Case

K.R v. Anderson Community School Corp., 81 F.3d 673

(7th Cir. 1996) (emphasis added)

K.R. is a multiply handicapped student in need of a full-time instructional assistant to attend school. If K.R. attended public school, she would indisputably be entitled to all services prescribed by her individual education plan ("IEP") under the Individuals with Disabilities Education Act, 20 U.S.C. secs. 1400 et seq. ("IDEA"), including the instructional assistant. However, K.R.'s parents have opted out of the public system and have voluntarily placed K.R. in a private parochial school. **The question, therefore, is whether the IDEA or its accompanying regulations require Anderson Community Schools to provide the instructional assistant at the private school.** . . .

I. BACKGROUND

It is not disputed that K.R. is a child with disabilities who is eligible under the IDEA for special educational and related services. K.R. was a six-year-old kindergarten student at the time this dispute arose. She suffers from myelomeningocele, spina bifida, and hydrocephalus with a shunt, which create difficulties with expressive language, motor skills, and mobility, requiring her to use a wheel- chair. She thus needs assistance with positioning for activities, reaching and grasping, self-help skills, motor movements, mobility, and expression. Implementation of her IEP (determined in conformity with the IDEA) requires, among other necessary related services, a full-time instructional assistant. . . .

The IEP provided for placement in a kindergarten class with related services for speech therapy, occupational therapy, transportation, and a full-time instructional assistant. During the conference, K.R.'s parents asked whether K.R. would receive all of the services if she attended St. Mary's School, a private parochial school. The public school told K.R.'s parents that it would not provide an instructional assistant if she attended private school. Nonetheless, K.R.'s parents voluntarily enrolled her at St. Mary's for kindergarten. During K.R.'s attendance at St. Mary's, the public school has provided K.R. with speech therapy, occupational therapy, and physical therapy at a public school site, as well as transportation to that site. Since the local system determined that it would not provide K.R. with an instructional assistant on site at the private school, and since St. Mary's chose not to provide the service itself, K.R.'s mother attended St. Mary's with her to fulfill the duties of an instructional assistant prior to the district court's decision. . . .

On May 25, 1995, the district court issued a permanent injunction and declaratory judgment holding that the public school was required to provide a full-time instructional assistant at the private school. *K.R. ex rel. M.R. v. Anderson Community Sch. Corp.*, 887 F. Supp. 1217 (S.D. Ind. 1995). The district court based its decision on a regulation that requires the special education services to private school students be "comparable" to the services provided to public school students.

II. DISCUSSION

The IDEA's statutory scheme is typical of a federal granting program. The statute provides federal grants to states, which in turn fund local school districts, for assistance in educating disabled students. The states that elect to participate in the program receive a grant of not more than forty percent of the average per pupil expenditure for all students nationwide multiplied by the number of disabled students in the particular state receiving the grant. 20 U.S.C. sec. 1411(a). According to the United States Department of Education ("DOE"), federal grants supply only about eight percent of the funds needed to provide disabled students with special services. Nonetheless, a state that accepts IDEA grants must have in effect a policy that "assures all children with disabilities the right to a free appropriate public education" and a plan that assures such an education will be available. 20 U.S.C. sec. 1412(1) & (2)(B). The **local school district must prepare for each disabled child an IEP that identifies the special education and related services that are necessary to meet that child's needs, and the district must then offer to provide those services at full public expense.** 20 U.S.C. secs. 1412(4), 1414(a)(5). The district **must place the child in a private school at public expense if it is unable to provide the necessary services in a public school.** 20 U.S.C. sec. 1413(a)(4)(B). . . .

The regulations help clarify the public school's obligation with respect to disabled students in private schools. **If the parents voluntarily place their child in a private school, "the public agency is not required by this part to pay for the child's education at the private school or facility. However, the public agency shall make services available to the child** as provided under secs. 300.450-300.452." 34 C.F.R. sec. 300.403. In turn, Section 300.452 states, "[e]ach [local educational agency] shall provide special education and related services designed to meet the needs of private school children with disabilities residing in the jurisdiction of the agency." 34 C.F.R. sec. 300.452. Section 300.451 further requires the local agency to ensure that, "[t]o the extent consistent with their number and location in the State, provision is made for the participation of private school children with disabilities in the program assisted or carried out under this part by providing them with special education and related services. . . ." 34 C.F.R. sec. 300.451. . . .

It is abundantly clear from the distinctions drawn in both the statute and the regulations that neither Congress nor the DOE intended for public schools to provide students such as K.R. with services comparable to what she would receive in the public school. . . **The public school need only provide "a genuine opportunity for equitable participation,"** 34 C.F.R. sec. 76.651(a)(1), and it must consult with representatives of the student to determine, among other things, which children will receive benefits and what benefits will be provided. . . .

Given the statutory scheme as outlined above, which clearly affords public schools discretion in providing services to private school students, **interpreting "comparable" in Section 76.654 as requiring identical services would render**

that regulation void as inconsistent with the statute. . . . For example, public schools may legitimately regulate the provision of expensive services, such as full-time assistants, in order to ration limited resources across more students. In light of the statutory provisions, **"comparable" must be interpreted in a manner that permits public schools discretion in providing services to voluntarily placed private school students**. . . .

IV.

The only **remaining question is whether the public school in this case properly exercised its discretion** as outlined in the cross-referenced regulations. **The standard is whether the student was provided with a genuine opportunity for equitable participation.** We agree with the Fourth Circuit--the only other Circuit to have addressed this issue--**that the essential component is that of opportunity. . . . Where the public school makes available the necessary service at a public institution, giving the disabled student a genuine opportunity to participate, and nothing in the record indicates that it has otherwise abused its discretion, the public school has discharged its obligation.** . . . K.R. was offered the service of a full-time instructional assistant at Anderson Community School. We have no reason to doubt the opportunity was genuine: nothing in the record demonstrates that K.R. was prevented from attending the public school by anything other than a desire to attend private school; and nothing demonstrates that the public school would have failed to provide the instructional assistant had K.R. decided to return. K.R. was thus provided with a genuine opportunity that she rejected. . . .

V. CONCLUSION

We conclude that the IDEA and its regulations do not require a public school to make comparable provisions for a disabled student voluntarily attending private school as for disabled public school students. Rather, public schools are given discretion under the law and **need only provide voluntarily placed private school students a genuine opportunity for equitable participation**. Here, Anderson Community School afforded K.R. a genuine opportunity for the services of an instructional assistant at a public school, and she declined. Further, the public school's provision of other related services demonstrates that it reasonably exercised its discretion rather than eschew its responsibility once K.R. chose to attend private school. The decision of the district court is therefore reversed.

D. *IDEA: Related Services Requirement*

Case
Cedar Rapids Comm. Sch. Dist. v. Garret F., 526 U.S. 66 (1999)
(footnotes other than number 1 omitted; emphasis added)

The Individuals with Disabilities Education Act (IDEA). . . . was enacted, in part, "to assure that all children with disabilities have available to them . . . a free appropriate public education which emphasizes special education and related services designed to meet their unique needs." . . . Consistent with this purpose, the IDEA authorizes federal financial assistance to States that agree to provide disabled children with special education and "related services." . . . **The question presented in this case is whether the definition of "related services" in §1401(a)(17) [fn1] requires a public school district in a participating State to provide a ventilator-dependent student with certain nursing services during school hours.**

I. BACKGROUND

Respondent Garret F. is a friendly, creative, and intelligent young man. When Garret was four years old, his spinal column was severed in a motorcycle accident. Though paralyzed from the neck down, his mental capacities were unaffected. He is able to speak, to control his motorized wheelchair through use of a puff and suck straw, and to operate a computer with a device that responds to head movements. Garret is currently a student in the Cedar Rapids Community School District (District), he attends regular classes in a typical school program, and his academic performance has been a success. Garret is, however, ventilator dependent, and therefore requires a responsible individual nearby to attend to certain physical needs while he is in school.

During Garret's early years at school his family provided for his physical care during the school day. When he was in kindergarten, his 18-year-old aunt attended him; in the next four years, his family used settlement proceeds they received after the accident, their insurance, and other resources to employ a licensed practical nurse. In 1993, Garret's mother requested the District to accept financial responsibility for the health care services that Garret requires during the school day. The District denied the request, believing that it was not legally obligated to provide continuous one-on-one nursing services. . . .

II. TITLE

The District contends that §1401(a)(17) does not require it to provide Garret with "continuous one-on-one nursing services" during the school day, even though Garret cannot remain in school without such care. . . However, the IDEA's definition of "related services," our decision in *Irving Independent School Dist.* v. *Tatro,* 468 U.S. 833 (1984), and the overall statutory scheme all support the decision of the Court of Appeals.

The text of the **"related services"** definition, see n. 1, *supra* , **broadly encompasses those supportive services that "may be required to assist a child with a disability to benefit from special education."** . . . As a general matter, services that enable a disabled child to remain in school during the day provide the student with "the meaningful access to education that Congress envisioned." *Tatro* , . . . (" `Congress sought primarily to make public education available to handicapped children' and `to make such access meaningful' " (quoting *Board of Ed. of Hendrick Hudson Central School Dist., Westchester Cty.* v. *Rowley* , . . .).

This general definition of "related services" is illuminated by a parenthetical phrase listing examples of particular services that are included within the statute's coverage. §1401(a)(17). **"Medical services" are enumerated in this list, but such services are limited to those that are "for diagnostic and evaluation purposes."** *Ibid.* The statute does not contain a more specific definition of the "medical services" that are excepted from the coverage of §1401(a)(17).

The scope of the "medical services" exclusion is not a matter of first impression in this Court. In *Tatro* **we concluded that the Secretary of Education had reasonably determined that the term "medical services" referred only to services that must be performed by a physician, and not to school health services**. . . . Accordingly, **we held that a specific form of health care (clean intermittent catherization) that is often, though not always, performed by a nurse is not an excluded medical service**. We referenced the likely cost of the services and the competence of school staff as justifications for drawing a line between physician and other services, *ibid.* , but our endorsement of that line was unmistakable. It is thus settled that the phrase "medical services" in §1401(a)(17) does not embrace all forms of care that might loosely be described as "medical" in other contexts, such as a claim for an income tax deduction. . . .

The District may have legitimate financial concerns, but our role in this dispute is to interpret existing law. Defining "related services" in a manner that *accommodates* the cost concerns Congress may have had, . . . is altogether different from using cost *itself* as the definition. Given that §1401(a)(17) does not employ cost in its definition of "related services" or excluded "medical services," accepting the District's cost-based standard as the sole test for determining the scope of the provision would require us to engage in judicial lawmaking without any guidance from Congress. It would also create some tension with the purposes of the IDEA. The statute may not require public schools to maximize the potential of disabled students commensurate with the opportunities provided to other children, see *Rowley* , . . . ; and the potential financial burdens imposed on participating States may be relevant to arriving at a sensible construction of the IDEA, see *Tatro* , . . . But Congress intended "to open the door of public education" to all qualified children and "require[d] participating States to educate handicapped children with nonhandicapped children whenever possible." . . .

This case is about whether meaningful access to the public schools will be assured, not the level of education that a school must finance once access is attained. It is undisputed that the services at issue must be provided if Garret is to remain in school. Under the statute, our precedent, and the purposes of the IDEA, the District must fund such "related services" in order to help guarantee that students like Garret are integrated into the public schools.

[Court ruling:] The judgment of the Court of Appeals is accordingly

Affirmed.

Footnote

1   "The term 'related services' means transportation, and such developmental, corrective, and other supportive services (including speech pathology and audiology, psychological services, physical and occupational therapy, recreation, including therapeutic recreation, social work services, counseling services, including rehabilitation counseling, and medical services, except that such medical services shall be for diagnostic and evaluation purposes only) **as may be required to assist a child with a disability to benefit from special education, and includes the early identification and assessment of disabling conditions in children."** 20 U. S. C. §1401(a)(17). . . .

Appendix

The heart of the IDEA, 20 U.S.C. section 1415, as it existed in August of 2004 reads in relevant part (emphasis added):

§ 1415. Procedural safeguards

(a) Establishment of procedures

Any State educational agency, State agency, or local educational agency that receives assistance under this subchapter **shall establish and maintain procedures** in accordance with this section **to ensure that children with disabilities and their parents are guaranteed procedural safeguards** with respect to the **provision of free appropriate public education** by such agencies.

b) Types of procedures

The **procedures required by this section shall include**—

(1) an opportunity for the parents of a child with a disability to **examine all records relating to such child and to participate in meetings with respect to the identification, evaluation, and educational placement of the child, and the provision of a free appropriate public education** to such child, and to **obtain an independent educational evaluation of the child**;

(2) procedures to protect the rights of the child whenever the parents of the child are not known . . . including the assignment of an individual . . . to act as a surrogate for the parents;

(3) **written prior notice to the parents** of the child whenever such agency—

(A) **proposes to initiate or change**; or

(B) **refuses to initiate or change**;   the **identification, evaluation, or educational placement of the child**, in accordance with subsection (c) of this section, or the **provision of a free appropriate public education** to the child;

(4) procedures designed to ensure that the notice required by paragraph (3) is in the native language of the parents, unless it clearly is not feasible to do so;

(5) an **opportunity for mediation** in accordance with subsection (e) of this section;

(6) an **opportunity to present complaints** with respect to any matter relating to the identification, evaluation, or educational placement of the child, or the provision of a free appropriate public education to such child;

(7) procedures that require the parent of a child with a disability, or the attorney representing the child, to provide notice. . . . and

(8) procedures that require the State educational agency to develop a model form to assist parents in filing a complaint in accordance with paragraph (7).

(c) Content of prior written notice

The notice required by subsection (b)(3) of this section shall include— . . . .and

(7) sources for parents to contact to obtain assistance in understanding the provisions of this subchapter.

(d) Procedural safeguards notice

(1) **In general A copy of the procedural safeguards available to the parents of a child with a disability shall be given to the parents**, at a minimum—

(A) upon initial referral for evaluation;

(B) upon each notification of an individualized education program meeting and upon reevaluation of the child; and

(C) upon registration of a complaint under subsection (b)(6) of this section.

(2) **Contents**

The **procedural safeguards notice shall include a full explanation of the procedural safeguards, written in the native language** of the parents, unless it clearly is not feasible to do so, and written in an easily understandable manner, available under this section and under regulations promulgated by the Secretary relating to—

(A) independent educational evaluation;

(B) prior written notice;

(C) parental consent;

(D) access to educational records;

(E) opportunity to present complaints;

(F) the child's placement during pendency of due process proceedings;

(G) procedures for students who are subject to placement in an interim alternative educational setting;

(H) requirements for unilateral placement by parents of children in private schools at public expense;

(I) mediation;

(J) due process hearings, including requirements for disclosure of evaluation results and recommendations;

(K) State-level appeals (if applicable in that State);

(L) civil actions; and

(M) attorneys' fees.

(e) Mediation

(1) **In general**

Any State educational agency or local educational agency that receives assistance under this subchapter **shall ensure that procedures are established** and implemented **to allow parties** to disputes involving any matter described in subsection (b)(6) of this section **to resolve such disputes through a mediation process** which, at a minimum, shall be available whenever a hearing is requested under subsection (f) or (k) of this section.

(2) **Requirements**

Such procedures shall meet the following requirements: . . . .

(G) Discussions that occur during the mediation process shall be confidential and may not be used as evidence in any subsequent due process hearings or civil proceedings and the parties to the mediation process may be required to sign a confidentiality pledge prior to the commencement of such process.

(f) Impartial due process hearing

(1) **In general**

Whenever a complaint has been received under subsection (b)(6) or (k) of this section, the **parents involved in such complaint shall have an opportunity for an impartial due process hearing**, which shall be conducted by the State educational agency or by the local educational agency, as determined by State law or by the State educational agency. . . .

(g) Appeal

If the hearing required by subsection (f) of this section is conducted by a local educational agency, any party aggrieved by the findings and decision rendered in such a hearing may appeal such findings and decision to the State educational agency. Such agency shall conduct an impartial review of such decision. The officer conducting such review shall make an independent decision upon completion of such review.

(h) Safeguards

Any party to a hearing conducted pursuant to subsection (f) or (k) of this section, or an appeal conducted pursuant to subsection (g) of this section, shall be accorded— . . . .

and

(4) the right to written, or, at the option of the parents, electronic findings of fact and decisions (which findings and decisions shall be made available to the public consistent with the requirements of section 1417(c) of this title (relating to the confidentiality of data, information, and records) and shall also be transmitted to the advisory panel established pursuant to section 1412(a)(21) of this title).

(i) Administrative procedures

(1) In general

(A) **Decision made in hearing** . . . .

(B) **Decision made at appeal** . . . .

(2) Right to bring civil action

(A) In general

Any party aggrieved by the findings and decision made under subsection (f) or (k) of this section who does not have the right to an appeal under subsection (g) of this section, and any party aggrieved by the findings and decision under this subsection, **shall have the right to bring a civil action with respect to the complaint presented pursuant to this section, which action may be brought in any State court of competent jurisdiction or in a district court of the United States** without regard to the amount in controversy.

(B) **Additional requirements** . . . .

(3) Jurisdiction of district courts; attorneys' fees

(A) In general

The district courts of the United States shall have jurisdiction of actions brought under this section without regard to the amount in controversy.

(B) Award of attorneys' fees

In any action or proceeding brought under this section, **the court, in its discretion, may award reasonable attorneys' fees as part of the costs to the parents of a child with a disability who is the prevailing party.**

(C) Determination of amount of attorneys' fees

Fees awarded under this paragraph shall be based on rates prevailing in the community in which the action or proceeding arose for the kind and quality of services furnished. No bonus or multiplier may be used in calculating the fees awarded under this subsection.

(D) **Prohibition of attorneys' fees and related costs for certain services.** . . .

(E) **Exception to prohibition on attorneys' fees and related costs**

Notwithstanding subparagraph (D), an award of attorneys' fees and related costs may be made to a parent who is the prevailing party and who was substantially justified in rejecting the settlement offer.

(F) Reduction in amount of attorneys' fees . . . .

(G) Exception to reduction in amount of attorneys' fees . . . .

The provisions of subparagraph (F) shall not apply in any action or proceeding if the court finds that the State or local educational agency unreasonably protracted the final resolution of the action or proceeding or there was a violation of this section.

(j) Maintenance of current educational placement

Except as provided in subsection (k)(7) of this section, **during the pendency of any proceedings conducted pursuant to this section, unless the State or local educational agency and the parents otherwise agree, the child shall remain in the then-current educational placement of such child, or, if applying for initial admission to a public school, shall, with the consent of the parents, be placed in the public school program until all such proceedings have been completed.**

(k) Placement in alternative educational setting

(1) **Authority of school personnel**

(A) **School personnel under this section may order a change in the placement of a child with a disability**—

(i) **to an appropriate interim alternative educational setting, another setting, or suspension, for not more than 10 school days (to the extent such alternatives would be applied to children without disabilities)**; and

(ii) **to an appropriate interim alternative educational setting for the same amount of time that a child without a disability would be subject to discipline, but for not more than 45 days if**—

(I) the child carries or possesses a weapon to or at school, on school premises, or to or at a school function under the jurisdiction of a State or a local educational agency; or

(II) **the child knowingly possesses or uses illegal drugs or sells or solicits the sale of a controlled substance while at school or a school function under the jurisdiction of a State or local educational agency.**

(B) **Either before or not later than 10 days after taking a disciplinary action** described in subparagraph (A)—

(i) **if the local educational agency did not conduct a functional behavioral assessment and implement a behavioral intervention plan** for such child before the behavior that resulted in the suspension described in subparagraph (A), the **agency shall convene an IEP meeting to develop** an assessment plan to address that behavior; or

(ii) **if the child already has a behavioral intervention plan, the IEP Team shall review the plan and modify it, as necessary, to address the behavior.**

(2) Authority of hearing officer

A hearing officer under this section may order a change in the placement of a child with a disability to an appropriate interim alternative educational setting for not more than 45 days if the hearing officer—

(A) **determines that the public agency has demonstrated by substantial evidence that maintaining the current placement of such child is substantially likely to result in injury to the child or to others;**

(B) **considers the appropriateness of the child's current placement;**

(C) **considers whether the public agency has made reasonable efforts to minimize the risk of harm in the child's current placement, including the use of supplementary aids and services;** and

(D) **determines that the interim alternative educational setting meets the requirements of paragraph (3)(B).**

(3) Determination of setting

(A) In general

The **alternative educational setting** described in paragraph (1)(A)(ii) **shall be determined by the IEP Team**.

(B) Additional requirements

Any **interim alternative educational setting** in which a child is placed under paragraph (1) or (2) **shall—**

(i) be selected so as to enable the child to continue to participate in the general curriculum, although in another setting, and to continue to receive those services and modifications, including those described in the child's current IEP, that will enable the child to meet the goals set out in that IEP; and

(ii) **include services and modifications designed to address the behavior described in paragraph (1) or paragraph (2) so that it does not recur.**

(4) Manifestation determination review

(A) In general

If a disciplinary action is contemplated as described in paragraph (1) or paragraph (2) for a behavior of a child with a disability described in either of those paragraphs, or if a disciplinary action involving a change of placement for more than 10 days is contemplated for a child with a disability who has engaged in other behavior that violated any rule or code of conduct of the local educational agency that applies to all children—

(i) not later than the date on which the decision to take that action is made, the parents shall be notified of that decision and of all procedural safeguards accorded under this section; and

(ii) **immediately, if possible, but in no case later than 10 school days after the date on which the decision to take that action is made, a review shall be conducted of the relationship between the child's disability and the behavior subject to the disciplinary action.**

(B) **Individuals to carry out review**

A review described in subparagraph (A) shall be conducted by the IEP Team and other qualified personnel.

(C) **Conduct of review**

In carrying out a review described in subparagraph (A), the **IEP Team may determine that the behavior of the child was not a manifestation of such child's disability** only if the IEP Team—

(i) **first considers, in terms of the behavior subject to disciplinary action, all relevant information, including—**

(I) evaluation and diagnostic results, including such results or other relevant information supplied by the parents of the child;

(II) observations of the child; and

(III) the child's IEP and placement; and

(ii) **then determines that—**

(I) **in relationship to the behavior subject to disciplinary action, the child's IEP and placement were appropriate and the special education services, supplementary aids and services, and behavior intervention strategies were provided consistent with the child's IEP and placement;**

(II) **the child's disability did not impair the ability of the child to understand the impact and consequences of the behavior subject to disciplinary action;** and

(III) **the child's disability did not impair the ability of the child to control the behavior subject to disciplinary action.**

(5) **Determination that behavior was not manifestation of disability**

(A) **In general**

If the result of the review described in paragraph (4) is a determination, consistent with paragraph (4)(C), that the behavior of the child with a disability **was not a manifestation of the child's disability, the relevant disciplinary procedures applicable to children without disabilities may** be applied to the child in the same manner in which they would be applied to children without disabilities, except as provided in section 1412(a)(1) of this title.

(B) **Additional requirement**

If the public agency initiates disciplinary procedures applicable to all children, the agency shall ensure that the special education and disciplinary records of the child with a disability are transmitted for consideration by the person or persons making the final determination regarding the disciplinary action.

(6) **Parent appeal**

(A) **In general**

(i) **If the child's parent disagrees with a determination that the child's behavior was not a manifestation of the child's disability or with any decision regarding placement, the parent may request a hearing**.

(ii) The State or local educational agency shall arrange for an expedited hearing in any case described in this subsection when requested by a parent.

(B) **Review of decision**

(i) In reviewing a decision with respect to the manifestation determination, the hearing officer shall determine whether the public agency has demonstrated that the child's behavior was not a manifestation of such child's disability consistent with the requirements of paragraph (4)(C).

(ii) In reviewing a decision under paragraph (1)(A)(ii) to place the child in an interim alternative educational setting, the hearing officer shall apply the standards set out in paragraph (2).

(7) **Placement during appeals**

(A) **In general**

When a parent requests a hearing regarding a disciplinary action described in paragraph (1)(A)(ii) or paragraph (2) **to challenge the interim alternative educational setting or the manifestation determination, the child shall remain in the interim alternative educational setting pending the decision of the hearing officer or until the expiration of the time period** provided for in paragraph (1)(A)(ii) or paragraph (2), **whichever occurs first, unless the parent and the State or local educational agency agree otherwise**.

(B) **Current placement**

If a child is placed in an interim alternative educational setting pursuant to paragraph (1)(A)(ii) or paragraph (2) and school personnel propose to change the child's placement after expiration of the interim alternative placement, during the pendency of any proceeding to challenge the proposed change in placement, the child shall remain in the current placement (the child's placement prior to the interim alternative educational setting), except as provided in subparagraph (C).

(C) **Expedited hearing**

(i) **If school personnel maintain that it is dangerous for the child to be in the current placement (placement prior to removal to the interim alternative education setting) during the pendency of the due process proceedings, the local educational agency may request an expedited hearing**.

(ii) In determining whether the child may be placed in the alternative educational setting or in another appropriate placement ordered by the hearing officer, the hearing officer shall apply the standards set out in paragraph (2).

(8) **Protections for children not yet eligible for special education and related services**

(A) **In general**

A child who has not been determined to be eligible for special education and related services under this subchapter and **who has engaged in behavior that violated any rule or code of conduct of the local educational agency, including any behavior described in paragraph (1), may assert any of the protections provided for in this subchapter if the local educational agency had knowledge (as determined in accordance with this paragraph) that the child was a child with a disability before the behavior that precipitated the disciplinary action occurred.**

(B) **Basis of knowledge**

A local educational agency **shall be deemed to have knowledge that a child is a child with a disability if**—

(i) **the parent of the child has expressed concern in writing** (unless the parent is illiterate or has a disability that prevents compliance with the requirements contained in this clause) **to personnel of the appropriate educational agency that the child is in need of special education and related services**;

(ii) **the behavior or performance of the child demonstrates the need for such services**;

(iii) **the parent of the child has requested an evaluation of the child pursuant to section 1414 of this title**; or

(iv) **the teacher of the child, or other personnel of the local educational agency, has expressed concern about the behavior or performance of the child to the director of special education of such agency or to other personnel of the agency**.

(C) **Conditions that apply if no basis of knowledge**

(i) **In general. If a local educational agency does not have knowledge that a child is a child with a disability (in accordance with subparagraph (B)) prior to taking disciplinary measures against the child, the child may be subjected to the same disciplinary measures as measures applied to children without disabilities who engaged in comparable behaviors** consistent with clause (ii).

(ii) **Limitations. If a request is made for an evaluation of a child during the time period in which the child is subjected to disciplinary measures under paragraph (1) or (2), the evaluation shall be conducted in an expedited manner. If the child is determined to be a child with a disability**, taking into consideration information from the evaluation conducted by the agency and information provided by the parents, **the agency shall provide special education and related services in accordance with the provisions of this subchapter, except that, pending the results of the evaluation, the child shall remain in the educational placement determined by school authorities.**

(9) **Referral to and action by law enforcement and judicial authorities**

(A) **Nothing in this subchapter shall be construed to prohibit an agency from reporting a crime committed by a child with a disability to appropriate authorities or to prevent State law enforcement and judicial authorities from exercising their responsibilities with regard to the application of Federal and State law to crimes committed by a child with a disability.**

(B) **An agency reporting a crime committed by a child with a disability shall ensure that copies of the special education and disciplinary records of the child are transmitted for consideration by the appropriate authorities to whom it reports the crime.**

(10) **Definitions**

For purposes of this subsection, the following definitions apply:

(A) **Controlled substance**

The term "controlled substance" means a drug or other substance identified under schedules I, II, III, IV, or V in section 202(c) of the Controlled Substances Act (21 U.S.C. 812(c)).

(B) **Illegal drug**

The term "illegal drug"—

(i) means a controlled substance; but

(ii) does not include such a substance that is legally possessed or used under the supervision of a licensed health-care professional or that is legally possessed or used under any other authority under that Act [21 U.S.C. 801 et seq.] or under any other provision of Federal law.

(C) **Substantial evidence**

The term "substantial evidence" means beyond a preponderance of the evidence.

(D) **Weapon**

The term "weapon" has the meaning given the term "dangerous weapon" under paragraph (2) of the first subsection (g) of section 930 of title 18. . . .

SCENARIOS
STATE AND APPLY THE RELEVANT LEGAL RULE(S) TO THE FACTS.

1. Cheerleader disclosed to Coach at the start of basketball season that she was six month's pregnant and due to deliver in mid-February. Based on her physician's written statement of good health and normal pregnancy, Coach was willing to permit her to participate in practices and at games with the necessary modifications that her physical condition dictated. However, Coach told her absolutely that she would not be able to participate in the state cheerleading competition that began the third week in April because the routines would be too complex and strenuous for her to have learned due to a lack of practice time and top-notch physical shape when the squad began working in earnest after the basketball season in the third week of March. If Cheerleader had a normal delivery the third week of February and filed suit to challenge Coach's total denial of her participation in the cheerleading competition (that School participated in as a member of the high school athletic association-sponsored event), what would be the legal issue and how would a court likely consider and apply the relevant legal standard?

2. Student was a seventh grade boy weighing 200 pounds and standing six foot tall who had been determined emotionally disabled under the IDEA. His outbursts were difficult to predict and because he had physically manhandled one of his teachers as well as several students, a 60 year-old male aide, who was retired military and of similar physical stature to Student, was employed and assigned exclusively to assist in the control of Student. When Student became exceedingly violent one spring day with efforts contained in his individualized education program (IEP) having no effect on getting him under control, school security officers were called. Before they arrived, Student had managed to knock out the aide, throw the teacher into a corner, and intimidated other students by picking up a desk and threatening to visit it upon their skulls.

When released from juvenile detention two days later, Student was brought to school by his father who absolutely refused to agree to home education pending the start of IDEA procedures to either expel him from school or develop a more restrictive IEP. Principal called two security officers who, along with Principal, escorted Student and his father to their car where father was told to keep the child at home until Principal informed the father when Student could return. Principal then began the manifestation determination process, but due to delays caused by the parents, as well as illness of two IEP committee members, the committee did not meet until two weeks later and determined that Student's violent outburst was a manifestation of his disability. The committee recommended certain psychological tests to be performed and set a date two weeks in the future to assess the need for a more restrictive educational setting for Student. A day later, an attorney representing the father appeared at the superintendent's office and demanded that Student be returned to his previous classroom setting pending the culmination of the process.

What is the legal issue and what options, if any, are available to the school district at this point in time?

CHAPTER
11

ATTENDANCE AND INSTRUCTION

The very heart of education, attendance and instruction, is not without its judicial controversies. In general, courts have been called upon to settle disagreements regarding the power of the state to compel education and its instructional content versus the rights of parents to control and influence the upbringing of their children.

I. ATTENDANCE

A. *Compulsory Education*

States, through their respective constitutional powers to establish educational systems, have in various ways legislated compulsory attendance statutes. The general mandate is to attend public schools or, in the alternative, nonpublic schools that offer instruction at least equivalent to that of public schools. Some states carefully define and regulate what is required to be equivalent while others take a more *laissez faire* approach and leave it up to the courts to determine the meaning of equivalent instruction. Compulsory attendance is usually enforced either through the criminal courts where parents are found guilty if proven to have failed to send their children to a public school or provide equivalent instruction in a nonpublic school, or through the juvenile courts where children under the age of eighteen are adjudicated as delinquents if proven to be habitually absent.

The two United States Supreme Court decisions that follow established the legal framework and rationale for reaching the proper balance between the power of state government and rights of parents in compelling education.

Case
Pierce v. Society of the Sisters of the Holy Names of Jesus and Mary, 268 U.S. 510 (1925) (emphasis added)

These appeals are from decrees, based upon undenied allegations, which granted preliminary orders restraining appellants from threatening or attempting to enforce the Compulsory Education Act . . . under the initiative provision of her Constitution by the voters of Oregon. . . .

The challenged act, effective September 1, 1926, requires every parent, guardian, or other person having control or charge or custody of a child between 8 and 16 years to send him 'to a public school for the period of time a public school shall be held during the current year' in the district where the child resides; and failure so to do is declared a misdemeanor. . . The manifest purpose is to compel general attendance at public schools by normal children, between 8 and 16, who have not completed the eighth grade. And without doubt enforcement of the statute would seriously impair, perhaps destroy, the profitable features of appellees' business and greatly diminish the value of their property.

Appellee the Society of Sisters is an Oregon corporation, organized in 1880, with power to care for orphans, educate and instruct the youth, establish and maintain academies or schools, and acquire necessary real and personal property. . . . The Compulsory Education Act of 1922 has already caused the withdrawal from its schools of children who would otherwise continue, and their income has steadily declined. The appellants, public officers, have proclaimed their purpose strictly to enforce the statute. . . .

Appellee Hill Military Academy is a private corporation organized in 1908 under the laws of Oregon, engaged in owning, operating, and conducting for profit an elementary, college preparatory, and military training school for boys between the ages of 5 and 21 years. . . By reason of the statute and threat of enforcement appellee's business is being destroyed and its property depreciated; parents and guardians are refusing to make contracts for the future instruction of their sons, and some are being withdrawn. . . .

No question is raised concerning the power of the state reasonably to regulate all schools, to inspect, supervise and examine them, their teachers and pupils; to require that all children of proper age attend some school, that teachers shall be of good moral character and patriotic disposition, that certain studies plainly essential to good citizenship must be taught, and that nothing be taught which is manifestly inimical to the public welfare.

The inevitable practical result of enforcing the act under consideration would be destruction of appellees' primary schools, and perhaps all other private primary schools for normal children within the state of Oregon. Appellees are engaged in a kind of undertaking not inherently harmful, but long regarded as useful and meritorious. Certainly there is nothing in the present records to indicate that they have failed to discharge their obligations to patrons, students, or the state. And there are no peculiar circumstances or present emergencies that demand extraordinary measures relative to primary education.

Under the doctrine of *Meyer v. Nebraska*, . . . we think it entirely plain that the Act of 1922 unreasonably interferes with **the liberty of parents and guardians to direct the upbringing and education of children under their control**. As often heretofore pointed out, rights guaranteed by the Constitution may not be abridged by legislation that has no reasonable relation to some purpose within the competency of the state. **The fundamental theory of liberty** upon which all governments in this Union repose **excludes any general power of the state to standardize its children by forcing them to accept instruction from public teachers only**. The child is not the mere creature of the state; those who nurture him and direct his destiny have the right, coupled with the high duty, to recognize and prepare him for additional obligations. . . .

Generally, it is entirely true, as urged by counsel, that no person in any business has such an interest in possible customers as to enable him to restrain exercise of proper power of the state upon the ground that he will be deprived of patronage. But the injunctions here sought are not against the exercise of any proper power. Appellees asked protection against arbitrary, unreasonable, and unlawful interference with their patrons and the consequent destruction of their business and property. Their interest is clear and immediate. . . .

The decrees below are affirmed.

The *Pierce* court, citing its decision in *Meyer v. Nebraska*, reinforced the doctrine that parents possess the liberty "to direct the upbringing and education of children under their control." Proponents of parent rights in later cases will use this doctrine in an attempt to gain greater control of their children's education within the public schools.

Case
Wisconsin v. Yoder, 406 U.S. 205 (1972) (emphasis added)

[**Facts:**] Respondents Jonas Yoder and Wallace Miller are members of the Old Order Amish religion, and respondent Adin Yutzy is a member of the Conservative Amish Mennonite Church. They and their families are residents of Green County, Wisconsin. Wisconsin's compulsory school-attendance law required them to cause their children to attend public or private school until reaching age 16 but the respondents declined to send their children, ages 14 and 15, to public school after they completed the eighth grade. The children were not enrolled in any private school, or within any recognized exception to the compulsory-attendance law, and they are conceded to be subject to the Wisconsin statute.

On complaint of the school district administrator for the public schools, respondents were charged, tried, and convicted of violating the compulsory-attendance law in Green County Court and were fined the sum of $5 each. Respondents defended on the ground that the application of the compulsory-attendance law violated their rights under the First and Fourteenth Amendments. The trial testimony showed that respondents believed, in accordance with the tenets of Old Order Amish communities generally, that their children's attendance at high school, public or private, was contrary to the Amish religion and way of life. . . .

Amish objection to formal education beyond the eighth grade is firmly grounded in these central religious concepts. They object to the high school, and higher education generally, because the values they teach are in marked variance with Amish values and the Amish way of life; they view secondary school education as an impermissible exposure of their children to a "worldly" influence in conflict with their beliefs. . . .

The Amish do not object to elementary education through the first eight grades as a general proposition because they agree that their children must have basic skills in the "three R's" in order to read the Bible, to be good farmers and citizens, and to be able to deal with non-Amish people when necessary in the course of daily affairs. They view such a basic education as acceptable because it does not significantly expose their children to worldly values or interfere with their development in the Amish community during the crucial adolescent period. While Amish accept compulsory elementary education generally, wherever possible they have established their own elementary schools in many respects like the small local schools of the past. . . .

[**Rationale:**] **There is no doubt as to the power of a State, having a high responsibility for education of its citizens, to impose reasonable regulations for the control and duration of basic education.** See, e. g., *Pierce v. Society of Sisters.* . . . **Providing public schools ranks at the very apex of the function of a State.** Yet even this paramount responsibility was, in *Pierce,* made to yield to the **right of parents to provide an equivalent education in a privately operated system.** There the Court held that Oregon's statute compelling attendance in a public school from age eight to age 16 unreasonably interfered with the interest of parents in directing the rearing of their offspring, including their education in church-operated schools. As that case suggests, **the values of parental direction of the religious upbringing and education of their children in their early and formative years have a high place in our society**. . . Thus, **a State's interest in universal education, however highly we rank it, is not totally free from a balancing process when it impinges on fundamental rights and interests, such as those specifically protected by the Free Exercise Clause** of the First Amendment, and the traditional interest of parents with respect to the religious upbringing of their children so long as they, in the words of *Pierce*, "prepare [them] for additional obligations." . . . . **It follows that in order for Wisconsin to compel school attendance beyond the eighth grade against a claim that such attendance interferes with the practice of a legitimate religious belief, it must appear either that the State does not deny the free exercise of religious belief by its requirement, or that there is a state interest of sufficient magnitude to override the interest claiming protection under the Free Exercise Clause.** . . .

We come then to the quality of the claims of the respondents concerning the alleged encroachment of Wisconsin's compulsory school-attendance statute on their rights and the rights of their children to the free exercise of the religious beliefs they and their forebears have adhered to for almost three centuries. In evaluating those claims we must be careful to determine whether the Amish religious faith and their mode of life are, as they claim, inseparable and interdependent. **A way of life, however virtuous and admirable, may not be interposed as a barrier to reasonable state regulation of education if it is based on purely secular considerations; to have the protection of the Religion Clauses, the claims must be rooted in religious belief**. . . .

Giving no weight to such secular considerations, however, **we see that the record in this case abundantly supports the claim that the traditional way of life of the Amish is not merely a matter of personal preference, but one of deep religious conviction**, shared by an organized group, and intimately related to daily living. . . .

The impact of the compulsory-attendance law on respondents' practice of the Amish religion is not only severe, but inescapable, for the Wisconsin law affirmatively **compels them, under threat of criminal sanction, to perform acts undeniably at odds with fundamental tenets of their religious beliefs**. . . . As the record shows, compulsory school attendance to age 16 for Amish children carries with it a very real threat of undermining the Amish community and religious practice as they exist today. . . .

The State advances **two primary arguments** in support of its system of compulsory education. It notes . . . that **some degree of education is necessary to prepare citizens to participate effectively and intelligently in our open political system if we are to preserve freedom and independence**. Further, **education prepares individuals to be self-reliant and self-sufficient participants in society**. We accept these propositions.

However, the evidence adduced by the Amish in this case is persuasively to the effect that **an additional one or two years of formal high school for Amish children in place of their long-established program of informal vocational education would do little to serve those interests**. Respondents' experts testified at trial, without challenge, that the value of all education must be assessed in terms of its capacity to prepare the child for life. It is one thing to say that compulsory education for a year or two beyond the eighth grade may be necessary when its goal is the preparation of the child for life in modern society as the majority live, but it is quite another if the goal of education be viewed as the preparation of the child for life in the separated agrarian community that is the keystone of the Amish faith. . . .

The State, however, supports its interest in providing an additional one or two years of compulsory high school education to Amish children because of the possibility that some such children will choose to leave the Amish community, and that if this occurs they will be ill-equipped for life. The State argues that if Amish children leave their church they should not be in the position of making their way in the world without the education available in the one or two additional years the State requires. However, on this record, that argument is highly speculative. There is no specific evidence of the loss of Amish adherents by attrition, nor is there any showing that upon leaving the Amish community Amish children, with their practical agricultural training and habits of industry and self-reliance, would become burdens on society because of educational short-comings. . . .

Insofar as the State's claim rests on the view that a brief additional period of formal education is imperative to enable the Amish to participate effectively and intelligently in our democratic process, it must fall. **The Amish alternative to formal secondary school education has enabled them to function effectively in their day-to-day life under self-imposed limitations on relations with the world, and to survive and prosper in contemporary society as a separate, sharply identifiable and highly self-sufficient community for more than 200 years in this country**. In itself this is strong evidence that they are capable of fulfilling the social and political responsibilities of citizenship without compelled attendance beyond the eighth grade at the price of jeopardizing their free exercise of religious belief. . . .

However read, the Court's holding in *Pierce* stands as a **charter of the rights of parents to direct the religious up-bringing of their children**. And, when the interests of parenthood are combined with a free exercise claim of the nature revealed by this record, more than merely a "reasonable relation to some purpose within the competency of the State" is required to sustain the validity of the State's requirement under the First Amendment. To be sure, **the power of the parent, even when linked to a free exercise claim, may be subject to limitation under *Prince* if it appears that parental decisions will jeopardize the health or safety of the child, or have a potential for significant social burdens.** But in this case, the Amish have introduced persuasive evidence undermining the arguments the State has advanced to support its claims in terms of the welfare of the child and society as a whole. **The record strongly indicates that accommodating the religious objections of the Amish by forgoing one, or at most two, additional years of compulsory education will not impair the physical or mental health of the child, or result in an inability to be self-supporting or to discharge the duties and responsibilities of citizenship, or in any other way materially detract from the welfare of society**. . . .

[Court ruling:] For the reasons stated we hold, with the Supreme Court of Wisconsin, that the First and Fourteenth Amendments prevent the State from compelling respondents to cause their children to attend formal high school to age 16. **Our disposition of this case, however, in no way alters our recognition of the obvious fact that courts are not school boards or legislatures, and are ill-equipped to determine the "necessity" of discrete aspects of a State's program of compulsory education. This should suggest that courts must move with great circumspection in performing the sensitive and delicate task of weighing a State's legitimate social concern when faced with religious claims for exemption from generally applicable educational requirements.** It cannot be overemphasized that we are not dealing with a way of life and mode of education by a group claiming to have recently discovered some "progressive" or more enlightened process for rearing children for modern life.

Nothing we hold is intended to undermine the general applicability of the State's compulsory school-attendance statutes or to limit the power of the State to promulgate reasonable standards that, while not impairing the free exercise of religion, provide for continuing agricultural vocational education under parental and church guidance by the Old Order Amish or others similarly situated. The States have had a long history of amicable and effective relationships with church-sponsored schools, and there is no basis for assuming that, in this related context, reasonable standards cannot be established concerning the content of the continuing vocational education of Amish children under parental guidance, provided always that state regulations are not inconsistent with what we have said in this opinion.

Affirmed.

Nine years after the *Wisconsin v. Yoder* ruling, the West Virginia Supreme Court in *State v. Riddle*, 285 S.E.2d 359 (W.Va. 1981), upheld the misdemeanor conviction of two parents who home-schooled two elementary-age children based on religious reasons.

The parents cited the *Yoder* case in support and argued that their religious rights under the Free Exercise Clause of the First Amendment entitled them to ignore the state compulsory attendance law with impunity, including its requirement that instruction in the home must be "conducted by a person or persons who, in the judgment of the county superintendent and county board of education, are qualified to give instruction. . . ." The *Riddle* court noted that the parents had utilized a formal correspondence course whose curriculum contained all the subjects taught in the public schools, but stated at 364 - 366(emphasis added):

Court ruling: [I]s the State of West Virginia required to forebear in the enforcement of the compulsory attendance law upon the suggestion of any parent who wishes to keep his child home from school that there is a conflict between school attendance and freedom of religion? Emphatically, we answer the question in the negative. . . .

As the Supreme Court indicated in *Yoder*, a **delicate balancing test must be applied** when compelling state interests that run into conflict with the free exercise clause. . . .

There can be little doubt that **on occasion the state's interest will override even the most sincerely held religious convictions**. . . . In numerous instances courts have required life-saving medical treatment for children in the face of parental objections grounded in sincerely held religious convictions. . . .

Consequently, notwithstanding the strong language in *Yoder*, since that case arouse out of an entirely different factual context, **this Court holds that sincerely held religious convictions are never a defense to total noncompliance with the compulsory attendance law**. . . .

We find it inconceivable that in the twentieth century the free exercise clause of the first amendment implies that children can lawfully be sequestered on a rural homestead during all of their formative years to be released upon the world only after their opportunities to acquire basic skills have been foreclosed and their capacity to cope with modern society has been undermined as to prohibit useful, happy or productive lives.

Case
Swanson v. Guthrie Indep. Sch. Dist. I-L, 135 F.3d 694
(10th Cir. 1998) (emphasis added)

Annie Swanson and her parents as next friends (Plaintiffs) appeal the district court's grant of summary judgment to Defendants. Annie had filed suit claiming that Defendants' refusal to allow her to attend public school on a part-time basis violated her rights under the Free Exercise Clause of the United States Constitution, her parents' constitutional right to direct her education, and her rights under Oklahoma state law. We affirm the judgment of the district court.

[Facts:] Annie has been home-schooled by her parents since she started school. **The purpose behind the home-schooling is religious--Annie's parents wish to be able to teach her Christian principles that are excluded from the public-school curriculum**. When Annie reached the seventh grade, her parents decided that she would benefit by taking a few classes at the public school. Annie's parents believed the public school's ability to teach certain classes (particularly foreign- language classes, vocal music, and some science classes) was superior to their instructional capability in those areas, and that attending some classes at the public school would better prepare Annie for college.

Annie's parents spoke to the then-superintendent of schools and received permission for her to attend two seventh-grade classes for the last nine weeks of the school year. She attended those classes, performed very well in them, and caused no disruption to the school system. Annie then pre-registered for two classes for the eighth grade. Before she began school, however, Defendant Bowman was hired as the new superintendent. He refused to allow Annie to attend the eighth grade on a part-time basis, and told her parents they would need permission from the school board. He also made some statements that Mrs. Swanson interpreted as criticism of Christian home-schoolers.

In August 1994 the school board held a regularly-scheduled meeting at which the Swansons were allowed to present their position. The board deferred a decision on adopting a policy concerning part-time attendance, but did vote to require Annie to register as a full-time student if she wished to attend eighth-grade classes before such a policy could be adopted. At the September meeting of the school board the board voted to adopt the following part-time-attendance policy:

It is the policy of the Guthrie Board of Education that **all students enrolling in Guthrie Public Schools must do so on a full- time basis**. Full-time basis shall be defined as attending classes for the full instructional day within the public school system or in con- junction with another state accredited institution such as vocational- technical school or a college or university for concurrent enrollment. The only exceptions to this policy shall be for fifth-year seniors and special education students whose IEP's require variations of student schedules. . . .

Analysis: Free-Exercise Claim
The question at issue in this case is the validity of the rule or regulation enacted by the school board, as it impacts on Plaintiffs' right to the free exercise of their religion. Plaintiffs maintain that the part-time-attendance policy is a burden, albeit indirect, on the full and free exercise of their religious beliefs concerning the way in which children should be raised and educated. . . .

As a general proposition, a law (or policy) that is neutral and of general applicability need not be justified by a compelling governmental interest even if that law incidentally burdens a particular religious practice or belief. . . . On its face, the policy enacted by the school board in this case is neutral and of general application--it applies to all persons who might wish to attend public school on a part-time basis, and prohibits such part-time attendance (with certain specific exceptions, such as fifth-year seniors and special- education students). It applies to students who are home-schooled for secular reasons as well as those home-schooled for religious reasons, and it applies to students attending private schools whether or not those private schools are religious or secular in orientation. . . .

We are therefore left with the fact that the board's policy is a neutral policy of general applicability. . . . The board's policy therefore does not violate traditional free-exercise principles. . . .

Hybrid-Rights Claim

Plaintiffs point out that parents have a constitutional right to raise and educate their children, and that the **part-time-attendance policy infringes on this right as well as on the free-exercise right discussed above**. . . .

We have no quarrel with Plaintiffs' assertion that Annie's **parents have a constitutional right to direct her education, up to a point**. For example, they have a right to send her to a private school, whether that school is religious or secular. *See Pierce v. Society of Sisters.* . . .

Numerous cases, however, have made it clear that this constitutional right is limited in scope. Federal courts addressing the issue have held that **parents have no right to exempt their children from certain reading programs the parents found objectionable, or from a school's community-service requirement, or from an assembly program that included sexually explicit topics**. *Immediato v. Rye Neck School Dist.*, 73 F.3d 454 (2d Cir.) . . . (1996); *Brown v. Hot, Sexy and Safer Productions, Inc.*, 68 F.3d 525 (1 st Cir. 1995) . . . (1996); *Fleischfresser v. Directors of School Dist. 200*, 15 F.3d 680 (7 th Cir. 1994); *Mozert v. Hawkins County Bd. of Educ._*, 827 F.2d 1058 (6 th Cir. 1987) . . . .

Other courts have determined that home-schooled children may be subjected to standardized testing to assess the quality of education the children are receiving, even over the parents' objections. *Murphy v. State of Arkansas_*, 852 F.2d 1039 (8 th Cir. 1988).

In addition, states may constitutionally require that teachers at religiously-oriented private schools be certified by the state. *Fellowship Baptist Church v. Benton*, 815 F.2d 485 (8 th Cir. 1987). **The case law in this area establishes that parents simply do not have a constitutional right to control each and every aspect of their children's education and oust the state's authority over that subject.** . . .

The claimed constitutional right Plaintiffs wish to establish in this case is the right of parents to send their children to public school on a part-time basis, and to pick and choose which courses their children will take from the public school. Plaintiffs would have this right override the local school board's explicit decision to disallow such part-time attendance (except where the school would receive state funding for the part-time attendee). However, **decisions as to how to allocate scarce resources, as well as what curriculum to offer or require, are uniquely committed to the discretion of local school authorities**, as the cases cited above demonstrate. . . .

[Court ruling:] The above discussion establishes that Plaintiffs have shown no colorable claim of infringement on the constitutional right to direct a child's education. Accordingly, **we hold that this is not a hybrid- rights case**. . . . Based on the foregoing, **we hold that Defendants were not required to show a compelling state interest** in this case, despite Plaintiffs' attempt to invoke the hybrid-rights doctrine. . . .

Parental Right to Direct Education

In addition to arguing the parental-rights issue as a component of the hybrid-rights claim, **Plaintiffs maintain that the part-time attendance policy violates the right to control Annie's education, separate and apart from the claimed free-exercise violation**. For the reasons stated in the hybrid-rights discussion, however, we hold that the parental right to control a child's education does not extend as far as Plaintiffs would wish. **There is no federal parental right that would force a local school board to allow parents to dictate that their children will attend public school for only part of the school day**. . . .

[Conclusion:] Plaintiffs have attempted to portray this case as one involving religious discrimination against Christian home-schoolers. The record provided to the district court and this court, however, indicates that it involves only financial distinctions between certain part-time students and all home-schoolers, secular or religious, as well as private-school students. **Since this case involved only a neutral rule of general applicability, it was sufficient for Defendants to prove a reasonable relationship between the part-time-attendance policy and a legitimate purpose of the school board**. Plaintiffs have not argued that Defendants failed to meet this low threshold, and it is clear that Defendants have satisfied it. Therefore, the district court's decision dismissing all of Plaintiffs' claims is AFFIRMED.

Case
Eukers v. State, 728 N.E.2d 219 (Ind.App. 2000) (emphasis added)

Following a bench trial, Georgene Eukers was found guilty of violating Indiana Code section 20-8.1-3-34, regarding compulsory school attendance, a Class B misdemeanor. Eukers now appeals her conviction. We affirm.

[Issue:] Eukers raises the following restated issue for our review: **whether the delegation of authority by the legislature to local school corporations to establish attendance policies, the violation of which constitutes a criminal offense, is an unconstitutional delegation of the legislative function**.

[Facts:] The facts most favorable to the judgment reveal that Eukers is the mother and custodial parent of M.E. M.E. is a student at Darrough Chapel Elementary School in Kokomo, Indiana. The Kokomo-Center Township Consolidated School Corporation has an **attendance policy which provides that after a student receives ten (10) absences, a student must obtain a doctor's excuse for any subsequent absences**. After a student accumulates twenty unexcused absences, the school attendance officer notifies the county prosecutor, who may elect to bring formal charges against the student's parent. Eukers signed a document prior to M.E.'s enrollment in school which indicated that she understood the school's attendance policy.

Between September of 1997 and January of 1998, M.E. accumulated twenty-three absences. Consequently, the State charged Eukers with violating Indiana Code section 20-8.1-3-34. Following a bench trial, Eukers was found guilty as charged and sentenced to one hundred eighty days in the Howard County Jail, suspended, and one year of probation. This appeal ensued.

Eukers contends that the legislature, by permitting Indiana's school districts to establish their own attendance polices, has impermissibly delegated "the purely legislative function of defining the elements and acts which constitute criminal activity . . . to the individual school attendance districts." . . . Eukers argues that the school's attendance policy violates Article I, sections 16, 18, and 23 of the Indiana Constitution. . . Essentially, Eukers argues that the Powers Act is an unconstitutional delegation of authority by the General Assembly to school corporations. . . .

Unconstitutional Delegation of Authority

A. General Powers Act

The General School Powers Act (the "Powers Act") statutorily invests local school corporations with broad managerial autonomy to formulate and implement educational policies. Ind. Code §§ 20-5-1 to –6. The Powers Act provides both general and specific powers to school corporations. With regard to specific powers, the Powers Act provides in pertinent part that:

> [i]n carrying out the school purposes of each school corporation, its governing body acting on its behalf shall have the following specific powers: . . . To prepare, make, enforce amend and/or repeal rules, regulations and procedures for the government and management of the schools. . . .

Ind. Code § 20-5-2-2(17).

One of the most elementary regulations of a school is an attendance policy. We believe that the broad language of the Powers Act authorizes public school officials to promulgate and enforce school attendance policies. . . .

After adopting the attendance policy, the school board placed it in a handbook that was mailed to the parents of all students who attended school in the Kokomo-Center Township Consolidated School District. The **attendance policy contained in the handbook provides in pertinent part** that:

[t]he first ten (10) absences must be covered by either phone calls, notes and/ or doctor's statements to be considered excused. . . . Any additional absences following ten (10) absences, which may have previously been covered by a phone call, note, and/or doctor's statement, will be unexcused unless covered by a doctor's statement. Continued unexcused absences may result in a formal referral for educational neglect. A student/parent conference will be required when absences become frequent or excessive.

We have stated that the "legislature cannot effectively confer upon school authorities power to conduct schools and make all rules necessary for the

orderly process of education, yet deny them the power to effectively enforce such rules." *Salem Community Sch. Corp. v. Easterly,* . . . 275 N.E.2d 317, 322 (1971). **Therefore, the Powers Act also provides schools with the authority to enforce their attendance policies, such as requiring a child with unexcused absences to attend Saturday school or after-school detention.** Although school officials may take disciplinary action against a child for unexcused absences, **school officials have no recourse against the parent.**

B. Compulsory Attendance Act

However, the General Assembly has provided the State with a means of punishing a parent for failing to require their child to attend school by enacting the Compulsory Attendance Act . . . Indiana Code section 20-8.1-3-1 provides that "[t]he **legislative intent [of the Attendance Act] is to provide an efficient and speedy means of insuring that children receive a proper education whenever it is reasonably possible.**" Furthermore, **we have held that the fundamental legislative purpose of the Attendance Act was to prevent parents from denying their children certain minimal education.** *Salem Community Sch. Corp.*, 275 N.E.2d at 322 (citing *State v. Bailey*, 157 Ind. 324, 61 N.E. 730 (1901)).

The Attendance Act provides in pertinent part that:

> **[i]t is unlawful for a parent to fail, neglect, or refuse to send his child to a public school for the full term as required under this chapter unless the child is provided with instruction equivalent to that given in the public schools.** This section does not apply during any period when the child is excused from attendance under this chapter. Ind. Code § 20-8.1-3-34. "A person who knowingly violates this chapter commits a Class B misdemeanor." Ind. Code § 20-8.1-3-37.

Thus, a parent who fails to ensure that his or her child attends school is subject to a possible criminal penalty in Indiana.

C. Prosecutorial Discretion

Under the current statutory scheme in Indiana, a prosecutor who is aware of a parent who has allowed his or her child to accrue a single unexcused absence may criminally prosecute a parent. See Ind. Code § 20-8.1-3-34 to-37. In addition, a prosecutor may decline to press charges against a parent whose child has violated a school's attendance policy. **The statutorily triggering event for possible criminal prosecution is one unexcused absence, not the violation of a particular school's attendance policy.** Thus, a violation of a school's attendance policy does not *per se* subject a parent to criminal liability.

Moreover, the discretion whether or not to prosecute a parent for violating Indiana Code section 20-8.1-3-34 lies solely with the prosecutor, even though an attendance officer of a school may have provided the information that a child has an unexcused absence. It is well-settled that the decision whether to prosecute lies within the prosecutor's sole discretion. . . . Thus, **a school's attendance policy does not unconstitutionally impinge on the legislature's exclusive power to establish and define criminal offenses**.

Conclusion: Based on the foregoing, we hold that the delegation of authority to school districts to establish attendance policies is not unconstitutional because the prosecutor is vested with sole discretion by the legislature in deciding whether to prosecute a parent under 20-8.1-3-34, and this discretion operates independently of a school's attendance policy.

Affirmed.

B. Truancy

While state compulsory education statutes prohibit "truancy," they often leave it to the court's to define the term. In the case of *InInterest of A.D.F.*, 335 S.E.2d 144 (Ga.App. 1985), the court noted at 146:

Definition of truancy:

The law does not define truant but the dictionary does. To be "truant" is to be "one who stays away from business or any duty; especially, one who stays out of school without leave." Websters New Intl. Dictionary, 2d Edition.

The court in *Simmons v. State*, 371 N.E.2d 1316, 175 Ind.App. 333, 341 stated (emphasis added):

No Indiana case defines "habitual truant" as such. The term has been defined by foreign jurisdictions to mean that conduct "which amounts to a refusal to attend school in defiance of parental authority." *In re Alley* (1921), 174 Wisc. 85, 182 N.W. 360. "Habitual truancy" has also been defined as:

The willful unexcused refusal of a pupil to attend school in defiance of parental authority and in violation of an applicable compulsory school attendance law. *Chicago Board of Education v. Couba* (1976), 41 Ill. App. 3d 858, 354 N.E.2d 630.

The common thread in cases defining "habitual truancy" is the "willful refusal to attend school in defiance of parental authority". *Ex parte Drye* (1930), 250 Mich. 210, 229 N.W. 623; *State v. Freudenberg* (1917), 166 Wisc. 35, 163 N.W. 184.

The unrefuted evidence is that Vickie missed, during the period from November 3, 1975, to February 25, 1976, twenty-eight (28) of sixty-two (62) school days for which absences no excuse was offered. To no avail she was repeatedly told by her parents not to miss school. Thus, there was sufficient evidence to allow the Juvenile Referee to reasonably, by a fair preponderance of the evidence, find Vickie habitually truant, and thus a delinquent child.

It appears that due to judicial definition, a child has to be in defiance of "parental authority" to be truant. Therefore, if parents authorize a child to "skip school," or to go on vacation with them during the school year, the child may not be "truant" for purposes of juvenile delinquency proceedings, but the parent could be charged, depending on the prosecutor's discretion, for a refusing to comply with the compulsory attendance law.

II. INSTRUCTION

The Supreme Court in the following case addressed the respective rights of the state in deciding instructional issues and the rights of parents to control the education of their children.

Case
Meyer v. State of Nebraska, 262 U.S. 390 (1923) (emphasis added)

[Facts:] Plaintiff in error was tried and convicted in the district court for Hamilton county, Nebraska, under an information which charged that on May 25, 1920, while an instructor in Zion Parochial School, he unlawfully taught the subject of reading in the German language to Raymond Parpart, a child of 10 years, who had not attained and successfully passed the eighth grade. The information is based upon 'An act relating to the teaching of foreign languages in the state of Nebraska,' approved April 9, 1919 (Laws 1919, c. 249), which follows:

'Section 1. No person, individually or as a teacher, shall, in any private, denominational, parochial or public school, teach any subject to any person in any language than the English language.

'Sec. 2. Languages, other than the English language, may be taught as languages only after a pupil shall have attained and successfully passed the eighth grade as evidenced by a certificate of graduation issued by the county superintendent of the county in which the child resides. . . .

[Issue:] The problem for our determination is whether the statute as construed and applied unreasonably infringes the liberty guaranteed to the plaintiff in error by the Fourteenth Amendment:

'No state ... shall deprive any person of life, liberty or property without
due process of law.'

While this court has not attempted to define with exactness the liberty thus guaranteed, the term liberty has received much consideration and some of the included things have been definitely stated. Without doubt, **it denotes not merely freedom from bodily restraint but also the right of the individual to contract, to engage in any of the common occupations of life, to acquire useful knowledge, to marry, establish a home and bring up children, to worship God according to the dictates of his own conscience, and generally to enjoy those privileges long recognized at common law as essential to the orderly pursuit of happiness by** free men. . . . **The established doctrine is that this liberty may not be interfered with, under the guise of protecting the public interest, by legislative action which is arbitrary or without reasonable relation to some purpose within the competency of the state to effect**. Determination by the Legislature of what constitutes proper exercise of police power is not final or conclusive but is subject to supervision by the courts. . . .

The American people have always regarded education and acquisition of knowledge as matters of supreme importance which should be diligently promoted. The Ordinance of 1787 declares:

> 'Religion, morality and knowledge being necessary to good government and the happiness of mankind, schools and the means of education shall forever be encouraged.'

Corresponding to the right of control, it is the natural duty of the parent to give his children education suitable to their station in life; and nearly all the states, including Nebraska, enforce this obligation by compulsory laws.

Practically, education of the young is only possible in schools conducted by especially qualified persons who devote themselves thereto. The calling always has been regarded as useful and honorable, essential, indeed, to the public welfare. **Mere knowledge of the German language cannot reasonably be regarded as harmful. Heretofore it has been commonly looked upon as helpful and desirable**. Plaintiff in error taught this language in school as part of his occupation. **His right thus to teach and the right of parents to engage him so to instruct their children, we think, are within the liberty of the amendment.**

. . . Evidently the Legislature has attempted materially to interfere with the calling of modern language teachers, with the opportunities of pupils to acquire knowledge, and with **the power of parents to control the education of their own**. . . .

That the state may do much, go very far, indeed, in order to improve the quality of its citizens, physically, mentally and morally, is clear; but the individual has certain fundamental rights which must be respected. . . .

The power of the state to compel attendance at some school and to make reasonable regulations for all schools, including a requirement that they shall give instructions in English, is not questioned. Nor has challenge been made of the state's power to prescribe a curriculum for institutions which it supports. Those matters are not within the present controversy. . . . **No emergency has arisen which renders knowledge by a child of some language other than English so clearly harmful as to justify its inhibition** with the consequent infringement of rights long freely enjoyed. **We are constrained to conclude that the statute as applied is arbitrary and without reasonable relation to any end within the competency of the state.**

As the statute undertakes to interfere only with teaching which involves a modern language, leaving complete freedom as to other matters, there seems no adequate foundation for the suggestion that the purpose was to protect the child's health by limiting his mental activities. It is well known that proficiency in a foreign language seldom comes to one not instructed at an early age, and experience shows that this is not injurious to the health, morals or understanding of the ordinary child.

[Court ruling:] The judgment of the court below must be reversed and the cause remanded for further proceedings not inconsistent with this opinion.

REVERSED.

Although the *Meyer* case focused on the liberty interest rights of the teacher that were violated by the Nebraska statute, it acknowledged the right of parents to "engage" the teacher and to "control the education of their own."

Case
Leebaert v. Harrington, 332 F.3d 134 (2ⁿᵈ Cir. 2003) (emphasis added)

Plaintiff-Appellant Turk Leebaert . . . **argues that his constitutional right to direct the upbringing and education of his child requires the defendants, upon his request, to excuse his minor son, Corky Leebaert, from attending health education classes** at a public school administered by the defendants. Leebaert further **argues that the right to excuse his son is, as a matter of constitutional law, "fundamental."** His son may therefore be required to attend classes teaching the health curriculum only if the requirement to do so withstands constitutional "strict scrutiny" which, Leebaert contends, it does not. . . .

[Facts:] The seventh-grade health-education curriculum . . . includes instruction on health and safety, alcohol, tobacco and drugs, and family life. The defendants . . . maintain that only six of the forty-five days on which the seventh-grade health education classes are taught . . . are related to family-life instruction or AIDS education, and that, pursuant [to the applicable statute], the school permits parents . . . to excuse their children from those six classes by notifying the principal of their request. The remainder of the health education program at the school is mandatory and defendants insist that it is not unconstitutional for the school to require Leebaert's son to attend. . . .

Leebaert identified . . . aspects of the school's health curriculum as contradicting his sincerely held [religious] beliefs [including]:

> Defining self esteem; Grieving and feelings about death. . .; The definition of love. . .; Myths and facts about tobacco, marijuana and alcohol; . . . Discussions of behaviors which demonstrate respect for self and others; Discussing responses to being sexually harassed. . . .

[Issue:] The question before us, then, is whether Leebaert's asserted right – the right to excuse his son from mandatory public school classes – is fundamental. Leebaert argues that it is, asserting that it stems from a pair of cases decided in the first quarter of the twentieth century. . . .

In defining the scope of the parental right to direct the upbringing and education of children, the First and Tenth Circuits have held that it does not include a right to exempt one's child from public school requirements.

In *Brown v. Hot, Sexy and Safer Productions, Inc.*, 68 F.3d 525 (1st Cir. 1995), the First Circuit **held that a parental challenge to a public school's AIDS awareness and sex education program was not rooted in a constitutionally protected right**. . . The court distinguished the right established in *Meyer* and *Pierce* from the right asserted by the plaintiffs, which the court understood as the right to dictate public school curricula:

The *Meyer* and *Pierce* cases, we think, evince the principle that the state cannot prevent parents from choosing a specific educational program – whether it be religious instruction at a private school or instruction in a foreign language. . . . **We do not think, however, that this freedom encompasses a fundamental constitutional right to dictate the curriculum at the public school . . . . If all parents had a fundamental constitutional right to dictate individually what the schools teach their children, the schools would be forced to cater a curriculum for each student whose parents had genuine moral disagreements with the school's choice of subject matter.** We cannot see that the Constitution imposes such a burden on state educational systems. . . .

Similarly, in *Swanson v. Guthrie Independent School District No. I-L*, . . . the Tenth Circuit **held that a public school's policy against part-time attendance did not implicate parents' constitutional right to direct their children's education.** . . .

. . . *Meyer, Pierce*, **and their progeny do not begin to suggest the existence of a fundamental right of every parent to tell a public school what his or her child will and will not be taught**. As the *Brown* and *Swanson* courts correctly perceived, recognition of such a fundamental right . . . **would make it difficult or impossible for any public school authority to administer school curricula responsive to the overall educational needs of the community and its children**. . . .

[Court ruling:] We . . . conclude here that the **defendants mandatory health curriculum must withstand no more that rational basis review to pass constitutional muster, which concededly it does**. . . .

We affirm the judgment of the district court.

A. School Board "Censorship"

Case

Board of Education, Island Trees Union Free School District No. 26 v. Pico, 457 U.S. 2799 (1982) (emphasis added)

[Issue:] The **principal question presented is whether the First Amendment imposes limitations upon the exercise by a local school board of its discretion to remove library books from high school and junior high school libraries**. . . .

In September 1975, petitioners Ahrens, Martin, and Hughes [school board members] attended a conference sponsored by . . . a politically conservative organization of parents concerned about education legislation in the State of New York. At the conference these petitioners **obtained lists of books described by Ahrens as "objectionable,"** . . . and by Martin as **"improper fare for school students,"** . . . . In February 1976, at a meeting with the Superintendent of Schools and the Principals of the High School and Junior High School, the Board gave an **"unofficial direction" that the listed books be removed from the library shelves and delivered to the Board's offices, so that Board members could read them**. When this directive was carried out, it became publicized, and the Board issued a press release justifying its action. It characterized the removed books as "anti-American, anti-Christian, anti-Sem[i]tic, and just plain filthy," and concluded that "[i]t is our duty, our moral obligation, to protect the children in our schools from this moral danger as surely as from physical and medical dangers." . . .

A short time later, the Board **appointed a "Book Review Committee,"** . . . . The **Board substantially rejected the Committee's report** later that month, **deciding that only one book should be returned to the High School library without restriction**, that **another should be made available subject to parental approval**, but that **the remaining nine books should "be removed from elementary and secondary libraries and [from] use in the curriculum."** . . . The Board gave no reasons for rejecting the recommendations of the Committee that it had appointed. . . .

The Court has long recognized that local school boards have broad discretion in the management of school affairs. . . . **We are therefore in full agreement with petitioners that local school boards must be permitted "to establish and apply their curriculum in such a way as to transmit community values," and that "there is a legitimate and substantial community interest in promoting respect for authority and traditional values be they social, moral, or political."** . . .

At the same time, however, we have necessarily recognized that the discretion of the States and local school boards in matters of education **must be exercised in a manner that comports with the transcendent imperatives of the First Amendment**. In *West Virginia Board of Education v. Barnette,* . . . (1943), we held that under the First Amendment a student in a public school could not be compelled to salute the flag. . . .

Of course, **courts should not "intervene in the resolution of conflicts which arise in the daily operation of school systems" unless "basic constitutional values" are "directly and sharply implicate[d]" in those conflicts.** . . But we think that the First Amendment rights of students may be directly and sharply implicated by the removal of books from the shelves of a school library.** . . .

In sum, just as **access to ideas** makes it possible for citizens generally to exercise their rights of free speech and press in a meaningful manner, **such access prepares students for active and effective participation in the pluralistic, often contentious society** in which they will soon be adult members. Of course all First Amendment rights accorded to students must be construed "in light of the special characteristics of the school environment." *Tinker v. Des Moines School Dist.* . . . **But the special characteristics of the school library make that environment especially appropriate for the recognition of the First Amendment rights of students**. A school library, no less than any other public library, is "a place dedicated to quiet, to knowledge, and to beauty." . . . The school library is the principal locus of such freedom. . . .

Petitioners emphasize the inculcative function of secondary education, and argue that they must be allowed unfettered discretion to "transmit community values" through the Island Trees schools. But that sweeping claim overlooks the **unique role of the school library**. It appears from the record that use of the **Island Trees school libraries is completely voluntary on the part of students**. Their selection of books from these libraries is **entirely a matter of free choice**; the libraries afford them an opportunity at self-education and individual enrichment that is wholly optional. **Petitioners might well defend their claim of absolute discretion in matters of curriculum by reliance upon their duty to inculcate community values. But we think that petitioners' reliance upon that duty is misplaced where, as here, they attempt to extend their claim of absolute discretion beyond the compulsory environment of the classroom, into the school library and the regime of voluntary inquiry that there holds sway.**

[Court ruling:] **In rejecting petitioners' claim of absolute discretion to remove books from their school libraries, we do not deny that local school boards have a substantial legitimate role to play in the determination of school library content.** We thus must turn to the **question of the extent to which the First Amendment places limitations upon the discretion of petitioners to remove books from their libraries**. . . .

. . . Petitioners rightly possess **significant discretion to determine the content** of their school libraries. But that discretion **may not be exercised in a narrowly partisan or political manner**. If a Democratic school board, motivated by party affiliation, ordered the removal of all books written by or in favor of Republicans, few would doubt that the order violated the constitutional rights of the students denied access to those books. The same conclusion would surely apply if an all-white school board, motivated by racial animus, decided to remove all books authored by blacks or advocating racial equality and integration. **Our Constitution does not permit the official suppression of ideas**. Thus whether petitioners' removal of books from their school libraries denied respondents their First Amendment rights **depends upon the motivation behind petitioners' actions**. If petitioners intended by their removal decision to deny respondents access to ideas with which petitioners disagreed, and if this intent was the decisive factor in petitioners' decision, then petitioners have exercised their discretion in violation of the Constitution. .

. . . On the other hand, respondents implicitly concede that an unconstitutional motivation would not be demonstrated if it were shown that petitioners had decided to remove the books at issue because those books were pervasively vulgar. . . . And again, respondents concede that if it were demonstrated that the removal decision was based solely upon the "educational suitability" of the books in question, then their removal would be "perfectly permissible." . . . **In other words, in respondents' view such motivations, if decisive of petitioners' actions, would not carry the danger of an official suppression of ideas, and thus would not violate respondents' First Amendment rights**.

As noted earlier, nothing in our decision today affects in any way the discretion of a local school board to **choose** books to add to the libraries of their schools. Because we are concerned in this case with the suppression of ideas, our holding today affects only the discretion to **remove** books. In brief, **we hold that local school boards may not remove books from school library shelves simply because they dislike the ideas contained in those books and seek by their removal to "prescribe what shall be orthodox in politics, nationalism, religion, or other matters of opinion."** *West Virginia Board of Education v. Barnette*, . . . Such purposes stand inescapably condemned by our precedents. . . .

The Supreme Court's *Pico* ruling was a plurality decision, which means that a majority of the court failed to agree on the same rationale, even though five justices did agree to uphold the circuit court's ruling to remand the case to the district court for a trial on the issue of the motivation of the school board members for removing the books from the library. Three justices (Brennan, Marshall and Stevens) agreed with the rationale expressed above, and two other justices (Blackmun and White), based on individually separate reasoning, concurred with the three that the case should be returned to the trial court.

The Eleventh Circuit in *Virgil v. School Board of Columbia County*, 862 F.2d 1517 (11th Cir. 1989), upheld the school board's removal, due to objections based on vulgarity and sexual content, of a previously adopted textbook containing the works of Chaucer and Aristophanes, because it was "reasonably related to legitimate pedagogical concerns" under the legal standard adopted by the Supreme Court in *Hazledwood School District v. Kuhlmeier*, 484 U.S. 260 (1988). *Hazlewood* upheld the principal's removal of student-drafted articles from the school-sponsored newspaper that was published as part of the school's journalism curriculum, finding that the decision was rationally based on legitimate educational concerns.

In *Virgil*, the Eleventh Circuit applied *Hazlewood* because it determined that the removal of the textbook was based on a curricular decision of the school board and that the board's motivation was "related to the explicit sexuality and excessive vulgar language," a legitimate educational concern. Lastly, the court found that the action was reasonable because (1) a "substantial number" of the students who used the book were under the age of majority, (2) the book remained available in the school library, and (3) teachers were not prohibited from assigning, nor students from reading, the works contained in the book or discussing the themes of such in class or on school property.

B. Parent Suits to Remove Books

When parental attempts to get school boards to remove perceived objectionable books from the school curriculum have failed, they have tried to use courts to accomplish the same end, but have been largely unsuccessful.

One legal theory employed is that the material in the text violates their First Amendment right of free exercise of religion. For example, in *Mozert v. Hawkins County Board of Education*, 827 F.2d 1058 (6th Cir. 1987), the plaintiffs, who belonged to various churches and denominations, consisted of seven families comprised of fourteen parents and seventeen children and described themselves as "born again Christians," attacked the school's use of the Holt, Rinehart and Winston *Basic Reading* series that was used in grades one through eight because the stories therein conflicted with their religious beliefs and convictions by teaching such things as mental telepathy, evolution, secular humanism, futuristic super nationalism, pacifism, magic, religious tolerance, and a false view of death.

The *Mozert* court phrased the **legal question to be decided as "whether a governmental requirement that a person be exposed to ideas he or she finds objectionable on religious grounds constitutes a burden on the free exercise of that person's religion."**

The court found that the plaintiffs failed to allege or prove that any of the students involved were "ever required to affirm his or her belief or disbelief in any idea or practice mentioned" in the stories contained in the Holt reading series. Neither was there any evidence that the students were required to believe, as fact, in the material, nor was there evidence that the students, other than being required to read and discuss the material, were disciplined for disputing the information contained in the readings. Lastly, there was no proof that the required reading and discussion of the material was forbidden by their religion. As a result, the court ruled that "the plaintiffs failed to establish the existence of an unconstitutional burden" on their free exercise of religion, and reversed the ruling of the district court.

The second theory utilized by parents to attack material in textbooks used by public schools is that such use constituted an illegal establishment of religion under the First Amendment. This theory proved as unavailing as the one alleging a violation of free exercise or religion rights. For example, in 1994 both the Seventh and Ninth Circuits defeated attempts to prove that the use of Holt, Rinehart and Winston's *Impression* reading series constituted an establishment of the "religions" of Satanism, Wicca, and witchcraft.

In *Fleischfresser v. Directors of School District 200*, 15 F.3d 680 (7th Cir. 1994), the court referred to the plaintiffs' allegation of the presence of some "amorphous religion" in the reading series as speculative and stated that such "amorphous character makes it difficult for us to reconcile the parents' claim with the purpose of the Establishment Clause." However, the court still applied the three-part test enunciated in the Supreme Court's *Lemon v. Kurtzman* case and determined that the reading series had a secular purpose (noting that schools "traditionally rely on fantasy and 'make-believe to hold a student's attention and to develop reading skills, . . . creativity and imagination"), did not have a primary effect of advancing religion (at most, any connection to religion were "secondary, if not trivial,"), and the school board, having reserved the right to review the series before making the purchase, did not amount to excessive entanglement between government and religion.

The Ninth Circuit in *Brown v. Woodland Joint Unified School District*, 27 F.3d 1373 (9th Cir. 1994), did not decide that Wicca was a religion, but in applying the *Lemon* test, modified with the endorsement test, assumed, for purposes of the argument, that Wicca was a religion. The *Brown* court determined that the *Impression* series had a secular purpose (both parties stipulated such), did not have the primary effect of endorsing religion in the mind of a reasonable, objective student observer, and did not create in excessive entanglement with religion by having created a committee to review parental complaints.

Lastly, the attempt to persuade the judiciary that some public school curricula violated the Establishment Clause by creating the religion of secular humanism also failed at the circuit court level in *Smith v. Board of School Commissioners of Mobile County*, 827 F.2d 684 (11th Cir. 1987), which reversed the district court's opinion that certain social studies and home economics textbooks improperly established secular humanism as a religion. The Eleventh Circuit assumed, without deciding, that secular humanism was a religion and considered only the primary effect prong of the *Lemon* test in that both parties had agreed that the secular purpose and excessive entanglement prongs had not been violated. It determined that the books' contents were "essentially neutral" toward religion, and hence the Establishment Clause was not violated.

SCENARIOS
STATE AND APPLY THE RELEVANT LEGAL RULE(S) TO THE FACTS.

1. Parent, a very wealthy and influential person, liked to work behind the scenes and keep himself out of the limelight. Due to his "recruitment" of three school board candidates and generous donations to their campaigns, he was successful in getting them elected to a five-person school board. The first item on Parent's "wish list" for school reform was cleansing the school's libraries and textbooks of the notion that man had descended from apes and that natural evolution as posited by Darwin was the source of human creation. Due to his influence, the three board members that he helped elect were able to pass policy (on a split vote of three to two) that required (1) the removal of books, articles, and even parts of books and periodicals from the library containing reference to the above-indicated material, and (2) the pasting over of any reference to evolution in every textbook and ancillary material used by teachers.

Suit was filed by a group of parents on behalf of their children to enjoin implementation of the policy.

2. Parent, an attorney, sued School District on behalf of child in an effort to nullify her middle school child's receipt of an "F" grade for a six-weeks grading period for refusing, with her consent, to attend health class and participate in the state-mandated AIDS portion of the curriculum. Parent had unsuccessfully attempted, based on philosophical grounds against sex education in the schools and the court-recognized right of parents to direct the education of their children, to get School District to substitute a parent-approved curriculum for the AIDS instruction.

3. Parent threatened suit School District for its refusal to remove certain books from the library and for declining Parent's demand to forbid the use of the board-adopted reading series in the elementary school which Parent contended promoted non-traditional thinking and values such as witchcraft, paganism, mythology, and magic. What is the legal issue and how would a court likely consider and apply the relevant legal standard?

CHAPTER 12

FIRST AMENDMENT RELIGION CLAUSES: PERSONAL FREE EXERCISE OF RELIGION AND GOVERNMENT NEUTRALITY TOWARD RELIGION

The First Amendment to the United States Constitution (as applied to the states and their public schools by the Fourteenth Amendment) prohibits government from the "establishment of religion" and from denying persons the "free exercise of religion." In essence, in order to preserve the fundamental right of individuals to freely practice their religious faith, the government is required to maintain neutrality by not establishing religion. The courts have the task of interpreting the meaning of these clauses, which they have done by creating legal standards and applying them to the countless religiously-related fact situations that continue to occur in public schools.

The Supreme Court, in the case of *Abington v. Schemp*, 374 U.S. 203, 226 (1963), expressed the underlying purpose for the religion clauses as follows:

> The very purpose of a Bill of Rights was to withdraw certain subjects from the vicissitudes of political controversy, to place them beyond the reach of majorities and officials, and to establish them as legal principles to be applied by the courts. One's right to . . . freedom of worship . . . and other fundamental rights may not be submitted to vote; they depend on the outcome of no elections.

> . . . The place of religion in our society is an inviolable citadel of the individual heart and mind. We have come to recognize through bitter experience that it is not within the power of government to invade that citadel, whether its purpose or effect be to aid or oppose, to advance or retard. In the relationship between man and religion, the State is firmly committed to a position of neutrality. Though the application of that rule requires interpretation of a delicate sort, the rule itself is clearly and concisely stated in the words of the First Amendment. . . .

In the first school prayer case, *Engle v. Vitale*, 370 U.S. 421, 427 (1962), the Supreme Court traced government establishment of religion back to England and the early American colonies, including Virginia, and gave the following account:

> But the successful Revolution against English political domination was shortly followed by intense opposition to the practice of establishing religion by law. This opposition crystallized rapidly into an effective political force in Virginia, where the minority religious groups such as Presbyterians, Lutherans, Quakers and Baptists had gained such strength that the adherents to the established Episcopal Church were actually a minority themselves. In 1785-1786, those opposed to the established Church, led by James Madison and Thomas Jefferson, who, though themselves not members of any of these dissenting religious groups, opposed all religious establishments by law on grounds of principle, obtained the enactment of the famous "Virginia Bill for Religious Liberty" by which all religious groups were placed on an equal footing so far as the State was concerned.

I. MEANING OF "ESTABLISHMENT OF RELIGION"

The Supreme Court in *Everson v. Board of Education*, 330 U.S. 1, 16, stated:

The "establishment of religion" clause of the First Amendment means at least this: neither a state nor the Federal Government can set up a church. Neither can pass laws that aid one religion, aid all religions, or prefer one religion over another. Neither can force nor influence a person to go to or to remain away from church against his will or force him to profess a belief or disbelief in any religion. No person can be punished for entertaining or professing religious beliefs or disbeliefs, for church attendance or non-attendance. No tax in any amount, large or small, can be levied to support any religious activities or institutions, whatever they may be called, or whatever form they may adopt to teach or practice religion. Neither a state nor the Federal Government can, openly or secretly, participate in the affairs of any religious organizations or groups, and vice versa. In the words of Jefferson, the clause against establishment of religion by law was intended to erect "a wall of separation between church and State." . . . .

A. School Board Action or Acquiescence

If a public school board either acts to bring religion to its domain (or silently acquiesces to a religious custom or practice occurring within the area of its control), it can find itself reading a lawyer's letter stating, "You are violating the Establishment Clause. If immediate steps are not taken to cease your practice, my client will be forced to file suit, and you will pay my fees when my client prevails."

B. Employee Action

If a principal, teacher, instructional aide or other school employee acts on his or her own initiative, independent of school board policy or administrative regulation, to bring religion to a public school-sponsored activity, the school district, as a legal, corporate entity, can be dismissed from a suit by showing that it had not created or acquiesced to the particular religious action initiated by its employee. However, because the employee is deemed by the courts to be a "state actor," the employee is subject to suit under Section 1983 of the 1871 Civil Rights Act. Unless the board had a clear policy that prohibited the religious act, the employee would be deemed to have acted within the scope of employment and the board will find itself paying the legal defense and holding the employee harmless for any costs, damages, and attorney's fees. (In practice, the school will pay a substantial deductible amount with the liability insurance carrier paying the bulk of the costs; the carrier may raise rates and, perhaps, refuse liability coverage in the future.)

C. The Establishment Clause Legal Standards

In 1971, the U.S. Supreme Court fashioned a three-part standard to apply to situations where states or their schools were alleged to have established religion. *Lemon v. Kurtzman*, 403 U.S. 602 (1971). The Court placed the burden on the government to prove all three of the following tests:

1. it had a secular purpose for its action;

2. the action's primary effect did not advance or inhibit religion; and

3. no excessive entanglement occurred between government and religion in the administration of the action.

Beginning in the mid-1980's, less than a majority of Supreme Court justices, led by Justice Sandra Day O'Connor, have argued that the so-called *Lemon* standard should be modified or replaced by an endorsement test where the government would have to prove that a **reasonable observer would believe that the purpose or effect of the government's action neither endorsed nor disapproved of religion**.

In the graduation-prayer case, *Lee v. Weisman*, 505 U.S. 577 (1992), the Supreme Court applied a governmental coercion standard wherein the public school would bear the burden of proving that **the school's action did not coerce or require a student to participate in a religious activity.**

D. *Judicial Application of the Standards*

A number of federal circuit courts in school Establishment Clause cases have applied all three legal standards. For example, the Fifth Circuit did so in the "Clergy in the Schools" case of *Doe v. Beaumont Ind. Sch. Dist.*, F.3d (5th Cir. 2001), and as a result, reversed a finding of summary judgment because there were issues of fact yet to be determined, and remanded the case to the trial court for further proceedings.

Case
Doe v. Beaumont Ind. Sch. Dist., 240 F.3d 462 (5th Cir. 2001)
(emphasis added)

[Facts:] . . . In 1996, the Beaumont Independent School District instituted a volunteer program in its elementary and middle schools called "Clergy in the Schools." The District solicited volunteers from area clergy of all local faiths, the majority of which are Protestant Christian. Participants conducted group counseling on secular issues including race, divorce, peer pressure, discipline, and drugs. The program's stated goals were to provide (1) meaningful dialogue between the clergy and students regarding civic values and morality; (2) a safe school atmosphere; and (3) volunteer opportunities.

. . . the District took several steps to avoid constitutional concerns regarding the content of the counseling sessions. It schooled the clergy regarding legal strictures, instructing them not to wear clerical garb, identify their religious affiliations, engage in religious discussions, or quote the Bible. Requests for prayer were to be deflected to outside of the school. The District also prohibited discussions regarding sex or abortion. School officials attended the meetings along with the clergy and students.

Participation by students in the program was voluntary, although no parental consent was required. Students who wished to participate could do so, but participation was also solicited on a random basis. . . .

The record reflects a number of volunteer opportunities for adults, which are administered through its "School Volunteer Program." Those programs include a sorority that conducts fairs and a child safety program; several corporate volunteer programs; senior citizen volunteering, some of which includes mentoring; and

DARE, an anti-drug program involving police officers. There are also volunteer programs involving mentoring funded by sources outside the Beaumont public schools. . . .

Before the District initiated the program, one of the parent plaintiffs read about the program in the newspaper. She requested that the District integrate professionals from secular counseling professions into the program. After the District refused her request, she and the other Doe plaintiffs brought suit to enjoin the program from going forward. They alleged that it violated the Establishment Clause of the First Amendment as well as the Texas Constitution. . . .

[Issue:] The **ultimate question in this Establishment Clause case is equality of treatment: whether the school board preferred religion over non-religion**. It follows, at trial, that the district court must not confine its analysis to only "Clergy in the Schools." **Rather, the court can and should examine the targeted program in its full context, viewing it as it actually operates in its setting, including other programs similar in purpose and function. If the set of programs together comprise a mosaic that is neutral with regards to religion, then the Establishment Clause is not offended.** The program's mission and means pose questions of fact, subsidiary to the ultimate question of whether the school district has impermissibly preferred religion over non-religion, which preclude the grant of summary judgment. . . .

[Legal Standard--Three Lines of Analysis:] In evaluating the merits of the Doe plaintiffs' Establishment Clause claim, we consider their allegations in light of three lines of analysis developed by the Supreme Court. **First, the three-part inquiry of *Lemon v. Kurtzman* asks (1) whether the purpose of the practice is not secular**; (2) whether the **program's primary effect advances or inhibits religion**; and (3) whether the **program fosters an excessive government entanglement with religion.** The **second test, the "coercion" test, measures whether the government has directed a formal religious exercise in such a way as to oblige the participation of objectors.** The **final test, the "endorsement" test, prohibits the government from conveying or attempting to convey a message that religion is preferred over non-religion.** We will apply the latter two tests to the program's effects, rather than its purpose or structure, thus focusing on the plaintiffs' strongest contention that the program is non-neutral. . . .

[Application of the Legal Standard Secular Purpose:]

Under *Lemon*, we first analyze whether the Clergy in the Schools program had a secular purpose. Courts normally defer to a government's statement of secular purpose. That purpose, however, must be sincere and not a sham.

The District's **stated purposes of the program - to provide dialogue between the clergy and students regarding civic values and morality, a safe school atmosphere, and volunteer opportunities - are secular goals.** It is permissible for a school to promote discussions on morality, safety, and volunteering from the community. That these goals may overlap with some religious views is of no moment. . .

We are not persuaded that these indicia [presented by the plaintiffs] are sufficient to demonstrate as a matter of law that the purpose of the Program was not secular. Superintendent Thomas's requests regarding tutoring and prayer at church, as well as the volunteers' prayers before meetings, were not part of the program and the summary judgment record indicates no hidden purpose in conducting it. The record does demonstrate that following the two violations of the program's stated goal - the PTA president's distribution of the information sheet and the Bible quotation used by one of the volunteers - the District sent out literature to the volunteers clarifying the secular purposes of the program. . .

. . . **We cannot find here as a matter of law that the stated purposes of the program were not permissible or pretextual**. Thus, we cannot find as a matter of law that the program ran afoul of the purpose prong of Lemon. We leave this issue for trial. The parties may adduce such evidence as they can bearing on the question of whether the stated purposes were pretext.

[Primary Effect:] The second prong of *Lemon* examines whether the program at issue has the primary effect of advancing or inhibiting religion. The Court has identified several types of impermissible effects. Two are relevant here. **First, we ask whether the program will cause state-sponsored inculcation of religious beliefs**. In the context of this program, **this inquiry dovetails with the coercion test of *Lee v. Weisman***, asking whether the District has directed a religious activity in such a way as to compel participation. These impermissible effects turn on whether the Program encourages religious indoctrination or involves religious services.

The Supreme Court has assumed that a religious organization may be unable to follow the secular guidelines of a program only if the organization is "pervasively sectarian." An interfaith group of clergy in the program's setting is not "pervasively sectarian." The volunteers are working in a secular setting with other volunteers who subscribe to different faiths. Thus, **we presume that the volunteers will comply with the program's secular guidelines**. The plaintiffs' only evidence to the contrary, the Bible quotation by one volunteer, is not sufficient to demonstrate state-sponsored inculcation.

Similarly, **because the counseling does not constitute a religious exercise, the Program does not violate the coercion test**. We cannot imply from the presence of a minister that the message cannot be secular - a commonsense observation that is also the law. If no religious activity is at issue, any speculation as to whether students might feel pressured to participate is irrelevant. We conclude that the summary judgment record does not support a conclusion that the program violates the coercion test.

We turn to the second group of impermissible effects: the **core question of non-neutrality**. The Court has required that a government allocate benefits among secular and religious organizations in a neutral manner. A non-neutral program is impermissible because it could convey the message that the religion-oriented recipients are uniquely qualified to carry out those services. **Put another way, it is impermissible for the government to "endorse" religion by conveying a message that religion is preferred over non-religion**. . . .

A government-sponsored activity such as a volunteer program may indicate non-neutrality or endorsement. **The key question is in what context we assess that activity - by a narrow examination of each individual extracurricular program, or from the perspective of the District's entire menu of volunteer mentoring and counseling programs**. The Supreme Court has allowed clerical figures to perform secular duties as long as the government neutrally allowed those duties to be performed by secular or religious figures. The District argues that it allows and sponsors mentoring opportunities for both religious and secular figures. . . .

This record, developed as it was on limited summary proceedings, lacks sufficient detail regarding the overall set of volunteer programs operated by the District to sustain a summary judgment in either direction. We therefore leave this issue for trial **and instruct the district court to consider the entire set of volunteer programs operated by the District - including, but not limited to the "Clergy in the Schools" program - in answering the question of whether the District preferred religion over nonreligion**.

The **endorsement analysis** under *Allegheny*, which begins with the element that carries religious symbolism, also **requires us to examine the volunteer program as a whole**. In a visual display, every element carries with it complete symbolic content. The elements are prototypical symbols, conveying a whole message within a single visual marker. In our case, an individual clergy member, wearing no vestments and untitled, is not a symbol. Instead, the most basic symbolic element in our case is the clergy's presence as a counseling group. We agree with the Does that the presence of a group of clergy participating in a program called "Clergy in the Schools" carries some symbolic weight. Even if the clergy do not wear their clerical vestments, the program suggests that they have been chosen as a group because of a perceived expertise in the fields of civic values and morals.

Again, **we look at that symbol not in a vacuum, however, but within its relevant context**. In *Allegheny*, the Court did not focus on a government's decision to display a Chanukah menorah in isolation, but considered it within the context of the government's inclusion of other elements including a Christmas tree and a sign saluting liberty. The Court determined that the particular setting "negated" any message of endorsement of religion.

[Excessive Entanglement:] The *Lemon* test's third prong bars excessive entanglement. **Administrative cooperation alone does not constitute such a violation. Only programs that require "pervasive monitoring" run afoul of the Establishment Clause**. The Court has held that to require from religious officials the performance of administrative duties consistent with and not more onerous than those required from non-religious officials in analogous programs does not constitute excessive entanglement.

In *Agostini v. Felton*, **the Court found no excessive entanglement where a school district sending public school teachers to parochial schools under Title I provided training regarding the secular nature of the program, required the removal of religious symbols from private school classrooms, and made unannounced visits to classrooms about once a month**. The program here is very similar to the controls in *Agostini* in terms of training and visual symbols. The monitoring requirement could be characterized as "pervasive" because an administrator attends every session, rather than attending sporadically. **Because the District monitors all of its volunteer programs, however, that supervision imposes no unique administrative burdens**. That the District sent a mailing soliciting the clergy volunteers appears to have been a function of having no existing umbrella organization rather than an administrative need occasioned by the volunteers' religious professions. In the absence of a need for the District to undertake measures it does not follow with respect to other programs, we find no excessive entanglement. . . .

[Dicta:] Establishment Clause analysis requires that we be sensitive to the context and circumstances attending each case. If the clergy program is fairly viewed, on a fully developed record, as part of a larger framework of secular mentoring and counseling programs, it has not run afoul of the Establishment Clause. . . .

Facts decide cases at every level and of all types. . . . Facts and their resolution lie too close to the heart of the judicial function to treat them as little more than pieces of an erector set - available for use in a writer's envisioned design. . . .

We agree that the ultimate question is whether the school district impermissibly preferred religion over non-religion. **This agreement reflects our overarching agreement that the school district owes a duty to be evenhanded in its policies toward religion and non-religion, a duty of equality**. Relatedly, we agree that context is critical in assessing neutrality. . . .

[Court Ruling:] We reverse the grant of summary judgment and remand to the Chief Judge of the Eastern District of Texas for further proceedings, including trial if necessary.

Notes:
1. Consider the totality of similar programs offered students. Under "The Issue" section, the Court states that "the district court must not confine its analysis to only 'Clergy in the Schools.' Rather, the court can and should examine the targeted program in its full context, viewing it as it actually operates in its setting, including other programs similar in purpose and function. If the set of programs together comprise a mosaic that is neutral with regards to religion, then the Establishment Clause is not offended." Hence, the Court is giving an opening to the school (when the case goes back to trial court) to show that, in the big picture of outside volunteer programs which it offers its students, the "Clergy in the Schools" program has a

religiously neutral effect without appearing to endorse religion.

2. For each situation where a public school employee or board of education has acted to bring religion into the domain of the school district, consider three questions:

(1) Did the act have a secular purpose, with the primary effect neither advancing nor inhibiting religion, and without creating an excessive administrative entanglement with religion?

(2) Did the act's purpose or effect endorse or promote religion in the eyes of a reasonable observer?

(3) Did the act coerce or obligate students or employees to participate?

Case
Bauchman v. West High School, 132 F.3d 542
(10th Cir. 1997) (emphasis added)

[Facts:] Rachel Bauchman was a sophomore at Salt Lake City's West High School during the 1994-95 school year. During that same year, Ms. Bauchman auditioned for and was admitted into Mr. Richard Torgerson's *a capella* choir class (the "Choir"), an elective course offered for credit.

. . . Ms. Bauchman, who is Jewish, generally alleges Mr. Torgerson "engaged for many years, and continues to engage, in the advocacy, promotion, endorsement and proselytizing of his [Mormon] religious beliefs and practices" during his public school classes and Choir performances. More specifically, she claims (1) as a member of the Choir she was required to perform a preponderance of Christian devotional music; (2) Mr. Torgerson selected songs for the religious messages they conveyed; (3) the Choir was required to perform Christian devotional songs at religious sites dominated by crucifixes and other religious symbols; (4) Mr. Torgerson selected religious sites for Choir performances with the purpose and effect of publicly identifying the Choir with religious institutions; (5) Mr. Torgerson berated and ostracized students, like herself, who dissented against his religious advocacy; (6) Mr. Torgerson covertly organized a Choir tour for select Choir members to perform religious songs at religious venues in southern California; and (7) Mr. Torgerson deliberately scheduled the Choir to sing two explicitly Christian devotional songs during West High School's 1995 graduation.

Ms. Bauchman also presents a long list of Mr. Torgerson's alleged unconstitutional practices as a public school teacher beginning some seventeen years prior to Ms. Bauchman's enrollment in his class. She alleges the remaining defendants had knowledge of but consistently failed to take any effective measures to stop Mr. Torgerson from promoting religion in his Choir classes. . . .

[The Evolution of the Legal Standard:] Our attempt to glean an appropriate standard for this case from existing, muddled Establishment Clause precedent begins with *Lemon v. Kurtzman* . . . which is recognized as the benchmark case for Establishment Clause analysis. Applying *Lemon*, government action does not violate the Establishment Clause so long as it (1) has a secular purpose, (2) does not have the principal or primary effect of advancing or inhibiting religion, and (3) does not foster an excessive entanglement. . . .

Beginning in the 1980s, however, the *Lemon* analysis came under vigorous attack by Justices and commentators alike. Acknowledging *Lemon's* weaknesses, Justice O'Connor seized the opportunity in *Lynch v. Donnelly* to draft a concurring opinion encouraging the Court to refine the *Lemon* analysis to focus more on whether the government is "endorsing" religion.

. . . Applying Justice O'Connor's refined analysis, the **government impermissibly endorses religion if its conduct has either (1) the purpose or (2) the effect of conveying a message that "religion or a particular religious belief is favored or preferred."**

Justice O'Connor's "endorsement test" is now widely accepted as the controlling analytical framework for evaluating Establishment Clause claims. . . **It would be wrong, however, to suggest the Court is unanimous in its adoption of the endorsement test**. Moreover, even the Justices who have adopted the endorsement test do not agree on how it should be applied. . . .

Nevertheless, the uncertainty surrounding the present Court's position regarding the appropriate scope of the endorsement test and the appropriate Establishment Clause analysis, in general, cautions us to apply both the purpose and effect components of the refined endorsement test, together with the entanglement criterion imposed by Lemon when evaluating Ms. Bauchman's Establishment Clause claim. . . .

[Application of the "Refined" Endorsement Legal Standard, Plus Lemon's Entanglement Prong:] Ms. Bauchman's factual allegations concerning violation of her Establishment Clause rights fall into three categories: the performance of religious music, the performance at religious sites, and the public ridicule and harassment she experienced as a result of the defendants' collective response to her objections. . .

We first consider whether allegations regarding the singing of religious songs at religious sites, alone, state a claim under the criteria we have set forth. . . Ms. Bauchman simply alleges Mr. Torgerson selected and required her to perform a preponderance of "Christian devotional" songs in places dominated by crosses and other religious symbols. We will not infer an impermissible purpose or effect in the absence of any supporting factual allegations. . . However, we will evaluate whether Ms. Bauchman's allegations concerning the selection and performance of songs alone suggest religious endorsement or the school's excessive entanglement with religion.

[Endorsement:]

Vis a` Vis Purpose

. . . certain principles governing our inquiry into the government's actual purpose are beyond dispute. Namely, **the Constitution does not require that the purpose of every government-sanctioned activity be unrelated to religion**. . . . **Courts have long recognized the historical, social and cultural significance of religion in our lives and in the world, generally**. **Courts also have recognized that "a variety of motives and purposes are implicated" by government activity in a pluralistic society**. . . . Accordingly, there is a legitimate time, manner and place for the discussion of religion in the public classroom. . . .

Here, **we discern a number of plausible secular purposes** for the defendants' conduct. For example, it is recognized that a significant percentage of serious choral music is based on religious themes or text. . . Any choral curriculum designed to expose students to the full array of vocal music culture therefore can be expected to reflect a significant number of religious songs. . . Plausible secular reasons also exists for performing school choir concerts in churches and other venues associated with religious institutions. Such venues often are acoustically superior to high school auditoriums or gymnasiums. . . . Moreover, by performing in such venues, an instructor can showcase his choir to the general public in an atmosphere conducive to the performance of serious choral music. . . .

We see no reason to conclude that defendants' selection of religious songs and religious performance venues serves an impermissible purpose simply because some of those songs and venues, which undisputedly represent only part of the Choir's repertoire and performance venues, may coincide with religious beliefs different from those of Ms. Bauchman. . . Accordingly, Ms. Bauchman's complaint fails to state an Establishment Clause claim under the purpose component of the endorsement test.

Vis a` Vis Effect:

To state a claim under this component of the endorsement test, Ms. Bauchman **must allege facts indicating the Choir curriculum or Choir activities have a principle or primary effect of advancing or endorsing religion**. . . . [t]he Constitution does not forbid all mention of religion in public schools. **The Establishment Clause prohibits only those school activities that, in the eyes of a reasonable observer, advance or promote religion or a particular religious belief. This is an objective inquiry, not an inquiry into whether particular individual might be offended by the content or location of the Choir's performance**, or consider such performances to endorse religion.

We believe a reasonable. . . . observer aware of the purpose, context and history of public education in Salt Lake City . . . would perceive the following with respect to Ms. Bauchman's allegations . . .: the Choir represents one of Salt Lake City's public high schools and is comprised of a diverse group of students; many of the Choir's songs have religious content -- content predominately representative of Judeo-Christian beliefs; in contrast to a church choir, this Choir also performs a variety of secular songs; the Choir's talent is displayed in the diverse array of songs performed and in a number of different public (religious and nonreligious) settings, all of which reflect the community's culture and heritage. Certainly, any given observer will give more or less meaning to the lyrics of a particular song sung in a particular venue based on that observer's individual experiences and spiritual beliefs. **However, the natural consequences of the Choir's alleged activities, viewed in context and in their entirety by a reasonable observer, would not be the advancement or endorsement of religion**. Ms. Bauchman's complaint therefore fails to support a claim that the Choir curriculum or Choir activities have a principle or primary effect of endorsing religion.

[Entanglement:] The entanglement analysis typically is applied to circumstances in which the state is involving itself with a recognized religious activity or institution. . . For the reasons discussed above, we have rejected the notion that Ms. Bauchman's allegations regarding the Choir's singing of religious songs in religious venues alone support a claim that defendants' conduct endorses religion. **Instead, we believe a reasonable observer would conclude the selection of religious songs from a body of choral music predominated by songs with religious themes and text, and the selection of public performance venues affiliated with religious institutions, without more, amount to religiously neutral educational choices. Consequently, we perceive no state involvement with recognized religious activity**. . . .

[Extraneous Allegation:]

Having determined Ms. Bauchman's allegations concerning the singing of religious songs at religious sites do not implicate the Establishment Clause, we must next address the relevance, if any, of her remaining **allegations that she was subjected to public ridicule and harassment as a result of defendants' conduct**. Certainly, Ms. Bauchman's allegations she was criticized and retaliated against for opposing the religious content of the Choir curriculum, taken as true, evidence a lack of sensitivity, crudeness and poor judgment unbefitting of high school students, their parents, and especially, public school teachers and administrators. **However, such claims do not rise to the level of a constitutional violation**. Nor can they be used to breathe constitutional life into otherwise unactionable conduct. The fact that the defendants did not change their behavior in accordance with Ms. Bauchman's demands and reacted negatively and/or offensively to those demands simply cannot be viewed as support for her claim that the Choir's performance of religious music at religious venues furthered a religious purpose, advanced or favored religion or a particular religious belief, or otherwise entangled the public school with religion. We reject this "backdoor" attempt to substantiate an otherwise flawed constitutional claim and conclude the district court properly dismissed Ms. Bauchman's Establishment Clause claim.

[The Ruling:] We acknowledge, as has the United States Supreme Court, that jurisprudence in this arena "is of necessity one of line-drawing, of determining at what point a dissenter's rights of religious freedom are infringed by the State." . . . However, for the reasons stated above, we conclude Ms. Bauchman has failed to demonstrate a real constitutional threat by way of her complaint or proposed amended complaint. We therefore AFFIRM the district court's dismissal of Ms. Bauchman's § 1983 claims. . . .

Notes:

1. The court references the difficulty in applying the appropriate legal standard as "existing, muddled Establishment Clause precedent." It then gives the history of the standard starting with *Lemon v. Kurtzman* in 1971 and evolving into Justice O'Connor's "refined endorsement test" which it described as being "now widely accepted as the controlling analytical framework for evaluating Establishment Clause claims. . . It would be wrong, however, to suggest the Court is unanimous in its adoption of the endorsement test. Moreover, even the Justices who have adopted the endorsement test do not agree on how it should be applied. . . ."

2. In responding to the student's allegations that she was ridiculed, harassed, and criticized for objecting to the religious music in the curriculum, the court said "such claims do not rise to the level of a constitutional violation." These allegations may have been made in an attempt to establish coercion or simply to gain the sympathy of the court. It did not work, however, and the court recognized that a negative or offensive response by school officials to her conduct does not equate to a violation of the Establishment Clause (even though such response, according to the court, was insensitive, crude, and poor judgment).

Case
Adler v. Duval County School Board, 250 F.3d 1330
(11th Cir. 2001), *cert. denied* (emphasis added)

[Background:] On March 15, 2000, this Court ruled that Duval County's facially-neutral policy permitting high school seniors to vote upon the delivery by a student of a message entirely of that student's choosing as part of graduation ceremonies did not violate the Establishment Clause. . . . 206 F.3d 1070 (11th Cir.) (en banc)

. . . Meanwhile, on June 19, 2000, the Supreme Court rendered its decision in *Santa Fe Independent School District v. Doe*, 530 U.S. 290 . . . , which invalidated a Texas school board's policy permitting students to vote upon the delivery of a "statement or invocation," subject to officials' approval, at each home high school football game.

On October 2, 2000, the Court vacated our decision and remanded it for further consideration in light of *Santa Fe*. The case was returned to us on December 19, 2000, and we proceeded to rehear the case *en banc*.

Having carefully reviewed the Supreme Court's opinion . . . , **we conclude that *Santa Fe* does not alter our previous *en banc* decision, and accordingly we reinstate that decision and the judgment in favor of Duval County**. . . .

[Facts from the First Duval County Decision:] . . . The Duval County policy provides in relevant part:

1. The use of a brief opening and/or closing message, not to exceed two minutes, at high school graduation exercises shall rest within the discretion of the graduating senior class;

2. The opening and/or closing message shall be given by a student volunteer, in the graduating senior class, chosen by the graduating senior class as a whole;

3. If the graduating senior class chooses to use an opening and/or closing message, the content of that message shall be prepared by the student volunteer and shall not be monitored or otherwise reviewed by Duval County School Board, its officers or employees;

The purpose of these guidelines is to allow students to direct their own graduation message without monitoring and review by school officials.

[Issue from the First Duval County Decision:] . . . We defined the issue then before us as **"whether the Duval County school system's policy of permitting a graduating student, elected by her class, to deliver an unrestricted message of her choice at the beginning and/or closing of graduation ceremonies is facially violative of the Establishment Clause."** . . . Analyzing this policy under the Supreme Court's opinions in *Lee v. Weisman*, 505 U.S. 577 . . . (1992) and *Lemon v. Kurtzman*, 403 U.S. 602 . . . (1971), we concluded that the policy did not violate the Establishment Clause on its face.

[Rationale from the First Duval County Decision:] Although we offered multiple reasons for that decision, our *Lee* analysis turned on several key facts. **First**, we emphasized that under Duval County's policy **school officials have no power to direct that a message (let alone a religious message) be delivered at graduation ceremonies**, or control in any way the content of any message actually to be delivered. As we explained:

> [U]nder the Duval County graduation policy . . . neither the School Board nor its principals may ordain, direct, establish, or endorse a religious prayer or message of any kind. Indeed, by the very terms of the policy, a religious message may not even be offered at graduation. The Duval County policy explicitly divorces school officials from the decision-making process as to whether any message--be it religious or not--may be delivered at graduation at all. Moreover, decisional control over the most crucial elements of the graduation policy rests with the students and not the state.... Under the policy, the School Board and its agents have no control over who will draft the message (if there be any message at all) or what its content may be. The School Board also does not suggest in any way, let alone require, that the graduating class consider religious or any other criteria in deciding whether to have a

student message or in selecting a particular student speaker. And most notably, if the graduating class chooses to have a message, the content of the message shall be prepared by the student speaker alone and no one else. The Duval County School Board is expressly prohibited by the very terms of its policy from influencing or editing the message in any way. [The] decision [as to content] rests solely with the elected student speaker--with neither the senior class nor the school exercising any sort of editorial oversight. Therefore, on the face of the policy itself, the students unambiguously understand that any student message is utterly divorced from any state sponsorship.

206 F.3d at 1076.

Second, we rejected the argument that the state's role in providing a vehicle for a graduation message by itself transformed the student's private speech into state-sponsored speech. We accepted the assumption that the school board "exerted overwhelming control over the graduation ceremony," **but stressed that the board "did not have control over the elements which are most crucial in the Establishment Clause calculus: the selection of the messenger, the content of the message, or most basically, the decision whether or not there would be a message in the first place."** . . .

Citing these and other facts, we found as well that the policy met all three prongs of the *Lemon* test. **We concluded that the policy had a secular purpose, including "affording graduating students an opportunity to direct their own graduation ceremony," and "permitting student freedom of expression."** . . . We also noted that the **text of the policy did not reveal a religious purpose**, and that the limited pieces of background evidence highlighted for the contention that the policy's secular purpose was a sham could not "strip the policy of [its] secular purpose. No matter what an individual board member may have hoped--and they said nothing on the record about codifying this policy--Duval County's policy is facially neutral and undeniably evinces a secular purpose." . . . We closed our prior *en banc* opinion by defining our holding narrowly, stating that Duval County's policy of "permitting graduating students to decide through a vote whether to have an unrestricted student graduation message at the beginning and/or closing of graduation ceremonies does not facially violate the Establishment Clause." . . .

[The Supreme Court's Santa Fe Decision:] Three months after we issued our prior *en banc* opinion, the Supreme Court decided *Santa Fe*. By a 6-3 vote, the Court found that a school district policy permitting students to vote upon the delivery by a student of a "statement or invocation" prior to high school football games violated the Establishment Clause. **Because the facts of *Santa Fe* are fundamentally different in many crucial respects from the facts of this case, they are worth presenting in some detail**.

For a period of time leading up to and including the 1992-93 and 1993-94 school years, the Santa Fe school district allowed students to read overtly Christian prayers from the stage at graduation ceremonies and over the public address system at home football games. The prayers were characterized as "invocations" or "benedictions" for these events, and typically were given by officers of the student council. Similar prayers were recited by the student council "chaplain" prior to the start of football games.

In 1994, responding to the Supreme Court's decision in *Lee*, the district drafted a written policy that prohibited clerics from delivering invocations or benedictions at graduation ceremonies, but otherwise did not prohibit prayer at school functions. After graduation ceremonies that year, the district amended its written policy to say that a school "may permit the graduating senior class(es), with the advice and counsel of the senior class sponsor, to elect to choose student volunteers to deliver nonsectarian, non-proselytizing invocations and benedictions for the purpose of solemnizing their graduation ceremonies." The same policy was adopted for football games.

In April 1995, several students and parents filed suit in federal court, in part to prevent the district from violating the Establishment Clause at imminent graduation exercises. . . .

In response to a court order, Santa Fe again revised its policies dealing with prayer at school functions. Policies enacted in May and July 1995 for graduation ceremonies provided the format for the District's August 1995 policy regarding high school football games. That August policy authorized two student elections, the first to determine whether an "invocation" should be delivered, and the second to select the spokesperson to deliver it. On August 31, 1995, according to the parties' stipulation, "the district's high school students voted to determine whether a student would deliver the prayer at varsity football games."

Subsequently, in October 1995, the school district slightly modified the August policy. The October version of the policy was (in the Supreme Court's words) "essentially the same as the August policy, though it omits the word 'prayer' from its title, and refers to 'messages' and 'statements' as well as 'invocations.' " . . . The October policy provided in relevant part:

The board has chosen to permit students to deliver a brief invocation and/or message to be delivered during the pre-game ceremonies of home varsity football games to solemnize the event, to promote good sportsmanship and student safety, and to establish the appropriate environment for the competition. . . .

After the Fifth Circuit held that both the August and October policies violated the Establishment Clause, the Supreme Court granted the District's petition for certiorari, limited to the following question: "Whether petitioner's policy permitting student-led, student-initiated prayer at football games violates the Establishment Clause." . . . The Court did not propose to address, and did not address in its ensuing opinion, the district's graduation policies.

[Santa Fe's Application of the Coercion Test:] A majority of the Court found that the October policy violated the Establishment Clause. **The Court analyzed the policy under the principle of** *Lee* **that "government may not coerce anyone to support or participate in religion or its exercise, or otherwise act in a way which establishes a [state] religion...."** ... Initially, **the Court determined that messages delivered by students pursuant to the policy would constitute state-sponsored speech rather than private speech.** The Court offered essentially four reasons for that finding: (1) the student's speech would be **authorized by a government policy that explicitly and implicitly encouraged one particular kind of message,** ... 2) it would **take place on school property at a school event,** ... (3) the government had **broad power to regulate the content of the student's speech,** and (4) the **electoral system would yield only a single speaker and would completely prevent dissenting viewpoints from being heard,** ...

Having found that student speech under the policy was, and would be perceived as, state-sponsored, the Court then found that the religious content of the "statement or invocation" permitted by the Santa Fe policy was impermissibly coercive. The Court explained that "[t]he electoral mechanism, **when considered in light of the history in which the policy in question evolved,** reflects a **device the District put in place that determines whether religious messages will be delivered at home football games."** ... The Court also reasoned that, even though the case was brought as a facial challenge, it was appropriate as part of the facial inquiry to consider the purpose of the policy... The Court stressed that **"the text of the October policy alone reveals that it has an unconstitutional purpose,"** and added that the **events leading up to the enactment of the October policy further conveyed the school board's purpose to ensure a place for prayer in school functions.** .... For these reasons, the Court concluded that the Santa Fe's football game policy was unconstitutional.

[Application of Santa Fe to Duval County:] In *Santa Fe* itself the Supreme Court reiterated just how case-specific Establishment Clause analysis must be under its precedent. As the Court explained:

> Whether a government activity violates the Establishment Clause is "in large part a legal question to be answered on the basis of judicial interpretation of social facts.... Every government practice must be judged in its unique circumstances. ..."

120 S.Ct. at 2282 (citation omitted). We spoke similarly in our prior *en banc* opinion:

[Student's Private Message v. State-Sponsored Religious Message:] Establishment Clause jurisprudence calls for the **difficult task of separating a student's private message, which may be religious in character, from a state-sponsored religious message, protecting the former and prohibiting the latter.** This determination is of "necessity one of line-drawing," ... "sometimes quite fine, based on the particular facts of each case," . . . Indeed, our courts have recognized that "at graduation time and throughout the course of the education process, there will be instances when religious values, religious practices, and religious persons will have some interaction with the public schools and their students." . . .

The Court in *Santa Fe* did not attempt to sweep with a broad brush; rather, it found based on the facts then before it that Santa Fe's policy allowing students to elect a speaker to give a "statement or invocation" of plainly religious bent, at every single home football game, subject to content review by school officials and potential state censorship of non- or anti-religious messages, violated the Establishment Clause. The facts of this case are fundamentally different, and in our view require exactly the same result today as they did at the time of our prior opinion.

Critical to the Supreme Court's conclusion was its finding that the speech delivered by students pursuant to the Santa Fe policy was state-sponsored rather than private. In reaching that conclusion, the Court relied in substantial part on two facts: (1) the speech was "subject to particular regulations that confine the content and topic of the student's message," . . . and (2) the policy, "by its terms invites and encourages religious messages," .. Those two dispositive facts are not present here, and that makes all the difference.

First, the Duval County policy does not contain any restriction on the identity of the student speaker or the content of the message that might be delivered. Indeed, school officials are affirmatively forbidden from reviewing the content of the message, and are expressly denied the opportunity to censor any non-religious or otherwise disfavored views:

> "If the graduating senior class chooses to use an opening and/or closing message, the content of that message shall be prepared by the student volunteer and shall not be monitored or otherwise reviewed by Duvall County School Board, its officers or employees. The purpose of these guidelines is to allow students to direct their own graduation message without monitoring or review by school officials."

> . . . This is in sharp contrast to the Santa Fe policy, under which any message was subject to content regulation by the state. The Santa Fe policy dictated that the process of selecting a speaker and delivering the message was subject to the " 'advice and direction of the high school principal.' " 120 S.Ct. at 2273 n. 6. As part of that process, school officials were effectively authorized to review the message itself to ensure that it was " 'consistent with the goals and purpose of th[e] policy.' " . . . The policy therefore created virtually no check on school officials' power to regulate the proposed student message, giving almost unfettered discretion to state officials acting under the guise of determining that the message would be " 'appropriate.' " . . .

The ability to regulate the content of speech is a hallmark of state involvement,

and the Supreme Court returned repeatedly to that theme in *Santa Fe*. The Court highlighted that "[t]he statement or invocation ... is subject to particular regulations that confine the content and topic of the student's message." . . . The Court observed that "Santa Fe's student election system ensures that only those messages deemed 'appropriate' under the District's policy may be delivered." . . . And the Court expressly characterized the Santa Fe policy as "not a content-neutral regulation" because of its "content restrictions." . . . (emphasizing that "the policy mandates that the 'statement or invocation' be 'consistent with the goals and purposes of this policy' and that accordingly "the District has failed to divorce itself from the religious content of the invocations"). The ability of the state to regulate the content of the students' message was a critical factor in the Court's reasoning, and is indisputably not present in this case. **Under the Duval County policy, if the senior class elects to have a message, the student elected to give that message is totally free and autonomous to say whatever he or she desires, without review or censorship by agents of the state or, for that matter, the student body.** No reasonable person attending a graduation could view that wholly unregulated message as one imposed by the state.

Second, unlike Santa Fe's policy, the Duval County policy does not "by its terms, invite and encourage religious messages." . . . On the contrary, the policy is entirely neutral regarding whether a message is to be given, and if a message is to be given, the content of that message. Although the Supreme Court did not limit its analysis to the text of the Santa Fe policy, it placed heavy emphasis on the text's express and unambiguous preference for the delivery of religious messages.

The policy itself states that the purpose of the message is "to solemnize the event." A religious message is the most obvious method of solemnizing an event. Moreover, the requirements that the message "promote good citizenship" and "establish the appropriate environment for competition" further narrows the types of message deemed appropriate, suggesting that a solemn, yet nonreligious, message, such as commentary on United States foreign policy, would be prohibited. **Indeed, the only type of message that is expressly endorsed in the text is an "invocation"--a term that primarily describes an appeal for divine assistance**. In fact, as used in the past at Santa Fe High School, an "invocation" has always entailed a focused religious message. Thus, the expressed purposes of the policy encourage the selection of a religious message.

. . . **The fact that the text of the Santa Fe policy expressed a clear preference for religious messages was a key factor in the Court's determination that student speech delivered pursuant to that policy would be viewed as state-sponsored.** . . . ("[N]othing in the Constitution ... prohibits any public school student from praying.... But the religious liberty protected by the Constitution is abridged when the State affirmatively sponsors the particular religious practice of prayer.") . . . **In this case, the text setting forth the Duval County policy contains no language approving an "invocation" and no other provision that could fairly be read to require or approve a "religious" theme.**

These important facts demonstrate why *Santa Fe* is distinguishable from this case, and more particularly why the speech at issue here--unlike the speech contemplated by the Santa Fe policy--cannot reasonably be described as state-sponsored. These key facts also help illustrate why the speech permitted by Duval County cannot reasonably be described as state "coercion" of religion. . .

The Duval County policy, unlike the Santa Fe policy, does not subject the issue of prayer to an up-or-down vote; students do not vote on whether prayer, or its equivalent, should be included in graduation ceremonies. **Rather, students vote on two questions that do not expressly or inherently concern prayer: (1) whether to permit a student "message" during the ceremony, and (2) if so, which student is to deliver the message.** *Santa Fe* does not remotely state or suggest that the term "message" connotes prayer, nor could it plausibly give so narrow a meaning to so broad a term. Instead, the Court repeatedly focused on the Santa Fe policy's use of the additional term "invocation," and drew from that term and the school district's concessions the conclusion that Santa Fe's policy mandated a vote on prayer. Santa Fe that the terms "opening" and "closing" as used in Duval County's policy connote prayer. Indeed, those terms did not even appear in Santa Fe's policy. Simply put, "[w]hatever majoritarian pressures are attendant to a student-led prayer pursuant to a direct student plebiscite on prayer are not facially presented by the Duval County policy." . . .

Although it is possible that under Duval County's policy the student body may select a speaker who then chooses on his or her own to deliver a religious message, **that result is not preordained, and more to the point would not reflect a "majority" vote to impose religion on unwilling listeners**. **Rather, it would reflect the uncensored and wholly unreviewable decision of a single student speaker**. It cannot seriously be argued that Duval County's policy ensures that persons with "minority" views will never prevail in the student electoral process, whether we define "minority" in this context as persons opposed to the delivery of student-selected speech at graduation, persons opposed to the delivery of religious messages generally, or persons opposed to the delivery of a religious message that does not coincide with their chosen faith. In fact, the limited record before us proves just the opposite; in seven of the 17 instances reflected in the record, students voted for no message at all or for a student speaker who subsequently delivered an entirely secular message. . . .

For all of these reasons, the private speech delivered by a student pursuant to the Duval County policy does not become state-sponsored as a matter of law simply by virtue of the logic of *Santa Fe*.

Santa Fe also does not alter the analysis under the three-part test of *Lemon*. *Santa Fe* only addresses one part of the *Lemon* test: whether the policy at issue has a secular purpose. . . . The Court's treatment of this issue, however, underscores the differences between the Santa Fe policy and this policy. As discussed above, the text setting forth the Duval County policy does not evince a religious purpose. The text of the Santa Fe policy unambiguously did precisely that, a fact upon which the

Court placed great emphasis. . . ("the text of the ... policy alone reveals that it had an unconstitutional purpose"). . . .

In addition, in *Santa Fe*, school officials stated unabashedly that the policy was designed to permit a student vote for prayer at graduation. Quite simply, *Santa Fe* does not undermine our finding that Duval County's policy, on this record in this facial challenge, has a secular purpose.

. . . The Supreme Court did not rule that an election process itself is always incompatible with the Establishment Clause. Nor did it rule that a student elected to speak to the student body is necessarily a state-sponsored speaker. Rather, the Court stressed that it was not invalidating all student elections, but merely concluding on the facts before it "that the resulting religious message under this policy would be attributable to the school, not just the student." . . .

Second, the Court did not rule that, simply because the speech at issue is "authorized by a government policy and took place on government property at a government-sponsored school-related event," it always constitutes state-sponsored speech. On the contrary, the Court expressly acknowledged that "not every message delivered under such circumstances is the government's own." . . .What turns private speech into state speech in this context is, above all, the additional element of state control over the content of the message. ". . . But it is the element of potential censorship, and the attendant risk recognized by *Santa Fe* that non-religious messages (or messages hostile to religion) will be suppressed, that is conspicuously absent from the record of this case. Notably, in our prior *en banc* opinion, we explained how **affording students the opportunity to vote on whether or not to have a message that would be entirely of the student's choosing bore no more the imprimatur of the state than the process of selecting a homecoming queen**. . . .

[The Ruling:]
OPINION AND JUDGMENT REINSTATED.

Notes:

1. The Duval County case emphasizes the importance between a school board (a) providing for private student speech at school-sponsored programs, uncensored by school officials and (b) sponsoring religious speech. The tough issue, practically, for administrators, is not being able to "censor" what the student speaker plans to say in the school-sponsored speech forum, whether it be graduation, the school newspaper, a variety show, or student council election speeches. The Duval County court stressed that such censorship could convert a student's protected private religious speech into school-sponsored/approved speech thus violating the Establishment Clause. (Under the Supreme Court's 1988 *Hazlewood* case standard of "legitimate educational concern," school officials may censor student speech in school-sponsored speech forum if the standard is met. However, if it is the administrator's review of a religious message for a graduation program, a court could conclude that the message became approved and sponsored by the school, thus violating the Establishment Clause.)

2. Two years prior to the Duval County decision, the Eleventh Circuit ruled on whether a school's application of Alabama statute that allowed student-initiated, nonsectarian, non-proselytizing prayer violated the Establishment Clause. *Chandler v. James,* 180 F.3d 1254 (11th Cir. 1999). In addressing the issue of student-initiated religious expression versus school- sponsored religious speech, the *Chandler* court stated:

The discriminatory suppression of student-initiated religious speech demonstrates not neutrality but hostility toward religion because the: exclusion of religious ideas, symbols, and voices marginalizes religion.... Silence about a subject conveys a powerful message. When the public sphere is open to ideas and symbols representing nonreligious viewpoints, culture, and ideological commitment, to exclude all those whose basis is "religious" would profoundly distort public culture. . . The prohibition of all religious speech in our public schools implies, therefore, an unconstitutional disapproval of religion. . . . [*Id.* at 1261]

On the other hand, even genuinely student-initiated religious speech may constitute state action if the State participates in or supervises the speech. . . Religious speech in school by teachers, for example, is especially troublesome because "a teacher's [religious] speech can be taken as directly and deliberately representative of the school." . . . Teacher participation in student-initiated prayer "improperly entangles the State in religion and signals an unconstitutional endorsement of religion." . . . In upholding the Equal Access Act, which provides that schools must afford religious groups the same access to school facilities as secular groups enjoy, the Supreme Court relied in part on the act's express prohibition on teacher participation which "avoids the problems of the 'students' emulation of teachers as role models.' " . . . [Citing *Board. of Educ. v. Mergens*, 496 U.S. 226 at 251.] Therefore, student religious speech must be without oversight, without supervision, subject only to the same reasonable time, place, and manner restrictions as all other student speech in school. [*Id.* at 1264.]

3. Where school principal reviewed a co-salutatorian's graduation address and refused to permit him to include overly proselytizing content (but did permit him to keep several personal references to his religion and to distribute the complete draft just outside the site of the ceremony), the court ruled that his speech and free exercise of religion rights were not violated when the school acted to prevent the illegal establishment of religion. See *Lassonde v. Pleasanton Unified Sch. Dist.*, 320 F.3d 979 (9th Cir. 2003) where the court applied the endorsement and coercion tests and determined that "a reasonable dissenter could have felt that silence [of school officials in reaction to the proselytizing speech] signified approval or participation. . . [and that the school] had no means of preventing the coerced participation of dissenters attending their graduation ceremony other than censoring Plaintiff's speech." [*Id.* at 984.]

II. COMMUNITY ACCESS TO SCHOOL FACILITIES

Where a school board had an unwritten policy (which was initiated when a community group requested it be allowed to make Bibles available to students) that permitted the distribution of religious, political and other materials one day each year by outside groups on tables in the hallways, with clearly displayed disclaimers that renounced sponsorship and endorsement by the school, the court found no illegal establishment of religion. *Peck v. Upshur County Bd. of Educ.*, 155 F.3d 274 (4th Cir. 1998). The court found the policy neutral because its purpose was to create an open speech forum to further the school's education mission by exposing students to a broad spectrum of knowledge, even though the only materials so-far distributed were Bibles. However, the court warned that the created open forum could become so dominated by private religious speech as to become a genuine threat of religious establishment. By opening its buildings to outside entities, of course, the school takes the risk that "unpopular" groups with messages not held by the majority of the community would have access to the students.

Two Supreme Court decisions have upheld the right of outside groups to use school buildings for religious speech purposes where the schools had opened its facilities to outsiders for nonreligious speech. In *Lamb's Chapel v. Center Moriches Union Free Sch. Dist.*, 508 U.S. 384 (1993), the Court found that the school's permitted use of its buildings for "social, civic and recreational meetings and entertainments, and other uses pertaining to the welfare of the community," while denying access to any group for religious purposes, violated the speech rights of a church that desired to use the school to show a six-part film series on child rearing from a Christian perspective. In *Good News Club v. Milford Central School*, 533 U.S. 98 (2001), the Court ruled that the school, which permitted community use of its buildings, had violated the free speech rights of the plaintiff group due to its religious viewpoint when it sought access to an elementary building right after school so that it could conduct religious education for students wanting to attend.

Case
Wigg v. Sioux Falls Dist. 49-5, 382 F.3d 807 (8th Cir. 2004)
(emphasis added)

Elementary teacher Barbara Wigg sued Sioux Falls School District 49-5 and Superintendent Dr. John Keegan (collectively referred to as "SFSD") **to challenge SFSD's decision prohibiting her from participating in a Christian-based after-school program at schools in the school district**. Wigg sought a preliminary injunction, a permanent injunction, declaratory relief, and damages **claiming that SFSD's policy violated her First Amendment free speech rights. SFSD defended its decision on grounds that Wigg's participation would subject SFSD to First Amendment Establishment Clause liability**. Initially, the district court denied the temporary injunction motion; however, the court later granted Wigg a permanent injunction after concluding that Wigg could participate in the after-school program at schools in the district-other than the one in which she taught-without raising Establishment Clause concerns for SFSD. The district court also ruled that SFSD's Establishment Clause concerns allowed it to prohibit Wigg's participation in the after-school program at her present school. Both parties appeal. We affirm in part and reverse in part.

[Background:] Wigg, currently a second-and third-grade teacher at Laura B. Anderson Elementary School ("Anderson Elementary"), has worked in the school district at five different elementary schools since 1988. . . . Throughout her employment, Wigg has been active with children after school hours. For example, she has participated in after-school Girl Scouts and has taught private guitar and reading lessons.

The Good News Club ("the Club") is an after-school organization sponsored by Child Evangelism Fellowship. To participate in the Club, a child must provide a signed permission slip from a parent. According to the Club's literature, its purpose is to "evangelize boys and girls with the Gospel of the Lord Jesus Christ and establish (disciple) them in the Word of God and in the local church for Christian living." SFSD maintains **two pertinent policy provisions**.

First, SFSD follows a "Community Use of School Facilities" Policy **(Use Policy) that allows both school-sponsored and student-initiated groups, as well as community organizations such as churches, non-profit organizations, and non-sectarian youth groups, to use its facilities**. The purpose of the Use Policy is to foster community involvement. SFSD requires only that applicants verify that they are non-profit organizations and that they have liability insurance.

Second, SFSD maintains a "Religion in the Schools and at School Activities" Policy **(Religion Policy) that prohibits all SFSD personnel from participating in religious activities on school grounds or at school-sponsored activities**. The prohibition, however, does not apply when the organization has leased the facility according to the lease provision in the Use Policy. SFSD interprets this lease provision to apply only to temporary leases to a church seeking a permanent location.

In October 2002, the Club requested access to SFSD's facilities to hold its meetings. SFSD granted the request, and the Club currently meets at five elementary schools within SFSD, including Anderson Elementary. The Club meets at Anderson Elementary from 3:00 p.m. to 4:00 p.m. at the end of the school day. Wigg attended the Club's first meeting in Anderson Elementary's library on December 15, 2002. Nine students attended that meeting, including some from Wigg's combined second- and third-grade class. At the meeting, the students played a game, learned a Bible verse, and heard a Christian story.

. . . On January 17, 2003, SFSD affirmed its decision not to permit Wigg to participate because the school feared that allowing Wigg to participate in the Club would present Establishment Clause issues for SFSD. . . .

[Analysis:] Both Wigg and SFSD argue that the district court erred in deciding the substantive First Amendment issues in this case. **The arguments highlight the considerable tension among the clauses of the First Amendment-particularly when an issue arises in a public school setting**. Does a school's concern for avoiding accusations of establishment of religion justify inhibiting the free

speech and association rights of employees after work hours when the relevant activity takes place on school property? In this case, **we do not believe so.** . . .

SFSD urges us to conclude that its Religion Policy prohibiting Wigg's or any SFSD employee's participation in any religious-based organization having access to SFSD property is justified by SFSD's Establishment Clause concerns. The posture of this case suggests that we must answer whether the government's compelling interest in avoiding an Establishment Clause violation would justify viewpoint discrimination in a school setting.

To date, the Supreme Court has rejected Establishment Clause defenses in at least two free speech cases, *Widmar v. Vincent*, 454 U.S. 263 (1981), and *Lamb's Chapel v. Ctr. Moriches Union Free Sch. Dist.*, 508 U.S. 384 (1993). However, we, like the Court in *Good News Club v. Milford Cent. Sch.*, 533 U.S. 98 (2001), save this question for another day because **we conclude that, on these facts, SFSD has no valid Establishment Clause interest that justifies its restriction of its employees' private speech.** . . .

The First Amendment to the Federal Constitution provides that "Congress shall make no law respecting an establishment of religion, or prohibiting the free exercise thereof; or abridging the freedom of speech. . . ." The Fourteenth Amendment imposes those substantive limitations on the legislative power of the States and their political subdivisions. *Santa Fe Indep. Sch. Dist. v. Doe*, 530 U.S. 290, 301 (2000) (citations omitted).

With few exceptions, the First Amendment prohibits governments from infringing free speech rights in public forums. *Perry Educ. Ass'n v. Perry Local Educators' Ass'n*, 460 U.S. 37, 45 (1983). **The government has more discretion when the speech forum established by the government is considered limited. Then, the government is not required to allow persons to engage in every type of speech.** The government may reserve the forum for certain groups or discussion of certain topics, but it must "abstain from regulating speech when the specific motivating ideology or the opinion or perspective of the speaker is the rationale for the restriction." Rosenberger v. Rector and Visitors of Univ. of Va., 515 U.S. 819, 829 (1995). A viewpoint-discriminatory regulation is presumed to be unconstitutional. . . .

"The principle that government may accommodate the free exercise of religion does not supersede the fundamental limitations imposed by the Establishment Clause. It is beyond dispute that, at a minimum, the Constitution guarantees that government may not coerce anyone to support or participate in religion or its exercise, or otherwise act in a way which 'establishes a [state] religion or religious faith, or tends to do so.'" *Lee v. Weisman*, 505 U.S. 577, 587 (1992) . . . . However, "**there is a crucial difference between government speech endorsing religion, which the Establishment Clause forbids, and private speech endorsing religion, which the Free Speech and Free Exercise Clauses protect**." *Bd. of Ed. of Westside Cmty. Sch. (Dist.66) v. Mergens*, 496 U.S. 226, 250 (1990) (opinion of O'Connor,

J.). **Of utmost importance in Establishment Clause inquiries is whether the government regulation is neutral towards religion.** . . . **The "guarantee of neutrality is respected, not offended, when the government, following neutral criteria and evenhanded policies, extends benefits to recipients whose ideologies and viewpoints, including religious ones, are broad and diverse."** . . .

SFSD argues that permitting its employees to participate in religious-based programs held on school grounds would violate Establishment Clause principles **because it would appear that SFSD endorses a particular religion or religious activity**. However, **SFSD's policy** of prohibiting all employees-even on their own time-from participating in any religious-based programs held on school grounds **is an overly broad remedy**. In an effort to avoid an establishment of religion, **SFSD unnecessarily limits the ability of its employees to engage in private religious speech on their own time**. Although SFSD allows access to the Club, **SFSD impermissibly discriminates by limiting those who can attend based upon the subject matter of the speech**. As such, **SFSD's Religion Policy** preventing SFSD employees from participating in religious-based activities **is viewpoint discriminatory and, thus, per se unconstitutional**. . . . In support of its policy limiting SFSD employees from participating in religious-based programs, **SFSD argues that its Establishment Clause concern constitutes a compelling reason to justify the restriction**. However, **Wigg asserts that the Establishment Clause is not implicated because her participation constitutes private or free speech outside the sphere of her employment and without the imprimatur of SFSD**. . . .

We recently decided *Doe v. The Sch. Dist. of the City of Norfolk*, 340 F.3d 605 (8th Cir. 2003), dealing with Establishment Clause concerns in relation to a private speech issue. In *Doe*, a public high school student and parent filed a § 1983 Establishment Clause lawsuit against a school district, its superintendent, and a school board member because **the school board member, who was also a parent of a graduating student, recited a prayer at the school-sponsored graduation despite specific instructions prohibiting prayer at the ceremony.** We found **no Establishment Clause violation after determining that the school board member was acting as a private citizen when he recited the prayer although he gained access to the podium due in part to his position on the school board.** We particularly observed that **the parent's prayer was not state-sponsored and did not bear the "imprint of the state"-although it occurred at a school-sponsored event-because he was not acting in a representative capacity at that moment.** . . . We noted that the Supreme Court in *Santa Fe*, which prohibited student-led prayer prior to school-sponsored sporting events, provided a relevant inquiry asking "'**whether an objective observer, acquainted with the text, legislative history, and implementation of the statute, would perceive it as a state endorsement of prayer in public schools**.'" . . . The Court in *Santa Fe* determined that an objective observer would perceive that the school sanctioned the pre-game prayer. Utilizing this inquiry, we reached a contrary conclusion in *Doe,* noting that the school specifically advised all graduation participants, including the school-board-member parent, that prayer was not permitted during the ceremony and that the parent's comments were clearly only his own.

With the guidance of *Doe* and *Santa Fe*, **we conclude that Wigg's participation in the after-school Club constitutes private speech**. Wigg's private speech does not put SFSD at risk of violating the Establishment Clause: Wigg's speech did not occur during a school-sponsored event; she did not affiliate her views with SFSD (Wigg's counsel proposed a disclaimer explaining that any school district employees participating in the Club were acting as private citizens and did not represent SFSD in any manner); students participated in the meetings with parental consent; and nonparticipating students-unless supervised-exited the building before the meetings began. Under the inquiry provided in *Santa Fe*, *no reasonable observer would perceive Wigg's private speech as a state endorsement of religion by SFSD*. SFSD's desire to avoid the appearance of endorsing religion does not transform Wigg's private religious speech into a state action in violation of the Establishment Clause. Even private speech occurring at school-related functions is constitutionally protected, *Chandler v. Siegelman*, 230 F.3d 1313, 1317 (11th Cir. 2000); therefore private speech occurring at non-school functions held on school grounds must necessarily be afforded those same protections.

While we are aware that school districts like SFSD must tread carefully in a constitutional mine field of Establishment Clause, Free Speech Clause and Free Exercise Clause concerns, we reiterate that Establishment Clause cases stress the government's neutrality towards religion. . . . Wigg seeks nothing more than to be treated like other private citizens who are allowed access to Club meetings. SFSD's policy permitting participation by all interested parties-so long as they are not district employees-in after-school, religious-based, non-school related activities violates that mandate of neutrality. As such, we affirm the district court's order allowing Wigg to participate in the Club at other SFSD school locations, but we reverse the court's decision prohibiting Wigg from participating at Anderson Elementary.

III. EQUAL ACCESS ACT

The Equal Access Act of 1984, 20 U.S.C. sections 4071- 4074, applies to secondary schools that receive federal funds and maintain a "limited open forum," wherein "noncurriculum related" student groups are permitted to meet. Such schools are prohibited from denying equal access to, or discriminating against, student groups based on the content of religious or other speech at the meetings. The key sections of the Act read (emphasis added):

Sec. 4071. **Denial of equal access prohibited**

(a) Restriction of limited open forum on basis of religious, political, philosophical, or other speech content prohibited

It shall be unlawful for any public secondary school which receives Federal financial assistance and which has a **limited open forum** to deny equal access or a fair opportunity to, or discriminate against, any students who wish to conduct a meeting within that limited open forum on the basis of the religious, political, philosophical, or other content of the speech at such meetings.

(b) "Limited open forum" defined

A public secondary school has a limited open forum whenever such school grants an offering to or opportunity for one or more **noncurriculum related student groups** to meet on school premises during noninstructional time.

(c) Fair opportunity criteria

Schools shall be deemed to offer a fair opportunity to students who wish to conduct a meeting within its limited open forum if such school uniformly provides that -

(1) the meeting is **voluntary and student-initiated**;

(2) there is **no sponsorship of the meeting by the school, the government, or its agents or employees**;

(3) **employees or agents of the school or government are present at religious meetings only in a nonparticipatory capacity**;

(4) the meeting **does not materially and substantially interfere with the orderly conduct of educational activities within the school**; and

(5) **nonschool persons may not direct, conduct, control, or regularly attend** activities of student groups.

(d) Construction of subchapter with respect to certain rights

Nothing in this subchapter shall be construed to authorize the United States or any State or political subdivision thereof -

(1) to influence the form or content of any prayer or other religious activity;

(2) to require any person to participate in prayer or other religious activity;

(3) to expend public funds beyond the incidental cost of providing the space for student-initiated meetings;

(4) to compel any school agent or employee to attend a school meeting if the content of the speech at the meeting is contrary to the beliefs of the agent or employee;

(5) to sanction meetings that are otherwise unlawful;

(6) to limit the rights of groups of students which are not of a specified numerical size; or

(7) to abridge the constitutional rights of any person.

(e) Federal financial assistance to schools unaffected

Notwithstanding the availability of any other remedy under the Constitution or the laws of the United States, nothing in this subchapter shall be construed to authorize the United States to deny or withhold Federal financial assistance to any school.

(f) Authority of schools with respect to order, discipline, well-being, and attendance concerns

Nothing in this subchapter shall be construed to limit the authority of the school, its agents or employees, to maintain order and discipline on school premises, to protect the well-being of students and faculty, and to assure that attendance of students at meetings is voluntary.

Sec. 4072. - **Definitions**

As used in this subchapter -

(1) The term "secondary school" means a public school which provides secondary education as determined by State law.

(2) The term **"sponsorship" includes the act of promoting, leading, or participating** in a meeting. The assignment of a teacher, administrator, or other school employee to a meeting for custodial purposes does not constitute sponsorship of the meeting.

(3) The term "meeting" includes those activities of student groups which are permitted under a school's limited open forum and are not directly related to the school curriculum.

(4) The term "noninstructional time" means time set aside by the school before actual classroom instruction begins or after actual classroom instruction ends.

The Supreme Court upheld the constitutionality of the Equal Access Act due to its secular purpose of protecting private student speech, and ruled the school in violation when it denied access to a student group that sought to meet for religious purposes. *Mergens v. Board of Educ.*, 496 U.S. 226 (1990). In addressing the issue of whether the school had created a "limited open forum," the court stated that such a forum is created if the school sponsors clubs or permits groups to meet that are **not directly related to its curriculum offerings**. Since groups such as scuba diving, chess and a service club that worked with special education classes were allowed to meet, a "limited open forum" was created and, therefore, it violated the Act to prohibit a student-initiated religious group from meeting.

IV. FREE EXERCISE OF RELIGION

When government in the regulation of the public schools is alleged to interfere with a student's or parents free exercise of religion, the legal standard applied by the courts is a balancing test. The interests of the individual, who must show that government has burdened the practice of a legitimate religious belief, are weighed against the government's interests, which must prove compelling.

The Supreme Court, which invalidated the application of a state's compulsory education law to members of the Amish faith whose children ceased formal education before their sixteenth birthday, *Wisconsin v. Yoder*, 406 U.S.205, 214 (1972), stated:

There is no doubt as to the power of a state, having a high responsibility for education of its citizens, to impose reasonable regulations for the control and duration of basic education. . . Providing public schools ranks at the very apex of the function of the state. . . Thus, a state's interest in universal education, however highly we rank it, is not totally free from a balancing process when it impinges on fundamental rights and interests, such as those specifically protected by the free exercise clause of the first amendment. . .

. . . In order for Wisconsin to compel school attendance beyond the eighth grade against a claim that such attendance interferes with the practice of a legitimate religious belief, it must appear either that the state does not deny the free exercise of religious belief by its requirement, or that there is a state interest of sufficient magnitude to override the interest claiming protection under the free exercise clause. . . .

The *Yoder* court determined that the state of Wisconsin's interest in requiring Amish children to continue a formal education for an additional two years was not sufficiently compelling when viewed in light of the Amish faith and culture that provided its children with a continued vocational, agriculture-based education.

When faced with claims of school practices or regulations interfering with free exercise of religion, educators need to determine if the student/parent holds a legitimate religious (as opposed to a philosophical) belief and if that belief is burdened by the school's requirement. If so, then the school must be able to demonstrate a compelling interest to justify its insistence that the student follow its demand. Absent such an interest, the school would need to accommodate the religious belief of the student by modifying or dropping its requirement.

Schools, for example, regularly accommodate students of the Jehovah Witness faith by excusing them from activities such as Halloween and birthday parties, as well as recitation of the Pledge of Allegiance. Similarly, Christian Science students are excused from any study of medical treatment of disease. Lastly, in order to accommodate student members of the Worldwide Church of God, which requires attendance at week-long religious meetings, schools modify their attendance policies so that no penalties are applied. See *Worldwide Church of God v. Amarillo Indep. Sch. Dist.*, 511 F.Supp. 613 (N.D. Tex. 1981), affirmed *per curiam*, 670 F.2d 46 (5th Cir. 1982).

SCENARIOS
STATE AND APPLY THE RELEVANT LEGAL RULE(S) TO THE FACTS.

1. The chairman of the Christian Ministers Association, approached Public High School Principal at the start of the school year with the following two-part proposal:

a. Every Friday, a half hour before the start of classes a minister from the Association, who is a licensed counselor pursuant to State Code that regulates the profession, will come to the high school to be available to any student for personal counseling. The minister will then stay the entire morning so that students may be counseled during study hall periods. Parents would consent to the voluntary counseling which would have no religious content initiated by the minister. Only if the student requested religious viewpoints, prayer, or religious literature, would the minister oblige. No religious garb would be worn. Each student before each counseling session would receive, sign, and date a statement that s/he is there voluntarily with parental consent, that it is understood that there will be no religious content, oral or written, unless initiated by the student, and that the school is neither sponsoring nor promoting religion by allowing the minister to counsel. The parent, student, and minister would agree that the school's guidance counselor will from time to time, and no less than twice during the morning, enter the room to assure that the terms of the arrangement are being followed.

b. On the same Friday, just before the start of the first period and following recitation of the Pledge of Allegiance, the minister will share a Bible story and a nondenominational, inspirational message based thereon. Since it will be broadcast over closed circuit television in every classroom, the minister's will not wear any religious garb or symbols. Christ may be referenced, but only in relation to universal human values. No prayer will be offered. Any student who does not desire to listen may either sit and ignore the message or leave the room and return following its delivery. Before the presentation, a statement will be made that the school is neither sponsoring nor promoting the message.

School adopted the proposals and suit was filed to enjoin the implementation of each.

2. Student was a sixth grade female and a child of conservative Christian parents. The teachings of their church required all members of the faith to dress conservatively, which meant that everyone wore long-sleeved shirts with males wearing pants and females dresses both of which must cover the ankles. Physical education was a state-mandated course for all children in public schools. Parent requested that School allow his daughter to be exempted from the requirement that physical education dress must be short-sleeved shirts and shorts and that she be permitted to wear the clothing required of her religion. After consideration, School disallowed Parent's request stating that (a) the wearing of the dress would pose too great a threat to her safety and that of class members who could get tangled in the material, and (2) if she failed to comply, she would fail the course.

Parent on child's behalf filed suit to permit daughter to wear religiously appropriate dress in the class and not be penalized with a failing grade.

CHAPTER
13

COLLECTIVE
BARGAINING

While the National Labor Relations Act, which governs private sector collective bargaining, does not apply to bargaining between public school districts and their teacher and non-teacher employees, federal courts have addressed bargaining-related issues impacting school employees throughout the country, regardless of the particular state's bargaining law or lack of such. These issues include the right of employees to meet, organize, and express their concerns to school management, the ability of school-recognized unions to collect "agency shop" or "representation fees" from non-members whom it represents, the right of the recognized unions and schools to negotiate exclusive provisions in contracts that discriminate against competing unions, and the right of individual employees to have union representation during an employer's investigatory interview that could lead to discipline of the employee.

Secondly, although collective bargaining statutes raise legal questions that are very state-sensitive, state courts have weighed in on such general topics as strikes and binding arbitration of grievances.

I. RIGHT TO FORM AND PARTICIPATE IN LABOR UNIONS

Because of the First Amendment right of freedom of speech and association, public school employees under the United States Constitution may form an organization, solicit and accept membership, collect dues, elect officers, promote and advocate the improvement of wages, fringe benefits, working conditions, and other labor-related issues, as well as to *seek* recognition of the school employer and *seek* to bargain and reach agreement with said employer on said issues. The school employer is not compelled *under the Constitution* to recognize and bargain with a labor union. However, state statutes may place such an obligation on school employers.

The Supreme Court has recognized the First Amendment right of speech and association of public employees to form unions for their mutual benefit, including the "agency shop" case of *Abood v. Detroit Board of Education*, 431 U.S. 209 (1977), which stated at 233-234 (emphasis added):

> Our decisions establish with unmistakable clarity that the **freedom of an individual to associate for the purpose of advancing beliefs and ideas is protected by the First and Fourteenth Amendments**. E. g., *Elrod v. Burns*, . . . (plurality opinion); *Cousins v. Wigoda*, ... *Kusper v. Pontikes*, ...*NAACP v. Alabama ex rel. Patterson*, ...

> Equally clear is the proposition that a **government may not require an individual to relinquish rights guaranteed him by the First Amendment as a condition of public employment**. E. g., *Elrod v. Burns*. . . . *Perry v. Sindermann*, ...

> One of the principles underlying the Court's decision in *Buckley v. Valeo*, ... was that **contributing to an organization for the purpose of spreading a political message is protected by the First Amendment**. Because "[making] a contribution . . . enables like-minded persons to pool their resources in furtherance of common political goals. . . the Court reasoned that limitations upon the freedom to contribute "implicate(s) fundamental First Amendment interests**," . . . .

> The fact that the appellants are compelled to make, rather than prohibited from making, contributions for political purposes works no less an infringement of their constitutional rights. **For at the heart of the First Amendment is the notion that an individual should be free to believe as he will, and that in a free society one's beliefs should be shaped by his mind and his conscience rather than coerced by the State**. . . . And the freedom of belief is no incidental or secondary aspect of the First Amendment's protections:

> "If there is any fixed star in our constitutional constellation, it is that **no official, high or petty, can prescribe what shall be orthodox in politics, nationalism, religion, or other matters of opinion** or force citizens to confess by word or act their faith therein."

West *Virginia Bd. of Ed. v. Barnette,* . . . .

These principles prohibit a State from compelling any individual to affirm his belief in God, . . . or to associate with a political party, . . . as a condition of retaining public employment. They are no less applicable to the case at bar, and they thus prohibit the appellees from requiring any of the appellants to contribute to the support of an ideological cause he may oppose as a condition of holding a job as a public school teacher. . . .

In states that do not require recognition of and bargaining with the exclusive labor union chosen by its members, school employers may voluntarily recognize and negotiate with a labor union (provided state law does not prohibit its public schools from doing so). As long as the school employer does not breach the terms of any contract with a voluntarily recognized union, it can unilaterally establish the conditions that will govern the process, including the ability of the local union to affiliate with outside unions or individuals.

Case
Michigan City Area Schools v. Siddall, 427 N.E.2d 464
(Ind.App. 1981) (emphasis added)

This is an action for injunctive relief in a labor dispute involving **non-teaching** employees of the Michigan City Area Schools (the school).

[Facts:] It appears that during the late summer of 1979 the school board adopted a voluntary policy for collective bargaining with its non-teaching employees (hereafter referred to as the classified employees). In August a number of these employees: bus drivers, custodians, cooks and maintenance people, refused to perform their work assignments. **The central issue in dispute was the school's refusal to recognize and negotiate with the individual selected by the classified employees to represent them.**

The voluntary recognition and bargaining policy adopted by the school was **expressly conditioned upon two factors. It would not recognize a classified employee organization if the organization had any members who were not employees of the school, and it would not negotiate with "representatives" who were neither employees of the school nor attorneys.** In explanation of these requirements the policy stated,

"The intent of this definition is for the school corporation to recognize only local classified school employee organizations made up solely of full-time classified employees and/or part-time classified employees, while recognizing any individual employee's right to join any organization of the employee's choice."

The policy statement provided that **the school would bargain collectively on certain subjects with a properly selected representative.** The policy statement also expressed **the school's retained right to revoke or change the policy declaration at any time with the proviso that no such action would affect any collective bargaining contracts that might have been entered into.**

The classified employees indicated their desire to be represented in negotiations by an employee of the Indiana State Teachers' Association who was neither an employee of the school nor an attorney.

When the school refused, the strike ensued. The school then sought an injunction to prohibit the strike activity and the classified employees counterclaimed seeking to restrain the school from interfering with their choice of bargaining representatives. After a hearing, the trial court permanently enjoined the classified employees from participating in a strike, restrained the school from interfering with or in any way preventing the classified employees from selecting the person or persons of their choice "to be their bargaining representative," and ordered the parties to engage in collective bargaining.

The school appeals contending that the orders restraining it from interfering with the choice of bargaining representative and mandating it to bargain collectively are contrary to law. Despite the practical wisdom in the trial court's decision, we are required to sustain the appeal.

[Issue:] In order to properly consider the issues presented it is necessary to briefly consider the legal posture of the parties.

Under the common law there is no legal duty for employers and employees to engage in the collective bargaining process. . . In addition, **the public employees involved in this dispute are not covered by the Indiana Teacher Bargaining Act**, IC 20-7.5-1-1 *et seq.,* **or the National Labor Relations Act**, as amended. 29 U.S. C.A. § 152(2).

On the other hand, the School Powers Act, IC 20-5-2-2(7), authorizes school boards to employ such persons as it needs in the work categories occupied by the classified employees and fix their salaries and compensation. **We have previously held that such authority is sufficient to validate collective bargaining contracts entered into by the parties**. *Gary Teachers Union v. School City of Gary* (1972), . . ., 284 N.E.2d 108.

Furthermore, **it is clear that an individual's constitutionally protected freedoms of speech and association permit the classified employees to join a labor organization of their choice, although no duty is thereby imposed upon the school to deal with the organization or its representatives**. . . .

That fact is critical. **If there is no legal obligation statutorily or at common law to engage in good faith collective bargaining with a duly chosen agent of a group of employees, there is no *illegal* interference with an employee's constitutional freedom of speech or association** where an employer does no more than refuse to recognize and engage in collective bargaining with some employee selected organization or its agents. In the absence of legal obligation the employer has the same freedom of choice to deal with or reject dealing with a "bargaining" agent that any party has in electing whether or not he wishes to deal with another party's admittedly authorized agent or servant. . . .

The only remaining question, then, is the impact of the school's policy statement

upon what must otherwise be held its freedom of choice to engage in voluntary bargaining. . . .

The policy adopted by the school board, as already outlined, stated that it would recognize for purposes of voluntary collective bargaining an organization of its classified employees in an appropriate unit, set forth a mechanism for determining such units and affirmed that it would engage in collective bargaining with the employees' duly selected representative. **It expressly conditioned its willingness, however, by restricting its obligation under the policy statement to organizations consisting exclusively of its employees and the use of bargaining representatives (negotiators) who were either employees of the school or attorneys**. Regardless of the practical wisdom of either or both such restrictions, **there appears to us to be no reason to invalidate them** and the employees have advanced none except the assertion that they should be entitled to choose whomsoever they desired.

[Rationale:]   The school has no legal obligation to engage in collective bargaining with the classified employees. However, it may do so voluntarily, and accordingly could properly declare qualifications or restrictions establishing a basis upon which it would agree to bargain collectively.

It follows that **since the classified employees did not comply with the policy conditions, there was no enforceable duty requiring the school to engage in collective bargaining**. The court's injunction was, therefore, in this regard contrary to law.

Moreover, **since the school was free to impose the conditions referred to, it did not illegally interfere with the employees' constitutional right to select whomsoever they desired as agent by refusing to deal with that agent**. The point being that the school had no obligation to bargain collectively under the circumstances. Since there was, therefore, no evidence of illegal interference it was error for the court to enjoin the school from interfering with the employees' selection of bargaining representatives. . . .

[Court ruling:] The judgment is therefore reversed and the cause is remanded to the trial court for such further proceedings consistent herewith as may be necessary.

Reversed and remanded.

In the case of *Indiana State Teachers Association v. Board of School Commissioners of the City of Indianapolis*, 101 F.3d 1179 (7th Cir. 1996), the court was faced with the situation where a school had voluntarily recognized and bargained with a local union of non-teacher employees for many years (AFSCME), and then refused to allow an election for the collective bargaining representative that was desired by a rival union (ISTA). In response to the ISTA's claim of a denial of Fourteenth Amendment equal protection (there was no allegation of a denial of free speech or association), the court found that the Equal Protection Clause did not apply. The rationale of the court was that the unequal treatment of the two unions by the school board, when the two unions were in factually unequal circumstances, was not a denial of equal protection. Said the court at 1182:

There is nothing irrational or vicious about preferring a known quantity to the unknown. . . . Trust and commitment are not unknown or misplaced in labor relations any more than in other relational or transactional settings. The situation of the AFSCME local, with which the school board has been dealing without the expense and frictions of an election for almost twenty years, and of the Association or any other union that wants to replace the AFSCME local is, far from being prima facie equal, radically unequal. . . .

II. AGENCY SHOP OR REPRESENTATION FEES

A. *Legality When State Statute Silent*

Case
Fort Wayne Education Assoc. v. Goetz, 443 N.E.2d 464
(Ind.App. 1983) (emphasis added)

[Facts:] Plaintiff-appellant Fort Wayne Education Association, Inc. (Association) is appealing the judgment rendered against it in five small claims actions it had instigated for the collection of representation fees from non-member teachers employed by Fort Wayne Community Schools. Each action was premised on a provision in the Master Contract negotiated by the Association, as exclusive representative of the Fort Wayne teachers, with the Board of School Trustees (Board). **The pertinent contract clause provided a non-mandatory payroll deduction system for the collection of a representation fee, such fee being an assessment by the Association against teachers who were not members of the organization for the purpose of defraying the costs of collective bargaining, grievance adjustment, contract administration and other expenses related to services rendered as their exclusive representative**. Essentially, the fee was a sum slightly less than regular membership dues paid to the Association and its parental affiliates, Indiana State Teachers Association and National Education Association, reflecting a deduction for amounts used for political purposes. The five nonmember teachers totally refused to pay the representation fee, and the Association brought suit against them, all five actions being consolidated on motion of the teachers.

The parties stipulated to certain facts (which the court adopted as its sole findings of facts) upon which the trial court rendered judgment for the teachers, concluding Indiana does not provide statutory authorization for an agency shop provision and, further, the Association can not reap payment on the basis of unjust enrichment.

We reverse. . . .

[Issue:] We are presented with an issue that has generated a great deal of controversy in the area of labor relations, in both private and public sectors. That **issue is whether nonunion members can be compelled to pay their share of**

the costs generated by the labor organization which represents their interests in dealing with management. Typically, these fee-payment arrangements are negotiated into collective bargaining agreements governing the relationship between the employer and the employees. Such provisions, commonly denoted as union security agreements, are generally viewed as promoting stability within the working relationship. . . .

Here, the Association negotiated what the parties refer to as an "agency shop" provision. **An agency shop is defined as requiring,** *as a condition of employment,* **nonunion member employees to pay fees to a union for services rendered as their bargaining representative but not otherwise requiring membership.** . . . . Thus, in the case before us, one must necessarily note that **nowhere in this particular agreement is a teacher's continued employment conditioned on payment of the representation fee.** Rather, **the fee provision manifests only the Board's recognition of the Association's claim for equitable compensation and legitimates that claim solely to the extent the Board will provide for payroll deductions for the convenience of the Association** *if voluntarily authorized by each nonmember.* Thus, we are dealing with a **modified form of agency shop.** The Fort Wayne teachers preliminarily challenge the constitutionality of the affixation of such an obligation to their jobs.

[Rationale:]

1. *Constitutionality*

It can no longer be gainsaid that public school teachers possess the constitutional right to associate in labor organizations, as provided by the First Amendment. . . .*cf. Abood v. Detroit Board of Education,* (1977) 431 U.S. 209, . . . ("Our decisions establish with unmistakable clarity that **the freedom of an individual to associate for the purpose of advancing beliefs and ideas is protected by the First and Fourteenth Amendments.**" *Id.* at 233, ...) **Equally clear is an individual's right of choice not to associate himself with a particular organization or ideology.** *Id.* at 234--35, ... However, in the action herein, **the Master Contract provision does not require membership in the Association. It merely requires that nonmember teachers carry their financial burden in return for the benefits they receive from the Association's activities as their exclusive representative.** This monetary assessment is not, of itself, unconstitutional. As the United States Supreme Court has stated, and recently reaffirmed, **"We ... hold that the requirement for financial support of the collective-bargaining agency by all who receive the benefits of its work ... does not violate ... the First ... Amendmen[t].**" *Railway Employees' Department v. Hanson,* (1956) 351 U.S. 225, 238, ...

The rationale in support of agency shop agreements is the elimination of "free riders," those nonmembers who partake of the benefits engendered by their labor representative without paying their share of the costs. . . . This policy was recently articulated in the public school teachers' case of *Abood:*

"The designation of a union as exclusive representative carries with it great responsibilities. The tasks of negotiating and administering a collective-bargaining agreement and representing the interests of employees in settling disputes and processing grievances are continuing and difficult ones. They often entail expenditure of much time and money. . . . The services of lawyers, expert negotiators, economists, and a research staff, as well as general administrative personnel, may be required. Moreover, **in carrying out these duties, the union is obliged 'fairly and equitably to represent all employees ..., union and nonunion,' within the relevant unit. . . . A union-shop arrangement has been thought to distribute fairly the cost of these activities among those who benefit, and it counteracts the incentive that employees might otherwise have to become 'free riders'---to refuse to contribute to the union while obtaining benefits of union representation that necessarily accrue to all employees**." . . .

Abood, supra, 431 U.S. at 221--22, . . . This justification for agency shops, however, is of no avail **unless authorized by statute** because our General Assembly has particularly prescribed the regulation of teachers' labor relations.

2. *Indiana General Powers Act*

Indiana's General Powers Act, Ind.Code 20-5-1-1 *et seq.,* grants to school corporations the power to conduct the educational program in their respective districts. Ind. Code 20--5--2--1 is a general grant, and Ind. Code 20-5-2-2 enumerates a nonexclusive list of specific powers. *See* Ind.Code 20-5-2-2(19). Within this specific list is the power to prepare rules and regulations for the governance of employees. Ind.Code 20-5-2-2(17). A sister state recently held this authorization was sufficient to uphold a fee arrangement as is present here. In *Jefferson Area Teachers Assoc. v. Lockwood,* (1982) . . . 433 N.E.2d 604, *U.S. appeal pending,* a teacher was held liable on a small claims complaint for collection of a service fee equal to 50% of dues. The court held that inasmuch as the board of education had statutory authority to make rules and regulations for the governance of its employees and as the teacher had signed a contract expressly agreeing to abide by such rules, the service fee in the Master Agreement was enforceable.

Our General Powers Act also bestows upon local school boards the ability to "exercise any other power and make any expenditure in carrying out its general powers and purposes . . . or in carrying out the powers delineated in this section which is reasonable from a business or educational standpoint in carrying out school purposes of the school corporation. ..." IC 20-5-2-2(19). Further, the Act "shall be supplemental and in addition to all other laws, Ind.Code 20-5-6-2, and "shall be liberally construed to permit the governing body of school corporations to conduct its affairs in a manner consistent with sound business practice. ..." Ind.Code 20-5-6-3. **It is therefore apparent the legislature endowed Indiana school boards with a great amount of discretion in running their individual systems**. However, **it is not apparent from the statute that the Fort Wayne Board abused that discretion when it entered into the agency shop agreement with the Association. In fact,**

courts acknowledge the sound business practice inherent in negotiating such a provision. *See, e.g., Abood, supra,* . . . . In addition, we must also consider statutes which may abridge the Board's discretion, more particularly, the Certificated Educational Employee Bargaining Act (CEEBA).

3. *Certificated Educational Employee Bargaining Act*

CEEBA, codified at Ind.Code 20-7.5-1 *et seq.,* is prefaced by a long declaration of the legislature regarding labor relations in school corporations. Ind.Code 20-7.5-1-1. This proclamation recognizes the right of school employees to organize and accepts the principles and procedures of collective bargaining, both measures being viewed as conducive to harmonious working relationships. A similar legislative policy statement was one of the primary bases for sustaining the imposition of a financial obligation upon non-union police officers in *Tremblay v. Berlin Police Union,* (1968) . . . 237 A.2d 668. The court in that case upheld the contract provision, despite a statute expressly prohibiting coercion to become a member of a labor organization, because of the legislature's public policy pronouncement and the absence of a statute prohibiting union shops, and because the ultimate decision to hire and fire personnel and other such discretionary functions remained in the employer police department. This is not dissimilar to the situation in our case.

After the Indiana General Assembly's prefatory policy statement in IC 20-7.5-1-1, begins the list of the specific statutory rights and responsibilities of the employers and employees, foremost being the duty to bargain collectively. Ind. Code 20-7.5-1-3. Only "salary, wages, hours and salary and wage related fringe benefits" are mandatory subjects of bargaining, Ind.Code 20-7.5-1-4; however, **one of the mandatory subjects of discussion, which *may* be bargained, is working conditions**. Ind.Code 20-7.5-1-5. **And, in the private sector, an agency shop provision, generally defined as a "condition of employment," is just such a working condition**. . . .

In addition to all of the foregoing, Indiana law explicitly provides the right to "form, join or assist employee organizations" to school employees, Ind.Code 20-7.5-1-6(a), and declares it an unfair practice for a school employer to encourage or discourage *membership* in any such organization through discrimination of any sort. Ind.Code 20-7.5-1-7(a)(3). **Conspicuously absent is any statutory right to refrain from "assisting" or "participating" in a labor organization**. Statutory phraseology such as this was the foundation for quashing agency shop clauses in some situations. . . .

In this context, we must remember that Indiana's right-to-work law itself, Burns' Ann.St. § 40-2701 *et seq.,* was repealed in 1965. . . . This law had provided "the right to refrain from forming, joining, continuing membership in, or *assisting* labor organizations." . . . Nevertheless, this court ruled the right-to-work law itself did not ban agency shop agreements in Indiana. . . . No comparable legislation has since been re-enacted for the private sector, and CEEBA was enacted for teachers in 1973, with only the provision that *membership* can not be required for school employees. IC 20-7.5-1-7(a)(3). **The statutes are silent with reference to any other forced participation in a labor organization. Even those laws for the private sector speak explicitly only of the right to organize, and not the right to refrain from such association**. Ind.Code 22-6-1-4, 22-7-1-2.

Neither is there any express statement regarding union security clauses, although it is implicit the National Labor Relations Act is effective in Indiana, IC 22-7-1-2, which act *does* provide for such agreements. **The Indiana legislature, while not *expressly* allowing agency shop provisions in CEEBA, must have been aware of the repeal of Indiana's right-to-work law when they passed the school employees' statute eight years later. Their failure to impose a similar right-to-work provision in CEEBA is indicative that anything less than union membership is certainly allowable, particularly in view of the language in IC 20-7.5-1-7(a)(3) which restricts unfair practices to coercion in *membership* only**. . . .

The teachers have also relied upon a recent Indiana case bearing directly upon the subject of agency shop clauses in teachers' contracts. It is factually and legally distinguishable from the case here. In *Anderson Federation of Teachers, Local 519 v. Alexander,* (1981) Ind.App., 416 N.E.2d 1327, **the clause in question made payment of service fees a condition of employment** [and] teachers failing to pay were subject to discharge. Chief Judge Buchanan **properly declared this provision invalid because school corporations can not bargain away the terms of teacher discharges**. However, he went on to say, "[we do not] suggest that such agreements between schools and teachers' unions are invalid *per se.* **We say only that construing the provisions of the CEEBA *in toto,* they forbid school corporations to make any collective bargaining agreement---for union security purposes or otherwise---in which the schools undertake the mandatory discharge of a given class of teachers**." . . . . The Fort Wayne Master Contract does not make the payment of dues a condition of employment. Therefore, the Anderson case is inapplicable. . . .

Because the statutes have been questioned, we also feel compelled to examine the legislative history of CEEBA to determine the intent of the General Assembly with regard to teachers' labor relations and union security. . . . We find this legislative background most persuasive in determining the Indiana General Assembly did not intend to prohibit contract clauses as negotiated here.

After searching inquiry into the pertinent cases and Indiana statutes, **we hold the Fort Wayne Board and the Association had the power to negotiate the agency shop clause in question, which clause recognized nonmember teachers' responsibility to pay a representation fee to the Association and did not delegate or abridge the Board's discretionary authority to manage the employment relationships with such nonmembers**.

4. *Questions Involving Political Expenditures*

We emphasize the fact the contract here **does not force nonmembers to pay for anything other than their share of the exclusive representative's costs of** providing services for the bargaining unit. **They can not be required to pay for political activities**. *Brotherhood of Railway & Steamship Clerks v. Allen,* (1963) 373 U.S. 113, . . . *Abood, supra.* The teachers herein have triggered a scrutiny of this issue. . . . Here, the case never reached this stage of adjudication because the trial court declared the provision invalid. However, the parties stipulated to the amount used for political activities. . . . The teachers' contention the Association has failed to carry its burden of proof is therefore without merit.

Finally, the teachers present us with one last issue. They recognize the Association has formulated an **internal rebate procedure** whereby teachers can contest the use of funds. This procedure is engaged upon payment to the organization; then, the nonmember teacher petitions for a rebate of improperly expended assessments. The teachers contend they cannot be compelled to submit to procedures in an organization which they have refused to join. This argument was evidently presented in order to forestall any such contentions by the Association in its reply brief. First of all, we reiterate that the teachers have factually agreed to the amount properly spent by the Association. Next, we note the Association has never insisted the teachers use this internal rebate procedure so the argument is akin to Don Quixote tilting with windmills. . . .

[Court ruling:] For all the foregoing reasons, we reverse the judgment of the trial court and direct it to enter judgment in favor of the Association.

In 1995 the Indiana General Assembly amended the Collective Bargaining Law to make representation fee language in labor-management master contracts unenforceable. Numerous bargaining agreements have retained the language to this day, but due to the amendment, teacher associations may not sue to collect the fee from non-paying teachers who are not union members.

III. VALID DISCRIMINATION AGAINST MINORITY UNION

Case
Perry Education Assoc. v. Perry Local Educators Assoc., 460 U.S. 37 (1983)
(emphasis added)

Perry Education Association is the **duly elected exclusive bargaining representative** for the teachers of the Metropolitan School District of Perry Township, Ind.

A collective-bargaining agreement with the Board of Education **provided that Perry Education Association, but no other union, would have access to the interschool mail system and teacher mail-boxes** in the Perry Township schools. **The issue in this case is whether the denial of similar access to the Perry Local Educators' Association, a rival teacher group, violates the First and Fourteenth Amendments.**

[Facts:]   The Metropolitan School District of Perry Township, Ind., operates a public school system of 13 separate schools. Each school building contains a set of mailboxes for the teachers. Interschool delivery by school employees permits messages to be delivered rapidly to teachers in the District. **The primary function of this internal mail system is to transmit official messages among the teachers and between the teachers and the school administration**. In addition, **teachers use the system to send personal messages, and individual school building principals have allowed delivery of messages from various private organization**.

Prior to 1977, both the Perry Education Association (PEA) and the Perry Local Educators' Association (PLEA) represented teachers in the School District and apparently **had equal access to the interschool mail system**. In 1977, PLEA challenged PEA's status as de facto bargaining representative for the Perry Township teachers by filing an election petition with the Indiana Education Employment Relations Board (Board). PEA won the election and was certified as the exclusive representative, as provided by Indiana law. Ind. Code 20-7.5-1-2(1) (1982).

The Board permits a school district to provide access to communication facilities to the union selected for the discharge of the exclusive representative duties of representing the bargaining unit and its individual members without having to provide equal access to rival unions. Following the election, **PEA and the School District negotiated a labor contract in which the School Board gave PEA "access to teachers' mailboxes in which to insert material" and the right to use the interschool mail delivery system to the extent that the School District incurred no extra expense by such use.** The labor agreement noted that **these access rights were being accorded to PEA "acting as the representative of the teachers" and went on to stipulate that these access rights shall not be granted to any other "school employee organization"** - a term of art defined by Indiana law to mean "any organization which has school employees as members and one of whose primary purposes is representing school employees in dealing with their school employer." The PEA contract with these provisions was renewed in 1980 and is presently in force.

The **exclusive-access policy applies only to use of the mail-boxes and school mail system**. PLEA is not prevented from using other school facilities to communicate with teachers. PLEA may post notices on school bulletin boards; may hold meetings on school property after school hours; and may, with approval of the building principals, make announcements on the public address system. . . .

[Issue:]   PLEA and two of its members filed this action under 42 U.S.C. 1983 against PEA and individual members of the Perry Township School Board. Plaintiffs **contended that PEA's preferential access to the internal mail system violates the First Amendment and the Equal Protection Clause of the Fourteenth Amendment**. . . .

The primary question presented is whether the First Amendment, applicable to the States by virtue of the Fourteenth Amendment, **is violated when a union that has been elected by public school teachers as their exclusive bargaining representative is granted access to certain means of communication, while such access is denied to a rival union**. . . . The First Amendment's guarantee of free speech applies to teacher's mailboxes as surely as it does elsewhere within the school. . . . **But this is not to say that the First Amendment requires equivalent access to all parts of a school building in which some form of communicative activity occurs**. "[N]owhere [have we] suggested that students, teachers, or anyone else has an absolute constitutional right to use all parts of a school building or its immediate environs for . . . unlimited expressive purposes." *Grayned v. City of Rockford*. . . (1972). **The existence of a right of access to public property and the standard by which limitations upon such a right must be evaluated differ depending on the character of the property at issue**.

[Rationale:] **In places which by long tradition or by government fiat have been devoted to assembly and debate, the rights of the State to limit expressive activity are sharply circumscribed. At one end of the spectrum are streets and parks which "have immemorially been held in trust for the use of the public and, time out of mind, have been used for purposes of assembly, communicating thoughts between citizens, and discussing public questions."** . . . . In these quintessential public forums, the government may not prohibit all communicative activity. For the State to enforce a content-based exclusion it must show that its regulation is necessary to serve a compelling state interest and that it is narrowly drawn to achieve that end. . . . **The State may also enforce regulations of the time, place, and manner of expression which are content-neutral, are narrowly tailored to serve a significant government interest, and leave open ample alternative channels of communication.** . . .

A second category consists of **public property which the State has opened for use by the public as a place for expressive activity**. The Constitution forbids a State to enforce certain exclusions from a forum generally open to the public even if it was not required to create the forum in the first place. . . . **Although a State is not required to indefinitely retain the open character of the facility, as long as it does so it is bound by the same standards as apply in a traditional public forum**. Reasonable time, place, and manner regulations are permissible, and a content-based prohibition must be narrowly drawn to effectuate a compelling state interest. . . .

Public property which is **not by tradition or designation a forum for public communication is governed by different standards**. We have recognized that the "First Amendment does not guarantee access to property simply because it is owned or controlled by the government." . . . **In addition to time, place, and manner regulations, the State may reserve the forum for its intended purposes, communicative or otherwise, as long as the regulation on speech is reasonable and not an effort to suppress expression merely because public officials oppose the speaker's view.** . . .

The **school mail facilities at issue here fall within this third category**. . . . The internal mail system, at least by policy, is not held open to the general public. It is instead PLEA's position that the school mail facilities have become a "limited public forum" from which it may not be excluded because of the periodic use of the system by private non-school-connected groups, and PLEA's own unrestricted access to the system prior to PEA's certification as exclusive representative.

Neither of these arguments is persuasive. The use of the internal school mail by groups not affiliated with the schools is no doubt a relevant consideration. **If by policy or by practice the Perry School District has opened its mail system for indiscriminate use by the general public, then PLEA could justifiably argue a public forum has been created**. This, however, is not the case. As the case comes before us, there is no indication in the record that the school mailboxes and interschool delivery system are open for use by the general public. Permission to use the system to communicate with teachers must be secured from the individual building principal. There is no court finding or evidence in the record that demonstrates that this permission has been granted as a matter of course to all who seek to distribute material. We can only conclude that the schools do allow some outside organizations such as the YMCA, Cub Scouts, and other civic and church organizations to use the facilities. **This type of selective access does not transform government property into a public forum**. . . .

Because the school mail system is not a public forum, the School District had no "constitutional obligation per se to let any organization use the school mail boxes." . . . In the Court of Appeals' view, however, the access policy adopted by the Perry schools favors a particular viewpoint, that of PEA, on labor relations, and consequently must be strictly scrutinized regardless of whether a public forum is involved. **There is, however, no indication that the School Board intended to discourage one viewpoint and advance another**. We believe it is more accurate to characterize the access policy as based on the status of the respective unions rather than their views.

Implicit in the concept of the nonpublic forum is the right to make distinctions in access on the basis of subject matter and speaker identity. These distinctions may be impermissible in a public forum but are inherent and inescapable in the process of limiting a nonpublic forum to activities compatible with the intended purpose of the property. The touchstone for evaluating these distinctions is whether they are reasonable in light of the purpose which the forum at issue serves. . . .

The differential access provided PEA and PLEA is reasonable because it is wholly consistent with the District's legitimate interest in ""preserv[ing] the property . . . for the use to which it is lawfully dedicated."" . . . **Use of school mail facilities enables PEA to perform effectively its obligations as exclusive representative** of all Perry Township teachers. **Conversely, PLEA does not have any official responsibility in connection with the School District and need not be entitled**

to the same rights of access to school mailboxes. . . . The tasks of negotiating and administering a collective-bargaining agreement and representing the interests of employees in settling disputes and processing grievances are continuing and difficult ones." . . . Moreover, exclusion of the rival union may reasonably be considered a means of insuring labor peace within the schools. **The policy "serves to prevent the District's schools from becoming a battlefield for inter-union squabbles."** . . .

Finally, **the reasonableness of the limitations on PLEA's access to the school mail system is also supported by the substantial alternative channels that remain open for union-teacher communication to take place**. These means range from bulletin boards to meeting facilities to the United States mail. During election periods, PLEA is assured of equal access to all modes of communication. There is no showing here that PLEA's ability to communicate with teachers is seriously impinged by the restricted access to the internal mail system. . . .

[Court ruling:] The Court of Appeals invalidated the limited privileges PEA negotiated as the bargaining voice of the Perry Township teachers by misapplying our cases that have dealt with the rights of free expression on streets, parks, and other forums generally open for assembly and debate. Virtually every other court to consider this type of exclusive-access policy has upheld it as constitutional. . . and today, so do we. The judgment of the Court of Appeals is

Reversed.

IV. EMPLOYEE RIGHT TO REPRESENTATION AT INVESTIGATORY INTERVIEWS

Case
NLRB v. Weingarten, Inc., 420 U.S. 251 (1975) (emphasis added)

The **National Labor Relations Board held in this case that respondent employer's denial of an employee's request that her union representative be present at an investigatory interview which the employee reasonably believed might result in disciplinary action constituted an unfair labor practice** . . . **because it interfered with, restrained, and coerced the individual right of the employee**. . . **"to engage in** . . . **concerted activities for** . . . **mutual aid or protection** . . . ."

. . . The Court of Appeals for the Fifth Circuit held that this was an impermissible construction . . . and refused to enforce the Board's order that directed respondent to cease and desist from requiring any employee to take part in an investigatory interview without union representation if the employee requests representation and reasonably fears disciplinary action. . . . We reverse.

[**Facts:**] Respondent operates a chain of some 100 retail stores with lunch counters at some, and so-called lobby food operations at others, dispensing food to take out or eat on the premises. Respondent's sales personnel are represented for collective-bargaining purposes by Retail Clerks Union, Local 455. Leura Collins, one of the sales personnel, worked at the lunch counter at Store No. 2 from 1961 to 1970 when she was transferred to the lobby operation at Store No. 98. Respondent maintains a companywide security department staffed by "Loss Prevention Specialists" who work undercover in all stores to guard against loss from shoplifting and employee dishonesty.

In June 1972, "Specialist" Hardy, without the knowledge of the store manager, spent two days observing the lobby operation at Store No. 98 investigating a report that Collins was taking money from a cash register. When Hardy's surveillance of Collins at work turned up no evidence to support the report, Hardy disclosed his presence to the store manager and reported that he could find nothing wrong. The store manager then told him that a fellow lobby employee of Collins had just reported that Collins had purchased a box of chicken that sold for $2.98, but had placed only $1 in the cash register. Collins was summoned to an interview with Specialist Hardy and the store manager, and Hardy questioned her.

The Board found that **several times during the questioning she asked the store manager to call the union shop steward or some other union representative to the interview, and that her requests were denied**. Collins admitted that she had purchased some chicken, a loaf of bread, and some cake that she said she paid for and donated to her church for a church dinner. She explained that she purchased four pieces of chicken for which the price was $1, but that because the lobby department was out of the small-size boxes in which such purchases were usually packaged, she put the chicken into the larger box normally used for packaging larger quantities. Specialist Hardy left the interview to check Collins' explanation with the fellow employee who had reported Collins. This employee confirmed that the lobby department had run out of small boxes and also said that she did not know how many pieces of chicken Collins had put in the larger box. Specialist Hardy returned to the interview, told Collins that her explanation had checked out, that he was sorry if he had inconvenienced her, and that the matter was closed.

Collins thereupon burst into tears and blurted out that the only thing she had ever gotten from the store without paying for it was her free lunch. This revelation surprised the store manager and Hardy because, although free lunches had been provided at Store No. 2 when Collins worked at the lunch counter there, company policy was not to provide free lunches at stores operating lobby departments. In consequence, the store manager and Specialist Hardy closely interrogated Collins about violations of the policy in the lobby department at Store No. 98. **Collins again asked that a shop steward be called to the interview, but the store manager denied her request**. Based on her answers to his questions, Specialist Hardy prepared a written statement which included a computation that Collins owed the store approximately $160 for lunches. Collins refused to sign the statement. The Board found that Collins, as well as most, if not all, employees in the lobby department of Store No. 98, including the manager of that department, took lunch from the lobby without paying for it, apparently because no contrary policy was ever made known to them. Indeed, when company headquarters advised Specialist Hardy by telephone during the interview that headquarters itself was uncertain whether the policy against providing free lunches at lobby departments was in effect at Store No. 98, he terminated his interrogation of Collins. The store manager asked Collins not to discuss the matter with anyone because he considered it a private matter between her and the company, of no concern to others. Collins, however, reported the details of the interview fully to her shop steward and other union representatives, and this unfair labor practice proceeding resulted.

[Issue:] The Board's construction that 7 creates a statutory right in an employee to refuse to submit without union representation to an interview which he reasonably fears may result in his discipline was announced in its decision and order of January 28, 1972, in *Quality Mfg. Co.* . . . In its opinions in that case and in *Mobil Oil Corp.*, 196 N. L. R. B. 1052, decided May 12, 1972, three months later, the Board shaped the contours and limits of the statutory right.

First, the right inherent in 7's guarantee of the right of employees to act in concert for mutual aid and protection. In *Mobil Oil*, the Board stated:

"An employee's right to union representation upon request is based on Section 7 of the Act which **guarantees the right of employees to act in concert for `mutual aid and protection.' The denial of this right has a reasonable tendency to interfere with, restrain, and coerce employees in violation of Section 8** (a) (1) of the Act. Thus, **it is a serious violation of the employee's individual right to engage in concerted activity by seeking the assistance of his statutory representative if the employer denies the employee's request and compels the employee to appear unassisted at an interview which may put his job security in jeopardy."** . . .

Second, the right arises only in situations where the employee requests representation. In other words, the employee may forgo his guaranteed right and, if he prefers, participate in an interview unaccompanied by his union representative.

Third, the employee's right to request representation as a condition of participation in an interview is limited to situations where the employee reasonably believes the investigation will result in disciplinary action. Thus the Board stated in *Quality*:

"We would not apply the rule to such run-of-the-mill shop-floor conversations as, for example, the giving of instructions or training or needed corrections of work techniques. In such cases there cannot normally be any reasonable basis for an employee to fear that any adverse impact may result from the interview, and thus we would then see no reasonable basis for him to seek the assistance of his representative." 195 N. L. R. B., at 199.

Fourth, exercise of the right may not interfere with legitimate employer prerogatives. The employer has no obligation to justify his refusal to allow union representation, and despite refusal, the employer is free to carry on his inquiry without interviewing the employee, and thus leave to the employee the choice between having an interview unaccompanied by his representative, or having no interview and forgoing any benefits that might be derived from one. . . .

Fifth, the employer has no duty to bargain with any union representative who may be permitted to attend the investigatory interview. The Board said in Mobil, "we are not giving the Union any particular rights with respect to predisciplinary discussions which it otherwise was not able to secure during collective-bargaining negotiations." . . . The employer has no duty to bargain with the union representative at an investigatory interview. "**The representative is present to assist the employee, and may attempt to clarify the facts** or suggest other employees who may have knowledge of them. **The employer, however, is free to insist that he is only interested, at that time, in hearing the employee's own account of the matter under investigation.**"

[**Rationale:**]   The Board's holding is a permissible construction of "concerted activities for . . . mutual aid or protection" by the agency charged by Congress with enforcement of the Act, and should have been sustained.

The action of an employee in seeking to have the assistance of his union representative at a confrontation with his employer clearly falls within the literal wording of 7 that "[e]mployees shall have the right . . . to engage in . . . concerted activities for the purpose of . . . mutual aid or protection." *Mobil Oil Corp. v. NLRB*, 482 F.2d 842, 847 (CA7 1973). This is true even though the employee alone may have an immediate stake in the outcome; he seeks "aid or protection" against a perceived threat to his employment security. The union representative whose participation he seeks is, however, safeguarding not only the particular employee's interest, but also the interests of the entire bargaining unit by exercising vigilance to make certain that the employer does not initiate or continue a practice of imposing punishment unjustly. The representative's presence is an assurance to other employees in the bargaining unit that they, too, can obtain his aid and protection if called upon to attend a like interview. . . .

The Board's construction plainly effectuates the most fundamental purposes of the Act. In 1, 29 U.S.C. 151, the Act declares that it is a goal of national labor policy to protect "the exercise by workers of full freedom of association, self-organization, and designation of representatives of their own choosing, for the purpose of . . . mutual aid or protection." To that end the Act is designed to eliminate the "inequality of bargaining power between employees . . . and employers." . . . Requiring a lone employee to attend an investigatory interview which he reasonably believes may result in the imposition of discipline perpetuates the inequality the Act was designed to eliminate, and bars recourse to the safeguards the Act provided "to redress the perceived imbalance of economic power between labor and management." . . . .

The Board's construction also gives recognition to the right when it is most useful to both employee and employer. A single employee confronted by an employer investigating whether certain conduct deserves discipline may be too fearful or inarticulate to relate accurately the incident being investigated, or too ignorant to raise extenuating factors. A knowledgeable union representative could assist the employer by eliciting favorable facts, and save the employer production time by getting to the bottom of the incident occasioning the interview. **Certainly his presence need not transform the interview into an adversary contest**. . . .

[Court ruling:] . . . The responsibility to adapt the Act to changing patterns of industrial life is entrusted to the Board. The Court of Appeals impermissibly encroached upon the Board's function in determining for itself that an employee has no "need" for union assistance at an investigatory interview. ". . . But the Board's construction here, while it may not be required by the Act, is at least permissible under it, and insofar as the Board's application of that meaning engages in the "difficult and delicate responsibility" of reconciling conflicting interests of labor and management, the balance stuck by the Board is "subject to limited judicial review. . . . In sum, the Board has reached a fair and reasoned balance upon a question within its special competence, its newly arrived at construction of 7 does not exceed the reach of that section, and the Board has adequately explicated the basis of its interpretation.

The statutory right confirmed today is in full harmony with actual industrial practice. Many important collective-bargaining agreements have provisions that accord employees rights of union representation at investigatory interviews. Even where such a right is not explicitly provided in the agreement a "well-established current of arbitral authority" sustains the right of union representation at investigatory interviews which the employee reasonably believes may result in disciplinary action against him. . . .

The judgment is reversed and the case is remanded with direction to enter a judgment enforcing the Board's order.

It is so ordered.

The *Weingarten* doctrine that an employee has the right, upon request of the employee, to a union representative when it is reasonably believed that the employer's investigatory interview will lead to disciplinary action clearly applies in states that have mandatory bargaining laws for public sector employees. In states that have not passed required bargaining legislation, but that do not prohibit bargaining, it is likely that courts would not apply the doctrine unless language in particular public sector bargaining agreements could be interpreted similar to the National Labor Relations Act's language construed by the *Weingarten* court.

V. BINDING ARBITRATION OF GRIEVANCES

Generally, states leave the decision whether to arbitrate a question arising under a labor contract up to the school district and the exclusive representative of the teacher or non-teacher employee union. If it is a state whose legislature has enacted statutes governing dismissal of the particular employee group, the law will either expressly permit the school districts and relevant employee union to arbitrate such matters or the law will be silent.

Where the state statute is silent, courts may go either of two ways when faced with the question of a matter being arbitrable. The Indiana Court of Appeals, for example, in *Michigan City Education Assoc. v. Board of School Trustees of Michigan City Area Schools,* 577 N.E.2d 1004, (Ind.App 1991) ruled that in the absence of express statutory authority permitting arbitration, a collective bargaining agreement permitting such was void because the school board could not bargain away its statutory right and duty to be the sole decision-maker in the dismissal of teachers by delegating such authority to a third-party arbitrator.

On the other hand, the New Jersey Supreme Court has taken the view that where there was a statute governing the dismissal of non-teacher employees, but the statute was silent as to arbitration of grievances, the school board in a collective agreement may waive its right to be the sole decision-maker in dismissals and agree to arbitration, but must do so in clear and unmistakable terms.

Case
Cambden Board of Education v. Alexander, ___ N.J. ___
(NJ, A-34/35, August 12, 2004) (emphasis added)

The Camden Board of Education (Board) voted not to renew certain custodians and mechanics (defendants) at the conclusion of the 1999-2000 school year. **Defendants sought to arbitrate the non-renewal of their appointments under the grievance provision of the applicable collective negotiation agreement (CNA). The question before the Court is whether arbitration should be permitted.**

. . . The parties agree that that statute does not preempt them from contractually granting greater protection to fixed-term employees by subjecting non-renewals to a just cause requirement, and submitting non-renewal grievances to binding arbitration. . . . Thus, the question -- can this matter be negotiated – is not in issue. **This case is about whether the parties, in fact, did negotiate for arbitration to apply in this non-renewal setting**.

As members of Local 1079 Custodial and Maintenance Employees of the Communications Workers of America, AFL-CIO (Union), defendants were protected by the CNA negotiated by the Union. The CNA's grievance provision, and two related provisions, follow:

Article III: Grievance Procedure

A. Definition

A "Grievance" shall mean a complaint by an employee or the Union that there has been to him/her a personal loss, injury or inconvenience because of a violation, misinterpretation, or misapplication of this Agreement.

B. Procedure

6. (a) The following procedure will be used to secure the services of an arbitrator: The Union will make a request to the Public Employment Relations Commission for a panel of arbitrators no later than 45 days after receipt of the Board's decision. (b) The arbitrator shall limit himself/herself to the issue submitted to him/her and shall consider nothing else. He/she can add nothing to, nor subtract anything from, the Agreement between the parties or any policy of the Board of Education. The recommendations of the arbitrator shall be binding on the parties. Only the Board and the aggrieved and his/her representatives shall be given copies of the arbitrator's report and findings and recommendations. This shall be accomplished within (30) days of the completion of the arbitrator's hearings.

Article IV: Employee Rights

A. No employee shall be disciplined or reprimanded without just cause. Any such action asserted by the Board, or any agent or representative thereof, shall be subject to the Grievance Procedure herein set forth. . . .

Toward the end of the 1999-2000 school year, each defendant received from a supervisor a letter warning that due to excessive absenteeism, "disciplinary action maybe [sic] taken which may include but not be limited to not being recommended for reappointment for the 2000-2001 school year." Thereafter, on the recommendation of the chief school administrator, the Board voted on June 28, 2000, not to renew defendants' appointments. We note that the Board permitted defendants to appear and to be heard prior to its vote. . . . **Each defendant not renewed for the 2000-01 school year then sought to arbitrate the merits of his non-renewal under the CNA's grievance procedures**.

Although the Board and Union agreed to waive the preliminary steps of the CNA's grievance procedure and to proceed directly to the arbitration stage of Article III, **the Board nonetheless preserved the issue of arbitrability**. The Board sought to restrain the arbitrations, initially before the Commissioner of Education, and thereafter in Superior Court. . . .

II.

The New Jersey Constitution grants public employees "the right to organize, present to and make known to the State, or any of its political subdivisions or agencies, their grievances and proposals through representatives of their choosing." N.J. Const. art. I, ¶ 19. Unlike private-sector employees, public employees are not given the right to "bargain collectively." . . . Public employees instead may engage in collective negotiations. . . .

The issue is whether the parties negotiated to provide for arbitration of the non-renewal of fixed-term employees. That issue is a legal question of contract interpretation for a court to decide: has the CNA made this public-sector dispute substantively arbitrable? . . .

III

A.

To resolve the instant question of contract interpretation, we begin by noting that the CNA's language does not specifically include disciplinary non-renewal, nor does it specifically exclude that subject. . . .

In a matter closely resembling the instant appeal, the Appellate Division considered whether a fixed-term employee's allegedly disciplinary non-renewal was subject to arbitration because the pertinent collective negotiations agreement made "discipline" subject to arbitration. See Marlboro Twp. Bd. of Educ. v. Marlboro Twp. Educ. Ass'n, . . . (holding that non-renewal of bus driver who had excessive absences over long period was not subject to grievance procedure), . . . (1997).

The court held that it would not "rewrite" the contract to provide for arbitration in the context of the Board's right to non-renew its fixed-term employee when clear language to that effect was not present in the collective negotiation agreement. . . .

In another case, the Supreme Court of New Hampshire similarly held that grievance language employed in the collective agreement between a school board and union (specifically, a reference to "discipline" and "discharge" of employees) was not specific enough to override a New Hampshire statute giving the school board authority not to renominate probationary teachers. Appeal of Westmoreland Sch. Bd., . . . (1989). . . .

Just as those courts determined in the above cases, **it appears to us from a fair review of the language of the CNA that non-renewals, disciplinary or not, were not implicitly made subject to arbitral review**. The CNA's language does not convey a clear waiver of the Board's rights in respect of non-renewals conferred by [New Jersey's collective negotiations act]. A waiver would have been accomplished had the agreement included specific language to that effect, . . . Given the statutory backdrop against which the parties' negotiation occurred, **we hold that more was necessary to effectuate clearly and unmistakably a waiver of the Board's authority** under [the collective negotiations statute]. In this public-sector employment dispute, a court should not deliver by fiat what was not obtained through negotiation.

B.

In addition, we note the counterintuitive result that is reached were we to presume that this CNA meant to allow a non-renewed, fixed-term employee access to arbitral review based on a theory that the Board's determination not to renew the contract was a pretext for discipline. **That access would bestow on the non-renewed, poorly performing employee, who claimed he or she was the subject of the supposed "disciplinary" action, greater rights than those given a competently performing individual whose contract simply was not renewed.** The poorly performing employee would have the benefit of a hearing on the "cause" for termination. A non-deficient employee, who could not allege a "disciplinary" motivation on the employer's part, would not. As was observed in a setting similar to the matter at hand, **"a disciplinee should be accorded no greater rights than those accorded to a faultless non-renewed employee."** Cresskill Bd. of Educ. v. Cresskill Educ. Ass'n, . . . (App. Div. 2003). . . .

In sum, the Board is entitled to depend on the authority the Legislature conferred on it, subject to constitutional limitations, unless its statutory right can be and, explicitly, has been negotiated away. **Arbitration is a voluntary device. Requiring that non-renewal be clearly and unmistakably subjected to arbitration under the terms of a collective negotiation agreement properly respects the Board's statutory prerogative over decisions concerning the non-renewal of fixed-term contracts of employment.** . . .

V.

In conclusion, the Board has the statutory right to renew, or not, a fixed-term employee for non-arbitrary and non-capricious reasons without being subject to review of that decision by an arbitrator. The CNA is silent about whether the parties intended the Board to give up that statutory right. In such circumstances, we hold that the CNA did not effectuate a waiver of the Broad's non-renewal right. Accordingly, the judgment of the Appellate Division is reversed, and the arbitrations are restrained. The arbitration award previously entered in favor of defendant, Derek Copeland, is vacated.

In an Indiana case, where the school board and teacher union had agreed to arbitrate teacher dismissals, the court was faced with the question of whether the collective bargaining law, non-permanent teacher dismissal statute, and the language of the collective agreement gave the arbitrator the authority to reinstate a teacher after finding violations of the agreement.

Case

North Miami Education Association v. North Miami Community Schools, 736 N.E.2d 749 (Ind.App. 2000)(emphasis added)

[Facts:] Statement of the Case: Appellants-Plaintiffs Nelda Sue Johnson (Johnson) and the North Miami Education Association (Association) (hereinafter referred to collectively as "Plaintiffs") appeal the trial court's Order granting the North Miami Community Schools' (School) motion to dismiss Plaintiffs' complaint and application to vacate an arbitrator's award because the arbitrator did not direct the School to reinstate Johnson as a teacher. The trial court found that the arbitrator did not exceed his power in making his award, and that Plaintiffs failed to allege any other statutory or factual basis that would allow the trial court to accept judicial review in order to vacate the Arbitration Award.

We affirm.

[Issue:] Plaintiffs raise one issue for our review, which we restate as: whether the trial court erred in granting the School's motion to dismiss the Plaintiffs' complaint and application to vacate the arbitrator's award because the Plaintiffs failed to allege either a statutory or factual basis to allow the trial court to exercise judicial review to vacate the Arbitration Award.

Facts and Procedural History:
Johnson was hired by the North Miami Community Schools at the beginning of the 1996--1997 school year as a nonpermanent teacher at the North Miami Junior-Senior High School. The North Miami Education Association is the exclusive representative for the employees of the North Miami Community Schools. The Association and the School negotiated a Collective Bargaining Agreement that covered August 1997 through August 1999.

Johnson's teaching contract was renewed for the 1997-1998 school year. However, during its regularly scheduled meeting of April 21, 1998, the School voted not to renew Johnson's contract as a non-permanent teacher for the 1998-1999 school year. The Association and Johnson stipulated that pursuant to Ind.Code § 20-6.1-4-14, the procedural due process safeguards were followed when the School voted to not renew Johnson's teaching contract. . . .

As a result of the School's decision to not renew Johnson's teaching contract, and **pursuant to the terms of the Collective Bargaining Agreement**, on May 22, 1998, the Association filed a grievance on Johnson's behalf. **The grievance asserted that the School had failed to abide by numerous provisions of the Agreement** when it refused to renew Johnson's contract for the 1998-1999 school year. As a remedy, **the grievance asked that Johnson's teaching contract be renewed, that references to her nonrenewal be expunged from her personnel file**, and that all other relief due her be granted.

After the grievance progressed through the contractual procedure of the Collective Bargaining Agreement without resolution, the **Association requested binding arbitration** of the grievance.

On August 4, 1998, an arbitration hearing was held before Stephen L. Hayford (Arbitrator). On October 26, 1998, the **Arbitrator** issued his Opinion and Award and **found that the School had violated four provisions of the Collective Bargaining Agreement, but determined that he had no authority to grant a remedy** reinstating Johnson's teaching contract.

On January 14, 1999, the Plaintiffs filed with the trial court their complaint and application for vacation of the Arbitrator's Award. . . .

On October 19, 1999, the trial court issued its Order granting the School's Motion to Dismiss because the Plaintiffs had failed to allege a factual basis or statutory authority that would allow the trial court to accept judicial review. Additional facts will be supplied when necessary.

Discussion and Decision: . . .
Specifically, Plaintiffs contend that because Indiana law allows school corporations and exclusive representatives to agree that teacher dismissals are subject to binding arbitration and the law provides arbitrators the power to reinstate teachers, the trial court erred in determining that the arbitrator had no power to reinstate Johnson despite the School's violations of the Agreement. We disagree.

Although the Arbitrator found that the School violated the Master Contract, and that these violations may have prejudiced Johnson's efforts to secure renewal of her teaching contract, **he also held that he was without authority to overturn the School's decision not to renew her contract**. Specifically, the Arbitrator's Award was as follows:

In the analysis above, the Arbitrator has determined that the actions of the Administration and the Board in the course of deciding not to renew the teaching contract of Nelda Sue Johnson, resulted in violations of Article X, Section D and Article XII, Sections A, B and E of the Master Contract. Accordingly, the instant Grievance is sustained.

In circumstances Master Contract violations like those found in this Case would warrant the reinstatement of [a] teacher terminated for alleged poor teaching performance. However, as explained previously, **because the decision not to renew the teaching contract of a nonpermanent teacher is a matter reserved by statute . . . to the sole discretion of the Board, the Arbitrator is without the**

authority to direct that Mrs. Johnson's nonrenewal be overturned. Instead the remedy in this Cause must be limited to the following. The Administration and the Board are directed, in the future, to comply fully with the provisions of Article X, Section D, and Article XII, Sections A, B and E of the Master Contract with regard to all bargaining unit teachers, nonpermanent, semi-permanent and permanent. No other remedy is directed.

Plaintiffs argue that the Arbitrator's decision and award was in manifest disregard of Indiana statutory law, and contains gross errors of judgment in law that are apparent on the face of the Award. Specifically, Plaintiffs rely on Ind.Code § 34-57-2-13 of the Uniform Arbitration Act to argue that the Arbitrator's award should be vacated. In relevant portion, that statute provides:

(a) Upon application of a party, the court shall vacate an award where:

* * * * *

(3) the arbitrators exceeded their powers and the award can not be corrected without affecting the merits of the decision upon the controversy submitted;

* * * * *

but the fact that the relief was such that it could not or would not be granted by a court of law or equity is not grounds for vacating or refusing to confirm the award. . . .

Plaintiffs begin with an analysis of three statutory amendments to the laws relating to arbitration of teacher dismissals to argue that the arbitrator understood and correctly stated the law, but disregarded the law in making his decision. **Collective bargaining agreements between school corporations and teachers are governed by Ind.Code § 20-7.5-1** *et seq.,* **and permit a school corporation and a teacher's association to bargain and include in a collective bargaining agreement provisions for the arbitration of teacher dismissals.**

First, Plaintiffs argue that the amended language of Ind.Code § 20-6.1-4-14.5 of the Teacher Tenure Act permits school employers and an exclusive representative to mutually agree to binding arbitration with respect to teacher dismissals. . . .

The Teacher Tenure Act (TTA) is the legislation that provides recourse in the dismissal of teachers in Indiana. Ind. Code § 20-6.1-4-1 *et seq.* **The policy of TTA "is to establish a uniform tenure system for all the schools of the state and must be construed liberally with that aim and end in view."** *Michigan City Educ. Ass'n v. Board of School Trustees of Michigan City Area Schools,* . . . (Ind. Ct.App.1991), *trans. denied* (quoting *School City of Lafayette v. Highley,* . . . (1938)). **The manifestation of the legislative intent underlying the TTA is present in the CEEBA by excluding the subjects of employment and discharge of teachers from collective bargaining, and providing that the school governing bodies** shall have responsibility and authority to hire and retain and to suspend and discharge teachers in accordance with applicable law. *Michigan City Educ. Ass'n,* 577 N.E.2d at 1008. Furthermore, as we read the amended language of Ind.Code § 20-6.1-4-14.5, **this statute is to be read not to limit the provisions of a collective bargaining agreement negotiated under IC § 20--7.5, and merely *allows* school employers and exclusive representatives, such as the Association in our case, to mutually agree to binding arbitration with regard to teacher dismissals. The statute does not contain any language with respect to an arbitrators' authority to renew a nonpermanent teacher's contract.**

Next, Plaintiffs argue that the amendment to Ind.Code § 20-7.5-1-5 of the CEEBA requires school employers and their exclusive bargaining representatives to "discuss" certain subjects, and permits them to "bargain collectively" with respect to the retention of certified employees. . . .

However, **our reading of this statute does not place a requirement on a school employer to collectively bargain with respect to the retention of a certificated employee.** The statute merely requires that the school employer *shall discuss and may but shall not be required* to collectively bargain the retention of a certificated employee.

Finally, Plaintiffs argue that the amendment to Ind.Code § 20-7.5-1-6 gives school employers the right to retain employees through collective bargaining procedures established in Ind.Code § 20-7.5-1-4 and 5.

This portion of the CEEBA dealing with the rights of school employers and school employees covers the rights of school employees to collectively bargain certain grievance issues with school employers. **However, this section does not grant authority to an arbitrator to overturn the decision of a school employer to not renew a nonpermanent teacher's contract.** Nevertheless, **Plaintiffs argue that the three amendments noted above clearly expressed an intent to permit collective bargaining of procedures that would alter the Teacher Tenure Act requirements related to the dismissal of teachers.**

Plaintiffs contend that while school employers are not required to collectively bargain for final and binding arbitration of teacher dismissals, Indiana law clearly allows them to do so, and therefore, the Arbitrator manifestly disregarded the law by finding that he did not have the authority to renew Johnson's contract. Furthermore, Plaintiffs claim that the School collectively bargained with the Association for a provision in their agreement to permit teacher dismissal disputes to be subject to grievance and arbitration procedures, and also permitted an arbitrator to reinstate a teacher who was terminated in violation of the Agreement.

Although we agree that the three amendments previously discussed permit school employers and employees to collectively bargain for final and binding arbitration of teacher dismissals, these statutes do not give an arbitrator the authority to reinstate a nonpermanent teacher's contract. Moreover, **our**

review of the Record does not yield any evidence that the Collective Bargaining Agreement between the School and the Association gave an arbitrator the authority to renew a nonpermanent teacher's contract. . . .

Indiana's Uniform Arbitration Act provides a mechanism for enforcing agreements to arbitrate and for securing judicial review and enforcement of arbitration awards. . . *see* Ind.Code §§ 34-4-2-1 to 34-4-2-22; . . . The purpose of arbitration is to afford parties the opportunity to reach a final disposition of differences in an easier, more expeditious manner than by litigation. . . . To facilitate this purpose, judicial review of arbitration awards is very narrow in scope. . . . **We set aside an award only when one of the grounds specified by the Uniform Arbitration Act for vacation of an award is demonstrated**. . . . A party who seeks to vacate an arbitration award under the Act bears the burden of proving the grounds to set the award aside. . . .

As we discussed above, the Uniform Arbitration Act provides that an arbitration award may be challenged on the ground that "the arbitrators exceeded their powers and the award can not be corrected without affecting the merits of the decision upon the controversy submitted." . . . The statutory provision does not attempt to limit the discretion and powers of a neutral arbitrator to whom a controversy has been duly submitted. . . .

The Uniform Arbitration Act does not declare which issues are subject to arbitration. . . . Rather, **arbitration arises through contract, and the parties are essentially free to define for themselves what questions may be arbitrated, remedies the arbitrator may afford, and the extent to which a decision must conform to the general principles of law**. *School City of East Chicago, Ind. v. East Chicago Federation of Teachers, Local No. 511, A.F.T.,* . . . (Ind.Ct.App.1981). Thus**, an arbitrator is limited by the bounds of the agreement from which he draws his authority and an arbitrator is expected to be aware of those limits**. . . .

Nonpermanent teachers are not accorded the same status, for purposes of right to employment in contract renewal, as are permanent teachers, but, rather, **nonpermanent teachers have no contractual right to continued employment**. *Aplin,* 413 N.E.2d at 1003. In *Vukovits,* this Court noted the **public policy established in Ind. Code § 20-6.1-4-14 that places the decision regarding the retention of nonpermanent teachers within the "unfettered discretion of the School Board."** *Vukovits v. Board of School Trustees of Rockville Community School Corp.,* 659 N.E.2d 174, 181 (Ind.Ct.App.1995), *reh'g denied, trans. denied.* Nonpermanent teacher's contract rights exist only with regard to a contract entered into for the present school year, and the decision to continue a nonpermanent teacher's contract is merely a decision to reemploy that teacher for another year. *Aplin,* 413 N.E.2d at 1003.

In the present case, **the Arbitrator found that in light of the clear language of Ind.Code § 20-6.1-4-14(i), and because the nonrenewal of Johnson's contract was not an act of discipline, he was without authority to evaluate the propriety of the School's decision to terminate Johnson's employment**. . . . [A]lthough

the Arbitrator determined that the Plaintiffs proved that the actions of the School, which led to the decision to not renew Johnson's teaching contract, resulted in four violations of the Collective Bargaining Agreement, and that those violations would usually warrant the reversal of the School's nonrenewal decision, the Arbitrator was statutorily barred from reversing the School's action.

[Court ruling:] Therefore, because the School properly followed the statutory procedures for not renewing Johnson's contract as a nonpermanent teacher and **because the relevant Indiana case law pertaining to Ind.Code § 20-6.1-4-14 states that the School has the unfettered discretion to not continue a nonpermanent teacher's contract for any reason considered relevant to the School's interest**, the Arbitrator's decision was proper.

Affirmed.

A. The Case of the "Sleeping" Arbitrator

Under a state's Uniform Arbitration Act, the school's assertion that an arbitrator slept during the presentation of the school's evidence was insufficient to vacate the arbitrator's ruling.

Case:

Ft. Wayne Community Schools v. Ft. Wayne Education Assoc., 490 N.E.2d 337
(Ind.App. 1986) (emphasis added)

Plaintiff-Appellant, Fort Wayne Community Schools (District), appeals the grant of summary judgment favoring Defendant-Appellee, Fort Wayne Education Association (Association) in an action to vacate an arbitration award in favor of the Association.

We affirm.

Issues

District raises three issues for our review which we consolidate and restate as follows:

> 1. whether the arbitration award should be vacated pursuant to IND. CODE 34-4-2-13(a)(2) and IND.CODE 34-4-13(a)(4) because the arbitrator allegedly slept while school district witness testified. . . .

Facts

Association is a bargaining agent for teachers in the Fort Wayne School District. The parties have a collective bargaining agreement, under which unresolved grievances are submitted to arbitration. A dispute arose over the adjustment of class size in the school district. District took the position any adjustment in class size should be made within two weeks of the official enrollment date. Association took the position the two week period was a valid starting point but classes should be reorganized, when necessary, throughout the entire school year.

Chief negotiators for each party were present at the hearing. Each party also presented witnesses to support their positions. One District witness was Dr. Charles Welch, District Director of Elementary Education. Several witnesses claimed the arbitrator slept when Dr. Welch testified about class size adjustment. Dr. Welch's affidavit indicates he was aware of the arbitrator's inattentiveness and tried unsuccessfully "by means of gestures" to make District's attorney aware of the sleeping. Dr. Welch informed the attorney of the arbitrator's sleeping after the hearing was completed.

The arbitrator ruled in favor of the Association. . . .

District then filed suit in the Allen Circuit Court to have the award vacated. Association filed a counterclaim seeking confirmation of the award. Both parties filed motions for summary judgment.

District claims it did not receive a fair hearing because the arbitrator slept during the testimony of Dr. Welch. . . .

Association claims District has failed to satisfy the requirements of IND.CODE 34-4-2-13(a) for vacating an arbitration award if the arbitrator was in fact sleeping during Dr. Welch's testimony. . . .

The trial court granted summary judgment for Association and District appeals.

Discussion and Decision:

. . . II. *Arbitrator's Misconduct*

District claims summary judgment for Association was improper because an issue exists as to whether or not the arbitrator slept during Dr. Welch's testimony. They further claim if the arbitrator did sleep during Dr. Welch's testimony, they received an unfair hearing and were therefore prejudiced. We disagree.

Although we do not condone the alleged sleeping of the arbitrator in this case, the fact he possibly slept is not dispositive here. An arbitrator's award may be set aside only for grounds specified in section 13(a) of the Indiana Uniform Arbitration Act. IND.CODE 34-4-2-13(a). *International Brotherhood, etc. v. Citizens Gas & Coke Utility* (1981), Ind.App., . . . A party who seeks to vacate an arbitration award under the Uniform Arbitration Act bears the burden of proving the grounds to set the award aside. . . .

The burden is heavy for one asserting a section 13(a) violation. In *Indianapolis Public Transportation, supra,* Judge Robertson stated:

This conclusion is in accord with the purpose of the Uniform Arbitration Act, which is to afford parties the opportunity to reach a final disposition of differences in an easier, more expeditious manner than by litigation. . . . In order to facilitate this purpose, judicial review of arbitration awards is limited. Thus, an award should only be set aside when one of the grounds specified by the Uniform Arbitration Act for vacation of an award is shown. . . .

414 N.E.2d at 969. Under section 13(a)(2) **District must not only show the action of the arbitrator constituted misconduct, they must further show prejudice resulting from the misconduct**. The showing of prejudice must be more than a mere allegation in order to meet the strict requirements of 13(a)(2). . . . Nor is it reasonable to infer prejudice from the facts. . . . Thus, because our review is limited, the party alleging prejudice must affirmatively show how he is in fact prejudiced. . . .

Comparing the affidavit of Dr. Welch and the decision of the arbitrator we find the substance of the documents substantially similar. Also, we note Dr. Welch was only one of several witnesses who testified on class size adjustment for District. . . .

Given this standard and the facts presented, the trial court did not err in granting summary judgment for Association on this issue. . . .

Accordingly, we find no reason to vacate or modify the award. The trial court is in all things affirmed.

B. Seven Rules of Arbitrating "Just Cause" Dismissals

School districts that agree to be bound by an arbitrator's decision when a grievance is filed alleging that an employee's termination or discipline was without just cause face two difficult hurdles. The first is complying with all of the rules that over the history of published arbitration decisions arbitrators have developed and applied to actions of school administrators in determining whether the dismissal was based on "just cause." This so-called "case law" of arbitration requires school administrators to pass all seven tests in order to succeed in proving that the discipline or dismissal was properly based on "just cause." The following standards were expressed by Arbitrator Carroll A. Daughtery in the arbitration case of *Grief Brothers Cooperage Corp.*, 42 L A 555 (1964):

1. Did the employer give the employee forewarning or foreknowledge of the possible or probable disciplinary consequences of the employee's conduct?

2. Was the employer's rule or directive to the employee reasonably related to the orderly, efficient, and safe operation of the employer's business, as well as to the employer's proper expectation of the employee's performance?

3. Before administering discipline, did the employer make an effort to discover if the employee in fact violated or disobeyed the employer's rule or directive?

4. Did the employer conduct a fair and objective investigation into the employee's believed violation of its rule or directive?

5. Did the employer gather substantial evidence or proof that the employee violated its rule or directive?

6. Did the employer apply its rules, directives, and penalties evenhandedly and

without discrimination to all employees?

7. Was the degree of discipline administered by the employer in this particular case reasonably related to both the seriousness of the employee's proven violation and the employee's service record with the employer?

If the arbitrator answers any one of the seven questions in the negative, the school loses, and the likely remedy in the case of a dismissal will be to reinstate the employee with back pay and full reimbursement of all other lost benefits, provided that the labor agreement can fairly be construed to permit the arbitrator sufficient authority to grant such a remedy.

C. Appeal of Arbitrator Decision

The second problematic hurdle in prevailing at arbitration involves trying to reverse the arbitrator's ruling on appeal. State law governing the appeal of arbitrator rulings in many states that adopted the "Uniform Arbitration Act," establishes a limited number of reasons for reversing an arbitrator, which usually include: (1) fraud or corruption in gaining the award, (2) improper exclusion of evidence, (3) misinterpretation or misapplication of relevant law, (4) exceeding authority given the arbitrator in the labor agreement, and (5) clear error in calculating data to arrive at the award. Even an arbitrator's mistake of law or misinterpretation of law is not a sufficient reason for reversal in Indiana. See, for example, Southwest Parke Education Assoc. v. Southwest Parke Community School Corp., 427 N.E.2d 1140 (Ind.App.1981), where the court stated at 1147 (emphasis added):

The courts of other states which have adopted the Uniform Act and which have in their acts a provision similar to IC 34-4-2-13 agree that generally an arbitrator's mistake of law or erroneous interpretation of the law does not constitute an act in excess of the arbitrator's powers.

VI. EMPLOYEE STRIKES WHEN STATUTE SILENT

In states with collective bargaining laws pertaining to certain employee groups, some have prohibited strikes whereas others have permitted strikes only after certain conditions are met. In a situation where the state has no statute pertaining to a particular school employee group that engages in a strike, the question faced by the court will be whether there is a right to withhold services from the school employer. The Indiana Supreme Court faced such an issue.

Case:
Anderson Federation of Teachers local 519 v. School City of Anderson,
251 N.E.2d 15 (Ind. 1990) (emphasis added)

On May 6, the Superior Court of Madison County found the appellant, Anderson Federation of Teachers, Local 519, in contempt of court for the violation of a restraining order which had been issued without notice on the 2nd day of May, 1968, directing the appellant, teachers' union, and its members to refrain from picketing and striking against the appellee school corporation. It is from this judgment of contempt that this appeal is taken.

The appellant is an organization of public school teachers employed by the appellee.

The appellee is a municipal corporation organized under the statutes of this state for the purpose of operating the public schools within the boundaries of the School City of Anderson, Indiana.

In the spring of 1968, the appellant and the appellees entered into negotiations concerning salary schedules for the following year. These negotiations apparently were not satisfactory to the appellant for on May 1, 1968, the appellant instituted a strike against the school corporation and established picket lines at the various schools operated by appellee. Evidence discloses that school children were unloaded in the public streets because of the presence of the picket lines. It was this action of picketing by the appellant which precipitated the temporary restraining order issued on May 2, 1968, and it was the continuation of this activity without regard for the restraining order upon which the trial court based its judgment after a hearing on May 6, 1968, that the appellant was in contempt of court for violating the restraining order.

The trial court was in all things correct in its finding and judgment of contempt of court. It is the contention of the appellant that Indiana's "Little Norris-LaGuardian Act," also known as the anti-injunction statute, the same being Burns' Ind. Stat. Ann. § 40--501, *et seq.,* is applicable in this case. This act prohibits the issuance of restraining orders and injunctions in matters involving labor disputes between unions and private employers. **We do not agree with the appellant that this act is applicable to disputes concerning public employees**. The **overwhelming weight of authority in the United States is that government employees may not engage in a strike for any purpose**.

The **Supreme Court of the United States clearly enunciated the proposition that public employees did not have a right to strike and that the injunctive processes might properly be used to prevent or halt such strikes** in the case of *United States v. United Mine Workers* (1947), 330 U. S. 258. . . .

In the *United Mine Workers* case it was contended that the specifications in Section 13 of the statute are in general terms and make no express exception of the United States, thus it was argued the restraining order and injunction were forbidden by the act and wrongfully issued. In dealing with this argument the Supreme Court of the United States, beginning at page 272 of the official opinion, stated:

"... **There is an old and well-known rule that statutes which in general terms divest pre-existing rights or privileges will not be applied to the sovereign without express words to that effect**. . . . Congress was not ignorant of the rule which those cases reiterated; and, with knowledge of that rule, Congress would not, writing the Norris-LaGuardia Act, omit to use 'clear and specific [language] to that effect' if it actually intended to reach the Government in all cases."

. . . We are in total accord with the above language and hold that it is equally applicable to the Indiana statute.

This same proposition has been followed generally in most of the other state jurisdictions **where it has been repeatedly held that strikes by public employees are or should be prohibited and that injunctions should be granted to halt or prevent them**. . . .

The Indiana Continuing Legal Education Forum in 1968 circulated a publication entitled MUNICIPAL EMPLOYEE NEGOTIATIONS AND STRIKES in which they point out that almost without exception the state and federal courts hold that strikes by public employees are illegal.

The publication also quotes from a letter written by President Franklin D. Roosevelt to the President of the National Federation of Federal Employees on August 16, 1937, in which he said:

"Particularly, I want to emphasize my conviction that militant tactics have no place in the functions of any organization of Government employees ... **A strike of public employees manifests nothing less than intent on their part to prevent or obstruct the operations of Government until their demands are satisfied. Such action, looking toward the paralysis of Government by those who have sworn to support it, is unthinkable and intolerable**."

In a New York Supreme Court case Justice Emilio Nunez in granting an injunction against striking teachers made the following observation:

"Upon the signing of the Condon-Wadlin Act, Governor Dewey stated, in part, that **'Every liberty enjoyed in this nation exists because it is protected by a government which functions uninterruptedly. The paralysis of any portion of government could quickly lead to the paralysis of all society. Paralysis of government is anarchy and in anarchy liberties become useless**.'"

Board of Education of the City of New York v. Albert Shanker and United Federation of Teachers, Local 2, Supreme Court (1967), 283 N.Y. S.2d 548, 552.

We thus see that both the federal and state jurisdictions and men both liberal and conservative in their political philosophies have uniformly recognized that to allow a strike by public employees is not merely a matter of choice of political philosophies, but is a thing which cannot and must not be permitted if the orderly function of our society is to be preserved. This is not a matter for debate in the political arena for it appears fundamental, as stated by Governor Dewey, public strikes would lead to anarchy, and, as stated by President Roosevelt, the public strike "is unthinkable and intolerable."

The Madison Superior Court is, therefore, in all things affirmed.

SCENARIOS
STATE AND APPLY THE RELEVANT LEGAL RULE(S) TO THE FACTS.

1. In a state whose laws are silent regarding collective bargaining between a school district and its non-teacher employees, School's bus drivers formed a union and elected officers in an effort to gain better salary, benefits, and working conditions. When School learned of Union's creation, Superintendent met with Union President and did the following in chronological order:

> a. Offered President a promotion to a management position with a 50 percent raise in salary in an effort to disorganize Union by removing its chief organizer and planner.

> b. Made it clear to President that there was "no way in God's creation that Union would ever be recognized by School Board and all the energy that had been and would be spent would be wasted."

> c. Told President that if he and the other three officers would resign from Union, Superintendent, via his connection with Relative, a big company president in town, could get them better paying jobs.

> d. Told President that she would never recommend that Union be recognized by School Board and that if President tried to gain recognition of Union from Board, he "would find out that unemployment compensation paid far less than his current pay."

Union filed suit in state trial court. Analyze each subsection separately.

2. Teacher taught in a state that statutorily required collective bargaining between school districts and their teaching employees. The Bargaining Law and School's Collective Bargaining Agreement with Teacher Union were silent regarding a teacher's ability to have union representation at a conference with management over a teacher's conduct or performance.

When Teacher had a growing number of parental complaints regarding his overly demanding teaching style and attitude toward his students, Principal did the following in chronological order:

> a. Called a conference with first-year Teacher for the following day during his preparation period, which Teacher voluntarily attended by himself, informed him of the concerns expressed by the parents, gave Teacher ideas on how he could improve the negative situation, stated that Teacher was expected to began immediately to turn the situation around, and said that a memorandum documenting the meeting would be placed in Teacher's personnel file.

> b. Giving Teacher two-days notice, called a conference several weeks after the first one to deal with further parent complaints and an apparent lack of improvement in resolving the same problems. When Teacher requested that Teacher Union representative be present for the meeting, Principal denied it, directed that he be

there alone (he came alone under protest), and at the conference presented Teacher with a formal memorandum stating the specific problems, methods to correct them, and performance targets and dates that improvement would be expected by.

c. Called a third conference with Teacher, refused his request for Teacher Union representation (he came alone under protest), and at the conference orally and in memorandum form stated that the he had not yet began to show improvement due to continuing parent complaints and Principal's classroom observation, that his job was in danger unless improvement was demonstrated in the next three weeks, which would be followed by his year-end formal evaluation, Principal would recommend that his contract not be renewed for the following year.

d. Denied Teacher's request for Teacher Union representation at the formal evaluation conference (where he came under protest) and recommended Teacher's dismissal due to insufficient improvement in remedying the noted problems.

Teacher Union and Teacher filed suit in state trial court to prevent School from proceeding with his dismissal. Analyze each subsection separately.